Man, Culture, and Society

REVISED EDITION

Edited by HARRY L. SHAPIRO

OXFORD UNIVERSITY PRESS
London   Oxford   New York
1971

OXFORD UNIVERSITY PRESS

Oxford   London   New York
Glasgow   Toronto   Melbourne   Wellington
Cape Town   Salisbury   Ibadan   Nairobi   Lusaka   Addis Ababa
Bombay   Calcutta   Madras   Karachi   Lahore   Dacca
Kuala Lumpur   Hong Kong   Tokyo

It is customary for the editor of a book to delay its prospective readers by telling them something of what they are about to read. It seemed to me that the chapters of this book spoke more eloquently of the ideas they contain than I could do for them. But as its editor, charged with a certain responsibility, I owe the readers some explanation of its purpose and the authors some protection from unjustified criticism. I begin, therefore, by completely absolving my colleagues in this venture of any share in such defects as may exist in the over-all planning—but not of the content and form of their own chapters. There are limits beyond which even a willing editor should not be expected to go. Within the frame that was set for them, the authors wrote as they wished.

My original intent—I think I have kept to it throughout the vicissitudes of the book—was to present a kind of basic anthropology for the general reader and for those who were being introduced to the subject for the first time. The coverage for each chapter was consequently chosen with this in mind. In a subject as diversified as anthropology, with its enormous array of detail, one volume can hope to do little more than present salient ideas and concepts. Even certain developments like the study of personality and culture, and national character, which are currently occupying the thoughts of many anthropologists, had to be curtailed or omitted to avoid undue bulk. I have, however, comforted myself for these omissions on the score that an introductory book should confine itself to the fundamentals, just as the properly constructed curriculum begins at the beginning. This seemed to me a useful, not to say a necessary, function and one that might provide an insight into what anthropology is about.

These chapters in their original version were designed to be independent units dispersed among other scientific topics in an ambitious project covering all science. This undertaking lapsed, but the chapters on anthropology survived and, thanks to the encouragement of the Oxford University Press, are now appearing as a book. The authors with exemplary good will took back their chapters, revised, or even rewrote, them, and accepted in most cases the editor's restrained suggestions for fitting them into their new guise. Three new contributors were invited to fill in areas that the new form required.

The few instances of overlapping between chapters can be attributed to this history. In most cases they were finally allowed to remain since they either served a purpose in the concept of the chapter as such or because the repetition in another context had a certain value which it seemed desirable to preserve.

Most introductory books of this kind are written by one author. The multi-authored ones are generally highly specialized and technical compendia or treatises. Anthropology, however, has become so diversified that few of its professionals attempt any longer to do research in all its phases or even to be proficient in them. Consequently a single author in treating all the branches of the subject is bound to be dependent on secondary materials. Sometimes this method has been employed brilliantly. The fact remains, however, that the authority that comes from an expert writing in his own specialty is sacrificed in that procedure. I have hoped, in this instance, by inviting scholars to write in their own competencies and according to a predetermined plan that I might achieve authority without sacrificing structural unity.

The language used throughout was kept deliberately as nontechnical as the subject permitted. It is my hope that any reasonably educated person will be able to read the book with understanding—and perhaps with pleasure and profit.

I owe many debts incurred during the protracted preparation of this book. The various writers have borne with delays, queries from me, revisions, and other vexatious details—all with exemplary patience and cooperation. I thank them one and all. To Mr. Charles E. Pettee of the Oxford University Press I am deeply indebted—no one but he knows how much. Mr. John Begg of the Oxford University Press has been most helpful in the design and illustration of the book. I am also grateful to Miss

Leona Capeless, also of the Oxford staff, for her editorial wisdom and very helpful suggestions. And I am deeply obliged to Mrs. Jane Orttung for her help in finding suitable illustrations. To my wife I dedicate whatever labor I have put into the book. She has been a constant source of encouragement.

HARRY L. SHAPIRO

January 1956

In the fifteen years since this book first appeared, new fossil discoveries, a host of archaeological excavations and the development of a variety of new concepts and techniques in anthropology have made it necessary to bring the original version up to date. Some of the chapters have been thoroughly revised or even rewritten by their authors. These include Cressman's "Man in the New World," Griffin's "The Study of Early Cultures" and Shapiro's "Human Beginnings." Two chapters have been replaced by current assessments of the accumulated data that have appeared since their predecessors were published. Gould presents a fresh appraisal of "The Old Stone Age" and Meadow has written an account of the emergence of civilization to replace the earlier chapter on the metal ages, which as a classificatory stage is now undergoing re-evaluation.

In addition a new chapter by a new author has been added to the roster. This is Rappaport's discussion of the relevance of ecology in the study of human cultures. The remaining chapters with some minor revisions have been retained in their original form when their continuing validity has warranted it.

Although the temptation to expand the coverage was strong, it was resisted with the single exception already mentioned in order to maintain the original purpose of the book.

I am again indebted to the various authors for their cooperation. To Miss Catherine Linnet of Oxford University Press I owe much for her patience and her invaluable guidance.

HARRY L. SHAPIRO

January 1971

Contributors

Ruth Benedict, COLUMBIA UNIVERSITY

V. Gordon Childe, UNIVERSITY OF LONDON, ENGLAND

L. S. Cressman, UNIVERSITY OF OREGON

Mary Douglas, UNIVERSITY COLLEGE, LONDON, ENGLAND

Daryll Forde, UNIVERSITY COLLEGE, LONDON, ENGLAND

R. A. Gould, AMERICAN MUSEUM OF NATURAL HISTORY

James B. Griffin, UNIVERSITY OF MICHIGAN

E. Adamson Hoebel, UNIVERSITY OF MINNESOTA

Harry Hoijer, UNIVERSITY OF CALIFORNIA, LOS ANGELES

Claude Lévi-Strauss, UNIVERSITY OF PARIS, FRANCE

R. Godfrey Lienhardt, UNIVERSITY OF OXFORD, ENGLAND

David G. Mandelbaum, UNIVERSITY OF CALIFORNIA, BERKELEY

Richard H. Meadow, HARVARD UNIVERSITY

George Peter Murdock, UNIVERSITY OF PITTSBURGH

Roy A. Rappaport, UNIVERSITY OF MICHIGAN

Robert Redfield, UNIVERSITY OF CHICAGO

Harry L. Shapiro, AMERICAN MUSEUM OF NATURAL HISTORY

Leslie Spier, UNIVERSITY OF NEW MEXICO

CONTENTS

ILLUSTRATIONS

Man, Culture, AND *Society*

HARRY L. SHAPIRO

I

Human Beginnings

AT LEAST FIVE MILLION YEARS AGO—toward the end of the Pliocene period —the curtain had already risen on man; not on man as we know him today: big brained, small jawed, and frequently balding, but on a creature with a small brain, a massive mandible, and trailing in many parts of his anatomy evidences of his emergence from the world of apes. But this date, derived from potassium-argon tests of the strata containing man-like fossils at Omo in East Africa and from a recently reported discovery at Lothagam Hill in northern Kenya, although it more than doubles the known evolutionary span previously assigned to the hominid line, by no means provides even an approximation of its full length. For this we should have to know the date of the primates that first began an adaptive change from an arboreal life to the bipedal existence on the ground that eventually led to the development of *Homo sapiens*. At present, according to Simon, the claimant that appears to be closest to this stage is Ramapithecus, a fossil found in the Siwalik Hills of India. It has been assigned to the upper Miocene, well over twelve million years ago. Of similar age and structure are Bramapithecus,* also from the Siwaliks, and Kenyapithecus discovered by Leakey in Africa. These possible earliest of hominids are represented only by jaw fragments and teeth, but the significant reduction of canine size, the characteristic cusp patterns, and the form of the dental arch, not only strongly suggest an early hominid pattern but imply the acquisition of bipedal posture as well.

To our minds, conditioned by a historical perspective that represents Greece and Rome as the ancient world, twelve million years seem an un-

---

* A recent re-examination of Ramapithecus and Bramapithecus by Simon has led to the suggestion that they are closely related.

3

conscionably long time. Actually in relation to the age of our planet and to the length of time that life has existed here, man is a johnny-come-lately. In the time-honored analogy of the clock, if the twenty-four hours of the day be taken as equivalent to the lapse of time since the beginning of life on earth, then the hominids would have to be shown as appearing only within the last ten minutes and our own type, *Homo sapiens,* within the last few seconds of the twenty-four hours. But if man's sojourn on earth by this comparison seems short, it has been long enough to produce far-reaching changes of an order unique in evolution.

There have been a number of attempts to identify the specifically human characteristics of man. He has been set apart from the other animals by his upright posture and highly developed brain. He has been distinguished as the creature that laughs, speaks, or thinks. He has also been described as the creature that has a culture. These attributes are all true, some at least in degree, but perhaps the fundamental fact that makes most of them possible and certainly sustains all of them is the technology that has become so much a part of man that it is virtually impossible to conceive of him without it. The simple ability to use tools is perhaps not a completely exclusive faculty of man. Apes are known to use sticks or boxes to attain a goal. But no other animal has employed tools so persistently as even primitive man has done, and it is only among man's closest primate relatives that anything like this propensity appears. But man not only uses stray objects as tools—as extensions of his arms and hands—but he makes them artfully and, in the course of human evolution, with increasing skill and variety. The purposeful chipping of a crude fist axe of the Lower Paleolithic, or even of the simpler pebble tool, is already far beyond the demonstrable capacity of any animal including the apes. And no other animal except man has shown the slightest ability to build on past achievement and to develop the accumulation of technology that culture and civilization represent.

We know virtually nothing about the precise way by which this tool-using and tool-making propensity of man became an established attribute of his. But we can be sure that without it his evolution as we know it could not have occurred. For it is on the basis of this ability to make tools that culture and society are constructed. And culture in turn has provided the milieu that more and more mediates raw nature as it affects man and thereby his evolution.

We do know, however, that man through the peculiar circumstances of his evolution inherited anatomical adaptations that made it possible for him to make and use tools. He inherited intact a remarkably generalized hand to which had been added the ability of grasping objects. He became adapted at the very outset of his career to walking on his legs, freeing his arms and hands from the responsibilities of locomotion and thus releasing them for other functions. He possessed a brain already larger than any other primate's and by inference more advanced. One cannot overstress the potentiality of these characteristics in making it possible for man to create for himself the tools and eventually the cultures which must have affected profoundly the continued evolution that transformed an ape-like hominid into modern man.

The hand that we have inherited is in certain respects a primitive organ. Compared with the hoofs, pads, and paws of various other mammals the human hand—indeed the primate hand—has retained much of its original structure with a minimum of change. It has long been agreed that it was the arboreal adaptation of the primates that provided the means of preserving this structure which in ground-living animals underwent such a variety of modifications, all of them sacrificing in greater or lesser degree that basic pattern. The necessity, in moving about in the trees, for grasping, for reaching, for holding branches—in short for using the hand and foot in the most flexible manner possible—made the ancient five-fingered hand a valuable mechanism. Its adaptation for such purposes was enhanced by the acquisition of the ability of opposing the thumb to the other fingers, thus permitting a true grasp. This highly adaptable hand with its opposable thumb has in certain primates undergone some deviations through response to specialized types of locomotion, but it has on the whole remained astonishingly intact. That timing had something to do with its preservation becomes obvious when we see the quite different kind of adaptation that became necessary when other mammals took to an arboreal career at later stages in their evolution after a compromise with ground living had deprived them of some degree of its original structure. Animals that use claws often make extremely adept arborealists, but they have for better or worse lost that supreme instrument, the hand.

Among the primates the hand has been used in a variety of ways to aid locomotion. Wherever grasping is an important adjunct the opposable thumb remains intact. Among the largest primates—the simians—a form of locomotion developed whereby the body was swung from hands used rather more like hooks than as reaching and grasping organs. This type of locomotion, known as brachiation, requires less of the thumb and we find, generally speaking, that the anthropoid apes have degenerate or reduced ones. This has suggested to some students of human evolution that the hominid or human line could hardly have emerged from a well-developed form of brachiating anthropoid ape.

The human hand, although a heritage of adaptation to arboreal life, is also admirably fitted for other functions that could not have been anticipated of primitive primates living in trees. In this the hand is like a number of other parts that have appeared in the course of evolution. Although in a sense designed to serve a specific function, the hand retained and acquired so great a range of potentiality that its possessors could make use of it in another context, thereby opening new possibilities of livelihood and even of evolution. Man had in the hand the means of making, holding, and using tools, which as I have previously suggested may be regarded as the trigger for further evolution.

But the hand could scarcely have acquired these new functions until it was released from its old ones. This occurred when man's ancestors adopted a new form of locomotion. It is again necessary to turn to the arboreal world of the primates to understand how man acquired his unique posture. Man is not, of course, the only animal that appears to be erect or that can rear up on its hind limbs. The kangaroo holds its body erect much of the time and even the trained dog can raise itself to mince on its hind legs, but these postures do not entail the full extension of the legs on the trunk. Nor can they be maintained for long or without subsidiary support. The kangaroo stiffens his tail to make, along with his hind legs, a sort of tripod for support as the so-called bipedal dinosaurs also did many millions of years before. Although arboreal life allowed the primates a variety of locomotion: crawling, hopping, leaping, running, and brachiating, all of them required some adaptation to semi-erect posture. For these animals committed to a grasping hand, locomotion in the trees meant moving in a vertical direction as often as in any other. Thus, whether leaper, hopper, or crawler, the primate that climbed up a tree went up head first with the body in an upright position, with the weight of the entire body supported by the hind limbs. It is significant that the foot of the primate, although frequently very hand-like in conformation and even in its grasping ability, is always more rigidly constructed and reveals greater adaptation for supporting the weight of the body than the hand ever does. Thus some degree of specialization of the hind limbs for weight support and a semi-erect posture appeared early among the primates and remained characteristic throughout their history. When and how this primate adjustment to partially upright posture became converted into a fully erect one is still obscure.

It has been said that brachiation by suspending the body from the arms maintains it habitually in what amounts to an upright posture and thus might have served as the introductory phase of upright locomotion on the ground. There are, however, some difficulties in this hypothesis. Some accomplished brachiators like the chimpanzees do not walk fully erect but use their arms as ever ready additional supports. The gorilla, who of all the anthropoid apes is most given to ground living, also uses his arms as he lumbers about with his body in a 45 degree angle to the ground. Indeed, it is even claimed that it is precisely because the gorilla is a re-formed brachiator that he must use this incompletely erect position since his over-developed arms and upper torso have shifted his center of gravity so far forward that the fully upright posture would be foreign to his anatomy. Thus those who claim that brachiation could hardly serve to pre-form the body for fully erect ground locomotion refer the transition to an earlier stage of primate evolution. Strauss has suggested a cerco-pithecid (Old World monkey) stage, but it might be mentioned that the living cercopithecids that did take to the ground became pronograde animals. The baboons run around quite handily, but with their bodies in a horizontal position. The truth may well be between these two views and that man's ancestors took to the ground when the simian radiation from a cercopithecid stock was taking place and some degree of brachiation had been adopted but not yet so developed as to block the use of a completely erect posture with the body at a 90 degree angle to the ground and the legs fully extended.

It is, of course, difficult to know with precision what it was that induced our primate ancestor to take to life on the ground. Whether it was his increasing size, together with an already existing ability to stand upright, that forced him gradually to give up what must have been an increasing struggle with gravity can only be inferred, or, as some have surmised, the consequence of a change in the environment that destroyed his arboreal milieu. But once on the ground and eventually fully adapted to upright locomotion, his range became enormously widened, eventually to embrace the whole world.

The third of the triad of gifts that have in part been responsible for man's evolution from its primate beginnings is a highly endowed brain. It is also the organ about whose evolution we know least. We can study its outer form and to some extent the proportions of its parts for whatever light this may shed on the nature of its evolving powers. But unfortunately the fossil evidence for this is scanty and, even if it were fuller, it would be valuable only for the lack of anything better. We cannot, therefore, assert with confidence that man's ancestors took to ground living because of their burgeoning intellectual equipment. Nor do we know very much about the role of the brain in guiding the initial stages of the emancipation of the hand. As far as the fossil evidence goes, it suggests that upright posture and some use of the hand as a tool were well established before brain volume had increased very much. Man's ancestors, of course, in common with other primates already enjoyed the use of a highly developed brain that had evolved through arboreal adaptation. But the remarkable increase in size and presumably the powers of the hominid brain seem, however, to have occurred after upright posture had been adopted. It is a reasonable hypothesis in our present state of knowledge to assume that just as arboreal life had initially stimulated the growth of the cerebrum and its cortex in the infra-human primate, that living on the ground and the use of the hands for manipulative, explorative, and creative purposes furnished an additional stimulus that later led to the enormous increase of the brain and its intellectual capacity in man. This, in turn, would have enabled the hand to perform more and more elaborate functions and thus for man himself to begin the arduous business of accumulating a culture. Here we would have what amounts to a kind of feed-back—the brain and culture mutually affecting each other, with the hand, at least in early stages, mediating the process to a large extent. We would expect, if this hypothesis is correct, that a substantial increase in brain size would follow on the acquisition of a human-like posture and the rudiments of a culture. This reconstruction would explain why we do not find the Australopithecines and other early hominids strikingly different from the anthropoid apes as far as brain size is concerned, although their skeletal structure had gone a very long way toward the erect posture characteristic of man. Up to the time of the discovery of the early African fossils, the most primitive hominid known was *Pithecanthropus,* whose brain size was roughly intermediate between the apes and *Homo sapiens* and whose posture was erect. The general assumption was that we would find in the precursors of *Pithecanthropus,* leading back to the ultimate point of departure from the primate stem a gradual transition, *pari passu* in both brain size and in adaptation to erect posture. We can now see there was nothing inevitable in this kind of transition except what our sense of symmetry might perhaps have suggested.

There are a variety of ways of looking at human evolution, but basic to them all is the actual fossilized anatomical record. This, if correctly interpreted, identifies the actual course of events and thus provides the basis for the many associated problems and questions that such a record might suggest. 'Correctly interpreted' is, of course, crucial. Over the century and more that scientists have been studying human or hominid fossils, many interpretations have been proposed and, as the record has become richer, discarded or modified. There is something of a jigsaw aspect to such reconstructions in so far as many of the connecting pieces are absent, for the fossil record is never absolutely complete. Thus, isolated fossils unlinked by a continuous and interlocking chain may be open to a number of interpretations as to their relationships and associations. There are limits, however, to such a diversity of interpretation since the nature and characteristics of the fossils themselves impose certain relationships that cannot be denied and thus limit the range of possible interpretations. One has only to read the literature of the past hundred years to become aware not only of the abandonment of earlier hypotheses but, of the increasing precision and refinement of those that have replaced them as the fossil record has become enriched. This is in the nature of science.

It is perhaps appropriate at this point to identify the fossil material with which we have to deal in this venture. Fossils, in a broad sense, include the remains of any organism as well as imprints of them dating from 'prehistoric times.' In the area of hominid evolution, however, virtually all such remains consist of bones or teeth that have been at least partially mineralized. It is this mineralization that has helped to preserve them over long periods of time, although under certain favorable conditions bones with very little mineralization will survive for extremely long stretches of time. Since the soft parts of the organism have never been found in the hominid record, we are reduced to skeletal and dental remains only. To add to this restriction, it is rare indeed to find complete, intact skulls or bones, and a complete skeleton is unknown. The most common hominid fossils are teeth, followed by bony fragments of the jaws and the vault of the skull. It follows from this that dental morphology has been explored with special interest and is consequently highly significant in establishing relationships. Cranial and facial fragments can be and often are important in reconstructing the skull which is another area of the skeleton commonly available.

Aside from the fragmentary nature of the fossil evidence upon which we depend, the paucity of these remains is in itself a major difficulty. I have already referred to the sporadic representations in the fossil record of the continuity of human evolution and the problems of establishing relationships from such a discontinuous array of fossils. But inherent in this problem lies another. A single fossil representative of a particular stage of evolution may or may not be completely typical of it. Where comparisons, however, are between widely disparate groups, variations from the norm can be ignored for characters where overlap is negligible or unlikely. As the fossil array is enriched and comparisons between more closely allied populations becomes necessary some overlap in normal variation might be expected and this problem may become acute. Fortunately, for some stages of hominid evolution as the fossil finds have enriched the record they have also provided additional samples of specific groups and to some extent increased our knowledge of the variations within the group, thus permitting more realistic assessments. An example of this is the recent reappraisal of the group of fossils known as the Australopithecines. Originally, as the individual fossils were found, they were identified as representative of distinct groups with the result that a large number of separate taxa were established. As the evidence has accumulated, it is now possible to see that many of the differences upon which the earlier classifications were based are largely individual variations. This has required a reappraisal and has led to a regrouping of these fossils into two major types: *Africanus* and *Robustus;* and in at least one interpretation as variants of a single species. This difficulty, however, remains in one form or another and has to be kept in mind.

If the details of the reconstruction of hominid evolution are subject to controversy and revision, the broad course of events, however, becomes more and more assured. In the following I shall stress the latter. Leaving aside the indentification of the precursors of the hominid line, there is little doubt that with the appearance of the Australopithecines at least five million years ago, that the hominids were already well established and that their adaptation to the basic hominid bipedal posture was firm and solid.

The fossils, now grouped together as the Australopithecines, first came to light with the discovery of an immature skull in South Africa in 1925. This child, burdened with the name of *Australopithecus africanus,* was at first identified by many students as an ape, despite Dart's and Broom's insistence that it was something more—something much closer to the origins of hominids themselves. Although *Australopithecus* had a brain slightly larger than an ape child of the same age might have had and its dental characteristics were suggestive of man's, its appearance otherwise was remarkably ape-like. Subsequent finds in the same part of Africa enriched our knowledge of this group of 'ape-men' but failed to dissipate the belief of many specialists that *Australopithecus* and his relatives were merely members of a group of apes that had evolved to a stage somewhat beyond other apes in the direction of man but still one that fell far short of this status and eventually came to naught. Perhaps much of this reluctance to attribute any more significance to these fossils was the consequence of a time-honored assumption that the dawn of hominid status would be heralded primarily by a brain appreciably larger than that any of the apes possessed. The Australopithecines up to this point did not seem especially noteworthy in that respect. Eventually as more and more fossils of this now quite extensive sub-family were excavated, bones of the skeleton began to appear and now there could be no doubt that upright posture was a settled characteristic of these creatures—a fact that certain cranial features had suggested.

Finds representing this important group are still being announced and we do not yet have complete or even adequate descriptions of a number of them. At present, it includes not only the South African fossils referred to above, but also the well-known *Zinjanthropus* discovered by Leakey in the Olduvai Gorge of East Africa. *Homo habilis* unearthed at the same site is also regarded by some experts as a member of this taxon, although others would place it morphologically with a more advanced group. The previously mentioned Omo and Lothagam Hill fossils would appear to be part of this assembly, and the Tell Ubeidiya remains discovered in Palestine belong here. It has even been suggested that *Meganthropus* found in Java, although part of the *Pithecanthropus* series, may be also closely related to the Australopithecines. It is clear that these representatives embrace a considerable range of types and that they shed far more light on the origins of the hominids than was at first admitted. Even if we may have to decide that the Australopithecines represent an abortive effort toward the evolution of a man, they do indicate the manner in which our own ancestors achieved a foothold on the hominid ladder. Walking erect on the ground now appears to have been established very early, and very probably precedes any striking modification of the brain. In fact, I am inclined to believe that it was precisely this shift in locomotion, coupled with its consequences for the hand, that provided one of the factors in the evolution of the hominid brain. In the light of this, it is noteworthy that crude stone tools have recently been reported in association with these fossils, greatly strengthening the claim that technology had a more significant role in the transition to hominid status than was formerly admitted.

We now know that Australopithecines and related types existed for a relatively long time, longer perhaps than any of the succeeding stages whose shorter spans indicate perhaps a speeding up of the tempo of human evolution as culture and language developed and played an increasing role in this process. If the later finds prove to be unquestionably Australopithecine in type, this group by present estimates would have existed for over four million years.

The transition from hominids of Australopithecine affiliation to a more advanced form is still not well documented by fossil remains. But, around the early part of the middle Pleistocene, perhaps 700,000 years ago, we encounter a distinct advance in another cluster of fossils that are collectively now known as *Homo erectus*. This name reflects the recognition that they belong to the same genus as modern man (*Homo sapiens*) but to a more primitive species. Among the best known are the Pithecanthropines. These fossils found in Java take their name from the first one to be discovered—*Pithecanthropus erectus*. When it was found in 1891 by Eugene Dubois, a Dutch physician in the Netherlands Colonial Service in Java, *Pithecanthropus* was especially noteworthy. It was then merely a generation since Darwin's publication of *On the Origin of Species*. The concept of a human evolution from a primate stock had only recently acquired wide acceptance and the fossil evidence to support it was just beginning to come to light, or better, to be recognized. Up to that time the only pre-*Homo sapiens* type of man known was Neanderthal. The impact of *Pithecanthropus* was therefore enormous. The skull cap with its heavy bony buttress above the eyes and its flattened crown was obviously more primitive than any known man's. But at the same time it had a cranial volume estimated at around 900 cc., very distinctly above any known ape's. This increased size had brought about an increase in the height of the skull vault. Associated with the cranial fragment was a beautifully preserved femur which in almost every detail of its morphology agreed with the conformation of a modern femur and therefore indicated that *Pithecanthropus* walked upright. *Pithecanthropus* thus seemed to represent something approaching the 'missing link' between man and his anthropoid ape ancestor. This view we now know is an inadequate conception of the process of human evolution. Man did not evolve out of developed anthropoid apes. But he does have a common ancestry with them. Therefore as we go back in time to this point of departure, we find the human stem different from what it is today. Similarly our collaterals, the living apes, must have been different when we trace them backward in time. The 'missing link' therefore would not be a stage halfway between living man and living apes, but a form long since extinct that was common to both.

In this view, the Pithecanthropines would represent a stage in advance of the Australopithecines of South Africa who also predate them in time. Subsequent discoveries by von Koenigswald have provided us not only with another skull very similar to the type find, but also a number of variants: *Pithecanthropus robustus* and *Meganthropus palaeojavanicus*. These more rugged and massive forms suggest that *Pithecanthropus erectus* himself represents a refined product of a line of development which at the least may be a local phenomenon or at most a reflection of a widespread progression.

Closely allied to the Pithecanthropines, particularly *Pithecanthropus erectus* is the population represented by a series of skulls, isolated fragments thereof, teeth, and miscellaneous long bones found at Chou Kou Tien, not far from Peiping in China. For some years virtually each season yielded more material until work in this fruitful area was closed down altogether by war. Recently the Chinese have once more resumed excavations. As far as one can count individuals from miscellaneous fragments, forty or more were represented in the total assemblage of fossils before they were lost at the beginning of World War II. These ancient skulls from Chou Kou Tien are now believed to belong to the same species as *Pithecanthropus;* their differences being regarded as no more than might occur within this zoological category. These differences, however they may finally be evaluated, all place *Sinanthropus** in advance of his Javanese relative. The former had a larger brain—about 200 cc. more on the average, a distinctly more developed forehead, a somewhat more refined cranial morphology, a less projecting jaw, and a dentition a little closer to our own. Like *Pithecanthropus, Sinanthropus* was adapted to upright locomotion—but not appreciably more.

If any further evidence of *Sinanthropus'* claim to a hominid status were required, their way of life would be ample. These people lived in caves, the floors of which they littered with the skeletal debris of animals they hunted and consumed. They used fire and employed stone tools of a primitive kind. Any additional attributes of culture can only be inferred, but it seems likely that people as advanced as this in technology must have also had a language. But of its nature we cannot even guess.

---

* The Chou Kou Tien fossils were originally classed as a distinct group by Davidson Black and named Sinanthropus Pekinensis. Their affinity with the Pithecanthropus led LeGros Clark to suggest Pithecanthropus Pekinensis as a more appropriate name.

The paramount fact, however, is that *Sinanthropus* is a *Homo erectus* ancestral to recent man. His close relationship to *Pithecanthropus* also lends validity to the latter's claim to a similar ancestral dignity. Together they demonstrate that already by the mid-Pleistocene, evolution had carried the hominids a long way from a stage comparable to the Australopithecine's. The brain which in the earlier forms seemed to lag somewhat behind the rapidly evolving lower limbs is now catching up and is already more than twice the size of that of the apes. Moreover, the effects of erect posture and expanding brain are clearly visible in the reduction of the muzzle, the shortening of the dental arch, modification of the teeth, heightening of the vault of the skull, and the gradual emergence of the brow.

Homo erectus enjoyed a wide distribution. He is represented not only by the Pithecanthropines in Java and China, but also by the Lantian skull found in Shensi, China, by a skull discovered in Bed II at Olduvai, in a more recent level than *Zinjanthropus* and *Homo habilis*. The fossils assigned to *Atlanthropus* discovered at Ternifine in North Africa, described by Arambourg, are strikingly similar to *Pithecanthropus* and are now included in *Homo erectus*. In Europe he is represented by the famous Heidelberg jaw.

The above are roughly contemporaneous, if we allow a period of about 300,000 years, but some representatives of this stage apparently continued down to fairly recent times, in fact, overlapping the earliest dates known for the fully developed *Homo sapiens*. The best known are the Solo skulls found in Java and dated to the final phase of the last ice age in the Pleistocene. Although the Solo skulls reveal a considerable increase in brain volume over the earlier *Pithecanthropus*, they retain a general resemblance to their predecessor in Java that warrants classing them as *Homo erectus*. It has been suggested that the Solo skulls reveal a line of development from the *Pithecanthropus* strain of *Homo erectus* to the *Homo sapiens* type of Australian aborigine.

Although the evidence available allows no other conclusion than the direct evolution of *Homo sapiens* from *Homo erectus*, tracing the transition however from one to the other is still fraught with difficulties. One of the problems centers on Neanderthal man. Historically, the first fossil discoveries (in the Neander Valley in Germany and at Gibraltar in Spain) that were recognized as predating modern *Homo sapiens* belonged to this type. Later, dozens of similar fossils were found in various parts of Europe and Asia, and there arose a distinct concept of Neanderthal man, with powerful projecting brow ridges and heavy massive jaw with little or no chin. Although the cranial capacity when measurable was often as great as in recent man and in some instances even larger, nevertheless, the general morphology of the skull with its relatively low height and heavy occipital torus seemed to represent an enlarged and somewhat refined form of what we now recognize as *Homo erectus*. This in itself might not have proved to be a difficulty to the acceptance of Neanderthal man as the direct precursor of modern man if it were not for the fact that this version of Neanderthal man was datable to the last glaciation and was succeeded rather abruptly in Europe by full developed *Homo sapiens* with the onset of the Upper Paleolithic about 45,000 years ago. Except possibly for the Tabun-skhul series of skulls found at Mt. Carmel in Palestine, nowhere were there populations that displayed a gradual transition to modern man. This led many students to doubt that this classic Neanderthal type gave rise to him. There was not enough time in the sequence to permit the evolutionary replacement of the one by the other.

This situation became more confused as various deviant but Neanderthal-like fossils began to come to light. These were less primitive in many ways and for the most part much earlier in time than the classic Neanderthal man. They include Swanscombe man and Steinheim man, dating back to the second interglacial, and Fontechevade, assigned to the last interglacial. Ehringsdorf of less determinable age was also clearly earlier than the classic and late Neanderthal. Without mentioning all these so-called progressive types, one more should be added to the list. This is the Vertesszollos man found in Hungary in 1965 and dated to the second glaciation. It is claimed to be more advanced in morphology than the classic Neaderthal, and to be one of the earliest sapiens-like forms yet discovered.

Since the possibilities this array could suggest are multiple, it should come as no surprise that a number of different interpretations have been suggested, and will be found in the current literature. One hypothesis accepts the classic Neanderthal as ancestral to modern man and cites the Tabun series as an evolutionary transition. Some partisans of this hypothesis tend to minimize the special features of the classic Neanderthal to place him closer to modern man than is warranted. Another regards the earlier so-called progressive Neanderthals as the ancestral group and relegates the later classic form to a specialized line that became extinct. Its anachronistic survival would then be attributed to isolation and specialized adaptation to a sub-glacial ecology.

Still another view tends to segregate Swanscombe man and possibly

Steinheim man from the progressive Neanderthals and to regard them as the transitional group to modern *Homo sapiens*. If this is correct, the emergence of modern *Homo sapiens* would have to be dated as far back as the second interglacial about 400,000 years ago and, perhaps earlier, if we include the Vertesszollos man. Such a date would overlap considerably the Pithecanthropines in the *Homo erectus* series. For such reasons, and others, we can at present only speculate about the precise course of events that led to the appearance of the man of today. Although the disappearance of earlier forms of man took place somewhat earlier in Europe than in several other areas, toward the end of the last glaciation, Europe and indeed other parts of the world as well were inhabited by populations that must be classified as *Homo sapiens*, and as far as we know by no others.

It is altogether possible, not to say likely, that in the course of human evolution some racial differentiation had occurred quite early. How far this process had gone, when it occurred, and how much of it has survived in the living races of man are questions difficult to answer. We can be quite sure that the hominids shared with other forms of life a tendency to vary. Consequently we might expect that given the proper conditions of isolation early man must have exhibited some degree of racial differentiation. This seems the more probable when we consider the wide geographic range of the early hominids and the necessity of their living in relatively small bands, circumstances ordinarily regarded as favorable for racial differentiation. On morphological grounds, Weidenreich has proposed more systematically than I am suggesting that the modern races of man were already forming early in human evolution and pursuing in specific geographic areas somewhat independent courses. To pursue his conception of the origin of human races would take us beyond the point I am making, namely, that the tendency to differentiate is inherent and expresses itself whenever it can. The more conventional view has long been that the living races first appeared with the dominance and spread of *Homo sapiens* at the beginning of the Upper Paleolithic which in Europe may be dated at about 40,000 years ago. Although we know relatively little about the rapidity with which human races may develop, this amount of time seems far too limited to produce the degree of differentiation we find today. Until, however, more fossil evidence is available, the solution to this problem will continue to be debatable.

The process, however, by which races have emerged is less uncertain, thanks to the researches of population geneticists. Their formulations drawn from the study of natural populations of insects, birds, and animals, from experimental conditions, and from genetic theory have contributed to our understanding of the dynamics of human race differentiation. This is possible because human genetics is fundamentally identifiable in principle with the genetics of all other forms of organic life.

When we think of race, we think in terms of groups of people, of populations the members of which share a common heredity but do not necessarily possess a common genotype. This is necessarily so because no two people, with the possible exception of identical twins, are ever exactly alike genetically. Consequently if every inheritable physical difference were given racial value, we would end up with virtually as many races as there are individuals. Race, then, is a classificatory device to deal with generalized *patterns* of inherited variations occurring within a species and maintained in existence by a population. Another way of saying this would be that race is the resultant of differences in gene frequencies. Differences between populations that are not inherited should play no part in such a system, contrary to widespread notions. Religion, language, customs, manners, values, and many other characteristics commonly confused with race differences are learned attributes and acquired during an individual's lifetime through exposure to social and cultural conditioning. The only legitimate criteria of race are those that are carried in the germ plasma and passed on from parents to child through physical inheritance. Since this is so, it follows that with every mating one individual draws from the population of which he is a member another individual whose genetic composition like his own is the resultant of a long history of matings within the population. If this is a random or unstructured process, their offspring then would represent a chance combination of the genetic potentialities contained within the population. And since the offspring, generation after generation, will continue to combine in a random fashion, we may conceive of the population as the stable continuing entity and the individuals that comprise it as merely ephemeral and chance genetic expressions that the population is capable of producing. Thus the combined genes of all the breeding members of the population form what is known as a gene pool. For some characters the genes may actually be estimated and their frequencies expressed in proportion to the whole.

Such a population is never uniform, in part because the environment of the individual members of the population may vary and to some degree affect the development of a trait but also because the gene pool is never homogeneous. This variety in the gene pool may arise from mutation or from other causes, but its existence produces some degree of heterogeneity in the components of a population—the *polymorphism* of the zoologist. The notion that the races of man were once homogeneous gains no support from this. In all probability human populations were always polymorphic.

Given such a population structure, how do racial differences become established? The answer to this depends on the interaction of several factors. If we keep in mind that any population's gene pool tends to vary, and as far as we know all of them have or there would be no evolution, we may discover here the *origin* of the differences. Thus if a population becomes separated into two or more groups that are unable to share each other's gene pool, each one will tend to develop independent genetic changes. And whatever accumulation of genetic change occurs in one will remain in that population and will not be shared with the others. In other words, the gene flow which distributes genetic modification in one population to others by intermixture is interrupted and the initial stages in differentiation are achieved. The degree of differentiation that now develops becomes a function, or effect, of the rate of mutation, or genetic change, the adaptive advantage of such changes, the size of the group, and the elapsed time during which isolation is maintained. The factors that produce isolation are numerous. The simplest and easiest to perceive is geographic, where groups or populations are separated by geographic barriers that reduce physical contact and consequently the opportunity for miscegenation. In a hunting economy where the size of a band is strictly limited in size by the difficulty of maintaining a large group in efficient relationship to the hunting area, populations may be widely spaced, separated by their peripheral hunting ranges and by the hostility engendered by territorial rights. In animal populations slight changes in breeding habits might effectively separate varieties that actually co-inhabit the same area. In man no such mechanism is known, but more subtle cultural or social structures have been thought to serve sometimes the same purpose. For example, a caste system by restricting to its own members the mating possibilities of one section of a population creates isolation for that section. Other social institutions or structures involving selectivity in mating might bring about comparable results. This is a subject that has been little investigated. It is, however, unlikely to be very significant in race differentiation since such systems do not last long enough to be very effective. The relatively frequent social reorganization characteristic of most cultures serves to break up any embryonic, or minor, distinctions that might be initiated by selective mating systems.

Although mutation is one of the principal sources of genetic distinction between populations, it is not the only one. Structural changes in the chromosomes that carry the genes may also contribute. Still another process common in human history has been suggested as highly significant. This may express itself, for example, when a daughter colony separates itself from the mother population and migrates to another region. If the migrating group is small, it may carry only a partial representation of the full complement of genes to be found in the original population. Or if all the variety of genes are present in the migrating group, their frequency percentages may differ. Such a consequence may be due to chance or even possibly the result of some selective influence, but in any case, the new population begins its corporate existence with a different gene pool from its parental one.

It is also conceivable that a disaster striking a small group might drastically cut down its numbers and thus alter the gene pool of the survivors. Such a group, when it recovered its former numerical strength, would consequently be genetically different from its prototype. The hazards to which small primitive groups were exposed were many. Warfare, famine, and epidemic must have struck frequently and devastatingly. One has only to recall the decimation created by the plagues of Medieval Europe, when as much as one-fourth of some populations perished, to realize how effective such events may be in altering the genic composition of a group. If susceptibility to disease were correlated with the genotype of an individual, the kind and extent of the destruction could profoundly affect the gene pool by selectively weeding out certain genes.

In addition to these possibilities of *originating* genetic differences between populations by the effect of chance alone or with overtones of selection, there is another mechanism in which chance is thought to play a principal role. This is commonly known as the Sewall Wright effect or random genetic drift. In certain circumstances it is supposed that random mating might account for the loss or fixation of a mutation. If the mutation rate is low and the size of the population small, the likelihood of loss by such a random process increases.

Reference was made previously to mutation as one of the principal sources of differentiation between populations. These genetic changes appear to occur in varying frequencies for different traits, but little is known about these rates in man. Nor do we know with assurance that the rate for a particular trait is the same in all human populations or different. The survival of these mutations is, however, differential, depending on the interaction of a number of processes.

The environment, too, affects the survival of a mutation. If a gene change produces a trait that is adaptive to a particular environment giving its possessor some degree of advantage in his reproductive rate, it is likely to survive and increase in frequency. This selective process reflects the manner in which a particular group becomes adjusted or adapted to its environmental niche and eventually emerges with features distinct from its related populations in other areas. Although stress used to be placed on non-adaptive features for purposes of racial classification, it is difficult to see how one can logically overlook or minimize the adaptive ones. I suspect that this distincton between adaptive and nonadaptive racial characters arose from the *apparent* lack of relationship between some characters and the environment. This, however, is a tricky distinction since ignorance of any connection is hardly warrant for its absence, especially since little systematic work in testing these relationships has been done. It has been suggested that even where a trait appears to be neutral, it may be affected by another trait that is more clearly adaptive. Despite a necessary caution in these judgments on the existence of non-adaptive traits, it would be equally unwarranted to deny out of hand that their occurrence was impossible. Until recently, for example, the abnormal sickle shape of the red blood corpuscles, which occurs widely among African populations, was considered neutral. New evidence brought forward by Allison* now suggests that it is associated with areas of endemic malaria and consequently its presence, at least in the heterozygous condition, is adaptive. On the other hand, the variations in the suture patterns in the pterion region of the skull elude any adaptive explanation.

Perhaps enough has already been brought forward to indicate how complex the dynamics of race formation may be. Although the process has been considerably clarified by recent investigation, much yet remains to be determined. But if the deails are still somewhat obscure, the major outlines are clearly defined by the interaction of genetic change, selection, and isolation. It is difficult to conceive of race differentiation progressing without all three. Consequently, the elimination of any one might check the process or interfere with its development. Of these three factors, only isolation appears to be susceptible of radical modification. Genetic change is an inherent attribute which we have no reason to think will cease or be effectively altered. Selection is a process that can operate directly or be mediated by culture or be directed deliberately by human agency, but it appears to be as effective now as in the past. Isolation, however, we may

* A. C. Allison. British Medical Journal, Feb. 6, 1954.

infer from our knowledge of man's history on the earth, is a condition which is rapidly vanishing. From the point of view of race formation in man, then, the earlier stages of his development were more suited for such differentiation than they are today. Back in early Pleistocene times the geographic spread of fossil finds indicates that man was already widely distributed, but he must have been thinly distributed for various reasons. He was a hunter or a food-gatherer which imposed on him the necessity of living in small groups within large foraging areas. His primitive culture made it difficult, if not impossible, to inhabit certain areas unsuited for a primitive economy. Geographic barriers loomed large against his technological poverty. Perhaps at no other time were human populations so small and so isolated one from another, thus providing optimum conditions for race formation.

With the agricultural revolution that the Neolithic ushered in, and with increasing tempo ever since, human aggregations in town and city have increased in size. Populations could now be settled on the land and by growing their own food be able to support themselves on a fraction of the area they formerly required. Thus communities increased steadily in number. Technology improved to permit utilizing areas formerly waste and traversing great distances with relative ease. Geographic barriers became progressively less ominous. Thus, in the last 10,000 years the earth has been filling up with the result that today hardly any populations survive in the kind of isolation most favorable for the initiation or preservation of race differences. In addition to the contacts created by mere crowding, man has also vastly increased his mobility. The massive migrations of historic and recent times, and the resulting reshuffling of genes, have led to an unprecedented gene flow. Whole new populations, the offspring of race mingling, have arisen in the modern world, creating intergrades and continuities and thus blurring the distinctions of race. It would, of course, be unwarranted to predict as some writers have that the future will witness a vast intermingling of all the present races and the elimination of all racial differences. But we can say that in our own times the tide has turned in that direction. Who knows how long or how far it will run?

In any appraisal of human biology, one factor emerges as unique. This is the effect of human culture on man's biological development. No other creature has created for himself anything like it. In a sense it is a new dimension—a new environmental niche—to which mankind while creating it must also adapt itself. We are, however, only at the threshold of a true understanding of its enormous significance.

JAMES B. GRIFFIN

II

The Study of Early Cultures

THE STUDY OF EARLY CULTURES is usually called archaeology in the Americas. Archaeology means the study or science of ancient things or the study of the long course of human cultural development. In Europe, the word prehistory is commonly used to apply to early cultures before writing or history, began. It is being increasingly applied to the study of pre-Columbian cultures in the New World as archaeological techniques and skills are increasingly used to interpret the historic settlements of European or early American societies such as has· been done at Williamsburg and Jamestown in the United States and Lewisburg in Canada.

Since recorded history only began to be effective in the Near East between 3000 to 2000 B.C. and in the other major Old World culture centers at later dates it can readily be appreciated that prehistory has the impressive task of interpreting the slow development of man's cultural achievements over some two million years of time. The archaeologist studies this unrecorded history by means of surviving specimens of human manufacture called artifacts, or by other data resulting from human occupation in an area. Artifacts are varied in nature from axes to art objects and from pottery to storage pits. Activities of people in an area, particularly of an agricultural society, may change the local vegetation and this can be reflected in the changes in the record of pollen preserved in favorable localities such as lake bottoms or bogs. Burial procedures, size of houses, and location of activities within houses can provide data on social and religious activities. Archaeology attempts to recover the cultural activities of past societies and how these societies functioned in their environments. It records and interprets these in terms of the changes which have taken place in time within any given geographical region, such as river valleys, coastal or mountain environments, to such large geographic units as the western or eastern hemispheres.

Ethnographic data on societies around the world for the past few hundred years and written records of past literate societies have been of great value in interpreting the tools, other artifacts, and behavioral patterns of prehistoric societies. Usually, the closer the observed or written record is in terms of time, area, and cultural tradition to that of the prehistoric society, the more accurate will be the interpretation of the prehistoric cultural complex. Knowledge of the cultural behavior of known social groups can furnish examples of activities, industries, and relationships which can be specifically searched for in excavations, or in the interpretation of the interrelations of artifacts to each other and to their physical context.

The rapid growth of archaeological excavation activity and the vast amount of data recovered have made the use of statistical analysis and computer programming a valuable, if not necessary, part of archaeological studies. There are many varieties of quantitative methods available for the description, classification, and defininition of the relationships of prehistoric artifacts. Such studies are able to accommodate large numbers of cultural variables and ascertain relations between variables. Placed in terms of time-space relationships, cultural variations may be more accurately observed and tested for meaningful causes-and-effect relations.

Increasing emphasis is placed on the study of complete functioning communities and their interactions. This would include all of those social, economic, and religious activities which were followed within a single society, and also during their interaction with contemporary groups which would be recognized from inter-group trade either of raw materials or finished goods. All of these activities and the items of material culture remains varied through time. All of these human activities must also be understood in terms of the relationships between the human group and the environment in which they lived. The importance of the environment in understanding how prehistoric societies functioned is a major reason for the heavy dependence upon knowledge from biology and the physical sciences to provide this data. The successful society is one which is able to procure adequate food and other basic necessities equal to or superior to that of neighboring groups. Natural forces produce changing environments and while these changes are normally gradual it was necessary for human activities to adapt to them. The interrelations are very complex and the measurement of the forces producing cultural change and development in prehistoric societies is very difficult. Changes can be recognized and their time and space relationships can be recorded but determining the processes which produced them is one of the vital tasks for future archaeological work.

Most archaeological data are recovered from areas of past human activity which are referred to as sites. Sites vary in size and complexity, from a location where a number of animals might have been killed and butchered, to a settled farming community occupied by several hundred people, to the remains of ancient cities, such as Pompei or Teotihuacan in central Mexico. Most people wonder how an archaeologist knows where to go to find evidences of former cultures. This is a relatively simple part of his work, for if one is interested in doing archaeology in a particular part of the world there are quite a number of leads to site locations. The publications and museum collections of former archaeological work will give the location of the sites excavated or merely surveyed. Historical documents often tell of former inhabitants in an area and sometimes place names will hint at occupation by an earlier people. Books and records published or preserved by other scientists or surveyors give leads to the location of sites. In Central America the native chicle-gatherers have called many sites to the attention of archaeologists. In almost every area there are a few people who have collected the relics of the past and preserved them in their own collections providing fertile sources of information. Finally, an archaeologist should survey an area himself to obtain a first-hand knowledge of site location and the variety of artifacts obtainable by surface collecting. After sifting this information, it is possible to recognize some of the historical and cultural problems of the area and to identify some of the sites most likely to provide data to answer initial problems.

THE SURVEY

If the archaeologist has determined that a certain geographic area seems favorable for intensive study he will delimit the area to be investigated, say the Lower Mississippi alluvial valley, the Viru valley in Peru, or the Tehuacan valley in Mexico. Physiographic maps are studied for the locations most often occupied by people, such as the junction of two streams. Soil maps, vegetation maps, climatic data, and other such aids to an understanding of an area's potential usefulness to man are examined. Detail maps such as the U.S.G.S. quadrangle sheets are of great help in the United States in pinpointing the exact location of a site.

Standardized forms are used to record information on the location, characteristics, ownership and many other facts necessary to an adequate judgment on the importance of a site to the problems in mind. Sites are numbered according to one of the standard schemes. The one most commonly used in the United States is a three-unit one with a number representing a specific state (Michigan is 21; Hawaii and Alaska are 49 and 50); a county abbreviation, such as Kt, and a number for the site reflecting its position in a numerical listing of sites within a county. Thus 21-Kt-1 is the Norton Mound Group in Kent County, Michigan. In this case the site is named after the property owner, a fairly common practice of archaeologists, but sites are also named for an adjoining or nearby physical feature; there is no one standard practice.

Aerial photographs have been of great help in locating sites. These may be particularly useful in dry areas with little vegetational cover where surface changes such as former irrigation canals or unusual elevation of ground resulting from long occupation of an area is noticeable, particularly if the photography is done at hours when such features cause shadows. Ancient excavations or construction features now covered by soil may show up in aerial photos because of different vegetational growth from that of the undisturbed ground so that former house floors, fortifications, and other features can be recognized at certain times of the year from the air more readily than on the ground. Infra-red photography from the air has recently been extensively employed in archaeological reconnaissance in the Arctic and other areas. Different species of plants and different quantities of organic material in soils will be distinguished by this film. This makes it possible to determine the size and conformation of sites with a great deal of accuracy.

There is, of course, no substitute for the ground survey, where areas favorable for human occupation are either explored on foot or viewed from a slow moving vehicle. In some instances where an entire area cannot be given such intensive inspection representative sections are soundly searched and estimates made as to the probable density of the occupation of the total area.

The individual site is of course the fundamental location unit of prehistoric occupation, and the inferences and judgments made about societal activities within and between sites depend on the correct analysis of the record of human occupation there. Site size, depth, and physical location are in themselves guides to population size, type of economy, and probable social activities. Collections of surface material will be made to

allow assessment of the time period of occupation, outside cultural relationships or trade, and any functionally different areas within the site.
If the site being surveyed is in an area where something is already known
about its prehistory there are often recognized a number of distinctive
artifact forms which will be of great aid in an initial understanding of the
site. When sites are large it is often advisable to prepare a grid system
over the site and then to collect intensively in a 'random sample' of the
squares which in theory should provide a statistically valid sample of
the materials from the site. This technique would seem to be most useful
in sites without much depth, where plowing has thoroughly disturbed the
occupied area. There are no magic schemes or figures that apply to all
sites and collections. For sites representing urban areas with a time span
of hundreds or even thousands of years different techniques are called
for than for deep cave or rock shelter sites.

Identification of features such as burial mounds, platform areas for
buildings, or fortification or house walls will be highly valuable in assessing the character of the site. For some sites steel probes which will penetrate some three to five feet may be of value, and even augurs when ju-
dicially employed can be an asset. A more common technique is the use
of test pits or trenches which should provide knowledge on the depth,
stratigraphy, and variability of a site.

There are various electronic aids which have been employed in survey
work. Metal detectors have been used for some time, and they are related
to the mine detectors developed during the last two major wars. The
proton magnetometer is a device that has been successfully used to deli-
neate subsurface archaeological features such as the excavated trench
of a fortification wall at the Angell site in southwestern Indiana. The instrument measures the intensity of the earth's gravitational field immediately beneath it so that variations in the readings as the instrument is
moved reflect subsurface soil changes.

The resistivity of soils to electrical currents passing through them has
been used by other fields of science before it was adapted to archaeology.
Soils are capable of conducting an electrical current because of their
mineral salts held in solution in the moisture in the soil. The more moisture held in soil the more efficient the soil is in conducting current. Thus
subsurface textural variations can be located, but the cause may not always be human activities.

A high sensitivity difference magnetometer was employed by University of California scientists to predict that beneath the main earth-covered

pyramid at the La Venta site in Tabasco, Mexico, there is a basalt pyramid.

A technique of survey by means of cameras and artificial lights inserted into hollow structures such as Etruscan tombs in Italy was an ingenious development to save time and money which might have been spent carefully excavating looted toombs. It has of course only limited applicability.

EXCAVATION

The major means of acquiring information on the past behavior of people is the collection of data by excavation. To avoid the unnecessary destruction of the archaeological record, one of the first principles is that excavation should be done only for specific problems of cultural importance and when excavation will contribute to an understanding of these problems. Unless a contribution is made to cultural history or to the understanding of the activities of a particular society, excavation may not be regarded as justified. In all deposits resulting from human living there is a valuable record, not only in the artifacts themselves but also in the nature of the association of the artifacts to each other and to the other deposits in the ground. The manner in which this record was deposited reveals the correct story and, if disturbed by excavation of any kind, is lost forever. When a site is dug, it is destroyed no matter whether the destroying is by commercial steamshovel, river erosion, or the archaeologist's trowel. In the last case, as complete a record as possible is made of all evidences of human handiwork, for anything in the site which shows human contact has significance.

It is easy to see why the excavation of a site should be done with great care by trained men competent to interpret the cultural deposits and the manner in which they were laid down. Excavation techniques vary according to the type of site being excavated. A cave or a rockshelter is quite different from a village site, which in turn presents different problems from large ceremonial structures. The ideal technique would be to remove the natural and human deposits in the same order in which they were accumulated. This ideal is rarely achieved because it is almost impossible to determine that order before excavation.

In excavating village sites, or large blocks within former cities, convenient-sized squares are usually accurately surveyed in a grid pattern. Such squares are then connected with a permanent landmark and are located on the detailed map of the site. All objects or features of the occupation of the site can then be placed on the site map accurately. Excavation in the village site is usually done by the skinning or peeling technique which removes successive horizontal layers until the deepest part of the occupational debris is reached. The depth of these horizontal cuts varies according to the nature of the site. If natural stratigraphy is present, the excavator should adjust his digging to recognize and take advantage of the resultant cultural groupings. By this technique it is relatively easy to recognize disturbances in the soil such as post-molds, pits, and fireplaces. In instances where either successive occupations for a long-continued one have complicated the site and caused the presence of many 'features,' it is common practice to also make a vertical cut which will often indicate when one pit or other soil disturbance has intruded upon another. (See Plate III.)

Burial mounds of moderate size have been excavated by the trench technique. This proceeds, like the vertical slicing of a cake, by removing successive slices of the mound, usually by starting at the top of the slice and working toward the bottom. In this way a vertical profile is kept, and it is rather easy to see disturbances or special features in the mound earth. Domiciliary mounds are usually excavated by a combination of trenching and peeling. A number of trenches are cut a short distance into the mound so that the structure of stratigraphy can be seen in the cross section. Then the flat-top surface is carefully cut down horizontally to each occupation level and the evidence of the former dwellings is uncovered. In more complex groupings of buildings and rooms as in the American Southwest, Middle America, or certain areas of the Old World, the individual rooms are cleared down to the floor before the room walls are studied, mapped, and removed. Caves and rockshelters are also adapted to the combined stripping and trenching techniques. (See Plates III and IV.)

The recovery of prehistoric and historic materials from the seas, lakes, and rivers poses special problems in equipment, training, and recording devices. Societies have been formed with special journals to accommodate underwater archaeological studies. Materials are obtained from marine disasters, caused by either nature or man; to land subsidence, rise in water level, or a combination of both. Such a specialty opens up new vistas for eccentric and mystical interpreters of past human behavior.

RECORDING OF THE DATA

It is, of course, essential that accurate records are made of all finds and features. One of these records should be a field catalogue in which the objects found are listed and described with the location from which each was obtained and its association with other specimens, or features, such as burials or fireplaces. In this catalogue the object is assigned a field. catalogue number. Special catalogues or notebooks may be used to record burials and associated artifacts, house floors, drawings of important designs, or other special features. Duplicate copies are made, and one dispatched to the institution sponsoring the excavation or to some other safe place. A written progress report of all the work should also be made in duplicate and should be a descriptive journal of the excavation. No excavation has ever been too fully recorded by these various techniques.

Photographs have come to play a very important part in the recording and interpretation of sites and their excavation. Photographs must always be taken of burials, structure floors, fire basins, significant soil or debris stratification, and of important finds. Photographs of objects which were taken at the time the specimen was found in the grave sometimes become the only visual record, for the specimen may not appear in the museum for one reason or another. Good photographs also serve to jog the memory of the archaeologist when he is writing his report.

Care should be taken to emphasize the indication of contemporaneity of the varied features found at a site such as the evidence for effective interaction of people within a house, or the connections between habitations in a settlement, or between activities of peoples at different loci within a settlement system. All of these and other relationships need to be clearly established so that the connections between things and people can be accurately observed and measured.

At some sites preservation of water-logged materials or fragile textiles or other organic materials will need to be done. These pose special excavation problems which need to be anticipated wherever possible. Because of transportation, storage, or other practical considerations it is sometimes necessary to study materials in the field and after preliminary analysis and recording to discard or rebury them.

PREPARATION OF THE REPORT

Even though excavation is a most important part of archaeological work it consumes but a small part of the total time and effort necessary to prepare and publish a report. After the field work is over, the excavated material and the records are taken to a laboratory for all of the necessary routine work which must be done before the items are studied. The items must be cleaned, preserved, and often repaired. They are then

given permanent catalogue numbers or some of the material once identified, may be discarded. The specimens are then classified in various
ways and descriptions prepared of typical classes of artifacts or features
and of various specimens. Classification may take a variety of forms for a
variety of functions. Methods of analysis vary and there are now a large
number of quantitative methods that can be applied to archaeological description and analysis. These activities are designed to recognize meaningful similarities or variations of objects and activities within sites and
between sites, between contemporary societies and with sequential societies. The purpose of this effort is to describe, and to gain some understanding of the degrees and kinds of relationships between societies.

There have been developed a wide variety of skills in the natural and
physical sciences which are of considerable assistance to the archaeologist
in his attempt to understand his data. Some of these skills are pertinent
to analyses and identification of the raw materials or of trade items used
by past societies, or the manufacturing techniques by which they were
made, and others are for the purpose of dating past events.

Identification of raw materials such as flint, stone, or obsidian to specific
sources can give valuable aid to the interpretation of past human activity.
Petrographic analysis has successfully been employed in England to prove
the "blue stones" at Stonehenge, in south-central England, came from
Carmarthenshire in Wales, a distance of about 140 airline miles. This
same technique has identified some twenty different rock varieties from
which Neolithic and Bronze Age axes were made. Some of the rock
sources are known. The distribution of the axes over wide areas from their
source of manufacture is an indication of a trade and exchange network.
Some flint sources are distinctive and tentative identifications can be made
on the basis of color and texture, and sometimes of small inclusions. Examples of such material would be the honey-colored flint from Grand
Pressigny in France, the multi-colored Flint Ridge flint from Ohio, or the
grayish-brown banded Dover flint from Tennessee.

More exact identifications have lately been made by trace-element
identification of obsidian sources by a number of different methods. This
has enabled archaeologists to trace trade routes and connections between
prehistoric societies with considerable success.

Amber from northern Europe has been known from Mediterranean
sites, such as the shaft graves at Mycenae, for many years; and some
chemical investigations that were destructive and time-consuming had
indicated its Baltic origin. This was done by the detection of succinic

acid, a characteristic organic acid of Baltic amber. It was later learned that sources in Galicia, Hungary, Rumania, and Sicily have ambers with succinic acid in as high a proportion as that of Baltic amber. Investigation of as little as two milligrams of amber by infrared spectrophotometers identified the spectral range in which important distinctions could be made between Baltic and non-Baltic amber.

Petrographic analysis of clays and mineral inclusions in pottery has been of considerable help in tracing trade connections in the American Southwest and in Mexico. Trace element analyses of pottery and glazes by a number of techniques have shown that the clays of some wine jars in ancient Athens were highly similar to the clays in many jars from two different islands in the eastern Mediterranean. In was also demonstrated that one of the distinctive trade wares in the Maya area almost certainly came from a specific site. Ideally, in analyses of this nature clay should be obtained from near the area of manufacture in order to make the identification of source, style, and manufacturing center as complete as possible. Similar identifications can be made of the metals used in tools and ornaments and in glass so that gradually there will be produced a body of sound knowledge of the distribution of raw materials and manufactured goods. Such precise identifications will put inferences about connections between prehistoric contemporary societies on a much more secure basis.

Recently developed techniques for the identification of the manner in which metal tools or other items were made, and their composition, are of value in determining the level of technical development. Knowledge of the changes in proportions of different ores in the manufacture of bronzes has indicated the change from initial use of almost pure copper in central and western Europe to a true tin bronze metallurgy. With a sound knowledge of chronology it is also evident that considerable variation in skill existed in the several areas of manufacture at any given period of time. It is also possible to identify techniques of manufacture of prehistoric copper implements in the United States by microscopic analysis. These were made by cold hammering and annealing. Similar techniques have aided in the study of the development of the use of iron.

One of the most fruitful products of the study of man and his culture with other fields of scientific investigation is the field of ethnobotany, which deals with man's utilization of the flora of an area and the effect on the flora of man's occupation. The study of prehistoric relationships may be called paleoethnobotany. Studies of man's exploitation of prehistoric

plant remains are of course most successful in dry areas where the specimens are best preserved. It is possible to determine the relative importance of different native plant foods through time; the procurement techniques may be reflected in recovered artifacts or inferred from historic
accounts of known collecting groups; the plants or seeds will indicate the
time of year when they were obtained and indicate whether occupation
was seasonal or on an annual basis.

The dramatic story of the gradual domestication of food plants in the
Near East and Mexico is a product of only the past twenty years or so. It
was this shift from food-collecting to food-producing societies in both the
Old and New Worlds which was so vitally important in the development
of the complex civilizations of those areas after some thousands of years
of gradual improvement of agricultural technology.

Similarly, the study of ethnozoology applied to prehistoric faunal remains has provided substantial and significant information on the relations of past societies to their environments. As with plants, animals
reflect climatic conditions and some of them may be rather sensitive indicators of temperature or moisture conditions. It is possible to identify age
and sex of animal remains with a great deal of accuracy. Knowledge of
the age of the animal can be a guide to the hunting skills and techniques
and to the time of year the animals were killed. This is of course of importance in determining when sites were occupied and the function of
any particular settlement. Butchering techniques reflect the methods of
food processing and may also reflect the ways meat was cooked. Burned
bones also may reflect cooking methods.

The only effective domestication of animals was in the Old World.
Intensive study is now under way by a number of mammalogists on the
history of this process and the regions where this took place.

The development of flotation techniques to recover fine vegetal and
small light bone material from refuse pits, house floors, and other village
debris has been highly successful. The techniques have resulted in the
recovery of a much wider range of seeds, nut hulls, small-fish bones, and
other food fragments or by-products and have substantially altered the
evidence of the food supply of some prehistoric populations.

Detailed study of desiccated human feces from dry caves and shelters
in western America, Mexico, and from Kentucky have contributed a great
deal to the understanding of the composition of the diet of prehistoric
people and something of the manner of food preparation. In addition,
studies could be made which could identify fossil pollen, pathologic re-

sults, nutritional properties, and the presence of parasitic organisms. Samples from Mesa Verde in southwest Colorado, in one case, contained eggs of the pinworm, *Enterobius vermiculares,* a rectal parasite, particularly of children. Another specimen contained eggs of the thorny-headed worm, probably ingested by eating insects or parasitized rodents. This worm could cause diarrhea and other serious involvements.

SOIL PROFILES

In recent years the study of soils, called 'pedology,' has been of considerable assistance to the archaeologist even though the primary purpose of this branch of knowledge has been to benefit agriculture. Soils are formed from the native rock of a region by mechanical weathering and by the disintegration of vegetal material which with rain water produces chemical weathering. The formation of soil is most rapid in temperate regions for it is in such areas that the chemical weathering is most effective. The decomposing vegetal material is called 'humus,' and under certain conditions it has an acid effect on the soil. The stages of soil formation and alteration are studied by means of vertical sections, which are technically referred to as profiles. Soil analysts can recognize horizontal zones with differing characteristics, which are called horizons.

Different climatic zones produce significantly different soils irrespective of the underlying rock formations from which they were derived. Because of this it is possible to recognize the climatic conditions which were in operation when a particular soil horizon was formed. Soils formed in coniferous forest areas with relatively cool summers and ample rainfall are called podsols. This combination produces an upper, or A, horizon of acid humus forming humic acids when carried down with the rain. The acids dissolve the bases and certain other components called sesquioxides to produce the lower part of the A horizon. When the humic acids can carry off no more sesquioxides, these are deposited as a brownish or reddish or black zone, which is called the B horizon. The leaching takes place in the A horizon, and in its lower zones the soil often assumes a light color. Horizon C is the unaltered parent material below the B horizon. Since podsols have the bases and sesquioxides carried downward, it is an acid soil which attacks organic matter such as bone, wood, shell, and other materials deposited in a site and hastens their decomposition.

Another soil type called the brown-earths forms in areas with a warm summer and moderate rainfall. In this soil the top humus layer is sufficiently aerated to oxidize the decaying vegetal material and the soil is thus either neutral or only slightly acid. Another soil type, largely of loess origin, is called 'chernozem,' or 'black-earth,' and is usually found in continental grassland areas such as the eastern plains of the United States or in southern Russia. This soil because of the continued presence of bases is never acid. In dryer steppe condition 'chestnut' soils are produced.

A mature soil profile takes a considerable period of time to develop and it will vary according to the climatic factors. In California some of the older cultural levels have been located which underlie mature soil profiles estimated by experts to be at least 4000 years old.

CHEMICAL ANALYSIS OF SOILS FOR IDENTIFICATION OF OCCUPIED AREAS

One of the results of soil study and analysis has aided archaeologists in the identification of sites. Soil chemists have provided a method for the determination of acid or base soils. Briefly, this method recognizes pure water as having a value of pH 7 in regard to its acid or base composition. Soils which provide a watery solution more acid than water have a pH value lower than 7; soils which are less acid than water will provide a pH value greater than 7. Most soils have values between 4 and 9. Inexpensive sets can now be purchased which enable anyone to determine the pH value of his soil, and this is of use to farmers and garden growers. It helps the archaeologist interpret his site, for an acid soil will cause disintegration of perishable material much more rapidly than will a base soil. When the acidity of the soil is known, the archaeologist has a better idea than before whether a poor condition of bone implements or refuse and burials is the result of a long period in the soil or of rapid decay. In Scandinavia there are certain large areas where the soil consistently shows a base reaction. Quite a number of sites have been located by making collections at regular intervals in likely locations. When the soil tests show an acid reaction or pH value less than 7, it is likely the spot represents a former human habitation area which by the deposition of organic material has changed the acid-base relationship. The presence of bones is an excellent clue to the location of a site. It is said that the soil of an area that was formerly densely occupied may contain as much as fifty times the normal amount of phosphate. Thus within a large site it is possible to determine the areas with maximum occupation. Certain restricted areas may have high concentrations of nitrates and may reflect fecal deposits or human latrine wastes.

Buried soils may have deposits of quite foreign origin such as volcanic ash layers. When such ash layers can be identified as to their specific source by trace element identification and the time of eruption determined by radiocarbon dates on organic material buried under the ash, then an excellent chronological tool has been gained which is applicable over the area of the ash fall. A recently developed guide to understanding the vegetational composition that helped to produce ancient soils is the study of biogenic opal or phytoliths. Most plants secrete silica bodies of distinctive shapes and sizes which are localized primarily in the aereal portion of vascular and epidermal tissues of plants. Studies of opaline residues in buried soils in the Midwest have aided in the recognition of a short-term intrusion of prairie vegetation into Ohio about 13,000 years ago. Such studies are just beginning but should make valuable contributions to vegetational and climatic history.

The Pleistocene Period and the Dating of Human History

An archaeologist should know enough geology to recognize when the expertise of a trained geologist is needed to interpret the association of natural features with the evidence of man's occupation. Geologists are particularly necessary in areas which were affected by the changes caused in the earth's surface during the Pleistocene period, or Ice Age. During the last one hundred and fifty years geologists have recognized four major and many minor periods within the last million or so years, when, in certain areas, particularly of the northern hemisphere there were large accumulations of snow and ice, much as in present-day Greenland. As the snow and ice accumulated in depth in those areas where weather conditions were most favorable, the edges of the ice mass moved outward until great areas in northern Eurasia and North America were covered by continental glaciers and mountain areas such as the Alps and Rocky Mountains had their glacial accumulations.

As the ice moved, it incorporated within its mass and on its surface the loose detritus of earth, sand, gravel, and even bedrock. It acted as a scouring agent during the thousands of years of its growth. When the climate became more moderate, these great ice fields gradually diminished in size, shrinking backward from their margins and depositing the earth and stone which had accumulated during its outward movement.

During the Pleistocene period then, there were factors at work which made great changes in the environment around the world in which man and his culture developed. In western Europe one major area of ice formation was in the Alps and another was in Scandinavia. It is in those areas that the first studies of glaciation were made. In addition to the four major ice advances and retreats (our present period may be the fourth interglacial), there were minor climatic changes accompanied by movements of the ice fronts.

The great amount of moisture needed to produce the great ice-sheets was drawn from the water on the earth and as a result the level of the oceans was lowered some 350 feet exposing large areas of the present continental shelf and making possible movements of plants and animals across such areas as the Bering Sea, the English Channel, and between mainland Asia and island groups off its eastern and southeastern coast. The weight of the ice on the land depressed some areas, but since the last removal of the ice they have been slowly rising. This phenomenon has been carefully studied in Scandinavia and in the Great Lakes area. The rise and fall of the general sea level due to the forming, and the melting of the glaciers, is called glacial 'eustasy,' while the uplift of the earth due to the melting of the ice mass is called the 'isostatic reaction.' In many areas of the world, beach lines and river terraces were formed during the glacial period which are now at varying distances above the present sea level or river floodplain. Human occupation often took place along these beaches or terraces because of the then available food supply. Such occupations may then be dated in terms of the period of formation of the beach or terrace. During the long and warm interglacial periods sea level was higher than it is today and the succession of such beaches has been intensively studied in the Mediterranean and the east coast of the United States.

The very gradual climatic fluctuations of the Pleistocene had a profound effect on the vegetation and animal forms upon which man depended for his existence. With colder conditions and the advance of the ice, those animal and plant forms adapted to warm or temperate climates were displaced or failed to survive and their places were taken by forms adapted to colder regimes. Thus, there are found in Europe such skeletal remains as the elephants, hippopotamus, rhinoceros, and a group of horses related to the zebra, all of which indicate a climate much warmer than the present. There are other remains, such as the mammoth, the reindeer, lemming, and the arctic fox which reflect much colder periods. Some animals are adapted to a forest environment such as the beaver, red deer, brown bear and lynx, while steppe or prairie conditions are indicated by the horse and certain antelope. At times under favorable conditions plant remains or fossil pollen are preserved furnishing additional evidence of the climatic conditions to which man had to adjust.

In the Old World the presence of man and his relatives during the early part of the Pleistocene is known from deposits dated by geological and physical-chemical techniques. These very early finds consist primarily of flint implements of various kinds, described in the following chapter and a few skeletal parts of early forms of man. During the last two glacial and interglacial periods, there is an increasing amount of human skeletal material and cultural data which is found in cave or rock shelter deposits, where it is often better preserved than in the open sites, and where the conditions of deposition and association of items are usually somewhat easier to interpret.

The association of man with a succession of events during the Pleistocene provided in most cases only a relative chronology in which events preceded or succeeded each other, but without, in most cases, providing a year-by-year record. Producing such a record was and is a long laborious procedure requiring the skills of interdisciplinary research and the gradual development of interpretive skills in various sciences.

CHRONOLOGY

Of the greatest importance to the archaeologist is the determination of the chronology of the area with which he is dealing. There are two end points on this ladder of human development. The top rung is the latest culture complex, which in the Americas is usually recognized by the presence of European manufactured trade items such as glass beads, iron knives, or brass. The bottom rung is represented by the earliest appearance of artifacts utilized by man to aid in his struggle for existence. It is essential that the most complete sequence of cultures be obtained so that the cultural story is a continuous one from the first to the last stage. When this is available, it is possible to record the changes in styles and in techniques that have been the result of local development and also to see the influences and materials that have come in from other areas and become a part of the local cultural growth.

The determination of the chronology or time period can be made either by means of relative or absolute chronology. The former is much more common. Relative chronology is obtained through stratigraphy, seriation, typology, and other techniques discussed later. It provides a sequence of artifacts and cultures but does not provide this time framework with accurate dates in terms of a year-by-year count. As a result one knows where a particular culture belongs in relation to others but the length of time it existed, or how many years ago, is not precisely known. In contrast, there is the much more accurate dating, or absolute chronology, afforded by a year-by-year count as in dendrochronology, the record of glacial varves, or by ancient coins, as in the Mediterranean area.

STRATIGRAPHY

Excavation of stratified sites, where one cultural level is found overlying an earlier one, provides one type of relative chronology. In such a case the fact that one culture is later than another is perfectly clear, but what is not known is the length of time that each existed or how long an interval of time separated them. In an attempt, perhaps, to infuse a bit of life into such relative chronologies archaeologists often assign a period of years to these culture groups or periods. The span of years is based on 'guesses' that utilize whatever evidence there is suggestive of a time factor. For example, some archaeologists who have excavated large shell-mound sites have taken the number of burials, and by knowing the average death rate of similar societies, have used it as a figure to determine the probable size of the group that deposited the shell-mound as a refuse accumulation. They have then estimated how much shell food these individuals would be likely to eat in a year, and then, taking the cubic content of the mound into consideration, have arrived at a possible figure for the age of the mound. Obviously, however, such estimates are not accurate, and there are so many unknown factors the result is hardly worth the labor of calculation. Other estimates have been given on the basis of comparable cultural units where the length of time is known. The horizontal extent of a site, the depth of material present, and the areal extent of a cultural division within a geographic region give some indication of its possible length of life.

FOSSIL POLLEN

Another method of determining relative chronology and connecting cultural material with climatic phases is by the study of fossil pollen. Like the study of glacial varves, it is most useful for comparatively recent times. In northern Europe, particularly, archaeological material has been found in peat deposits or in other beds with well-preserved botanical remains. The most important of the various botanical sources is tree pollen, which reflects the types of trees in existence during the formation of the deposits. The most valuable studies have been made where deposits of some depth were found which provided evidence for considerable changes in the forest flora and these in turn reflect significant climatic changes. In some instances peat deposits with good pollen contents have been obtained from directly on top of varved clay beds which could be dated, or on raised beach lines which also could be connected with a known chronology. Studies of ancient wooden trackways across bog areas in Britain have shown that their construction corresponds to pollen counts which indicate a wetter climate than that which immediately preceded and followed the trackways' construction.

Pollen analysis has not been studied very much in relation to archaeology in North America. The changes in flora, already amply demonstrated, have been correlated with radiocarbon dates to produce a sound understanding of the similarities and differences between the vegetational composition of various northern United States areas from Minnesota to New England. Important pollen studies have also been done in the Southwest and the Northwest Coast so that archaeologists can now correlate the cultural changes in prehistoric sites with floral and accompanying faunal changes.

SERIATION

This technique of arriving at a relative chronology is based on the principle of stylistic change which takes place through time in a given class of materials. In primitive cultures those manufactures which were easily and rapidly made and which also were sufficiently variable to reflect the style of the moment are the best for seriation. For this reason pottery, figurines, projectile points, axes, or other items from a considerable number of sites over a fair-sized area are arranged in a stylistic or logical sequence in relation to some known end point, which is usually either at the end or beginning of the series. This technique was successfully employed by Professor Kroeber of the University of California to determine the relative age of sites in the southwestern United States, Mexico, and Peru. In this manner it would be fairly simple to arrange examples of various automobiles in their order of production by means of their style if one had a fairly complete series of examples from the earliest to the latest.

TYPOLOGICAL METHOD

The crudity or excellence with which artifacts have been produced has sometimes been taken as evidence of relative age. This is sometimes justifiable and is supported by such examples as the early crude flint weapons of Europe's Old Stone Age. Such tools are, however, no cruder than rela-

tively modern Australian types. This criterion for age is not a reliable one
and should be employed with great care.

DISTRIBUTIONAL OR AGE-AREA METHOD

When culture traits are found in the same general area, those having
the greatest distribution are sometimes considered to be the oldest. This
assumption works best when dealing with closely related forms such as
the house types in the Southwest, where the small semi-subterranean
house was distributed over a wider territory than the large, complex multi-
roomed pueblo structure. At best, however, this method is only suggestive
and needs to be verified by stratigraphy.

PATINATION OR WEATHERING

Some attempts have been made to provide a relative age for artifacts
on the basis of the chemical or mechanical weathering shown by the
specimen as the result of exposure to climatic conditions or long burial.
These observed differences in such specimens cannot be measured by any
known technique, and there are usually too many unknown factors which
may have produced the changes.

Relative dating of obsidian artifacts has successfully been used for more
than ten years in a variety of environments. The thickness of the hydration layer formed on a freshly exposed surface by water from the atmosphere is carefully measured in microns. The thicker the hydration layer
the older the artifact found in a similar environment. The rate of hydration is controlled primarily by temperature and by chemical composition.
Different kinds of obsidians hydrate at different rates. The technique is
useful but the rate of hydration is determined by other dating methods
and is not as accurate a time clock as some of the other techniques available.

ABSOLUTE CHRONOLOGY

In some areas of the world there has been achieved the arrangement
of prehistoric cultures into a year by year chronology. In the southwestern
United States dendrochronology and in northern Europe glacial varve
chronology (both of these techniques are described later in this essay)
have provided the accuracy of dating which is desired in every area. In
the Maya area the archaeologists have the advantage of the Maya calendar which records the date of erection of various monuments and buildings. It is of great assistance in arranging the various sites or portions of

sites with regard to the Maya calendar, and within its own system is remarkably accurate as a year-by-year chronology. Unfortunately this Mayan calendrical system has not been satisfactorily correlated with our present chronology, although the margin of error within a number of different correlations is rather small.

GLACIAL VARVES

This method of determining chronology was the first which produced an accounting of geological events in terms of years. The different layers or lamina observed on the floors of former glacial lakes are called 'varves' in Swedish. It was Baron Gerard de Geer, a Swedish scientist who pondered on the meaning of these sediments during the latter part of the nineteenth century and initiated the development of techniques for interpreting this geological record. De Geer and his colleagues have demonstrated that the varves were deposited on the floors of glacial lakes or other relatively quiet water bodies. The melting of the glaciers during their recession was accelerated during the summer months and the runoff spread over the lake carrying with it sand and clay particles in suspension. The heavier coarser grains would naturally sink to the bottom first while the finer material might not have reached the bottom until winter, when the melting would cease. This process went on year after year. Not only can the yearly succession be observed by the change in the deposited material, but the coarser grains are almost always noticeably lighter in color than the finer sediments. By carefully studying and comparing these annual deposits from southern Scandinavia north to the more central mountainous area, a chronology from the present to some 10,000 years ago has been obtained. This chronology can be connected with the deposition of moraines and other surface features which can in turn be connected with human occupation areas. This resulted in unusually accurate dating of these successive cultural periods in the Baltic and North Sea areas.

This same method has been applied in northeastern North America but with less success because the most recent varve deposits cannot yet be connected with the Christian chronology. This is due to a gap of unknown time span between the varve series in the Connecticut Valley and the varve series northeast of Lake Huron. Most of the evidence of early man in North America (some 25,000 or so years ago) has come from the western part of the continent. Our time estimates of North American prehistory up to the appearance of radiocarbon dating were in some measure based on this none-too-accurate time scale in the Northeast and adjacent

Canada and on estimates of the length of time for the Niagara River to wear away the rock formations as Niagara Falls retreated southward.

Dendrochronology or Tree Ring Chronology

In the southwestern United States the study of the development of the prehistoric Indian cultures has been greatly aided by dendrochronology, which has permitted an arrangement of the archaeological material into the Christian calendar. This field was made possible through the work of an astronomer, Dr. A. E. Douglass, who was interested in determining the long-range effects of sun spots on the weather of the earth. To do this he utilized the annual growth rings of certain southwestern trees, particularly western yellow pine, which reflect climatic variation in the width of their rings and their growth pattern. This method of tree ring study is by no means a simple one and only trained individuals with considerable experience in handling, recording, and interpreting the ring sequence are competent to pass judgment on the age of prehistoric specimens.

The inner ring pattern of trees of modern or known cutting date is compared with the outer ring pattern of older specimens taken from buildings erected some 100 to 200 years ago. From such specimens Douglass was able to pass to the wood and charcoal specimens of late prehistoric age and gradually extend the sequence until it is now possible to date with great accuracy archaeological sites in certain areas of the Southwest as far back as the first year of the Christian era.

Dendrochronology has also been adapted to other areas, notably in northwestern Europe and Alaska and to some degree in Russia, Israel, and Japan. Since tree ring growth has as one of its important dimensions variations in climate, the variations of tree growth in the Southwest is also giving important information on prehistoric climatic variations with a precision rarely obtainable from any other non-historical source.

Bristlecone pine sections from the Southwest have been collected which contain over 7000 of the year-by-year growth rings. These calendar year records have been used to check the accuracy of radiocarbon dating. Processing sections of the bristlecone of known age in radiocarbon laboratories has resulted in the recognition of changes in the availability of Carbon-14 in the atmosphere in the past.

For some years the age of the earth and of its major geological periods have been dated by means of the radioactivity method. Through research in physics it is known that there is a constant and determinable rate for the disintegration of a radioactive isotope in minerals so that such minerals taken from a specific geological stratum can be used to date that stratum. For events within the span of time occupied by man, or near man, in the geologic past a number of decay ratios of radioactive isotopes have been particularly valuable. For older events the decay of potassium-40 to a gas, argon-40, can be measured, and the age of a rock formation can be obtained, such as has been done to date the volcanic tuff formations at Olduvai Gorge in Africa. Also applicable for the Pleistocene geologic period in which man's activity is concentrated is the rubidium-strontium method, which is valuable for some volcanic formations and for obsidian.

The most valuable time clock for most archaeological work has been radiocarbon dating, which was developed by Dr. W. F. Libby and his associates at the University of Chicago in the late 1940's. This dating method is based on the amount of the heavy isotope C^{14} found in dead organic material compared with the amount in living organic material as a measure of the time in radiocarbon years since the organism died. The half-life of carbon-14 has been measured by a number of different tests, and the most accurate value seems to be 5730 ± 40 years. If a specimen of charcoal or other organic material from a site is found to have three-quarters of the C^{14} content of living organisms the specimen will have died some 2865 radiocarbon years ago plus or minus a possible error of a variable number of years.

In the twenty years since the development of C^{14} dating, close to a hundred dating laboratories have been established all over the world. The many modifications which have been made in the basic assumptions that seemed valid in the original program have been aids to more accurate and more intelligent measurements of past human activities. The method has been particularly useful in measuring events over the past 30,000 years, and in many areas provided the first sound measure of elapsed time since specific prehistoric events took place. It is not sufficiently precise to allow archaeologists to speak of dated events at one or a number of sites as having taken place at the same time.

A method of obtaining relative age of bone materials from prehistoric sites is the study of their natural radioactivity. Fossil bones will have higher uranium and fluorine content than modern specimens. Studies of fluorine content helped to indicate that the assemblage of animal and human bone at the Piltdown site in England could not have been deposited at one time. Measurements of low-level beta activity in fossil bone in a flow counter incorporating anticoincidence counters by Jelinek (1965) and associates at the University of Michigan have indicated that while the natural radioactivity can be utilized in problems of relative chronology the tests must be conducted with rigorous methodological control.

Archaeomagnetism is the study of the remanent magnetism or archaeological remains. The earth's magnetic field changes continually both in intensity and direction. Recent variations in the relationship between true north and magnetic north and in the angle of dip of a magnetic needle have been recorded in a number of European and American cities. Most fired clays such as pottery, kilns, brick, fireplaces, or deep fired clay floor have a stable remanent magnetism that records the magnetic field of the earth at the time the specimen was fired. The technique, which has been successfully used in Europe and in Japan is just beginning to be developed in the United States by Professor Robert L. DuBois of the University of Oklahoma. He began in the Southwest because it is necessary to be able to date one or more clay samples on the directional curve by some accurate means such as dendrochronology or even radiocarbon. When such a time scale can be obtained fired samples from other sites when plotted on the directional curve will give a rather accurate measurement of the age of the sample. This method is said to be effective for about the last 35,000 to 50,000 years. It is also said to be accurate within fifty years or less, which is quite a bit better than radiocarbon dating.

Another dating technique using pottery and radiation activity is called thermoluminescence dating, which gives results spoken of as TL ages. This is still in the developmental stage but promising results have been obtained, particularly on pottery from the Mediterranean and Near East and from western Europe. It is also a valuable technique in distinguishing between genuine and spurious ceramic specimens.

CONCLUSION

It can thus be seen by this incomplete survey that the study of archaeology is a complex and involved undertaking. It ranges in its coverage of fields of knowledge from art history to zoology, from the study of prehistoric climates caused by celestial events governed by our solar system to the identification of ancient volcanic eruptions. Its immediate subject matter ranges from an understanding of the meaning of the flint chipping debris from a quarry or workshop to the understanding of the growth and development of the great civilizations of the Near East or of Middle America. The many interpretive techniques, which make interdisciplinary co-operation imperative, are time-consuming and expensive. The study of archaeology has an evolution of its own and adaptive mechanisms to enable it to keep pace with other human activities with which it competes in our contemporary society. The contribution of archaeology to modern knowledge, along with those of geology, biology, and other sciences, has changed remarkably man's view of himself and the universe in less than 150 years.

BIBLIOGRAPHY

Aitken, Martin L.
   Physics and Archaeology. Interscience Publishers, New York, 1961.
Binford, Sally R., and Lewis R. Binford
   New Perspectives in Archaeology. Aldine Publishing Co., Chicago, 1968.
Braidwood, Robert J.
   Prehistoric Men. Seventh edition. Scott, Foresman and Co., Chicago, Ill., 1967.
Brothwell, Don, and Eric Higgs
   Science in Archaeology. A Comprehensive Survey of Progress and Research. Thames and Hudson, Bristol, England, 1963.
Chang, K. C.
   Rethinking Archaeology. Random House, New York, 1967.
Clark, Grahame
   Archaeology and Society, Reconstructing the Prehistoric Past. Methuen & Co., London, 1957.
Clarke, David L.
   Analytical Archaeology. Methuen & Co., London, 1968.
Cleland, Charles E.
   The Prehistoric Animal Ecology and Ethnozoology of the Upper Great Lakes Region. Museum of Anthropology, University of Michigan, Anthropological Paper No. 29, Ann Arbor, 1966.
Deetz, James
   Invitation to Archaeology. The Natural History Press, Garden City, N.Y., 1967.
De Laet, Sigfried J.
   Archaeology and Its Problems. Phoenix House, London, 1957.
Heizer, Robert F.
   The Archaeologist at Work: A Source Book in Archaeological Method and Interpretations. Harper and Row, New York, 1959.

Hole, Frank, and Robert F. Heizer
    An Introduction to Prehistoric Archaeology. Holt, Rinehart and Winston,
    New York, 1965.
Kenyon, Kathleen M.
    Beginning in Archaeology. Second edition, revised. Phoenix House, Lon-
    don, 1961.
Levey, Martin, editor
    Archeological Chemistry. University of Pennsylvania Press, Philadelphia,
    1967.
Meggers, Betty J., editor
    Anthropological Archaeology in the Americas. Anthropological Society of
    Washington, Washington, D.C., 1968.
Meighan, Clement W.
    Archaeology: An Introduction. Chandler Publishing Co., San Francisco,
    1966.
Oakley, Kenneth P.
    Frameworks for Dating Fossil Man. Aldine Publishing Co., Chicago, 1964.
Pyddoke, Edward, editor
    The Scientist and Archaeology. Roy Publishers, New York, 1963.
Taylor, Joan du Plat, editor
    *Marine Archaeology. Developments During Sixty Years in the Mediter-
    ranean*. Hutchinson of London, 1965.
Taylor, Walter
    A Study of Archaeology. American Anthropological Association Memoir
    No. 69, Menasha, Wis., 1948.
Trigger, Bruce G.
    Beyond History: The Methods of Prehistory. Holt, Rinehart and Winston,
    New York, 1968.
Wheeler, Robert E. M.
    Archaeology from the Earth. Clarendon Press, Oxford, 1954.
Willey, Gordon R., and Philip Phillips
    Method and Theory in American Archaeology. University of Chicago
    Press, 1958.
Yarnell, Richard Asa
    *Aboriginal Relationships Between Culture and Plant Life in the Upper
    Great Lakes Region*. Museum of Anthropology, University of Michigan,
    Anthropological Paper No. 23, Ann Arbor, 1964.

R. A. GOULD

III

The Old Stone Age

THE IDEA OF THE OLD STONE AGE

GREEK AND ROMAN SCHOLARS KNEW that stone tools were made and used by various peoples, but this knowledge had to be rediscovered after the Dark Ages. In 1717 a manuscript written originally in the sixteenth century by Michel Mercatus, physician to Pope Clement VIII, was published which described chipped stone arrow and spear points. Mercatus took issue with the popular medieval idea that chipped stone tools were thunderbolts and suggested instead that they were used by men to sharpen hunting spears and other weapons. This view was presented even more forcefully by Antoine de Jussieu in 1723, with the remarkably modern-sounding argument that the native peoples of 'the American Islands and Canada' used such tools as stone axes, arrow points, and wedges. In 1790 John Frere discovered chipped stone hand-axes (today recognized as being of Acheulian type) in association with the bones of unknown animals (now known to be elephants) in a clay pit at Hoxne in Suffolk County, England. Frere asserted that these stone objects were 'weapons of war, fabricated and used by a people who had not the use of metals.'

Yet Frere's discovery was ignored for several years while debate raged between Catastrophists like Cuvier and Buckland and Fluvialists led by Charles Lyell. The Fluvialists argued that geologically ancient processes were basically the same as those of the present and proceeded at all times in a uniform way and a uniform rate consistent with those observed in the present. This was known as the doctrine of uniformitarianism, and it was opposed by the Catastrophists, who interpreted the earth's geologic strata as a series of distinct periods interrupted by great catastrophes, including the flood described in Genesis. During this period other scholars

47

like Tournal, Schmerling, and MacEnery were making additional discoveries like those of Frere and were building up a body of evidence to support the idea that men who made and used stone tools lived before 4004 B.C., the year set by Archbishop Ussher as the date of creation.

In 1806 Professor Rasmus Nyerup urged the formation of a National Danish Museum of Antiquities, stating that 'everything which has come down to us from heathendom is wrapped in a thick fog; it belongs to a space of time we cannot measure.' In an effort to dispel this fog of confusion, the historian Vedel-Simonsen first proposed what has since become known as the 'three-age system.' In 1813 he argued that the earliest inhabitants of Scandinavia used weapons of stone and wood. Later these people learned the use of copper, and finally they developed iron-working. This idea was not widely accepted, however, until C. J. Thomsen became the first curator at the National Museum in 1816 and began organizing the collections into three successive ages of Stone, Bronze, and Iron. Thomsen continued his efforts in this direction until his death in 1865, by which time his publications, exhibits, and contacts with colleagues in other parts of Europe had led to widespread application of this framework to other areas.

As the three-age system gained acceptance, it was quickly realized that certain refinements were needed if it was to remain useful both in Scandinavia and elsewhere. Thomsen and his student, J. J. A. Worsaae, both regarded the three-age system as a historical rather than an evolutionary scheme. Worsaae noted the abrupt shift in Denmark from the Stone Age to the Bronze Age and concluded that this new technology must have been brought into the area from somewhere else (as is known today, from the Middle East) rather than developed in a step-by-step fashion in Denmark. Another contemporary Schandinavian scholar, Sven Nilsson, promoted comparative studies of archaeological materials. Although he accepted Thomsen and Worsaae's idea of several waves of invaders bringing changes to prehistoric Scandinavian cultures, Nilsson also emphasized that culture as a whole evolved gradually, with the human race 'constantly undergoing a gradual and progressive development.'

More than anyone else, it was the Danes who systematized the field of archaeology during the first half of the nineteenth century. The scheme they devised became the basis for the classification of archaeological discoveries made by later scholars. The concept of the Stone Age as the earliest stage of human prehistory became increasingly subdivided. By the mid-nineteenth century enough new evidence had accumulated to cause French and English scholars to note a marked difference between the chipped stone industries of the earlier stone age and the ground and polished stone artifacts of the later periods. On this basis in 1865 Lord Avebury (formerly Sir John Lubbock) distinguished between the Paleolithic (Old Stone Age) and the Neolithic (or New Stone Age). As work in different parts of Europe continued, there grew an inevitable tendency toward specialization, with certain pioneer workers like Edward Lartet, Henry Christy, Victor Brun, Louis Lartet, Boyd Dawkins, and Gabriel de Mortillet focusing their attention on the paleolithic cultures of Europe.

Several classifications of the Old Stone Age resulted from these investigations. In particular, Mortillet's six-period classification of 1869, as shown by the historian of archaeology Glyn Daniel, 'remained the basis of Paleolithic classification until well into the twentieth century.' Mortillet's classification represented an adaptation of the 'type fossil' approach used in paleontology and geology to archaeological materials. That is, certain artifacts found in association with particular strata were regarded as characteristic of that strata wherever else they were found. From 1900 to about 1930 most paleolithic research was aimed at refining or elaborating Mortillet's original classification, with notable work being done by the Abbé Breuil, the Count Begouen, Norbert Casteret, R.A.S. Macalister, H. Obermaier, and D. Peyrony. Daniel speaks of this phase of paleolithic studies as 'the outgrowth of the geological-epochal treatment of Mortillet and the French School, and of the typological treatment of . . . the Scandinavian School.' That is, certain artifact assemblages were identified both as technological stages and as chronological periods based on geological and stratigraphic associations, or, as Daniel has succinctly phrased it, 'an uneasy marriage of geological and historical concepts.'

During the last thirty-five years an increasing number of archaeologists have criticized this technological-geological method of classification. Among other things they have emphasized that the subdivisions of the Old Stone Age do not denote cultures but technologies often based on only a single tool-type. Although the word 'culture' is frequently applied to such artifact assemblages, this usage is highly inappropriate in the sociological or anthropological sense. Of late there has been a tendency to attempt to reconstruct wider areas of ancient human behavior than technology alone. Most of this has centered on prehistoric economic systems and related areas of interest such as ecology, demography, settlement patterns, and trade. In 1944 V. Gordon Childe proposed that the labels of the three-age system be abandoned as chronological markers and be retained as technological terms. In some of his later work Childe suggested that the term 'Paleolithic' refer to ancient societies which depended for their livelihood on hunting and gathering wild foods and that the term 'Neolithic' refer to ancient agricultural societies. Thus when Childe spoke of the 'Neolithic Revolution' he did not mean a change from chipped to ground stone tools but a shift from a hunting to a horticultural economy. More recently, scholars like Robert Braidwood and Grahame Clark have refined and extended this economic approach to prehistory.

Other difficulties with the technological-geological classification arose when it was applied in areas outside Western Europe. As archaeological work proceeded, for example, in the Middle East and Africa, continuing debates arose over the wisdom of extending the terminology of the European classification to include materials which differed in many respects from the type specimens. Finally, evidence from excavations in Europe demonstrated that several epochs which had been thought to be sequential were, in fact, contemporaneous.

For these and other reasons archaeologists today are in the anomalous position of using terms derived from the old and somewhat unsatisfactory technological-geological classification while at the same time developing methods which will either eliminate the need for these terms or will broaden their meaning to include wider aspects of human behavior than technology alone. Thus the idea of the Old Stone Age is presently in a state of flux, with an increasing emphasis on studies that include ancient demography, climates, settlements, and other broadly ecological and anthropological topics. To archaeologists working along these lines the Old Stone Age has come to mean a way of life, broadly defined by an economy based entirely on hunting and gathering (including fishing) in which stone and bone tools are of primary importance in the technology. Within this framework there is a wide variety of adaptations according to differences in habitat and local resources, but, speaking in a general sense, this is a way of life which has characterized man's history from its beginning until the invention and spread of agriculture within the last 10,000 years. The Old Stone Age way of life has survived until the present or the recent past in a few remote areas which are poorly suited for agriculture, such as the Arctic shores of Greenland, Canada, and Alaska, the Kalahari Desert of Africa, and the Australian Desert. In short, the idea of the Old Stone Age is more useful today as a broad label for a way of life and its accompanying technology than as a time period in human history.

MAKING STONE TOOLS

What kind of material did ancient man look for when making stone tools? Primarily the concern was for a lithic material in which he could obtain a sharp working edge for purposes of cutting, scraping, and shaping materials like skin, wood, and bone. Certain types of stone with a high silica content—flint, chert, chalcedony, obsidian, and others—were best suited for this and figure heavily in the tool assemblages of ancient man. Where these materials were absent or scarce, men used varieties of stone with more pronounced grain and rougher texture—i.e. various quartzites and basalt—which were less than ideal for this purpose but nevertheless could serve. In historic times there have been many documented cases, particularly among American Indians and Australian Aborignes, of people who have found broken glass ideal for making many kinds of tools which were formerly made of stone.

Studies of ancient flint quarries and trade in lithic materials have shown how important the selection of appropriate raw materials was to Stone Age man. Much work remains to be done in this field, but analysis of lithic materials at archaeological sites to determine the sources of raw material (and thereby infer patterns of prehistoric trade and transport) is presently gaining importance. A new development along these lines, called 'neutron activation analysis,' offers the prospect of absolute precision in identifying lithic materials and their sources. This technique has recently been tested on obsidian artifacts made by ancient Indians in the eastern United States and, by this means, the source of the raw material has been located in Yellowstone Park, Wyoming. Similar studies have been carried out in the Mediterranean region.

A sharp blow with a stone on a nodule of flint, chert, or any of these silicious materials will produce a flake showing distinctive characteristics, including a striking platform, bulb of percussion, and ripple marks radiating from the point of impact, accompanied by radiating fissures and a bulbar scar. The nodule or core from which the flake was originally struck will show a corresponding negative bulb. Archaeologists look for these features when trying to recognize stone flakes which are the result of human activity, though it must be admitted that under special conditions stone flakes showing all or most of these features can occur entirely as the result of natural conditions. Usually an archaeologist also relies on the context in which stone flakes occur to tell him whether or not they are man-made. For example, stone flakes found in association with hearths and splintered animal bones suggest a human habitation, whereas stone flakes found on the ground surface unaccompanied by other cultural remains may be a much less certain case.

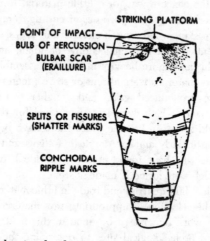

STRIKING PLATFORM

POINT OF IMPACT
BULB OF PERCUSSION
BULBAR SCAR
(ERAILLURE)

SPLITS OR FISSURES
(SHATTER MARKS)

CONCHOIDAL
RIPPLE MARKS

FIG. 1. Diagram showing the characteristics of the bulbar surface of a flint flake produced by percussion.

During the late nineteenth century there was speculation that man may have lived in pre-glacial times, during the Pliocene. Linked to this idea was the argument that the tools of these earliest men must have been cruder than even the simplest stone hand-axes, consisting of nothing more than rocks with naturally sharp edges which were simply picked up, used, and discarded, with no effort at trimming or shaping. The term 'eolith' (literally, 'dawn-stone') was coined to include such minimal artifacts, and controversies raged over this for many years and in fact continue to appear from time to time. Certainly there is nothing unreasonable about the notion that minimal artifacts like this could have existed, and in support of this idea one need only observe that some living examples of Stone Age man like the Australian Desert Aborigines use untrimmed rocks, sticks, and other materials for various tasks as a regular part of their behavior. Even after use most of these 'instant tools' are difficult or impossible to identify as tools unless they have been transported from where they occur naturally or are found in association with other cultural remains. An Aborigine may pick up a rock with a sharp edge to use as an impromptu hand-axe for wood-working or he may use an untrimmed stick as a club. But recognition of this fact should not lead to the assumption that man lived in the Pliocene. In fact, the 'eolithic' hypothesis is difficult if not impossible to test archaeologically and must remain somewhat speculative.

Archaeologists are on safer ground, however, when identifying stone artifacts which show patterns or regularities in flaking, either in the shape of the primary flake or in the secondary retouch. Broadly speaking, two main types of flaking were used to fashion chipped stone tools; *percussion-flaking* and *pressure-flaking*. Several varieties of each method are known, and experimental work by archaeologists is currently in progress to see if still more techniques can be inferred from the flaking patterns seen on ancient stone tools. These experiments have also revealed the existence of special techniques to augment flaking, such as the heat treatment of chert to permit finer work in pressure-flaking.

Perhaps the simplest form of percussion-flaking is the 'block-on-block' technique, where the worker takes a nodule of flint and strikes it directly against the edge of a larger stone. The Aborigines of the Western Desert of Australia today practice a modified form of this technique by picking up large rocks and striking them against chert nodules at quarries, dislodging numerous primary flakes from which only a few are selected for further trimming or use. The flakes produced by this method are usually coarse and thick; little if any effort is made to conserve the raw material.

A greater effort at conservation of flint or chert is evident with other types of percussion-flaking. Early hand-axes and large scrapers, that is, large, hand-held stone tools, were trimmed by direct percussion using small hammerstones. Tools of this sort have been referred to by archaeologists as core tools, as opposed to artifacts made from the flakes struck from cores, which are called flake tools. This distinction is useful but somewhat arbitrary, since it sometimes happens that the core itself is only a very large flake, while the flakes may be large enough to have been hand-held and used in much the same manner as the so-called core tools. Perhaps it is more helpful to distinguish between cores which were primarily intended as a source of flakes to be made into tools and cores which were meant to be actual tools. Percussion-flaking by means of a stick or a billet of antler gives even greater control than the use of a small hammerstone. Another economical method of percussion-flaking which can give rise to extremely regular trimming is the technique of indirect percussion, using a pointed punch of wood or bone in combination with a hammerstone. With this method the worker can direct the force of the blow with extreme precision. Archaeologists believe that some of the most technically outstanding flint-working by Stone Age man was accomplished by this method.

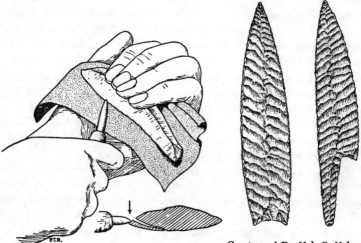

Courtesy of Dr. Nels C. Nelson

Fig. 2. Pressure flaking is a relatively evolved technique for the manufacture of stone tools. It is ordinarily used for shaping implements and for providing them with fine cutting edges.

On the whole, pressure-flaking affords even greater control and precision in stone-working than the percussion methods. It has been observed ethnographically among North American Indians (the most famous case being that of Ishi, the Yahi Indian who lived the last years of his life in San Francisco) and Aborigines in the Kimberley region of northwestern Australia. To accomplish this, the margins of the flake are ground with a stone to provide a narrow platform against which the worker presses with a piece of pointed wood, bone, or antler. By bearing down hard on this point he can remove a single narrow flake, and the process is repeated until a row of flakes has been removed. Another technique, inferred to have been practiced by the Indians of ancient Mexico, involves the use of a chest crutch to increase the amount of pressure brought to bear and a clamp to steady the piece being flaked. Perhaps the most bizarre-sounding

Fig. 3. Australian desert Aborigine trimming a stone adze-flake with his teeth.

type of pressure-flaking is that currently used by the Western Desert Aborigines of Australia, namely, pressing flakes off with the teeth. In this case the piece of stone to be trimmed is hafted to the end of a wooden tool such as a spearthrower or club, enabling it to be held securely as it is worked. This 'biting' technique of pressure-flaking was also reported for the Great Plains Indians of North America by Coronado's chronicler, Casteñada, in 1541.

WORLD PREHISTORY: A GUIDE TO THE READER

In describing the Stone Age of different parts of the world it is easy to become confused by the numerous sites and cultural sequences that have been discovered by archaeologists. Work has proceeded far enough, however, so that archaeologists may draw certain broad hypotheses about the early history of human culture. Although based on a wealth of available evidence, these generalizations are treated here as hypotheses because they will continue to require testing. In this chapter, the Old Stone Age archaeology of each major area of the Old World is treated separately, and it may be useful here to mention a few general trends of Stone Age technology as exemplified by the research done so far in each area. Perhaps the most evident development was the shift from general-purpose stone tools (where each tool performed a variety of functions) to more specialized tools; that is, real tool-kits with particular tools for particular functions. This transition occurred at different times in different places, but eventually it appears to have happened everywhere in the world except in Tasmania. Along with this trend, there was the appearance of tools for the purpose of making other tools. In this category are included such artifacts as drills, gravers, and burins (chisel-like implements used to split bone, antler, and wood). As this tendency toward specialization in stone tools increased, there was also a trend toward more localized traditions of tool-making. Thus one sees an increasing proliferation of localized tool-types and styles along with the appearance of such things as various ways of disposing of the dead, cave and rock art, settlement patterns, and other archaeologically complex phenomena.

Africa

Archaeological evidence so far obtained indicates that the earliest traces of human culture come from Africa. These occur in the form of pebble tools associated with fossil hominids (*Australopithecus*) and fauna of Lower Pleistocene age in a series of caves in South Africa, at Olduvai

Gorge in Tanzania (formerly Tanganyika), and at localities in Kenya, Ethiopia, Algeria, and Morocco. Because of its long sequence of stratified remains and the fact that most of the important finds there have been made *in situ* during controlled excavations, attention since 1959 has focused on the work of Dr. and Mrs. L. S. B. Leakey at Olduvai Gorge.

Pebbles of lava and quartz with flakes struck off either in two directions at one end (to make a somewhat pointed tool) or in a row on one side make up the Oldowan industry from Bed I at Olduvai Gorge. Associated with these simple stone choppers are a series of fossil hominids which have been termed *Zinjanthropus* and *Homo habilis* by the excavators but which are generally regarded as representatives of the genus *Australopithecus*, although *Homo habilis* is regarded as somewhat more evolved. The Bed I deposits at Olduvai Gorge have been dated by means of a new technique, the potassium-argon method, to between 1,750,000 and 2,000,000 years ago. Because of the unexpectedly great antiquity of these fossils, a certain amount of controversy at first surrounded this method of dating. Further tests were made, and these confirmed the earlier results; so that most archaeologists today accept these dates. In the lower part of Bed I a semicircular cleared area was encountered which the Leakeys and others have suggested may have been the base for a crude windbreak used by these early hominids.

Olduvai Gorge is remarkable not only for these earliest remains but also for the long sequence there of subsequent fossil and cultural materials. Bed I, the lowest geological level at the site, consists of volcanic tuffs up to 40 meters thick within which four levels of Oldowan culture have been identified. Above this lies Bed II, a formation made up largely of wind- and water-deposited sediments varying from about 20 to 30 meters in thickness. Bed III, 10 to 15 meters in thickness, lies above Bed II and consists largely of water laid sediments. Overlying this is a 45 meters' thick deposit of water-laid and aeolian sediments (Bed IV) indicative of a shift to a semi-arid environment. Finally, there is Bed V which contains evidence of pluvial phases (periods of increased rainfall) late in the Pleistocene.

Cultural materials occur in all of these levels. Oldowan tools were found in the lower part of Bed II, while higher up a percentage of tools showed signs of more systematic workmanship. This in fact marks the beginning of the Chelles-Acheul hand-axe industry. In Bed II some of these hand-axes are trimmed on both sides of each edge (called bifacial trimming by archaeologists) by percussion-flaking into beak-shaped or pear-shaped tools resembling some of the ancient hand-axes first observed by Frere, Mortillet, and other European scholars. Also found in Bed II was the 'Chellean skull'—fossil remains of a human form classified to the genus *Pithecanthropus* (and more recently assigned to the genus *Homo*). Potassium-argon dates for the horizon associated with this skull give an age of 490,000 years, but it must be cautioned that this method of dating has proved somewhat unreliable in dealing with more recent time levels. The early hand-axe industry of Bed II was also found to be associated with fossils of giant Middle Pleistocene fauna.

Beds III and IV contain increasing frequencies of hand-axes, and these show regularities of manufacture which eventually develop into an industry called the East African Acheulian. Whereas the earlier hand-axes (generally referred to as Chellean) were made by the block-on-block technique or by percussion-flaking with a hammerstone, Acheulian hand-axes are thought to have been fashioned by percussion-flaking with

TABLE 1.

Olduvai Gorge Sequence (Adapted from Oakley)

Cultural Stages			Bed Nos.	Geological Divisions
		Chelles-Acheul of East Africa		
E. African Acheulian	VI	11	IV	Upper Pleistocene
	V	10		
	IV	9		
	III	8		
	II	7		
	I	6	III	
E. African Chellean		5 ⎱ Transitional 4 ⎰		Middle Pleistocene
		3	II	
		2		
		1		
	Oldowan (pre-Chelles-Acheul)			
			I	Lower Pleistocene

wooden or bone strikers or even perhaps by the indirect percussion technique. The Acheulian sequence at Olduvai is also characterized by the presence of wedge-shaped bifaces called 'cleavers' by archaeologists. These are thought to have been used mainly for butchering and skinning animal carcasses, and they occur widely in Acheulian industries throughout Africa. Bed V at Olduvai contains a much more recent lithic assemblage known as the Kenya Capsian.

Looked at as a whole, the changes in stone tool traditions at Olduvai Gorge are gradual rather than abrupt. Even after the first Chelles-Acheul hand-axes appeared in Bed II, over 50 percent of the assemblage consisted of artifacts indistinguishable from Oldowan types. Similarly, the change from Chellean to Acheulian hand-axes involved gradual improvements, with more regular flaking and less sinuous edges, rather than the abrupt introduction of a new technology. Throughout this sequence there was also a tendency for the later people to use a wider variety of lithic materials in tool-making than was true at the beginning.

Much the same sequence for the Chelles-Acheul tradition has been found elsewhere in Africa. In the Vaal Valley region of South Africa a similar though not identical stone-tool sequence occurs, with the main differences from the East African sequence appearing in the Acheulian phases. Of special interest in this regard is a kind of prepared core technique involving the removal of a single large flake suitable for further trimming into a cleaver or biface. This has been named the Victoria West technique, and it represents a technological development similar in some ways to the Proto-Levalloisian technique which occurred among some Late Acheulian groups in Europe. However, present evidence suggests that these were not historically linked developments but occurred independently of each other, even though they are roughly contemporaneous.

Chellean artifacts from a locality at Stellenbosch in South Africa were formerly referred to as the Stellenbosch culture. Both at Olduvai and at other sites it is evident that stone flakes as well as choppers and hand-axes were used at all times. Even in Bed I contexts these flakes appear to have served as scrapers. Numerous stone flakes and pebble choppers are also reported from the South African caves known to contain various forms of *Australopithecus*. The presence of numerous shattered bones and fractured skulls of animals in some of the South African caves has led Raymond Dart, the scholar who made the first discovery of an Australopithecine in 1924, to propose that these early hominids used unworked animal bones, horns, and jaws as weapons. He termed this the 'Osteodontokeratic' culture. His argument for the existence of early bone tools is reasonable, but it shares some attributes of the 'eolithic' hypothesis proposed in the late nineteenth century and has proved hard to test scientifically.

In East Africa the peak of Acheulian craftsmanship appeared during the Acheulian IV (Leakey's Chelles-Acheul 9) in the form of extremely well-made hand-axes. Occupation sites from this period have been excavated at Isimila in Tanzania and at Olorgesailie, Lewa, and Kariandusi in the Rift Valley of Kenya. Food remains from this period were abundant at Olorgesailie, with giant baboon, extinct horse, and giant pig as the principal game hunted at different times. Polyhedral and spherical stone balls were also found here as well as at most other Acheulian occupations in East Africa, and Leakey has suggested that these were used as bolas stones in hunting.

Evidence for the use of fire does not appear until the final phase of Acheulian culture in South Africa. Important sites for the Final Acheulian stage in Africa include Kalambo Falls in northern Rhodesia, Montagu Cave in South Africa, and Hope Fountain and Broken Hill in Rhodesia. Of exceptional interest are the wooden artifacts at Kalambo Falls. Deposits at this site are thought to have been saturated by water since the Pleistocene, accounting for the remarkable preservation of wooden digging-sticks and other items in association with stone tools and debitage. A radiocarbon date of 57,000 years B.P. (before present) has been obtained for some of this wood. The stone tools discovered at Hope Fountain and in other sites nearby include core-choppers and flake tools which differ from more generally recognized Acheulian tools, but archaeologists believe this difference can be accounted for more easily by regarding the Hope Fountain sites as different seasonal or special activity areas of the same people rather than as a different group from the Acheulian hand-axe makers.

Relative to the rest of human prehistory, the picture described so far has been one of continuous and extremely slow development, involving gradual improvements in a few basic types of hand-axes, choppers, and other unspecialized stone tools comprising roughly 98.75 per cent of the time that tool-using man is thought to have existed. It is in the last 1.25 per cent of man's known existence that the most rapid changes and the greatest specializations in technology have occurred. E. S. Deevey has estimated that 2,000,000 years ago the total hominid population of the earth was between about 100,000 and 125,000 individuals, all thought to be Australopithecines living in Africa. Considering the abundance of other species, this was a modest- to small-sized population. The advent of stone tools is thought to have stimulated a sharp increase, so that by 300,000 years ago numbers would have been up to around 1,000,000 individuals. By this time *Homo erectus* had settled throughout Africa and Eurasia. By 25,000 years ago, with the appearance of fully modern man, *Homo sapiens*, numbers would have increased to around 3,300,000, with people having reached Australia and on the verge of spreading into the New World. By contrast, the population of the world in 1950 stood at around 2,400,000,000, with every indication pointing to even more rapid increases in the near future. In a general way, the rising estimates given by Deevey parallel the changes observed in the archaeological record, with the greatest rates of expansion occurring within the last 0.5 per cent of man's known history. When Deevey goes on to state that about 3 per cent of all the human beings who have ever lived are living today, he is echoing an impression which is apparent, too, from the archaeological record of a phenomenal increase of human development in technology, economy, and population in comparatively recent times over what it was during most of the sweep of human history.

In Africa south of the Sahara two main tool traditions emerged after the Final Acheulian: the Fauresmith culture in the open grasslands of South and East Africa and the Sangoan culture of the forests and riverine areas of Central Africa. The Fauresmith represented a continued dependence on well made bi-facial hand-axes essentially like those of the Final Acheulian but with differing methods of retouch. Fauresmith hand-axes tended to be smaller than their Acheulian predecessors, and discoidal cores appeared in the assemblage which were used for the removal of one or more flakes. Some of the Fauresmith flakes were long enough to be called blades or flake-blades by some archaeologists. At about the same time the Sangoan tradition, consisting mainly of stone picks, crude hand-axes, stone scrapers and utilized flakes, and high-backed cores, spread through Central Africa. Many of these tools are interpreted as being used for wood-working tasks, forming part of an over-all adaptation to life in heavily wooded country. At Kalambo Falls the Rhodesian Sangoan has been radiocarbon dated to around 40,000-43,000 years B.P. (before present).

Tendencies toward functional specialization and regional variation already evident in the Fauresmith and Sangoan traditions became even more pronounced in succeeding traditions. During a period of increased

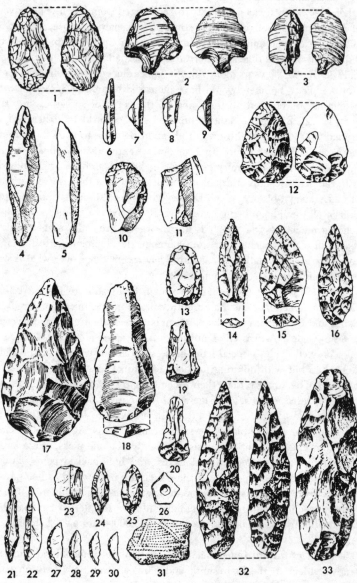

(*After Leakey, Burkitt, and Wulsin*)

rainfall late in the Pleistocene called the Gamblian Pluvial there appeared an artifact tradition known as the Proto-Stillbay. This appears to have developed from the Late Sangoan, and it culminated in a tradition called the Stillbay. Stillbay industries were characterized by bifacial points, notched scrapers, stone balls, and a variety of unspecialized chopping tools. Proto-Stillbay and Stillbay sites occurred throughout the open grasslands and savanna of East Africa and Rhodesia. In their fully developed form they included well-finished leaf-shaped points. At about the same time the Pietersburg tradition, noted for its triangular points and carefully finished core-scrapers, tended to occupy the bushveld country. At the Cave of Hearths in South Africa, Late Pietersburg materials have been dated by the radiocarbon method to about 13,000 years B.P.

Meanwhile, in Angola, the Congo, and parts of East Africa and Rhodesia which were heavily forested there arose another stone tool tradition with definite antecedents in the Sangoan—the Lupemban culture. The Lupemban retained many of the wood-working tools of the Sangoan, including picks, hand-axes, wedge-shaped tools, and a variety of scrapers. The Lupemban assemblage also included finely made, narrow points of stone. The Lupemban tradition was long-lived, as indicated by radio-

---

FIG. 4. *STONE AGE IMPLEMENTS FROM AFRICA*

Typical Stone Age tools from North (Nos. 1-11), East (Nos. 12 and 31), South (Nos. 13-30) and Equatorial (Nos. 32 and 33) Africa. No. 1, example of a S'Baïkian point; Nos. 2 and 3, typical Aterian points; Nos. 4-11, series illustrating the Lower Capsian culture—backed blades of Châtelperronian type (Nos. 4 and 5), small pointed blade (No. 6), triangles (Nos. 7 and 9), truncated blade (No. 8), end-scraper (No. 10), angle graver (No. 11); No. 12, point typical of the Stillbay culture from Kenya (East Africa); No. 13, 'duckbill,' or oval double side- and end-scraper of the Smithfield culture (South Africa); Nos. 14 and 15, Middle Stone Age types of points with faceted striking platforms from Glen Gray Falls (No. 14) and Fish Hoek (No. 15) in South Africa; No. 16, bifacial, leaf-shaped point of the Stillbay culture (South Africa); Nos. 17 and 18, typical implements of the Fauresmith culture of South Africa—hand-axe (No. 17) and flake with faceted striking platform (No. 18); Nos. 19 and 20, 'duck-bill' scrapers typical of the Smithfield culture (South Africa); Nos. 21-30, series of implements illustrating the Wilton culture of South Africa—perforator (No. 21), small backed blade (No. 22), small end-scraper (No. 23), double crescents (Nos. 24 and 25), Ostrich egg-shell bead (No. 26), crescents or lunates (Nos. 27-30); No. 31, pot-sherd with typical incised ornament of the Wilton culture (Kenya, East Africa); Nos. 32 and 33, Sangoan implements from the Belgian Congo (Equatorial Africa)—typical elongated laurel-leaf point (No. 32), and bifacial, pick-like implement (No. 33).

carbon dates of about 28,000 years B.P. from Kalambo Falls and 12,500 years B.P. from Mufo in Angola, in other words, encompassing nearly the whole of the Gamblian Pluvial period. At Mufo the Late Lupemban was succeeded by a tradition called the Lupembo-Tshitolian, which has been radiocarbon dated to about 9200 years ago. This change included the introduction of large numbers of small tools carefully fashioned from blades and flakes. These artifacts, termed microliths, were evidently hafted to handles of wood or bone and represent the introduction of composite tools in contrast to earlier traditions in which the stone tools were all held directly in the hand when used.

The Lupembo-Tshitolian actually represents only part of a wider change in stone tool traditions throughout Africa in which composite tools became important. In sub-Saharan Africa this change was most apparent in the industries of the Magosian culture. These industries included a variety of microliths such as backed blades and lunates (small crescents of flint) as well as small triangular and leaf-shaped points made by pressure-flaking, and burins. Flakes and blades were made by indirect percussion, sometimes from both ends of the core—a technique called bipolar flaking. Magosian industries were widespread throughout East and South Africa and may be derived from microlithic traditions appearing in North Africa at roughly the same time. At Kalambo Falls a Late Magosian assemblage has been radiocarbon dated to about 7600 years B.P.

In recent times the Magosian was succeeded by several relatively localized artifact traditions which include the Doian culture of southern Somalia, the Hargesian culture of the northern Somali Plateau, and the Wilton industries of East and South Africa. These traditions included small stone tools such as backed blades, burins, lunates, small scrapers (termed 'thumbnail scrapers' because of their small size), and arrowheads. The Doian people used pottery, but there is no evidence to show that they practiced agriculture of any kind. Wilton industries have been radiocarbon dated at several localities in East Africa; at Matjes River Cave to about 7700 to 5400 years B.P., at the Kafue Flats in Zambia to about 4200 years B.P., at the Lusu Rapids in Rhodesia to about 2100 years B.P., and at Nsongezi Rockshelter to about 1000 years B.P. Some Late Wilton industries have been found with Hottentot pottery. Meanwhile, in a rather limited area of South Africa, evidence of another late stone industry, called Smithfield, has been found. Although less microlithic than Wilton, this industry includes some microliths along with a few artifacts of bottle glass, indicating that it persisted into historic times. It is distinguished by the presence of elongated scrapers large enough to be hand-held. These and other late assemblages represent hunting cultures at a time when agriculture and husbandry had spread widely throughout sub-Saharan Africa and had largely displaced hunting as a primary way of life.

As mentioned earlier, there is some evidence for Oldowan artifacts in Africa north of the Sahara, principally at Ain-Anech in Algeria and at Casablanca in Morocco. However, no human fossils have been found accompanying these tools. Chellean industries occur at Sidi Abderrahman, near Casablanca, followed at this same site by a series of Acheulian materials. Acheulian materials also occur at Sidi Zin in Tunisia and at Ternifine in Algeria.

Following the Acheulian in North Africa there appears a stone tool tradition which differs rather sharply from post-Acheulian developments in sub-Saharan Africa and, in some ways, more closely resembles developments at that time in Western Europe. This is the appearance of the Levalloisian technique, in which a single flake was struck from a carefully prepared core. In industries employing this technique the flake was often given additional retouch for use as a point or scraper. In Europe this technique evolved out of the Acheulian and became a component of a diverse but widely recognized industry called the Mousterian. In North Africa the terminology of this industry, called Acheulio-Levalloisian, stresses its apparent African (i.e. Acheulian) origin. The industry has been found at stratified sites at the Kharga Oasis in Libya and along the Upper Nile in Egypt. In its earlier phase in the Libyan Desert, the Levallois cores were oval in shape and, when observed in the state before the flake had been struck off, resembled Acheulian hand-axes. Later these cores became smaller, with correspondingly smaller flakes and an increased use of secondary retouch. With the appearance of these Levalloisian industries, caves and rockshelters became important sites of human habitation in North Africa.

At the site of Bir-el-Ater in southern Tunisia a distinctive industry was discovered which appears to represent the most widespread development of the Levalloisian tradition in North Africa. Called the Aterian, it is distinguished primarily by the presence of tanged or stemmed artifacts. This tradition was distributed from the coast of Morocco to the Nile Valley and extended southwards deep into the Sahara. While climatic conditions then were probably wetter than at present, there is at least some evidence to suggest that the more southerly of these people were adapted to desert living. At Dar-es-Soltan in Morocco an Aterian industry has been radio-

carbon dated at >30,000 years B.P., while a Late Aterian assemblage at
Tibesti in Chad is dated by the same method to around 20,000 years B.P.
Most archaeologists agree that the characteristic stem on Aterian artifacts
was intended for hafting to a shaft or handle. The smaller ones were
probably spear or arrow heads, while the larger tanged artifacts are
thought to have been scrapers. Also present in the Aterian tradition were
minute hand-axes called 'petits coup-de-poings' by French archaeologists
who have excavated them.

Thus in North Africa clear evidence of hafting appears before the occurrence of microlithic industries. It can be argued, however, that composite tools made with microliths represent a different kind of hafting
from what occurred in the Aterian tradition. Following the Aterian in
North Africa a truly microlithic assemblage appeared which has been
termed, broadly, the Oranian (and sometimes, the Ibero-Maurusian).
Oranian materials are found mainly in the western half of North Africa
and include backed blades and lunates and other geometric microliths.
Further east, in Cyrenaica, evidence for an even earlier blade culture has
been found in the form of the Dabba tradition, in which burins and a
variety of tools made from backed blades abound. The sequence of Dabba
industries is perhaps best seen at Haua Fteah Cave in Cyrenaica. The
Dabba industries are thought to be derived from similar industries in the
Levant around or before 30,000 years ago.

In more recent times localized microlithic traditions appeared in North
Africa in much the same way as in sub-Saharan Africa. One of the most
important of these is the Capsian, first described in connection with a
large shell-mound occupation site at El Mekta in Tunisia. The industries
there included geometric microliths along with distinctive blade cores,
burins, and large blunt-backed points of a type generally referred to as
Chatelperronian. Also included in the assemblage were grinding stones,
bone awls, and beads made of ostrich egg shell. Radiocarbon dates of
around 8000 to 8400 years B.P. have been obtained for Capsian materials
at El Mekta. A blade-and-burin culture similar in many ways to the
Capsian has also been found in sub-Saharan Africa—the Kenya Capsian.
Sonia Cole calls the Kenya Capsian, 'one of the most controversial of all
cultures in East Africa.' The controversy in this case centers on the dating
of the Kenya Capsian, although there is also a question about whether or
not the Capsian of North Africa and the Kenya Capsian are actually related. Recent statements suggest that the Lower Kenya Capsian appeared
around 30,000 years ago while the Upper Kenya Capsian occurred much

later and may actually have been related to the Capsian of North Africa. Little can be said at this time about the origins of the Lower Kenya Capsian, but the Upper Kenya Capsian is better known from an extensive series of sites in the Kenya Rift Valley and northern Tanzania. Of special interest are the excavations by Leakey at Gamble's Cave in Kenya, where Upper Kenya Capsian lunates were found in a position indicating that they had served as barbs on a wooden arrow or spear tip. These finds and those of the smaller Aterian points in North Africa may be among the earliest evidence for the bow and arrow in the world, though the evidence is still open to debate. Stone scrapers, bone harpoon-points, fragments of red ochre, ostrich egg shell beads, and even some potsherds also occur in Upper Kenya Capsian deposits. The pottery shows some affinities to early Khartoum pottery tentatively dated to around 7000 B.C.

Europe

Despite the wealth of new information from Africa, most of the archaeological materials that pertain to the Old Stone Age still come from Europe. The study of Stone Age man was first undertaken in Europe, so there has been time for these materials to accumulate; and careful excavations have continued there on a large scale, thereby adding to the accumulation of data and compelling scholars to redefine their systems of artifact and cultural classification. Thus it is that many of the type-names for key artifact assemblages, such as the Chellean, Acheulian, Mousterian, Aurignacian, and others, originated in Europe, even if some of these artifact traditions may not have themselves.

The discovery of stone artifacts comparable in character and age to the Oldowan tools of Africa has, like these finds in Africa, been very recent. In 1958 four flakes and five pebble tools were discovered in association with Lower Pleistocene deposits (thought to be roughly contemporary with Bed I and lower Bed II at Olduvai Gorge) at Vallonet Cave in Provence (France). While the quantity of material recovered at this site was disappointing, and no human fossil remains were found, the evidence was sufficient to prove that men had lived in Europe during the Lower Pleistocene. In connection with this and other less well-documented finds, François Bordes has asked the question, "did this expansion [of *Australopithecus*] take place before the tool discovery stage, or later?" Present evidence suggests that the expansion of *Australopithecus* or a later form intermediate with *Homo erectus* proceeded from Africa to Europe and Asia, but there is insufficient evidence yet to answer Bordes's question.

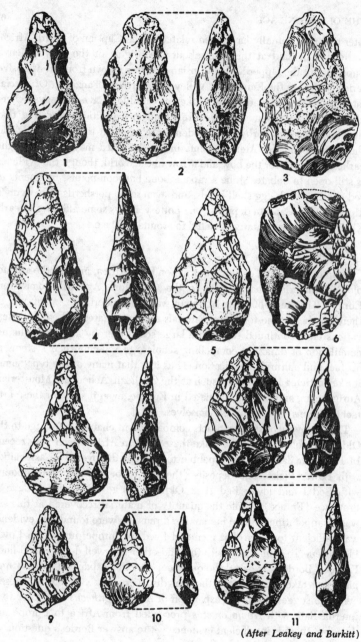

1   2   3
4   5   6
7   8
9   10   11

(After Leakey and Burkitt)

More recently, excavations at Vértesszöllös in north Hungary have uncovered charred and shattered bones of animals along with flint choppers,
chopping-tools, and scrapers associated with deposits estimated on geological and faunal grounds to be 500,000 to 200,000 years old. The stone
tools include artifacts which might qualify as Oldowan along with some
which show more careful workmanship. One of the excavators has suggested that this assemblage be termed the Buda industry.

No hand-axes occurred at Vallonet Cave and at Vértesszöllös, nor were
any found in the deposits at Clacton on the Essex coast of England. Primarily this latter industry consisted of choppers and chopping-tools made
of flint alcng with distinctive flakes, termed 'Clactonian flakes,' which
were trimmed for use as scrapers. There has been a lengthy controversy
concerning the antiquity of this assemblage, since early investigators
found it hard to reconcile the presence of a flake and chopper industry
with the existence of hand-axe traditions in Europe. But, thanks to intensive restudy, the status of the Clactonian as a definite tool tradition which
geological estimates place at somewhere between about 500,000 and 200,-
000 years ago has been confirmed to the satisfaction of most archaeologists.

An evolving hand-axe tradition similar in many ways to the Chelles-
Acheul sequence at Olduvai in Africa has long been regarded as characteristic of the Early Paleolithic of Western Europe. The earliest European
hand-axes were termed Abbevillian, after the discovery in the late nineteenth century of deposits containing ancient fauna and crude hand-axes
in a large gravel-pit at Abbeville on the Somme River. This is the only
stratified site in Europe where these artifacts have been found, and by
today's standards the excavations there left much to be desired. Estimates
based on the geology and fauna of the site place it at around 500,000
years ago, but these estimates must be regarded as gross approximations.
Abbevillian hand-axes have been found widely at other places in Western
Europe, but nowhere else *in situ*. One surface locality where these tools

---

Fig. 5. *LOWER PALEOLITHIC BIFACIAL IMPLEMENTS*

Abbevillian (Nos. 1-3) and Acheulian (Nos. 4-11) hand-axes. Nos. 1-3, typical
Abbevillian examples from Lower Pleistocene deposits in western Europe; No.
4, elongated ovate (Early/Middle Acheulian); No. 5, typical Acheulian ovate;
No. 6, cleaver—note the slightly curved but long cutting edge instead of a
point; No. 7, lanceolate hand-axe; No. 8, Middle Acheulian (IV) ovate showing S-twist; No. 9, sub-triangular type hand-axe of the Late Acheulian; Nos.
10 and 11, typical Micoquian (Final Acheulian) hand-axes.

occurred was Chelles, in France, where this hand-axe tradition was first recognized and given the name, Chellean. This name was dropped by European archaeologists after the discovery of *in situ* deposits at Abbeville, but its use has persisted in African archaeology.

In Europe there is less continuity between the early and late hand-axe traditions than is the case in Africa, owing mainly to ground disturbances caused by glacial phenomena. Developed Acheulian materials are known from a number of excavated sites, one of these being the type-site at Saint-Acheul near Amiens. Other important Acheulian sites include Cagny, also near Amiens, Swanscombe in England (also the locality where the fossil remains of Swanscombe Man were recovered), Combe-Grenal in the Dordogne Valley, and the neighboring localities of Torralba and Ambrona in northern Spain. The three last-named sites are of particular importance, since they have all been excavated recently under controlled conditions.

At Combe-Grenal nine layers of Upper Acheulian material have been excavated in deposits attributable to the latter part of the Riss (i.e. third major Pleistocene ice-advance) glaciation of Europe. At this site the Acheulian materials consist mainly of flakes and flake-tools (comprising 92 per cent to 95 per cent of the total collection), with hand-axes making up only a minor part of the assemblage. In earlier excavations at many other Acheulian sites there was a tendency to find hand-axes and to ignore flakes which, nevertheless, were probably present. Thus there has been a growing suspicion among archaeologists that the Acheulian—long regarded as the 'classic' example of a hand-axe culture—may have depended even more heavily on flake-tools than it did on hand-axes. Bordes has pointed out that a closer examination of the original finds at Saint-Acheul reveals a total of 92 cores, 20 hammerstones, 968 flakes, and 72 other types of tools, only 15 of which were hand-axes. The materials from Saint-Acheul derive from a lower (i.e. earlier) part of the Riss glaciation than those from Combe-Grenal, and Bordes has suggested that 'there is a turning-point in this Acheulian culture, when from this point onwards flake-tools become more numerous than the bifacial implements [i.e. hand-axes and cleavers].' Bordes sees some antecedents of Mousterian flake-tools in these Acheulian assemblages, although he notes that the Levalloisian technique is generally absent except at Cagny (a point on which the materials at this site differ in comparison with other Acheulian assemblages).

At Torralba and Ambrona a different aspect of Acheulian culture has been revealed. Both sites present evidence of ancient hunting practices of the people who made Acheulian tools. The fossil remains of about fifty straight-tusked elephants (the extinct *Elephas antiquus*) were uncovered at Ambrona along with hearths and stone tools. The tools, including numerous hand-axes, were made of stone of types not found near the site, so one can infer that they were brought to the site for the hunt. The hunters appear to have made use of the marshy condition of the Ambrona Valley at the time when Acheulian man occupied it to trap the elephants, perhaps by driving them into the bog by means of fires. The positioning of the elephant bones at the site has provided useful clues to inferring the methods used to butcher the animals. The fact of communal hunting of large game like this has also led to acceptance of the idea that these people must have been organized into fairly large bands or temporary groupings of bands. Although no human fossils were found at these sites, it is presumed on geological grounds and comparison with artifacts from localities in Africa and elsewhere that the men who lived and hunted in the Ambrona Valley were forms of *Homo erectus*.

During the Wurm or Fourth (and final) Pleistocene glaciation of Europe, there appeared a diverse stone-working tradition which has been collectively termed the Mousterian. The complex takes its name from the site of Le Moustier discovered in 1908 in the Dordogne Valley, but further work has revealed Mousterian artifacts at numerous localities in Europe and, it has been claimed, even as far afield as Russia, the Near East, and central China. A combination of radiocarbon and geological dating consistently places Mousterian materials between 100,000 and 35,000 B.C. In at least twenty sites in Europe as well as at several sites in the Near East, Mousterian artifacts have been found in association with the fossil remains of Neanderthal man.

Recent analyses by François Bordes have distinguished four major subtraditions or facies of the Mousterian in France:

1. Typical Mousterian—This facies consists mainly of points, most of them carefully made, and scrapers, many of which were made by the Levalloisian method. Hand-axes are rare.

2. Quina-Ferrassie Mousterian—This industry is sometimes called the Charentian, and it characteristically contains a high percentage of scrapers including some which are bifacially trimmed and others made on thick flakes with steep-sided edges. Very little of this material appears to have been made by the Levallois method.

3. Denticulate Mousterian—In this facies denticulate tools (that is,

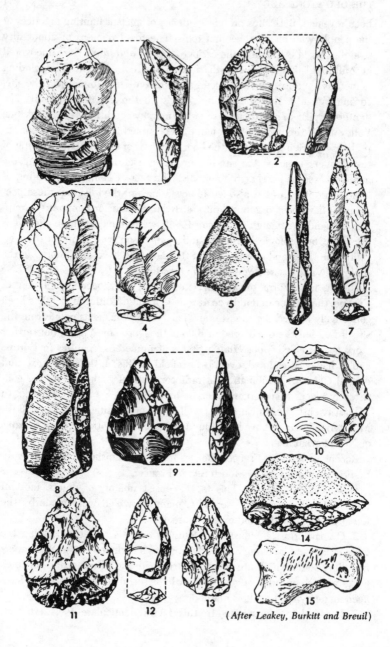

(*After Leakey, Burkitt and Breuil*)

tools with serrated or notched edges) dominate, while hand-axes and backed knives are absent and points and scrapers are uncommon. No human fossil remains have yet been found in association with materials of this facies of the Mousterian, nor is it certain the Levallois technique was used.

4. Mousterian of Acheulian Tradition—This tradition occurs in two sequential facies: type A and type B. Type A, the earlier, contains numerous hand-axes with Acheulian affinities. It appears to be partly contemporaneous with the Micoquian tradition, a Late Acheulian hand-axe industry of Western Europe. It also includes a wide variety of flake tools, mainly scrapers and points along with some burins, backed flakes, and end-scrapers. Type B, the later facies, contains few hand-axes but includes many denticulates and backed flakes and blades as well as some burins. At some sites a transitional assemblage between types A and B has been found, but, as in the case of the Denticulate Mousterian, no fossil human remains have yet been found in association with materials of the Mousterian of Acheulian tradition.

These four facies of Bordes's apply only to France, but materials identified as Mousterian with affinities to those in France, occur throughout Central Europe. In Germany the Mousterian assemblages include fine bifacially worked leaf-shaped tools called 'Blattspitzen' which, in terms of quality of workmanship, are unequaled until the appearance of the Solutrean leaf points much later. In western Germany, the materials of this tradition contain more evidence of the Levalloisian technique than is the case at the other localities.

Further to the east, side-scrapers are more common in Mousterian assemblages. Recent work suggests that in eastern Central Europe most of

---

FIG. 6. *LOWER AND MIDDLE PALEOLITHIC IMPLEMENTS*

Clactonian (Nos. 1 and 2), Levalloisian (Nos. 3-10), and Mousterian (Nos. 11-15) tools; all except Nos. 9-11 and No. 15 are flakes. No. 1, flake typical of the Early Clactonian (I); No. 2, well-worked Late Clactonian (III) flake tool; Nos. 3 and 4, Early Levalloisian (I/II) flakes; No. 5, Middle Levalloisian (IV) pointed flake with 'Chapeau-de-Gendarme,' or policeman's hat, type of faceted striking platform; Nos. 6 and 7, Middle Levalloisian blades; No. 8, Middle Levalloisian side-scraper; No. 9, small hand-axe of the Late Levalloisian Stage; No. 10, Middle/Late Levalloisian tortoise core (struck); No. 11, cordiform hand-axe of the Mousterian; Nos. 12 and 13, typical Mousterian points; No. 14, Mousterian side-scraper; No. 15, utilized bone from a Mousterian horizon in south-central France.

the Mousterian assemblages found so far are a regional variation of the Typical Mousterian described by Bordes. In general, the Mousterian of western Central Europe (mainly Germany) tends to show closer affinities to the Mousterian facies of France as described by Bordes than do the facies of eastern Central Europe. Also, the Levalloisian technique is poorly represented in the Mousterian industries of Central Europe generally, in contrast to the situation with the Mousterian of Western Europe.

The question among archaeologists today is: What do these different facies of the Mousterian mean in terms of human behavior? The issue has been put succinctly by Oakley, who asks, 'Are we really dealing with groups of people with different traditions, or with manifestations of several types of activity carried out by groups with the same tradition but in varying circumstances?' This question has not been answered yet, but archaeologists more and more are looking for ways to solve problems like this. Statistical analysis of artifact collections, experiments in stone-working, microscopic examination of stone tools for evidence of wear patterns, and ethno-archaeology (the study of present-day societies to determine patterns of tool use, settlements, butchering, and other 'archaeological' aspects of behavior) are among the varied approaches currently being tried by archaeologists in an effort to answer the kinds of questions being posed by the Mousterian data and other ancient Stone Age cultures.

Just as in Africa, there is evidence of increased specialization and proliferation of artifacts following the final phases of the Acheulian. This is shown by the varied nature of the different facies of the Mousterian, and recent statistical studies of Mousterian assemblages in Europe and the Near East have suggested that there are definite 'tool kits' within the Mousterian for special tasks like wood-working, hunting, skin-scraping, and others. Moreover, there is evidence for some kind of sacred life among the people in the form of pattern burial practices and occasional artifacts which appear to have ritual or talismanic significance. For example, Mousterian sites in Hungary have yielded an engraved pebble and a carved slab of mammoth ivory showing signs of having once been coated with ochre. At the sites of La Ferrassie in France, Mugharet-es-Skhūl at Mount Carmel (Israel), and Teshik-Tash in Uzbekistan (Russia) complex Neanderthal burials have been found. At La Ferrassie there were graves containing six individuals in what appears to be a family burial with two adults and four children arranged in a complicated pattern along with several stone artifacts. At Mount Carmel, ten individuals were buried within the cave, one of them grasping the jawbones of a wild boar. The

Teshik-Tash burial consisted of a Neanderthal boy buried in the midst of a cluster of goat frontlets with the horn-cores thrust into the soil.

In European terminology, Lower Paleolithic has traditionally referred to the early hand-axe and flake industries up to the Mousterian; the Mousterian has been included with the Middle Paleolithic; and the term, Upper Paleolithic, has been reserved for assemblages in which the backed blades and burins were important. These terms are useful as long as they are not too rigidly applied, since there is evidence at several localities for transitional assemblages which are not easily classified in one or another category. In the European Upper Paleolithic, the tendency toward technological and regional specialization observed during the Mousterian increased to an even greater degree along with altogether new developments such as cave art and sculpture. These developments were accompanied by the appearance of remains of unquestionably modern man, *Homo sapiens.*

Among European archaeologists the beginnings of the Upper Paleolithic are marked by the appearance of the early Perigordian culture in France. Early Perigordian assemblages include many artifacts which show Mousterian characteristics, such as Levalloisian-type flakes, Mousterian points, scrapers, and denticulates, but they also contain distinctive items like Châtelperron knives (large backed blades which come to a point), burins, and flake scrapers along with occasional bone awls and pendants made from animal teeth. In later levels of the Perigordian (termed Middle Perigordian) Mousterian types become rare while burins become both more common and more varied in form. Recent evidence also shows a sequence of development from the Châtelperron knife to a different form known as the La Gravette point during the transition from Early to Middle Perigordian. The Upper Perigordian saw the introduction of a new type of point with a long-tang and triangular cross section called the Font-Robert point and a distinctive type of small burin, called the Noailles burin, made on a flat and usually truncated blade. Large burins also continued into the Upper Perigordian, and bone points, fairly rare throughout the Perigordian, became more common in the final phase.

According to Bordes, while the Perigordian shows every sign of having developed out of the preceding Mousterian of Western Europe, another Upper Paleolithic blade-and-burin culture, the Aurignacian, appears to have arrived intact from somewhere else. In general, Aurignacian tools were made from smaller and finer blades than those of the Perigordian, and a number of other new tools appeared, among them thick but deli-

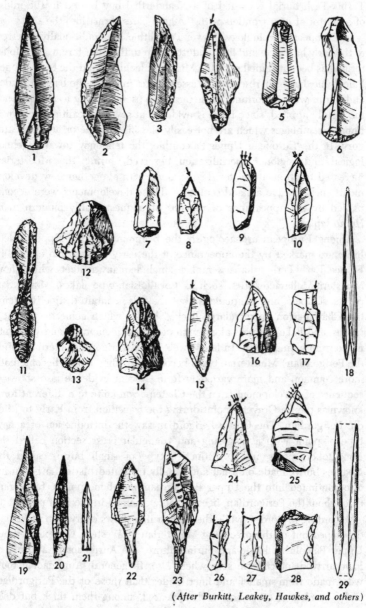

(*After Burkitt, Leakey, Hawkes, and others*)

cately retouched scrapers (carinate scrapers), distinctive 'hourglass'-shaped blades (called strangulated blades), split-base bone points, and nosed or beaked scrapers. Burins occurred but were less common than in Perigordian assemblages. Another distinctive artifact to appear in the Early Aurignacian was the Font-Yves point, a long leaf-shaped blade retouched on both margins. In later phases of the Aurignacian, split-base bone points were abandoned along with finely retouched blades, while burins became more common and varied. New types of bone points were developed along with a distinctive type of burin with a convex chisel-edge formed by removal of a series of small flakes instead of a single flake in the manner of earlier burins. This new type has been called the busked burin. Aurignacian materials in several classic sites including the Cro-Magnon Rockshelter in France have been dated generally to around 20,000 to 30,000 years ago during the mid- to late-Wurm (the fourth and final Pleistocene glaciation of Europe).

In Central Europe the Perigordian is perhaps best represented by recent excavations at the site of Dolni Vestonice in Moravia (Czechoslovakia). Here an industry similar to the Upper Perigordian of France has been dated by radiocarbon to around 24,000 years ago. This remarkable site contains numerous hearths within the outlines of what appear to have been huts or shelters constructed of animal bones and skins. A cluster of these huts lay on the edge of a swamp, and on the opposite side of the swamp were piled thousands of mammoth bones—evidence of intensive big-game hunting. At Szeleta Cave in the Bükk Mountains of Hungary there occurs an assemblage which contains backed blades somewhat like the Gravette type, endscrapers, sidescrapers, and leaf-shaped points (more Mousterian-than Solutrean-like in terms of their mode of retouch).

FIG. 7. *UPPER PALEOLITHIC IMPLEMENTS*
Lower Périgordian (Nos. 1-10 and 17), Aurignacian (Nos. 11-16 and 18), and Upper Périgordian (Nos. 19-29) tools. Nos. 1-3, Châtelperronian points (Lower Périgordian); Nos. 4, 8 and 17, angle burins; Nos. 5 and 6, end-of-blade scrapers; No. 7, double side and end-of-blade scraper; No. 9, flat burin; No. 10, screw driver or bec-de-flûte, burin; No. 11, 'strangulated,' or notched, blade; Nos. 12 and 14, steep scrapers (Aurignacian); No. 13, nose scraper; No. 15, angle burin on retouched blade; No. 16, core burin; No. 18, split-base bone point; Nos. 19-21, Gravettian points (Upper Périgordian); Nos. 22 and 23, Font Robert tanged points; No. 24, polyhedric burin; No. 25, beaked burin; Nos. 26 and 27, Noailles (small, multi-angle) burins; No. 28, end-scraper and perforator; No. 29, point with beveled base.

Termed the Szeletian, this culture also occurs in a number of localities in Czechoslovakia. Recent evidence suggests this may be a Central European counterpart to the Early Perigordian of Western Europe.

Aurignacian-like remains are widespread in Central Europe, with the principal excavated site at Istállóskö, in the Bükk Mountains not far from the Szeleta Cave. The site is rich in stone and bone artifacts, though burins are scarce and carinated scrapers absent. The upper layer of this site has been radiocarbon dated at about 29,000 B.C. Central European archaeologists term this industry the Olschewian and note its occurrence in cave sites in Yugoslavia, Czechoslovakia, southern Poland, Rumania, Bulgaria, and Germany. The Olschewian and Aurignacian appear to be closely related, although the nature of this relationship has not yet been worked out.

Although Solutrean materials have not been found in Central Europe, the site of Nietoperzowa Cave near Jermanovice, Poland, has yielded unifacially- and bifacially-worked leaf-shaped points along with some blades and cores which have been radiocarbon dated to around 38,000 years ago. These excavations show that Upper Paleolithic tendencies appeared early in Central Europe, but the relations of this industry to others in Europe remain uncertain.

Bordes sees the Perigordian and Aurignacian traditions as co-existing side by side in France until the relatively sudden appearance of a new culture, the Solutrean. The origins of the Solutrean remain a mystery to European archaeologists, although it evolved through a series of stages which archaeologists have termed Proto-Solutrean, Lower Solutrean, Middle Solutrean, and Upper Solutrean, respectively. The most distinctive artifact type in the Proto- and Lower Solutrean was a leaf-shaped point covered with delicate retouch on one face. This unifacial type of point remained common until the Middle Solutrean, when bifacial working became more common and large, well-made points started to appear. The bifacially-trimmed points of the Solutrean are often called 'laurel leaves' by archaeologists, and some were so large they must have served a ritual or display purpose of some kind. Some of the finer points were trimmed by pressure-flaking. These laurel leaf points continued into the Upper Solutrean, but along with them appeared some stemmed and barbed points. Throughout the Solutrean, burins were relatively uncommon while endscrapers and borers occurred frequently. Few bone tools appeared until the Upper Solutrean, at which time the first eyed needles appeared. The Lower Solutrean assemblage at the site of Laugerie-Haute in the Dordogne Valley of France has been radiocarbon dated at around 18,000 to 19,000 years ago.

The Solutrean was highly localized and did not occur in Central Europe. During their history the Solutrean people developed the art of flint-working to one of its highest levels, but they were followed by the Magdalenian culture in which flint-working was of little importance compared with work in bone. The origins of the Magdalenian are obscure. The early Magdalenian, as seen at Laugerie-Haute, contained almost no backed blades or flakes, thus weakening any likely connections with the Perigordian or Aurignacian, but it did contain numerous burins. Other tools, including beaked endscrapers and tiny multipointed gravers (called raclettes), occurred along with a variety of bone points, needles, and smoothing tools. Most of the bone points had bevelled bases, and some had incised marks on them in the shape of parallel lines or chevrons. Later in the Magdalenian thick endscrapers and raclettes decreased in number while a variety of backed bladelets appeared abruptly. Bone implements continued to develop, with the later phases containing bone and antler harpoon-tips with elaborately carved barbs. At first these had only a single row of barbs, but later on forms with a double row of barbs appeared.

In northern Germany there is evidence for a Magdalenian-like industry which has been termed the Hamburgian. It includes few burins but makes up for this with numerous borers and endscrapers. Magdalenian materials have been discovered at Petersfels Cave and other sites in Switzerland as well as in caves in Moravia. The Perigordian, Aurignacian, and Magdalenian are also well represented in the Cantabrian region of Spain as are the Middle and Upper Solutrean, particularly at the site of Castillo Cave.

Aside from the Solutrean, the Upper Paleolithic cultures of Europe are more renowned for their vivid and complex art styles than for their technology. In this regard, a wealth of new material has recently been discovered in Central and Eastern Europe and Russia as far east as the Ural Mountains. Archaeologists conventionally distinguish between two general types of Paleolithic art: parietal art—paintings and engravings situated on rock faces and the walls of caves as well as low-relief sculptures in stone or clay; and mobiliary art—carvings on tools and other portable objects as well as sculptured figurines. The location of much of Upper Paleolithic parietal art deep within caves beyond the zone of daylight and often in almost inaccessible crevices or passageways has led to speculation that it served magic or ritual purposes (for example, as rituals to increase

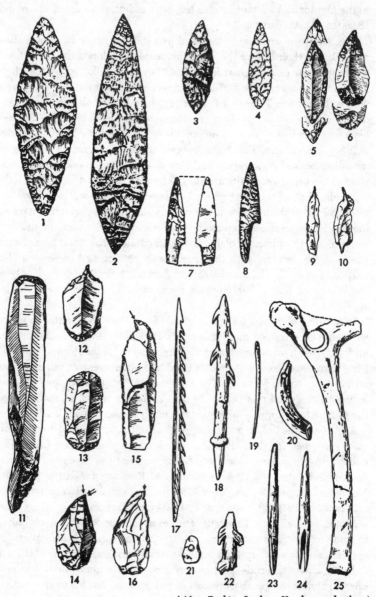

(*After Burkitt, Leakey, Hawkes, and others*)

or maintain the abundance of game or to bring luck in the hunt). More recently it has been proposed that the paintings are arranged in definite groupings within each cave suggesting an over-all pattern of organization, with particular animals and abstract signs as representations of either the male or female principle being arranged so as to reflect a coherent mythology based on the complementary opposition of the sexes.

In terms of chronology and cultural associations, the earliest dated parietal art occurs in the form of engraved blocks of stone at the site of La Ferrassie. These blocks, containing designs which probably depict sexual symbols and animals, were found in early Aurignacian levels at the site, as were similar blocks at the sites of Arcy sur Cure, Laussel, and Abri Cellier. Additional blocks with engraved and painted designs were found in the later Aurignacian levels of La Ferrassie. On the basis of radiocarbon and other types of dating these finds are estimated to be between about 30,000 and 25,000 years old. Examples of Perigordian parietal art also occur at Laussel and several sites at Sergeac. These include a 'Venus' figure, an engraved bison and horse, and a painted outline of a deer. The Solutrean apparently was poor in both parietal and mobiliary art, with the only certain example of painting with Solutrean associations being some black paint on a stone at Le Fourneau du Diable. The greatest proliferation of Paleolithic parietal art seems to have occurred during the Middle and Late Magdalenian. A low relief frieze of women and bison was discovered in association with Middle Magdalenian deposits at Angles sur l'Anglin, and frieze sculptures of animals at Abri Riverdit and Le

---

Fig. 8. *UPPER PALEOLITHIC IMPLEMENTS*

Solutrean (Nos. 1-10) and Magdalenian (Nos. 11-25) tools. Nos. 1 and 2, bifacial, laurel-leaf points (Middle Solutrean); Nos. 3 and 4, small, bifacial, leaf-shaped points (Middle Solutrean); Nos. 5 and 6, proto-laurel-leaf points (Lower Solutrean); Nos. 7 and 8, shouldered points (Upper Solutrean); No. 9, single-ended awl, or perforator; No. 10, double-ended awl, or perforator; No. 11, end-scraper on long blade (Magdalenian); No. 12, end-scraper and awl, or perforator; No. 13, double-ended scraper; No. 14, end-scraper and angle burin; Nos. 15 and 16, parrot-beak graver (Upper Magdalenian); No. 17, harpoon with single row of lateral barbs (Magdalenian V); Nos. 18 and 22, harpoons with double rows of lateral barbs (Magdalenian VI); No. 19, bone needle; No. 20, perforated horse tooth ornament (Aurignacian or Magdalenian); No. 21, small, perforated stone ornament; No. 23, javelin point with single beveled butt; No. 24, forked-base javelin point; No. 25, baton-de-commandement, or arrow straightener.

Cap Blanc, and engravings at Les Combarelles probably have the same associations, too. At Teyjat there are stalagmites with engravings and some paintings that are securely dated to the late Magdalenian. Today over a hundred caves with Paleolithic paintings and engravings are known to exist in Europe, with the greatest concentrations lying in the Dordogne region of southern France, the Pyrenees, and the Cantabrian Mountains of northern Spain.

Upper Paleolithic mobiliary art also shows enormous vitality and skill. Most famous, perhaps, are the 'Venus' figures—statuettes and bas-reliefs of women with voluptuous sexual characteristics. Fine examples of these are known from Upper Paleolithic sites in France, Austria, Italy, Czechoslovakia, and Russia. Also of interest are numerous pebbles with engraved designs, usually of animals, and sculptured or engraved bone artifacts of bone and antler. The Magdalenian was particularly rich in these latter items, but carved objects called *batons de commandements* (probably arrow- or spear-shaft straighteners) occurs as far back as the early Aurignacian.

Most archaeologists concur in the opinion that during the Magdalenian art reached a peak in the naturalistic rendering of animals, yet it appears that no sooner was this peak reached than parietal art ceased completely

---

FIG. 9. *TYPICAL EXAMPLES OF UPPER PALEOLITHIC ART*

Home art objects (Nos. 1-6, 10 and 11) and examples of cave art (Nos. 7-9 and 12-18). No. 1, spear-thrower carved in the form of an ibex; No. 2, small sculpture in the form of a horse's head; No. 3, painter's palette carved into the form of a fish; No. 4, engraving of a female figure carrying a bison's horn from Laussel (France), known as the 'Venus of Laussel'; No. 5, conventionalized engraving of a 'Venus' from Předmost (Moravia); No. 6, the so-called 'Venus of Brassempouy'; Nos. 7 and 8, typical tectiforms—possibly these represent dwellings of some type; No. 9, negative mutilated hands at Gargas (France); No. 10, highly conventionalized drawing on bone; No. 11, stylized drawing depicting a herd of reindeer (from Teyjat, France); No. 12, engraving of a horse (Phase 2) from Cantabria; No. 13, two mammoths at Font-de-Gaume (Phase 4) in the Dordogne—note the incomplete outlines; No. 14, bison partly engraved and partly painted in red (Phase 3) from Pindal, Cantabria; No. 15, engraving of a cave bear (Phase 2) from Combarelles, Dordogne District; No. 16, superpositions of paintings of different phases at Font-de Gaume, Dordogne: the head of a rhinoceros in red outline (Phase 1) is covered by a shapeless figure in black, which in turn is covered by oxen in flat black wash (Phase 3), and lastly by a feebly polychrome bison of Phase 4; No. 17, engraving of a hind (Phase 3) from the Cave of Castillo in Santander; No. 18, the famous 'sorcerer' from the Trois Frères Cave in southern France.

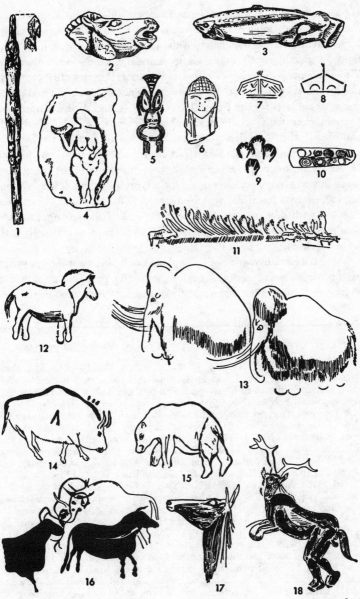

(After Burkitt)

for a time. Archaeological evidence from sites like Dolni Vestonice has shown that the people of the European Upper Paleolithic depended to a large extent for their livelihood on the hunting of large mammals living in the generally arctic or subarctic climates of the Würm glaciation. These mammals, which are either now extinct (mammoth) or moved northwards with the retreating ice sheets (reindeer, bison) figured prominently as subjects for the Paleolithic cave artists, and their disappearance from the scene with the advent of a changing climate may have led to the end of both the Magdalenian culture and the naturalistic art style it developed. As Grahame Clark has put it, 'In a sense therefore the Late Magdalenian artists, though marking the culmination of art many thousands of years old, were celebrating the adjustment of an advanced hunting culture to a particular set of environmental conditions. When these changed with dramatic suddenness at the end of the Ice Age, the economic infrastructure of the Magdalenian life collapsed and with it the art of the caves.'

There is a certain amount of cultural continuity between the final phase of the Magdalenian and the beginning of the post-glacial Azilian of France and Spain. Fine, naturalistic mobiliary art continued in the form

---

Fɪɢ. 10. *MESOLITHIC IMPLEMENTS FROM WESTERN EUROPE*

Azilian (Nos. 1-8), Asturian (No. 9), Tardenoisian (Nos. 10-46), and Larnian (Nos. 47-58) tools. Nos. 1 and 2, Azilian harpoons of stag horn; Nos. 3-5, small, rounded ('thumb-nail') scrapers typical of the Azilian culture; Nos. 6-8, Azilian painted pebbles; No. 9, Asturian pick made on a pebble; Nos. 10-20, Late Tardenoisian types from Belgium—small backed blade (No. 10), triangle (No. 11), perforator (No. 12), hollow-based points (Nos. 13 and 14), evolved types of trapezes (Nos. 15-17), trapezes, or transverse arrowheads (Nos. 18-20); Nos. 21-33, 37 and 38, Middle Tardenoisian types from Belgium—truncated blades (Nos. 21 and 22), rhomboid (No. 23), lunates or crescents (Nos. 24 and 25), triangles (Nos. 26 and 27), hollow-based points (Nos. 28, 32, 33, 37 and 38), small backed blades (Nos. 29-31); No. 34, microliths mounted in a slotted haft; Nos. 35 and 36, diagrams showing method of manufacturing microliths by the so-called notch technique; Nos. 39-46, Early Tardenoisian types from Belgium—obliquely truncated (non-geometric) blades (Nos. 39-44), backed blade (No. 45), trapezoid (No. 46); Nos. 47 and 48, utilized blades of the Early Larnian culture; No. 49, Late Larnian perforator made on a flake; Nos. 50 and 51, Upper Paleolithic-type steep scrapers (Early Larnian); Nos. 52 and 53, small perforators (Early Larnian); No. 54, coarse, utilized flake (Late Larnian); Nos. 55 and 56, small, rounded ('thumb-nail') scrapers (Early Larnian); No. 57, notched, or concave, scraper (Late Larnian); No. 58, Larne pick typical of the Late Larnian culture.

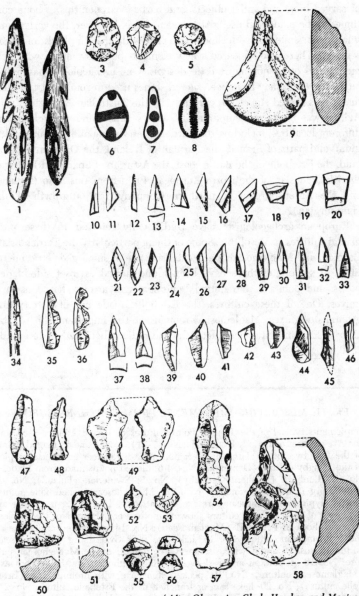

(*After Obermaier, Clark, Hawkes, and Movius*)

of carved bone and antler objects, and barbed harpoon-tips of bone continued to be made and used. At the same time, however, the variety and quality of stone tools declined sharply, with the emphasis on small scrapers. There also appeared a new element—pebbles painted with geometric and other non-naturalistic designs. One archaeologist has speculated that these may have been sacred stones used in somewhat the same manner as sacred stones are currently by the Australian Aborigines. The Azilian was partly contemporaneous with several different traditions in different localities, including the Tardenoisian in England, Germany, Belgium, and parts of France, the Larnian of Ireland, the Obanian of Scotland, the Ertebølle of the Baltic coast, the Asturian of Spain and Portugal, the Maglemosian of the North European Plain from Russia to England, and the Ahrensburgian of northern Germany (an outgrowth of the Hamburgian).

European archaeologists have traditionally referred to these postglacial cultures as Mesolithic. Some of them, particularly the Tardenoisian, Larnian, and Maglemosian made extensive use of small geometric microliths. At some sites these have been found hafted as inset side-blades, barbs, and points in the slotted bone shafts of arrows, harpoons, and knives. One of these cultures, the Ertebølle, made use of pottery and ground-stone axes. Maglemosian remains at the important site of Star Carr in England have been dated by the radiocarbon method to around 7500 B.C.

Fig. 11. *MESOLITHIC IMPLEMENTS FROM NORTHERN EUROPE*

Implements typical of the Tanged Point cultures of Period I (Nos. 1-6) and the Axe cultures of Periods II and III (Nos. 7-21). Nos. 1 and 2, tanged points of the Lyngby culture of the Baltic region; No. 3, reindeer antler axe or pick of the Lyngby culture (Denmark); Nos. 4-6, tanged points made from blades— No. 4: Hamburg (northern Germany), No. 5: Swiderian (Poland), No. 6: Ahrensburg (northern Germany); Nos. 7-9, Maglemosean barbed bone points; No. 10, typical Maglemosean core axe of flint; Nos. 11 and 12, transverse arrowheads of the Ertebølle culture showing method of hafting; No. 13, barbless bone fish-hook of Period II (Maglemosean); No. 14, perforated antler axe of the Maglemosean culture; No. 15, flake axe from Svaerdborg (Maglemosean culture); Nos. 16 and 17, flake scrapers (Period II) of the Maglemosean culture; No. 18, perforated antler sleeve showing method of hafting a core axe (Maglemosean culture); No. 19, pecked stone axe with ground edge (Ertebølle culture); No. 20, flake axe, or tranchet, of the Ertebølle culture; No. 21, pottery vessel (late Period III) of the Ertebølle culture.

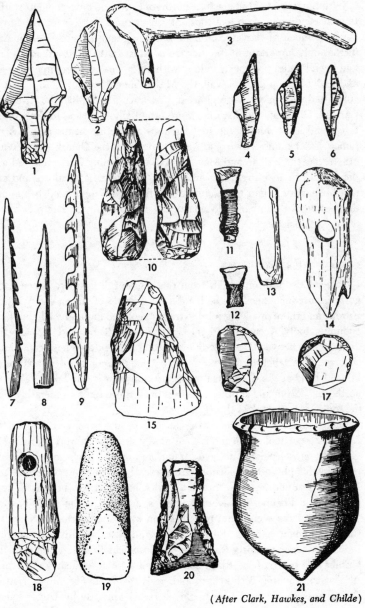

(After Clark, Hawkes, and Childe)

With the retreat of the glaciers, northern European environments shifted toward conditions more like those of recent times, with extensive forests covering much of the subcontinent. Solitary game like red deer became increasingly important in the diet (in contrast to the herd animals which had been hunted previously) along with other localized resources like fish and shellfish. In a general way, the Mesolithic cultures of Europe can be correlated with particular regions and resources. Some, like the Ertebølle, Larnian, Obanian, and Asturian were essentially maritime in their orientation and left behind large shell mounds and refuse heaps (such as the famous 'kitchenmiddens' or kjokkenmöddinger of the Danish coast) while others, like the Azilian and Maglemosian were mainly forest-adapted and depended heavily on red deer and horse. Thus when agriculture and animal husbandry began to reach Europe, they were integrated to varying degrees with a number of localized and economically rather specialized Stone Age societies.

Asia and the Near East

Lower Paleolithic materials from this region fall into two broad categories; those influenced by the hand-axe traditions of Africa and Western Europe and those involving a lithic tradition of making unifacial chopper/chopping tools. According to the studies of de Terra and Movius, the dividing line between these traditions during late Middle Pleistocene times occurred in northeastern India, marked by the presence of a mixture of bifacial hand-axe and unifacial chopper industries in the Soan Valley of northern Pakistan and at other localities in northern India (generally along the southwestern flank of the Himalayas).

Mousterian-like stone industries have been discovered widely in the Near East, particularly in the Levant at key sites like Jabrud (Syria), Mt. Carmel (Israel), Shanidar Cave (Iraq), and others. Archaeologists interested in this phase of prehistory are presently attempting to relate their Near Eastern findings with those of Bordes and other scholars in Western and Central Europe. In several instances, artifacts of the Near Eastern Mousterian have been found in association with Neanderthal or Neanderthal-like human remains. Further north and east, extensive Mousterian industries occur in thirty-three sites in European Russia (mainly in the Crimea and north of the Black Sea) as well as in several sites in Central Asia at the cave of Teshik-Tash and near Tashkent. The Mousterian of Russia appears to have been replaced rather abruptly by Upper Paleo-

(After Movius)

FIG. 12. Hand-axe and chopper/chopping-tool traditions in the Old World during late Middle Pleistocene times.

lithic blade-and-burin cultures, and archaeologists today are trying to determine how this dramatic replacement may have come about.

In the Far East, Lower Paleolithic industries are documented from several localities; at the Upper Irrawaddy River (Burma), Kota Tampan (northern Malaysia), Padjitan (Java), and, most important, from Choukoutien in China (near Peking). The sites at Choukoutien were excavated in the 1930's. They contained the earliest human fossils from continental Asia as well as a chopper/chopping-tool industry and evidence of hearths. When compared with developments in Europe and Africa, it is clear that *Homo erectus* (called Peking Man at Choukoutien) knew the use of fire—a factor which may have enabled him to spread into cooler climates than his Australopithecine predecessors—and possessed widely different lithic tool traditions (bifacial hand-axes in the west and unifacial chopper/chopping-tools in the east). Lower Paleolithic materials are known from elsewhere in China, too, with over sixty stratified sites known. These contain artifacts comparable to those from Choukoutien as well as somewhat later stone tools like thick, pointed flakes or "trihedral points" and limestone 'bolasstones' which are now referred to collectively as the Fenho Complex. Three human fossil teeth found with Fenho materials suggest that Fenho man was more like the Neanderthaloids of Europe and the Near East than *Homo erectus*.

The Upper Paleolithic cultures of China are poorly known, with the best evidence so far coming from the Upper Cave at Choukoutien. Artifacts of bone and shell were found in the Upper Cave along with remains of *Homo sapiens* and stone tools which showed relatively little change from the much earlier chopper/chopping-tool traditions. This evident conservatism in the stone tool industry makes it hard for archaeologists to decide whether or not to regard the Upper Cave culture as Upper Paleolithic in the same sense that the term is used elsewhere. Since excavations there were carried on before the advent of the radiocarbon method, the dating of the Upper Cave culture remains uncertain, though most archaeologists think it belongs in the transition from the final Pleistocene to Recent times.

Industries dating to Upper Pleistocene times have also been discovered at Niah Cave in Borneo in association with *Homo sapiens* and with at least one extinct species of mammal (giant pangolin). Meanwhile, in the Near East, Upper Paleolithic industries with closer affinities to those of Europe and Africa have been found. An industry called the Emiran has been excavated in Israel and Lebanon. It is thought to be transitional between the Mousterian and Aurignacian and has been dated by radiocarbon at the Lebanese site of Ksar 'Akil to <43,750 years B.P. In this re-

---

Fig. 13. *PALEOLITHIC IMPLEMENTS FROM SOUTHERN AND EASTERN ASIA*

Implements typical of the Lower Paleolithic assemblages from Burma (Nos. 1-5), Pakistan (Nos. 6-8) and Northern China (Nos. 9-13), Nos. 1 and 3, Anyathian choppers from Burma; No. 2, hand-adze of the Anyathian (Burma); No. 4, Anyathian chopping-tool from Burma; No. 5, large flake implement of the Anyathian (Burma); No. 6, chopper made on a pebble typical of the Soanian of Pakistan; No. 7, Soanian hand-adze made on a pebble (Pakistan); No. 8, pointed pebble-tool of the Soanian (Pakistan); implements of quartz from the *Sinanthropus* deposits at Choukoutien, Northern China—point (No. 9), side-scrapers (Nos. 10 and 11), and end-scrapers (Nos. 12 and 13).

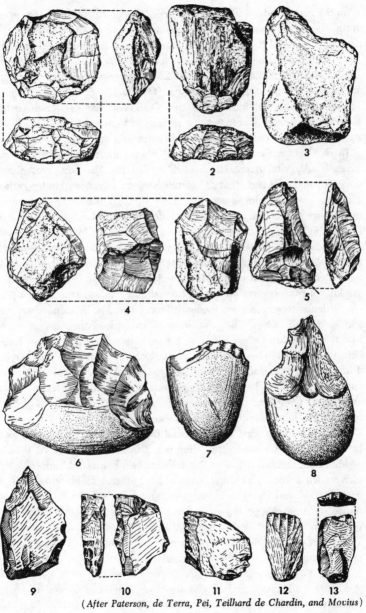

1 2 3

4 5

6 7 8

9 10 11 12 13

(*After Paterson, de Terra, Pei, Teilhard de Chardin, and Movius*)

gion the early blade- and -burin cultures (Upper Paleolithic in European terminology) appear early and alongside the late Mousterian industries. One of the first of these is the Amudian of Syria, long regarded as a pre-Aurignacian culture complex. Aurignacian-like materials have been recognized in Afghanistan at the site of Kara Kamar, where they have been radiocarbon dated to approximately 32,000 B.C. The Baradostian, another important blade-tool industry of the Near East, has been radiocarbon dated at the site of Shanidar Cave in Iraq to between 33,000 and 27,000 B.C., where it lies in a layer directly above Mousterian levels.

In the Levant the long sequence of blade cultures culminated in an exceptionally vital microlithic culture called the Natufian. Present evidence strongly suggests that the Natufians were advanced hunter-gatherers who gradually developed the arts of settled life and, presumably, agriculture as well. Their tool-kit included backed blades with a characteristic high gloss, indicative of use as sickle-blades in harvesting wild grains, and stone mortars, also useful in preparing grains. They also made a wide variety of bone tools, many of which were artistically carved in a manner rivaling that of the Magdalenians of Europe. Natufian remains are known from several important cave sites as well as from some open-air settlements where they evidently constructed substantial dwellings and even fortifications. The most dramatic example of these occurs at the lowest and next-to lowest levels at Tell-es-Sultan (Jericho) where Natufian-type flints have been found in association with stone walls, a rock-cut ditch, and large masonry towers dated to around 6700 B.C. Masonry huts and other structures have been discovered at the Natufian sites of Beidha and Nahal Oren, and large cemeteries rich in grave goods have been found at this latter site and also at the site of Shuqbah.

There is evidence that in late glacial times men with an Upper Paleolithic type of culture were spreading into Russia and Siberia. At the site of Malta in the Lake Baikal region remains of a blade-and-burin industry along with several dwellings, female statuettes, a child burial rich in grave goods, and the drawing of a mammoth have been found—all evidence of an advanced big-game hunting culture. Similar remains have been found at Buriet, on the Angora River. Further west in Russia, in the Don River basin, materials have been found at the site of Kostienki that point to connections with the Gravettian of Europe.

Upper Paleolithic and Mesolithic developments in east Asia are not generally well understood at this time. In India and Ceylon there are extensive microlithic stone tool industries, though the dating of these is uncertain. Most of these appear to be late, having survived alongside agricultural communities. In southeast Asia the chopper/chopping-tool tradition appears to culminate in the Hoabinhian culture. Hoabinhian sites occur both in caves and open-air localities and are marked by the presence of large split pebbles worked on one or sometimes both faces. At the Hoabinhian site of Gua Cha in Malaysia there is evidence both for ceremonial burial and cannibalism. Recent work at Spirit Cave in north Thailand has revealed Hoabinhian stone tools in association with plant remains and hearths dating to around 7000 B.C., suggesting the possibility of early plant domestication in southeast Asia.

Australia

The first scientific excavations in Australia occurred in 1929 at Devon Downs in the Murray River Valley near Adelaide. However, it has only been within the last ten years that Australian archaeology has developed as a discipline, with stratified sites being excavated in every state of the country including Tasmania. With these excavations, the antiquity of man in Australia has been found to be much earlier than was thought before. At Koonalda Cave on the Nullarbor Plain in South Australia there is evidence for a stone quarry which saw use as early as 16,000 B.C. Rock art, in the form of simple incised impressions, also occurs at Koonalda Cave and is thought to belong to this early occupation. In Arnhem Land, near Oenpelli, there has been excavated a series of rockshelters with radiocarbon dates for the earliest occupation running back to 24,800 years B.P. One startling discovery made during these excavations was the presence of edge-ground stone axes, a supposedly 'Neolithic' trait, in these earliest levels. These are probably the earliest such artifacts found anywhere in the world, although their presence does not imply an agricultural economy. Another important early site occurs at Kenniff Cave in Queensland, where an early human occupation has been dated by radiocarbon to about 14,000 B.C. Australian archaeologists now consider it quite possible that man has lived in Australia for as much as 30,000 to 40,000 years.

During the Upper Pleistocene the Australian landmass was separated by varying distances of water from the mainland of Southeast Asia. The earliest people to arrive must have come by water, although their points of arrival and routes of spread afterward remain open to speculation. The lithic materials from the earliest dated human occupations in Australia characteristically consist of unifacially worked scrapers, choppers, and cores with a distinctive 'horse-hoof' shape. These all appear to have been hand-held when used, although the ground-edge axes from Arnhem Land also point to at least some kind of hafting technology.

Present evidence indicates that in Western Australia around 4800 B.C. and in New South Wales around 3500 B.C. a new technology involving the manufacture and use of small, hafted chipped stone tools appeared. The assemblage containing these varied considerably from one part of the continent to another, with some sites containing a high percentage of small, discoidal scrapers while in other areas backed blades and small, unifacially retouched points called pirris were more common. Perhaps it is easiest to think of this new technology as an Australian small-tool tradition, since it did not always replace the earlier tradition of making large hand-held stone tools, but merely augmented it. In some parts of Australia some types of these small tools, often termed microliths, were still being made and used by the Aborigines at the time of European contact. Although it does not point to any significant change in the Aborigines' way of life, this was the most important technological change to appear in the archaeological record in Australia during post-Pleistocene times. All evidence to date indicates that the Australian Aborigines were always dependent entirely on hunting and gathering of wild foods for their livelihood.

Tasmania, unlike the rest of Australia, did not develop a small, hafted tool tradition. Generalized scrapers and flakes, all hand-held, continued in use among the Tasmanian Aborigines right into historic times. Recent archaeological work in Tasmania has traced human occupation of the island back to around 7500 to 8000 years ago, and it has been suggested on good evidence that the first Aborigines in Tasmania may have arrived there at a time in the Upper Pleistocene when sea levels were lower and the island was still connected to the Australian continent. This would have been around 11,000 years ago, and the result would have been cultural isolation from that time until the arrival of Europeans, with a persistence of the basic stone tool-kit seen elsewhere in Australia from much earlier times. If this hypothesis is correct, it points to a degree of cultural isolation unmatched anywhere else on earth. The Tasmanian Aborigines adapted to local environmental conditions and in that sense were unique, yet to a large degree it also appears that their culture represented a true historical survival of an Old Stone Age way of life. Thus the Tasmanian Aborigines were of great anthropological interest, and it is one of the great tragedies of mankind that inroads by Europeans had made these people extinct by 1876.

IV

The New Stone Age

ABOUT 18,000 YEARS AGO the last Ice Age is conventionally considered to
have ended; the Old World and the New began at last to assume the
form familiar from our atlases today. Consequently human societies had
to adapt themselves to quite novel conditions. But they had ample time;
for the change-over from Pleistocene to (geologically) Recent conditions
was not abrupt but a very slow process occupying several thousands of
years. The glaciers in high latitudes did not vanish overnight, but took
nearly 12,000 years to melt away. The changes in climate, vegetation,
and distribution of land and sea were equally gradual and varied greatly
in intensity in the several parts of our globe. The most general result
was an universal rise in sea level when the enormous quantities of water,
previously locked up in glaciers, flowed back to the oceans. One of the
incidental consequences was the separation of Britain from the continent
of Europe. But this general rise in sea level was no more sudden than
the melting of the glaciers that caused it. Moreover it was offset by a
rising of the land in areas that had been thickly covered with ice. The
weight of the ice on the mountains of Scandinavia and Scotland had
actually depressed the earth's crust there. So, when the weight was removed, the crust rebounded. The rate of the rebound was at first faster
than the general rise of sea level and accordingly delayed the separation
of Britain from the Continent and converted the Baltic into a brackish
lagoon (the Ancylus Lake). It went on after the rise of sea level had
caught up with it so that round the coasts of Scotland and Scandinavia
beaches formed when the sea had reached its maximum height are now
fifty or more feet above the present shore.

The changes in climate were also gradual and discontinuous. In gen-

95

eral of course, the weather in temperate latitudes became warmer, in the Mediterranean and subtropical zones drier. In northern Europe between 9000 and 6000 years ago the mean annual temperature was higher than today, but the climate of Britain, Denmark, and Sweden was more continental with sharper winters, but longer and warmer summers. For the next two thousand years the climate remained warmer but was nearly as damp as today, while thereafter drier conditions returned without a serious fall in the temperature for some 1500 years. It was only about 2600 years ago that the British and Danish climates deteriorated to their present notoriously damp and chilly level. In the Mediterranean area, on the contrary, and still more in North Africa, Asia Minor, and Iran the rainfall must have been diminishing all this time, but this desiccation may have been interrupted, like the deterioration of climate in northern Europe.

The climatic changes were followed by changes in plant and wild animal life. In the temperate zone of Europe forests invaded both the large tracts of steppe and tundra, that had fringed the river glaciers and ice-sheets, and also the northerly plains and mountains that had actually been covered with ice. Forest trees appeared everywhere in the same order, first birches, then pines, then oaks, and other deciduous trees. Further south, on the contrary, forests withered from drought, and prairies gradually turned into deserts—both processes being accelerated by the destructive activities of men. On the other hand, the regime whereby some great rivers—the Nile, the Tigris and Euphrates, the Indus and the Yellow River—regularly overflow their banks every year was now established, and the annual floods converted considerable tracts of incipient desert into swamps or potential gardens. Incidentally the silt brought down by these floods has actually built up considerable areas of dry land, e.g. part of the Nile Delta, in 'recent' geological times.

The first attempts of human societies to adjust themselves to these novel conditions resulted in the creation of what archaeologists call 'Mesolithic' cultures. Economically such do not differ essentially from the Paleolithic cultures from which they were derived. That is to say, the basis of life—the food supply—was still obtained exclusively by gathering, hunting, or catching what nature kindly supplied. Judging by the best known Mesolithic cultures—outside Europe such are really known only in North Africa and Palestine so far—more importance was now attached to gathering, i.e. collecting nuts, berries, roots, snails, shellfish, and so on, than in the Paleolithic. At least in northern Europe where conditions were very propitious, fishing too was intensively developed.

One result seems to have been that Mesolithic communities appear less nomadic than the Paleolithic; they tended to camp regularly for part at least of each year where a good supply of that sort of food could be confidently expected every season. In most European camps at least we find the bones of dogs, still very wolfish or jackal-like. Presumably ancestral dogs had already begun to attach themselves to men and even to help in the hunt in return for the offal that huntsmen would cast away. In Europe the dog would have been particularly useful in the new sort of chase imposed by the post-glacial landscape. For when forests invaded the tundras, the large herds of gregarious beasts that Paleolithic tribes had pursued so profitably vanished. Mesolithic groups had to pursue red and roe deer, wild oxen, wild pig, and other solitary game among the thickets, and in this pursuit the dog could easily make himself useful as he still does.

Another feature common to most Mesolithic societies is that they made considerable use of very minute implements of flints, termed microliths, that despite their small size are usually beautifully trimmed often to neat geometrical shapes. No one knows exactly how these were used, still less why their makers took such pains over shaping them. But their makers were of normal stature, not pygmies, and some were killed by arrows armed with microliths as heads. Of course not all Mesolithic tools are abnormally small and not all microliths are Mesolithic.

Far the most important advance in human control over external nature achieved during the Mesolithic stage, at least in Europe, was the creation of an effective kit of carpenter's tools. Such were obviously needed since forest was a dominating factor in the Mesolithic landscape throughout the temperate zone after trees had spread over the steppes and tundras. Yet by no means all Mesolithic societies devised utensils for dealing effectively with these encumbrances or utilizing the timber they would provide. The Azilians, for instance, of western Europe, lineal descendants of the reindeer-hunters termed Magdalenians, lacked carpenter's tools. For the same reason the principal groups who made microliths, the Tardenoisians, kept to sandy soils, windswept coasts, and treeless uplands. But tribes who hunted and fished beside the rivers and meres of the great North European Plain while it stretched, still uninterrupted by any substantial expanse of sea, from the Urals in the U.S.S.R.

to the Pennines in England, did develop a kit of adzes and chisels, and eventually axes and even gouges.

The earliest were made of bone or antler and may have developed out of wedges. The Indians of British Columbia used to split planks off the great trees of the Pacific coasts with the aid of wedges of bucks' antler. Wedges of reindeer's antler had apparently been used by Paleolithic hunters in southeastern Europe where trees survived during the Ice Age; the edges were sharpened by grinding and polishing. In the northern forests their Mesolithic successors seem to have got the idea of inserting a flint to form a sharper edge which could then be used for chopping and attaching the implement to a wooden handle to form an adze. East of the Baltic where flint was scarce, the blades of adzes and chisels had to be made of fine-grained rocks. In such a material, however, a really durable and trenchant edge could best be obtained by grinding and polishing—the process already applied to bone and antler. So, by transferring to stone a technique originally devised for bone, the ground stone adze-blade, or 'celt,' was created. A most potent instrument of production was thereby placed at man's disposal.

It is worth noting that at first these heavy wood-working tools were all mounted as adzes. So, today native carpenters throughout the Pacific use the adze in preference to the axe. With this equipment the hunter-fishers of northern Europe did produce some novel inventions, some of which have been preserved in peat bogs. These include the oldest extant paddles—other and earlier societies had been able to cross even straits, but neither their 'barques' nor their propellants survive. For transport over the snows a sledge was invented; a runner was unearthed in a Finnish bog. Eventually a local breed of wolfish dog was trained to draw these earliest vehicles.

There is at present no evidence to show whether other societies in the Mesolithic stage created independently or possessed such efficient carpenters' tools. The polished stone celt—axe- or adze-blade—used to be regarded as the criterion of the higher, Neolithic, stage, which is here defined by food-production. Nevertheless many recent 'savages' including not only many Red Indians but also some Australian aboriginal tribes used polished stone celts; indeed the economy of modern savages is generally more like that of European Mesolithic groups than that of their Paleolithic precursors. It just happens that owing to the extent of peat in northern Europe and the preservation in it of implements made of perishable material, the culture of the hunter-fishers on the great North

European Plain is far better known than that of any contemporary society elsewhere.

These Mesolithic North Europeans certainly developed a very efficient equipment for exploiting their territory's natural wealth in game, wild fowl, and fish, and utilized well available raw materials. Even during the pine-wood phase those living east of the Baltic had devised a type of bone arrowhead for slaying fur-bearing animals with minimum damage to the pelts. All fished with spears, harpoons, hook-and-line, and nets. Some had noticed the electrical property of amber—when rubbed with fur, it will attract dry leaves—and valued it as a magic substance.

Later, when the land bridges across the North Sea were submerged and the Baltic depression was filled with warm salt water, coastal tribes settled down all the year round where oyster banks offered a permanent and abundant supply of nourishment; near the Danish coasts—the land has risen since then—immense shell-mounds still survive to mark the sites of their encampments. By 4000 B.C. such sedentary folk had already discovered the art of converting clay into pottery and developed large and serviceable but rough vessels.

The characteristic fishing tackle, hunting weapons, transport devices, and even pot forms and techniques developed during the Mesolithic stage on the North European Plain, being well adapted to the exploitation of that environment, survived there for centuries. They recur beyond the Urals on the Plain's Siberian extension and to a remarkable degree even in the Woodland Zone of North America as far as Massachusetts. But meanwhile other societies, less easily situated but presented with ampler opportunities, had taken the revolutionary steps that mark the transition to a new economy and a higher cultural grade.

What the archaeologists call the Neolithic Stage and ethnographers term barbarism is characterized by 'food-production'—the cultivation of edible plants or the breeding of animals for food or the combination of both activities in mixed farming. Food-production constituted a real economic and technical revolution. Firstly, it put society potentially in control of its own food supply. Paleolithic and Mesolithic societies, like contemporary savages, had to rely entirely on what nature obligingly provided in the way of plant, animal, fish, or insect food. The supply was always limited, and the human population was limited by it. But, at least in theory, cultivators can augment the food supply by simply tilling more land, and so can provide for the support of a growing population. The herdsman has only to abstain from eating lamb and veal and to clear fresh pasture to obtain a like result—again of course in theory. Secondly, plant-cultivation and stockbreeding for the first time put men in control of sources of energy other than human muscle-power. The latter was the only force, apart from fire heat used in cooking and for hardening spears, available to earlier societies, unless perhaps the harnessing of dogs to pull sleighs by Mesolithic hunter-fishers in the north precedes the Neolithic revolution in time; sails certainly come later. But plants and animals are, to borrow a phrase from Leslie A. White, 'biochemical mechanisms,' and by breeding or cultivating them men make these mechanisms work for them.

Naturally the Neolithic revolution—the transition from pure hunting and collecting to farming—was really a complicated process actually spread over many centuries and perhaps millennia. It is unprofitable to speculate how the transition was effected; we have no direct archaeological evidence at all. We do not even know whether cultivation or stockbreeding came first. Many barbarian tribes today cultivate some plants but breed no animals for food, and to that extent the first alternative may seem the more likely. But the archaeological record from Europe, Hither Asia, and even China has so far revealed no trace of pure cultivators preceding the mixed farmers typical of the Neolithic in the Old World. This typical Neolithic economy was based on the cultivation of cereals—at first only wheat and barley—and on breeding horned cattle, sheep, goats, and pigs, or at least one of these species.

These cultivated cereals are derived from annual grasses that grow wild in rather dry and elevated steppe country. Possible cradles are Syria-Palestine with Iran and Cyrenaica, Abyssinia, and western China. So cereal cultivation cannot have originated independently in temperate Europe, upper Asia, or the tropics. Wild sheep again occur in North Africa, Hither Asia, Iran, and central Asia and could only be domesticated there. Beyond this we are not justified in making any assertion as to where the farming began, though recent discoveries do point rather explicitly to the hill countries of and bordering the Fertile Crescent as the cradle of wheat and barley cultivation.

The simple phrases, 'cultivation of cereals' and 'stockbreeding,' denote a number of quite complicated operations and a variety of alternative techniques. For the cultivation of cereals the ground should in the first instance be prepared for the seed by breaking up the surface. That is now done with a plow drawn by a tractor, horses, mules, or oxen. But the tractor is a very modern device, and it is more than doubtful whether any sort of plow was used by truly Neolithic societies. Two other devices are current among modern barbarians—the digging-stick or dibble in the Americas and the Pacific, the hoe in Africa. The first leaves no trace on the archaeological record; the use of hoes has been inferred for Neolithic Europe from objects supposed by some archaeologists to be stone hoe-blades or antler hoes and established for Egypt by representations of wooden hoes in later pictures. Today cultivation by either method is usually done by women and in small plots that may be interrupted by tree stumps or rocks rather than in fields. The term 'agriculture' should therefore be reserved for plow cultivation and is applicable only to the latest Neolithic farmers, if to any.

After sowing, the seed needs water if it is to grow. The source of the water divides cultivation into two contrasted branches—irrigation- and dry-farming respectively. The requisite water may be provided by a river or stream that naturally floods the plots by overflowing its banks at a convenient season. The Nile does this most obligingly every year; many rivers in Asia do so too but seldom so opportunely or reliably. Alternatively the life-giving fluid may be led to the plots by artificial channels from springs as well as rivers, but at least in the latter case it would be necessary to lift the water from the bed. Still irrigation cultivation has one great advantage; it not only waters the grain, but also renews the soils since the waters are usually charged with silt containing just those chemicals withdrawn from the earth by the crop. In really arid regions like Egypt, southern Iraq, Iran, and central Asia, as in Arizona and New Mexico, corn-growing has always had to depend on irrigation.

Elsewhere, even in north Syria and the Mediterranean basin as well as in the temperate latitudes of Europe and America, rain may be relied upon to water the crop. But then the farmer will be in for trouble. The elements withdrawn from the soil are not automatically replaced. So the soil soon becomes exhausted, and the yield declines. When this happens to a plot, some African tribes like the Lango today just abandon that plot and clear another patch of virgin soil. Then, when all handy plots have been in turn cropped to exhaustion, the whole group packs up, deserts the hamlet, and starts the cycle afresh somewhere else. This easy but extravagant mode of exploitation must once have been general. It was demonstrably practised by the Neolithic Danubians in central Europe and probably by other Neolithic Europeans too. Plainly such farmers were nearly as nomadic as Paleolithic hunters, perhaps even more so. Their migratory habits will explain the spread of their Neolithic techniques and economy over enormous areas and into territories where, in default of domesticable plants and animals, such practices could not arise spontaneously.

A slightly less wasteful method, slash-and-burn cultivation, is applicable in wooded or scrub country. When the cultivated plot will bear no more, it is allowed to return to bush for a few years, then cleared again, the scrub being burned on the plot. The ashes act as a fertilizer. On grass lands you may let the exhausted plot return to grass and serve as pasture, if you have domestic stock, and the droppings will manure it for you. In north Syria, Asia Minor, and the east Mediterranean where perennial supplies of drinking water for man and beast were obviously restricted and the cultivable land itself did not seem unlimited, one or other of these primitive 'rotations' must have been adopted very early; Neolithic settlements were really permanent hamlets or villages, occupied so long and reconstructed on the same site so often that their ruins now rise above the plains as mounds or *tells*. In temperate Europe, where the water supply is abundant and where to the first sparse population of Neolithic farmers the land itself seemed unlimited, such evidences of permanent habitation are lacking.

Thrift is compulsory for any farmer. His one crop must feed the family for the whole year and in addition provide seed for the next sowing. In practice it cannot have been too difficult on average land to produce more than was needed for domestic consumption. This excess of foodstuffs accruing to the household and the whole community is the basis of what economists call the social surplus. Naturally it is easier to produce a social surplus under a Neolithic economy than by hunting and collecting; for the storage of grain is very much easier than that of berries, grubs, fish, or meat. But provision for storing the crop was necessary. Granaries or silos are conspicuous features in any Neolithic settlement. The Neolithic Danubians erected regular barns, raised above the ground on posts. In Egypt straw-lined pits served as silos, and in Mesopotamia large jars were manufactured to hold the grain.

Specal implements were needed for harvesting the grain and converting it into flour. The oldest surviving reaping appliances are straight pieces of wood or bone armed with a short row of serrated flints. But even in Neolithic times a genuine angular curved sickle of wood or an animal's jawbone, still edged with flints, came into use. Grain could be pounded with pestle and mortar, but in the Old World it was more usually ground either with a bun-shaped stone on a saucerlike slab or with a sausage-shaped rubber on a flat slab. The latter was eventually ground down to the form of a saddle. The resultant 'saddle quern' remained the standard form of mill until the rotary quern was invented somewhere near the east Mediterranean about 600 B.C. (Till then, of course, and indeed much later each household ground its own flour every day in such hand-mills, as some of us today grind our coffee.)

In addition to cereals many Neolithic communities also cultivated beans or other leguminous plants and also flax—perhaps at first for its seeds rather than its fibres. Some in Hither Asia, the Mediterranean basin, and the Balkans began also to cultivate fruit trees, olives, figs, date-palms, and vines. Even in temperate Europe the native apple eventually may have been deliberately cultivated, as wild apples were demonstrably collected and dried in Neolithic times. Orchard husbandry must have exercised a stabilizing influence upon its practitioners. A *corn* plot is planted to yield a single crop; an orchard, once the trees mature, will bear fruit for many years. Its owners will not desert it willingly, while a corn-grower may lightheartedly leave his plot once the harvest has been gathered.

Stockbreeding did not involve so much fresh equipment as cultivation, but had more striking social repercussions. A herd of cattle or a flock of sheep represents capital more conspicuously than does seed *corn* or even fruit trees. If exploited primarily to provide milk (or even blood) and not treated just as a handy reserve of game to provide flesh, it will manifestly increase and multiply itself. Being easily moveable, livestock can conveniently be exchanged or stolen. Perhaps even in Neolithic times as in early historical periods, cows (or sheep or pigs) served as media for exchange, standards of wealth, and prizes for war. Cattle raiding indeed must have been an economic inducement to warfare; on the other hand, land, whether for hunting grounds or for tillage, is seldom acquired by savage or barbarous tribes through hostilities owing to super-stitious inhibitions. In Neolithic Europe anyhow, as more and more emphasis came to be laid on stockbreeding (in the temperate zone this would in fact be more productive than plot cultivation), weapons of war become increasingly prominent in the archaeological record. At the same time herding is traditionally a man's job, whereas plot cultivation with digging stick or hoe is normally entrusted to females. So pastoralism enhances the economic importance of the males and should favor a patriarchal organization of society. On the contrary where the cultivation of plots contributes the major portion to the food supply, the community's dependence on the produce of female labors is compatible with matriarchy. Finally pastoralism does not necessarily involve the degree of nomadism made familiar by the Biblical account of the Hebrew patriarchs. Cattle herders in Neolithic Europe, as in contemporary Africa, normally kept to one small territory; indeed the most sedentary community known in Neolithic Britain, the villagers of Skara Brae in Orkney, lived almost exclusively on the produce of flocks and herds. At worst, cattle breeding may involve a sort of annual migration termed transhumance, whereby a considerable part of the community leave the village for a season and escort the beasts to summer pastures.

We should expect that, at first, plants would be cultivated and livestock bred just to supplement the wild fruits, fish, and game provided by nature. Food-production should in fact have contributed less to society's food supply than food-gathering. Now a few very early Neolithic settlements in the Near East—in Iran, in the Fayum, and on the edge of the Nile Delta—do in fact seem to illustrate just this sort of economy. But in the most familiar Neolithic sites of Europe—the Swiss lake-dwellings, the English 'camps,' the great stone tombs of Denmark—farming is predominant; hunting, fishing, and collecting seem to have supplied only supplements and variety to menus—as indeed they still do, only more so. Indeed the earliest lake-villages in Switzerland seem more 'Neolithic' than those, still Neolithic, that immediately succeed them; for in the food refuse from the latter the proportion of game to domestic animals is higher than in the earlier villages. This observation confirms the inference already drawn that the Neolithic economy was introduced into Europe after having been developed in a different environment. The nomadism imposed on plot-cultivators as explained above now helps us to understand how the introduction may have been effected. Of course not only would such cultivators have to move on to new land as their plots become exhausted, their younger sons would have to open up fresh territory if an expanding population were to be accommodated. On the other hand the economy evolved in an arid climate would not work in temperate latitudes without modification, and its adjustment often looks like degradation.

In addition to actively co-operating with nature to increase the supplies of food, all Neolithic societies went on to manufacture substances that do not occur ready-made in nature. Thus all but the very oldest, like a few Mesolithic groups, made pottery; of course the preparation and storage of vegetable foods and milk imperatively demand water-tight containers. In converting clay that when moist is completely plastic, and that will disintegrate with an excess of moisture, into rigid and impervious earthenware, men—or rather women—were controlling a startling chemical transformation, a veritable transubstantiation.

Secondly all Neolithic societies that have left adequate evidence manufactured textile fabrics by spinning and weaving. The raw material—flax or wool—had to be cultivated or bred. (Most wild sheep carry mainly hair; woolly fleeces result from selective breeding. How far woolly sheep were available in the Stone Age is uncertain; they were probably unknown in Egypt but may have been bred already in Asia.) Then the fibers had to be converted into serviceable threads by spinning; for that only a spindle was needed. But the threads had to be woven together on a loom and that is quite a complicated mechanism comprising a rigid frame with at least two moveable parts. Being made entirely of wood, no Neolithic loom survives. After 3000 B.C. three distinct types are already traceable—one horizontal, attested for Egypt, and two vertical, current respectively in Hither Asia and temperate Europe. In pre-Columbian America on the contrary no such elaborate apparatus seems to have been known. Nets certainly and baskets probably were known to Mesolithic communities, and both techniques were generally familiar in the Neolithic Stage.

The dwellings of Neolithic farmers were generally—but not always—more substantial and commodious than those usually occupied by hunters and fishers whether today or in the remote Old Stone Age. Yet caves, when available, were still used as shelters and dwellings—in fact they are today. The Neolithic peasants, termed Danubians and inhabiting the löss lands of Central Europe, lived in very long, rectangular, gabled houses like the long houses of the Iroquois which doubtless accommodated the same sort of social group. The reed huts of barbarians in the marsh lands of Egypt and lower Mesopotamia were not beyond the powers of Paleolithic savages. But even the earliest farming village yet known (Jarmo in Iraq, occupied about 4500 B.C.) consists of substantial and commodious dwellings comprising several rooms. In the Near East, adobe was the favorite material for the walls; in Europe, split saplings or a screen of intertwined withies plastered with clay and dung (wattle-and-daub) sustained by posts. The roofs must normally have been of thatch. Apart from the Danubians' lodges which would house several natural families, a clan in fact, under one roof, many dwellings comprised two rooms, the main living room and kitchen generally measuring well over 100 square feet.

These dwellings must have been quite well furnished, but the fitments being mostly of wood have generally perished. But in Orkney where there were no trees, wooden articles had to be translated into durable stone. Hence, we know that late Neolithic houses in Europe were provided with fixed beds, that might be covered with canopies, very modern-looking dressers of at least two tiers of shelves, and various wall-cupboards or keeping places. Model stools and couches from the Near East bear similar testimony. Some light and warmth was provided by an open-fire, generally placed near the center of the room. Of course it served for cooking too, but for this purpose it was often supplemented by a clay baking oven such as are still used by peasants in the Balkans and Hither Asia. In cold climates, like south Russia, these ovens grew into regular stoves that, like their modern counterparts, surely served for heating as well as culinary purposes. Drains under the house floor usually carried off moisture, but there can have been no chimney to let out the smoke, only a hole in the roof, or more probably a gap under the eaves.

Only in Europe have whole Neolithic villages been uncovered. These comprised from eight to fifty houses, and such must have been the normal size for Neolithic communities. (See Plate V.) Until improved agricultural techniques had increased the yield per acre and indeed until wheeled carts had been invented, it would be inconvenient for more households to live together. For they must live close enough to the plots on the produce of which they depended, to be able to transport without undue labor to the common center the bulky grain which was their staple diet. So the number of persons who could comfortably inhabit a single hamlet was limited by the produce of the few plots in say four square miles that could be cultivated simultaneously under the rural economy already described. As soon as that limit was reached, the younger sons (or daughters) must hive off from the parental roof and found a new hamlet on virgin soil if they wanted to set up house on their own.

In such a community each household would normally provide its own equipment. In particular its female members not only ground the flour, prepared and cooked the food, spun the yarn, wove textile fabrics and made clothes therefrom, but also manufactured the domestic pots. On the other hand, there were public works in which the whole group must have co-operated. Streets—cobbled, paved, or corduroyed—for instance, are well attested. Some late Neolithic villages at least are defended by moats and palisades. On the Alpine lakes whole villages were built on piles along the shelving shore.

It is the essence of the Neolithic economy that each village or hamlet could be self-sufficing: both its food and the materials for the manufacture of essential tools and appliances could be obtained locally. Hence Neolithic communities tended to be rather isolated. In their isolation they had time to develop idiosyncrasies. On the one hand they could discover and exploit opportunities peculiar to their home land. On the other hand they developed seemingly arbitrary shapes for common tools, designs for decorating pots and weapons, rites for funerals, and so on. So archaeology reveals no single Neolithic civilization or culture—in the sense that we can speak today of an American or even a Western civilization—but an enormous number of cultures each distinguished by its own peculiar balance in farming, forms of tools, weapons, and ornaments, burial practices, artistic styles, and so on.

Yet the ideal of Neolithic self-sufficiency was never fully realized. Indeed even in the Old Stone Age the transportation of marine shells hundreds of miles from the coast revealed some interchanges between distinct communities. Among Neolithic societies interchanges were more frequent and more extensive. Mediterranean shells have been found in Neolithic villages and graves all over the Danube basin and beyond its northern watershed far down the Oder, Elbe, and Rhine. In Hither Asia shells and semiprecious stones were just as widely distributed. Moreover for the manufacture of axeheads, querns, and similar appliances specially suitable stones were often fetched from quite a long way. Indeed even in the Neolithic Stage small communities seem to have specialized in mining flint or quarrying choice rocks and in manufacturing from their winnings commodities for the market. Eventually a few people may have begun to supplement their livelihood by peddling the products to remoter groups. Both intercommunal specialization and trade in these senses are detectable in Neolithic times, but neither miners, axe-grinders, nor hucksters are likely to have been 'full-time specialists'; that is, their industrial or commercial activities would always have been combined with, and generally subsidiary to, the prime job of getting their own food by farming, hunting, or fishing. So our flint-miners, axe-manufacturers, and peddlers, attested in the New Stone Age, need not have lived, and probably did not live, on the social surplus (the food above domestic requirements produced by farmers, hunters, or fishermen) as industrial workers, clerks, professional men, and many others do today and had begun to do already in the prehistoric Bronze Stage.

Still, as we have said, there was already a social surplus. It must have been exceedingly small. From fully excavated villages like Skara Brae (Orkney) and Köln-Lindental (on the Rhine) we get the impression that it was pretty evenly distributed in early Neolithic times. Land and live-stock would be owned communally by large kinship groups. Co-opera-tion within the group would be organized as it is in a family. The vil-lage of Skara Brae could be regarded as a single house divided into seven tenements just as well as an aggregation of seven one-roomed houses. No chief would be needed to order about members of such groups, and, as far as early Neolithic times are concerned, there is no convincing archaeological evidence for chieftainship.

If plant cultivation preceded, and was for a time more important than stockbreeding, and if, as today, the plots were hoed by the women, the female section of the society would have made the principal contribu-tions to its food supply and might therefore be expected to have enjoyed a degree of authority. Confirmation for this assumption is considered by some to be provided by the observation that nearly all early Neo-lithic societies were accustomed to model or carve little statuettes of a female personage; they may represent a 'mother goddess' or a 'virgin,' and were almost certainly used in magic rites or religious ceremonies. In the later Neolithic of Europe such female figurines tend to disap-pear. Their place is sometimes taken by phalli or other male symbols. Now, at the same time stockbreeding, combined with hunting, had be-come relatively more prominent in the European economy. Since pas-toralism is associated with patriarchal organization, the contemporary disappearance of female figurines may reflect the diminution of that sex's status.

Again weapons of war, as contrasted with hunters' tools, are not con-spicuous in early Neolithic graves or settlements, and the latter were normally undefended. Later Neolithic villages, on the contrary, are often girt with defensive works; stone battle-axes and flint daggers figure prominently among later Neolithic relics in Europe. That coincides with the increased emphasis on stockbreeding, and, as we have suggested, cattle-raiding offered a motive for warfare. Moreover the still predatory methods of exploiting the soil might well have led to a competition for cultivable land keen enough to overcome superstitious scruples against annexing other people's territory.

In any case warfare, adequately attested for Late Neolithic Europe, would give opportunities for the rise of chieftains; it might result in the stratification of society. Under any Neolithic regime a man should be able to produce more than his keep. It would therefore be worth while retaining captives, taken in wars or raids, as slaves or reducing whole communities to a servile or tributary status. Late Neolithic developments might therefore result in the concentration of the social surplus in the hands of a small ruling or slaveholding class or of individual chiefs. That would prepare the way for a new economic order realized in the Bronze Age.

That farmers should be as much preoccupied with magic ceremonies to promote fertility as hunters is not surprising. The female figurines just mentioned were doubtless connected with such rites. The earth, in which the seed is planted and from which the new corn springs, is conceived as a great mother. But the dead too are implanted in mother earth. Surely their ghosts or spirits will be potent agents in the fertility process. In any case Neolithic farmers paid even more attention to the ritual burial of their deceased kinsmen than hunters and fishers. The body was normally doubled up when it was buried—the position of the embryo in the womb. Ample provision of food and drink and personal possessions—ornaments, weapons, and some tools—accompany the corpse. In northern and western Europe in late Neolithic times monumental tombs were constructed with enormous labor wherein the dead of many generations might 'sleep with their fathers.' The most imposing are termed megalithic (from the Greek μεγας great and λιθος stone) because they are built of extravagantly large stones any one of which may weigh up to eighty-six tons! Other tombs of the same plan and function built of small stones laid in rough courses without mortar and roofed by corbelling imply even greater ingenuity and scarcely less physical toil. Both megalithic and corbelled tombs were usually covered by a huge barrow that may contain as much stone as a modern parish church, and every stage in tomb building was accompanied by elaborate rites and ceremonies. Finally chambers of the same plan might be quarried out of the rock where it was suitable.

Collective tombs of the foregoing kinds are most densely distributed along the Atlantic coasts of Europe from southern Spain to Scotland and then across the North Sea to Holland, Denmark, and southern Sweden. In all areas the agreements in tomb plans seem too close to be fortuitous. Yet the grave goods, always poor, differ conspicuously in most provinces. Only one specialized type of collective tomb (the Paris cist) found in the

Paris basin, Brittany, Westphalia, and Sweden regularly yields such a
similar assemblage of relics as to be attributable to a single culture that
might have been diffused by an actual migration of people. For the rest,
unless one admits independent invention at a number of adjacent points,
the ideas of religion embodied in such collective tombs would seem to
have been adopted by several communities, already culturally distinct,
and to have been diffused by 'missionaries.'

It has been suggested that such 'missionaries' were really prospectors
who set out from somewhere in the eastern Mediterranean and traveled
westward by sea searching for gold, copper, tin, amber, and other commodities. As such prospectors would have been Bronze Age while the
tomb furniture in the British Isles and northern Europe is classically
Neolithic, considerable degradation of culture has to be postulated on
this hypothesis. (That Bronze Age in Egypt or Greece is contemporary with Neolithic in Britain and Denmark is in fact almost certain.)
But no early tomb in the east Mediterranean is really very like the northwest European family vaults; Egyptian tombs for instance were designed
to hold the body of a single pharaoh or noble, not for a whole clan or
lineage. Only the late 'tholos tombs' of Mycenaean Greece, built after
1550 B.C., have really significant parallels farther west. But the Spanish
and Portuguese tombs that really are strikingly like Mycenaean tholoi
have been shown by recent excavations to be late developments of the
funerary architecture of the Peninsula. The demonstrably older megalithic tombs which yield a Neolithic furniture find no really close analogies in the east Mediterranean. So, even diffusionists today are disin-
clined to look beyond the Iberian Peninsula for the starting point of the
'megalithic cult' and are even toying with the idea of an occidental origin
for the tholos tombs of Mycenae!

Megalithic tombs then seem to document a potent ancestor cult in
Neolithic Europe and dramatically illustrate the force of religion among
Neolithic societies and its role in promoting sustained social co-operation.

Naturally there is no one artistic style common to all the diverse cultures classifiable as Neolithic. And what survives of Neolithic art is much
less attractive to modern taste than the famous creations of reindeer-
hunters in France and Spain. No such realistic magic paintings are assign-
able to Neolithic societies. Such representations as survive are highly
conventionalized. They do not attempt to reproduce the sensuous detail
of the object as seen, but rather to suggest the object by abbreviated
symbolism. Aesthetically this may be a regression, but intellectually it

may indicate an advance—a new power of conceiving and expressing an abstract, general idea, transcending but embracing the concrete, individually different objects actually presented to the senses. It may then be the visual counterpart of more abstract forms of linguistic symbolism and so of more comprehensive reasoning.

Neolithic art is principally represented by geometric patterns mostly preserved on pots. We should class them as mere decoration, but we know from modern barbarians that apparently geometric decoration is really symbolic and charged with magic potency.

In conclusion, it may be well to repeat that the Neolithic Stage, though usually called an Age, does not represent a definite period of time. It began in Hither Asia perhaps 7000 years ago, but in Denmark probably no more than 4500. In Australia it never began at all. It survived in the Americas, except in Peru, till the advent of Europeans; in the Pacific to the nineteenth century; in parts of New Guinea till today. But in the Near East it gave place to a new technological stage, the Bronze Age, over 5000 years ago, in the Mediterranean basin not much later, in Denmark by 1500 B.C., even in north Russia about 1000 B.C. Any Bronze Age culture depended for its very existence on trade, and the great Bronze Age civilizations of the Near East actually drew supplies from an enormously wide area. Some features of Neolithic culture in barbarian Europe may therefore be really distant echoes of Oriental civilization. We have tried to discount this, but may not have succeeded altogether.

RICHARD H. MEADOW

V

The Emergence of Civilization

INTRODUCTION

A COMPREHENSIVE PICTURE of what have been designated the 'Chalcolithic (or Copper), Bronze, and Iron Ages' of the world would not be possible given the limited space available, even if the author were competent to undertake such a task. The dramatic increase over the last twenty years in the amount of data available to the archaeologist in all parts of the world makes specialization in one area, if not in one time period and/or point of view, almost a necessity. The discussion which follows is confined primarily to the area of southern Iraq between about 5500 and 2000 B.C. This 3500-year time span has been called the 'Chalcolithic and Early Bronze Ages.' It should be noted, however, that this terminology, based on the technical sophistication evident in the working of copper and its alloys is being replaced today by another which reflects smaller and more localized divisions of time.

In some areas of the Near East, the need for terms more limited in time and space has led to the division of the old metal age designations into smaller units such as: Early Bronze I, Middle Bronze III, or even Early Bronze IIIb. Such terminology may become confusing, however, when the end of the 'Early Bronze' period in one area (perhaps 'IIIC) corresponds in absolute time to the second part of the first period of the 'Middle Bronze' in another area (perhaps 'IB). Another response to the need for more precisely defined units has been the development of a new terminology based on the temporal divisions reflected in the stratigraphic columns from one or two major sites. Basic to this approach has been an attempt to define homogeneous culture areas on the basis of works of art, architecture, and most especially ceramics and metal.

112

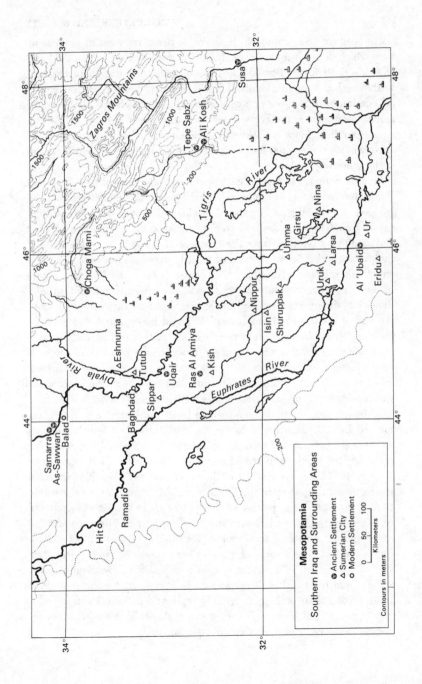

Mesopotamia
Southern Iraq and Surrounding Areas

⊛ Ancient Settlement
△ Sumerian City
○ Modern Settlement

0   50   100
Kilometers

Contours in meters

The 'culture area' approach, however, is being replaced by a point of view which depends upon the analysis of regions defined not on the basis of cultural attributes but on the basis of environmental characteristics. Within such geographical units, it is still necessary to break up the temporal continuum into more or less arbitrarily defined chunks, but intraregional continuity and development are emphasized instead of interregional parallels. Since questions of socio-cultural change seem easier to answer in such a regional framework, it is this last approach which is used in the following analysis.

Present evidence suggests that it was in the alluvium of the Tigris and Euphrates rivers that complex, stratified society—i.e. civilization first developed on a grand scale. By the third millennium B.C., both archaeological and contemporary written records indicate the prevalence of craft and administrative specialists, the existence of different social classes, and the presence of different degrees of wealth, perhaps cross-cutting the occupational and class groupings. The causes behind and the very nature of the development of such a social system are difficult to ascertain. Also difficult to discover is how fixed the hierarchical structure actually was by the end of the third millennium B.C. As might be expected, the evidence for social phenomena is often more explicit in the ancient texts than in archaeological remains. One can infer, however, the presence of some degree of social ranking from such characteristics as different settlement sizes, monumental art and architecture localized in specific areas, and varying degrees of pre- and post-mortem residential splendor.

Although most of the above societal traits are historically well documented by 2000 B.C., it was during the sixth, fifth, and fourth millennia B.C. that the processes of change took place which yielded the mixed bag of attributes used today to characterize 'Sumerian Civilization' (see Adams, 1966). Prior to 2600 B.C. there are few decipherable cuneiform inscriptions to supplement the archaeological records from southern Iraq. Before the Late Uruk period (c. 3200 B.C.) there are no contemporary texts at all, and the prehistorian must fall back upon inference and conscious testing of analogy to illuminate the otherwise meaningless archaeological record. The nature of past archaeological research in the Near East combined with the almost 'sudden' availability of decipherable documents from the third millennium B.C., has made that millennium seem more pivotal than perhaps it actually was. And if those thousand years can be considered fairly well known archaeologically, the 3000 years preceding them are, at best, very spottily documented.

The purpose of this chapter is to indicate some of the ways in which the environment of southern Mesopotamia imposed constraints on, provided guidelines for, and interacted with the socio-cultural processes which produced what has been called a 'civilized' and 'urban' Sumerian 'state.' Basic to the argument are two presuppositions. First, the cultural equipment and responses of the members of any society (taken as a convenient, yet arbitrary unit of analysis) can be characterized as 'old, new, or borrowed.' A group's pattern of actions within, reactions to, and modifications of its environment is unique since it has been moulded by what the members have been taught by and inherited from their elders, what they have borrowed from contemporaries, and what they have invented for themselves. Second, the environment which forms the milieu for life has social and cultural as well as physical dimensions. The clash of two populations is as much a fact of existence for a member of either as fickle rains and salty soil. The members of any population (defined on whatever level of magnitude is most convenient) must live with and react to such pressures as those brought by increasing population and outside aggression. These along with other factors including soil salination and environmental uncertainty sometimes can be shown to have been the result of human interference with the physical processes of Nature.

The following discussion will not so much describe the prehistory and early history of the area but emphasize the roles that a range of factors may have played in order to urge explicit investigation of those processes by archaeologists, philologists, and natural scientists. Some of the few investigations already undertaken and published will be summarized and evaluated.

NATURE OF THE EVIDENCE

Information about the development of society in ancient Sumer is derived mainly from three sources: philology, archaeology, and the natural sciences. It was the philologists who first recognized the existence of *Sumerian*, a language far older than the Neo-Assyrian and Neo-Babylonian known from the Biblically prominent cities of Assur and Babylon. By 1940, archaeologists had located and dug into the early historical levels of many of the important Sumerian sites. These include in the south: Uruk (= Erech, =Warka),* Nippur, Girsu (=Tello), Ur, Shuruppak (=Fara), and Kish; in the Diyala River drainage: Tutub (=Khafajah) and Eshnunna

---

* In parentheses are the commonly used alternate names for the ancient settlements.

(=Tell Asmar). From deep soundings at Uruk and Ur two prehistoric
Southern Mesopotamian periods were established: the 'Uruk' preceded by
the 'Ubaid.' During the early 1940's, excavations at Tell Uqair uncovered
a late 'Uruk' painted temple as well as earlier 'Ubaid' remains. The existence of prehistoric temples in the south was confirmed by excavations at
Eridu from 1947 to 1949, where the presence of remains earlier than and
distinct from those characteristic of the 'Ur-Ubaid' was revealed. Soundings at Nineveh and work at Tepe Gawra, Arpachiyah, and Hassuna had
established by 1946 a long sequence of occupation in the rain-fed steppe
of northern Mesopotamia. Expeditions led by Robert Braidwood in the
upland valleys of the Zagros, both in Iraq and in Iran, established that
domesticated plants were cultivated and domesticated animals used long
before the manufacture of fired ceramics in the area. These expeditions
in the late 1940's and early 1950's were carried out with the active participation of natural scientists. With this kind of collaboration and the
development of Carbon-14 dating, the time was ripe for a change in
attitudes toward Near Eastern pre-history. Instead of seeing earlier 'cultures' as the impoverished forebearers of later great civilizations, archaeologists were beginning to be able to view the later cultural manifestations as elaborations on a techno-economic base that had its roots deep in
the past.

With the recent publication (1969) of the results of excavations in Deh
Luran (West Khuzistan, Iran) and at Choga Mami (near Mandali in the
eastern steppe of Iraq), light has been shed on some of the processes of
human adaptation which eventually made settlement on a large scale
feasible in the Tigris-Euphrates delta. Both regions, however peripheral
to the main delta area, are key to an understanding of the techno-economic competence of the earliest farmers of the alluvium. Their importance is underlined by the extremely sketchy nature of the evidence
from the delta region itself during the period from about 5500 to 3000 B.C.
Data from before the sixth millennium are non-existent, and because of
the characteristics of sites selected for excavation, extensive clearing of
early strata generally has been impractical. Past interests have dictated
the excavation of the historic and late prehistoric levels of large urban
sites in a search for art, architecture, and cuneiform documents. More
than a sounding or two into the earlier prehistoric strata has been impossible given limitations of time, money, and the interests of the excavators. It is noteworthy that some of the best evidence for the pattern of
life in prehistoric Mesopotamia has come from such briefly occupied sites

as Tell as-Sawwan and Ras al Amiya. At both sites sufficient domestic structures were cleared to yield valuable data on the architecture and layout of early village settlements. Although extensive clearing was not carried out at Tepe Sabz, the successive pictures of environmental exploitation obtained from these Deh Luran excavations have increased our understanding of the processes of techno-economic change to a much greater degree than any previous work in the area.

As the natural sciences have complemented archaeology in the study of the early prehistoric periods, so philology has provided flesh to the archaeological skeleton from the late fourth millennium onward. Even more than vegetable and animal remains, ancient texts are subject to biases of location which are often reflected in their contents. Thus most of the cuneiform documents recovered are from individual archives specifically located within a temple, a palace, or occasionally in domestic or other structures. These groups of texts have generally been removed with little regard as to how they were deposited. It has been felt that the individual text itself would yield all the information necessary to place it in time and space. This may be true, to a degree, for religious or epic literature, but unfortunately one can only guess at what the arrangement of the specific economic texts in relation to one another might yield to the context-conscious epigrapher and/or excavator. Apart from the very uneven nature of the textual material (spotty in time and space), it is also necessary to realize that the documents now available reflect the ideology of a predominantly tradition-oriented literati. Many of the epics and religious texts represent accidentally preserved traditions passed down in the scribal schools in the form of copy books. It is the legal, economic, and some omen texts and letters which reflect the day-to-day activities of a limited segment of the populace living in and around the centers where the administrative apparatus was located and from which most of the texts have been recovered. Where the sphere of activity of the individual impinged upon the sphere of the religious or political bureaucracy, the results were recorded in cuneiform on clay.

A further problem, especially for the non-epigrapher, is interpretation of the ancient written material. As one eminent philologist has stated: 'Two different translators will occasionally arrive at somewhat different results; for all translating involves a choice between possibilities and allows the personal factor a certain amount of play' (Jacobsen, 1946:129-30). The result is that the non-specialist will read over one philologist's critique of another with the feeling of missing something important, especially when the interpretation of a text may depend upon only one or two signs. Difficulties of translation are compounded by the polyphonous nature of the script (one incised sign may stand for more than one value) with the result that each sign must be translated in the context in which it occurs. This may prove especially difficult when technical terms or weights and measures are come upon. However, a vast amount of data is potentially available through the epigrapher to the archaeologist interested in social structure and change if the latter exercises the utmost caution in selection and interpretation.

Similar caution must be exercised when using artifactual remains. Of all cultural debris, pottery has been singled out by the archaeologist as providing the best indication of cultural variation over time and space. Using primarily this non-perishable yet highly breakable product of human craftsmanship, and secondarily other durable remains, the archaeologist has attempted to delimit cultural boundaries. Decoration and vessel shapes especially and, to a lesser degree, the type of clay and finish have been used, often quite subjectively, to assign pottery from sites to specific 'ceramic traditions.' Conscious query of what similarities in artifactual remains actually indicates has been minimal. Complex processes such as 'evolution' and 'diffusion' have been invoked time and time again as explanations (sic) with little accompanying investigation into the 'how?' or the 'why?.' This is not to say that ceramic remains cannot be used to establish a relative chronology. A temporal and spatial framework is necessary before investigation of processes of interaction is possible. Such a structure, however, must be subject to continuous modification in detail since it merely reflects current opinion on the past processes which the archaeologist wishes to study. Archaeology is an often impressionistic yet always dynamic discipline. Only through constant and continuous revision is a modicum of historical 'truth' obtained. Techniques and standards of excavation are continually changing, as are the questions the archaeologist asks of his data. As in any academic discipline, present research, based on past accomplishment, underlines the need for future study.

Another problem, not confined to archaeology, is that of the time-lag between excavation and publication. Some excavation reports never find the printed page, others appear so tardily that they can almost be considered 'out-of-date.' Many excavations are reported in preliminary fashion in journals, with definitive publication appearing only years later. Such for instance, is the case with the site of Ur. Partially excavated by Sir Leonard Woolley between 1922 and 1934, preliminary reports came out promptly in the *Antiquaries Journal*, (1923-1934). Some volumes of the final report have appeared, but others still await publication. Portions of sites such as Kish were never published by their excavators; these become available only through the archival research of dedicated scholars. The small size of many excavations, the limitations inherent in the materials recovered, and the lack of a fully published record combine to make any attempt at a description of 'culture history' difficult, and an effort to reconstruct 'cultural processes' hazardous.

TABLE I: Approximate dating of the archaeological periods of southern Mesopotamia.*

Time (B.C.)	Period
c. 5500-5000	Eridu and Samarran
c. 4900-4500	Hajji Mohammad
c. 4400-4000	Ur-Ubaid I
c. 3900-3500	Ur-Ubaid II
c. 3500-3400	Early Uruk
c. 3400-3300	Middle Uruk
c. 3300-3100	Late Uruk (earliest writing)
c. 3100-2900	Jamdat Nasr
c. 2900-2750	Early Dynastic I
c. 2750-2600	Early Dynastic II
c. 2600-2500	Early Dynastic IIIa
c. 2500-2375	Early Dynastic IIIb
c. 2375-2230	Akkadian
c. 2230-2130	Post-Akkadian (Gutian)
c. 2130-2000	Ur III (2113-2006—height)

* Adapted from Porada, 1965.

THE TEMPORAL FRAMEWORK

The increase in data available from which to form a relative chronology, including the development of Carbon-14 dating, and the solidifying of an absolute chronology from contemporary textual material, has led both to recognition of the individuality of development in any given region and to realization of the arbitrary nature of the broad temporal divisions and designations imposed by the archaeologist. Yet, in order to study processes of interaction and change using archaeological remains, it is necessary to have firm control over description and definition in both time and space. Such control is presently derived primarily from comparison of the very remains which reflect the developments and interactions that the archaeologist wishes to study. Textual and Carbon-14 dating have helped

to break such circular reasoning, but attempts to fit strata of newly excavated sites neatly into arbitrarily established chronological periods
seem doomed to failure. Such periods are merely slices in the temporal
continuum. Hence when named periods are used in this discussion they
refer to portions of time which have indefinite boundaries. The developments they classify in one region may or may not be paralleled in another,
at the same or even at different times. Subject to these understandings the
periods of Mesopotamian prehistory and early history are listed in Table
I. The increasing fineness of the temporal divisions reflects both the availability of more diverse materials and a quickening tempo of change in
those classes of objects used to define a period.

It should be noted that Carbon-14 dates from recent excavations on the
Iranian plateau and in South Asia, as well as new work in Mesopotamia
itself, have raised the possibility that changes may be needed in the accepted chronology. The probability of fluctuating error in uncorrected
Carbon-14 determinations and the limited nature of both the Iranian and
Mesopotamian evidence combine to make the whole question exceedingly
complex. Specific problems of chronology will not be discussed, but it
must be emphasized that the temporal framework used here is not the
final word by any means.

GENERAL CLIMATE

Available evidence suggests little major change in the general climate of
the Near East since about 8000 B.C. Fluctuations in the timing and
amounts of rainfall have occurred, however. Since precipitation is reflected by vegetation cover (if there is little or no human interference),
pollen deposits trapped in ancient lake beds can give the specialist some
idea of past climatic conditions. Pollen cores from Turkey and Iran suggest that one period of deviation from today's vegetation pattern occurred
between 8000 and 4000 B.C. Longer periods without rainfall and/or higher
temperatures perhaps resulted in drier summers than today for much of
that 4000 years (Van Zeist, 1969: 43-44). Although such conditions would
have inhibited the growth of perennials, including the oak-pistachio
group which makes up the highland forests, annual vegetation which com-
pletes its growing cycle before summer (such as cereals and legumes)
could grow or be dry-farmed in areas with sufficient precipitation during
the growing season. For our purposes, therefore, and with due allowance
for man-produced alterations, the rainfall-temperature-vegetation complex
of the past 10,000 years can be illustrated by the patterns of the present.

ENVIRONMENT OF THE GENERAL AREA

Four main environmental types are recognized in the area of what to-day is Iraq and western Iran (Flannery, 1965 and 1969:73). These are: the high plateau, about 1500 meters elevation; intermontane valleys be-tween 450 and 1200 meters; the piedmont-steppe, 180 to 300 meters; and the alluvial desert, 30 to 150 meters. Altitude and latitude combine to effect distinctive vegetational complexes in each of these zones. Variations in rainfall and temperature between zones, as well as within them, pro-duce a mosaic of habitats. This pattern is further accentuated by differ-ences in the underlying land forms and geological materials as reflected in local soils, drainage, and mineral resources. Material resources useful to man were, then as now, sharply localized, and the demand for bitumen, flint, chert, obsidian, turquoise, and later copper and lapis lazuli, pro-moted the exchange of such substances over wide areas as early as the eighth millennium B.C.

The Alluvium: River Regimes

The alluvial desert of southern Mesopotamia begins at the ridge be-tween Ramasi and Baghdad. Near the present-day town of Hit the slope of the Euphrates shifts from 30 cm. to 11 cm. per kilometer, while near Balad, just northwest of Baghdad, the Tigris gradient drops abruptly from 50 cm. to 7 cm. per kilometer. These abrupt changes result in both rivers' depositing their considerable loads of silt in the northern end of the delta. The amount of water-borne deposit reaching the Persian Gulf is negligible. During peak water-carrying months in the late spring, both rivers tend to overflow their levees and often flood many thousand square kilometers of the alluvial plain with water three to six meters deep. Be-fore modern control such flooding was extremely destructive, especially as it often occurred just prior to or during harvest of the winter crops.

Today each of the twin rivers has a distinct character. Archaeological evidence suggests that the same was true in prehistoric and early historic times. The figures below give some idea of the differences. At Hit, the average maximum rise of the Euphrates has been measured at 3.5 meters during May, with upwards of a sevenfold increase in flow. The Tigris, on the other hand, rises an average of 5.8 meters in April, with flow increas-ing tenfold. A glance at a map of the area will indicate that the Euphrates has fewer tributaries than the Tigris; it also has further to flow after it emerges from the Anatolian plateau. The wider bed of the Euphrates further aids in loss of moisture through evaporation. The Tigris has many left bank tributaries which drain water from the Zagros; it carries more water than the Euphrates, has a wider catchment area, and is subject to more sudden flooding. Both rivers are at their lowest in September and October. During the winter, when the temperature drops and the rains come, evaporation decreases and flow increases, especially in the Euphrates.

Although the character of the alluvium undoubtedly differs today from its nature in prehistoric times, it seems reasonable to believe that the greater and earlier peaking of the Tigris, which would tend to flood cereal crops at the time of their harvest in April, played a major part in confining settlement to the Euphrates drainage. Other Tigris characteristics which may have played a similar limiting role in the upper plain are: high thick levees (preventing simple irrigation); a rapid meandering course (inhibiting communications); and extremely marshy peripheral areas (limiting effectively cultivated areas). In the delta region, the main course of the Tigris in prehistoric times may have been similar to what is today called the 'Shatt al Gharraf.' Between the eighth and sixteenth centuries A.D., the main body of the river flowed in this channel. Evidence from the ancient town of Girsu indicates that this or a similar channel was called 'the Tigris' during the seventeenth century B.C. This may have been due to modifications of a previous channel carried out by the leaders of Girsu about 2400 B.C. (See Buringh, 1957; Al Khashab, 1958; Jacobsen and Adams, 1958; de Vaumas, 1965.)

Uncertainty and Extremes

Life in the Tigris-Euphrates alluvium is characterized by uncertainty and extremes. The heat in the summer is intense. It is mitigated somewhat for the human population by low humidity and the northwest wind (Shimāl) which blows nine days out of ten. The Shimāl, however, increases water loss through evaporation. Plant life is seen only near the rivers and canals. Extensive cultivation of cereals during this period is rarely practical or possible and agriculture shrinks to small walled-garden plots which are constantly watered. During the winter, the southeast winds (the Sharqi) bring cooler and more humid weather. The rainfall from November through March, although low, is critical to a successful harvest. The occasional heavy downpours, however, play havoc with the landscape, turning the usually parched clays of fields, roads, and lanes into a morass of sticky mud. Travel is only possible on the raised levees of present or former watercourses that shed the rain which, however, inhibit drainage of the surrounding low-lying areas.

The average rainfall of the alluvium is generally well below the 200 mm. minimum considered necessary for dry farming along the Zagros watershed. Averages, however, have little meaning for much of the area. For example, although the 200 mm. isohyet (an average) includes part of the alluvium, the 300 mm. isohyet is considered the effective limit to dry-farming. It is only within the latter that one is assured of the necessary minimum amount of precipitation in eight years out of ten. An average dry farming production of 410 kilograms of cereal per hectare actually represents a range of 1000 to 0 (zero) kilograms per hectare depending upon the amount and timing of the rains.

Prerequisite for extensive cultivation in the alluvium is irrigation, but even that does not ensure security. The maximum extent of cultivation depends upon the maximum amount of water available at the correct time in any given growing season. The lack of correspondence between the growing season and maximum availability of river water as well as the fickle nature of winter rainfall severely limits cultivation. Chronic uncertainty about the crop yields in an area in any given year seems to be the rule. Periodic flooding, often during harvest season, and changes of course do not make the rivers any more dependable. Course shifts especially have played an important role in the prehistory and history of the alluvium. The main course of the Euphrates during the Sumerian period was almost certainly different from that of today and there is increasing evidence that both rivers have shifted their beds many times. (See references for preceding section and Adams, 1965; Flannery, 1969; Fernea, 1970: Appendix A.)

Tectonic Instability

Such bed shifting is perhaps linked to tectonic instability in the area. Evidence from the Diyala River and Susiana, both alluvial areas east of Mesopotamia proper, suggests a change from aggrading to down-cutting stream regimes within the past thousand years (see Adams, 1962 and 1965, for further details). One of the explanations for this change is crustal uplift in the Zagros Mountains which is thought to accompany continuing sinking of the alluvial plain of the Tigris and Euphrates. Lees and Falcon (1952) have suggested that the masses of silt deposited by the two rivers in the delta each year (estimated at more than 7 million cubic meters) have led not to a retreat of the Persian Gulf as formerly supposed but to the down warping of the land surface to accommodate the increasing weight. Localized compaction of silts beneath levees and ancient settlement mounds may produce similar settling. Hollows created by such movements turn into swamps, fed by the flooding rivers, until they are filled by alluvium and by dust carried by the Shimāl. There is evidence for localized uplift in the Diyala (Adams, 1965), Mandali (Oates, 1969), and Ur/Eridu (Flannery and Wright, 1966) areas. In the last case, the low ridge separating the Eridu depression from the alluvium around Ur is thought to have been thrust up since the Ubaid period.

Levees and the Changing Drainage Patterns

Levee formation, characteristic of aggrading regimes, provides a mechanism for the accumulation of large concentrated masses of silt. When a river overflows its banks, it tends to do so at many places simultaneously. Since the carrying capacity of overflow water is much less than that of the parent stream, sediment is deposited on the back slopes of the levee. Coarser sediments are deposited first, with fine silts deposited far down the levee slopes. The result is that a river in such a regime is raised above the level of the surrounding flood plain, permitting the formation of back-swamps. Water from the river drains into the depressions when the water table is high; as the level of the river drops, so will the water table. Under normal conditions, the back-swamps will drain through the relatively porous levees into the river when it is low. Irrigation, however, may upset this process.

Occasionally a watercourse will break its levee and find a new channel through low-lying areas. This is a common occurrence in the delta plain of Mesopotamia where much of the early settlement took place. There, the Euphrates in particular is characterized by many meandering branches with levees which are smaller and more easily breached than those in the steeper river plain to the north and east. Another characteristic of the south is that ground water tends to be nearer to the surface. Thus, although obtaining water for irrigation is easier, the dangers resulting from inadequate drainage are increased. Because the head waters of both rivers pass through gypsum and other salt-bearing strata, proper drainage of irrigated fields is essential if soil salination is to be avoided. (See, especially, Adams, 1965.)

Internal Variation

Also characteristic of the alluvium is internal diversity. Four types of subsistence zones (micro-environments) may be isolated within lowland Mesopotamia:

(1) Levee back slopes, margins of swamps, and depressions where extensive cultivation especially of cereals is undertaken in the winters.

(2) Artificial or natural low-lying areas near summer watercourses where garden and orchard cultivation is possible. (It is estimated that this category today represents no more than 10 per cent of the first.)

(3) Fallow fields, fringes of the western desert, marginal areas on the edge of cultivation and between major cities where grazing on weeds, stubble, and thin natural growth is available to the herdsman.

(4) Rivers and swamps where fish, reeds, and similar materials are available for food and building.

In the short run as well as the long run these zones will tend to overlap and grade into one another. Thus in the late spring, annual marshes turn into grazing grounds for animals. Similarly, loosing flocks to feed on young barley shoots is known from the area today (Adams, 1965:14). Silting, salination, and change in channels can alter the character of the landscape quite drastically in time, turning rich agricultural zones into areas fit only for grazing. Although there is presently no evidence of the character of the vegetation in the alluvium before interference by man, there is reason to suppose that it clustered around the perennial watercourses and in the swamps. Present vegetation along the rivers and channels includes tamarisk, poplar, willow, and wild licorice as well as the date palms. In the marshes, reeds, tall grasses, and sedge are found. Most of the rest of the vegetation consists of salt-resistant plants and weeds which thrive through human agency. 'Advantageous' weeds, those that are characterized by a niche different from that of the cereal crops, include shok (*Prosopis*) and camel thorn. Both are perennial legumes with deep root structures which tend to fix nitrogen in the soil. Although they cannot be destroyed by traditional plowing methods, these plants *do not compete* with the sown crops, as they mature very late. 'Disadvantageous' weeds, including the annual grains such as wild oats, legumes such as 'Khuzaima' (*Scorpiurus sulcata*), and thistles, not only *compete* for valuable soil nutrients but can overrun a field, cutting drastically into the yield. Thistles, especially, tend to impede, or even prohibit, harvesting. Many of these weeds, both advantageous and harmful, seem to have been imported into the lowland area during prehistoric times where they throve in the altered environment. Although not intentionally *cultivated,* such weeds are *domesticated* since they depend on a man-altered environment for their existence. Hans Helbaek (1969:406) suggests that the mechanism of their first introduction was unclean batches of seed brought in or traded by mountain cultivators.

Population Pressure and Changing Adaptation

As stated previously, irrigation is a prerequisite for extensive agriculture in the alluvium. The currently favored conceptual model of the origins of irrigation views this technology as an adaptation supplementing the yearly precipitation in areas of limited rainfall (Hole et al., 1969:355, and Adams, 1962:112). Movement of peoples into such marginal areas may have been caused, at least in part, by population pressure on resources (especially on land suitable for cultivation) in regions with more dependable and effective precipitation (see Binford, 1968; Flannery, 1969). With the widespread use of irrigation, areas previously defined as marginal on the basis of comparative population densities and technologies became more central, 'donating' aspects of culture instead of 'receiving' them. These concepts may be further elucidated as follows.

Technology, including tool-producing behavior, knowledge, and exploitation practices, delimits the sources of subsistence for a human population living within a 'habitat' (a conveniently chosen, naturally demarcated area). Aspects of technology, as part of culture, are learned from elders or contemporaries within the same local population, borrowed from neighbors, or invented in response to needs. If characteristics of the environment[*] within a region should change in such a way as to affect the food intake of individuals comprising a human population, then a stimulus for adopting changes in some aspects of the traditional technology will be present.

Ethologists, such as Wynne-Edwards (1962, 1965), have suggested that the population size of any species of animal, with a well-defined relationship to other species in a habitat at a given time, tends to stabilize well below the starvation level. The mechanisms thought to accomplish such

---

[*] Note that environment includes social and cultural as well as physical dimensions.

a leveling are both biological and behavioral; how much of the behavior is genetically determined, however, is debated. Similar mechanisms seem to have held the size of human populations to a low but slowly increasing level for the first 3 to 4 million years of man's existence. Within the past 20,000 years, however, basic alterations in the way of life of certain groups seem to have obviated the need for, overcome, or changed the nature of such mechanisms. Based on their past experiences, and using their ability to conceptualize and communicate, men became capable of consciously and/or unconsciously manipulating aspects of their environment.

In selected areas of the Old and New Worlds, conditions permitted and increasing population may have dictated 'broad spectrum' food gathering. Instead of moving around and foraging for a limited number of types of foods from a wide area, certain populations began to use a wider number of resources from a more circumscribed territory. It is thought that such practices led to sedentary settlement, cultivation of plants, and keeping of animals (Binford, 1968, and Flannery, 1969). In sum, population growth in specific habitats could have been a factor in precipitating population movements and/or technological change. Such a process would both reinforce trends towards the domestication of plants and animals, and spread the products and techniques to new areas.

With the development of cereal cultivation and animal husbandry specifically, moving into new habitats meant taking animals and seeds into areas perhaps less suited to their growth. Such movements would not only have favored change in the genetic make-up of the plants and animals through selection of those with more viable characteristics but also have stimulated cultural (including technological) change so that these organisms, crucial to the human group's own well-being, could continue to be productive sources of food. The evidence from sites which have yielded early plant remains (Braidwood, 1960, and Hole *et al.*, 1969) suggests that cultivation (like later irrigation) was originally a secondary adaptation; intensive gathering of wild cereals and legumes and hunting of wild animals provided the main sources of nutrition. Such a pattern continued at least through the sixth millennium B.C., when a shift took place in what was supplemental. Gathered foods seem to have become additions—albeit necessary ones—to a primarily cereal diet. In the archaeological record, the remains of wild plants and animals are supplanted by those of domestic species. Some sites show an increase in small seeds from wild plants; their great numbers suggest the gathering of wild fodder for animals.

BENEFITS OF A CHANGING TECHNOLOGY

Into the environment of southern Mesopotamia, man brought a complex of food grains, legumes, and animals which seem to have been originally cultivated (or herded) if not actually domesticated in the intermontane valleys of the Zagros and on the Anatolian plateau (see Helbaek, 1969; esp. 402-5). Upon movement into areas of lower elevation with earlier and more intensely hot summers and shorter and less frequent rains, the plants became increasingly dependent upon man for their survival. Changes in their genetic composition, manifested in more profitable harvests, permanently fixed the dependence of such domesticates on husbandry. Among the changes was one which toughened the rachis (upper stem) of the ripe cereal. The result was greater retention of grains during harvesting. The genetic change involved was rapidly fixed, since the proportion of a tough-rachis cereal recovered would be greater than that of the brittle-axis variety. Its chances of appearing in the next year's seed would therefore be greatly enhanced. With the increasing use of irrigation in some areas, certain plants developed in such a way as to become dependent upon this technology for their survival.

Irrigation, for example, seems to have promoted the formation of six-rowed hulled barley. The distribution of finds of this grain suggests that it required a higher water supply, especially during the hot, dry spring months, than was available in dry-farming regions. Helbaek (1969:421) reasons that this was because of the increased evaporation from the six-rowed as compared with the two-rowed variety grown in the highlands. Desiccation in the final stages of ripening also seems to have been the fate in dry-farming regions of free-threshing (bread) wheat. Early irrigation and selection by man permitted the appearance of both cereals, although, as will be noted below, increasing salinity substantially reduced the growing of wheat in some areas.

The certainty of cereal growth, even in years of poor rainfall, must have been a major asset of irrigation cultivation. When used on virgin land, or with some care in fallowing and/or drainage, irrigation will also tend to increase both the average yield of a field and the size of the useful parts of plants. Figures from a marginal dry-farming region such as Khuzistan in southwest Iran indicate that today the average yearly yield rises from 410 to 615 kilograms per hectare with irrigation (Adams, 1962: 110). Higher yields from irrigation are also reported from the Diyala River drainage (see Table IIA).

TABLE II

A: Modern yields from irrigation cultivation in the Diyala Basin, Iraq.

265 randomly sampled fields of wheat: 1,132 kgs ± 24.8 per hectare
77 randomly sampled fields of barley: 1,396 kgs ± 67.5 per hectare
Seeding rates: Barley: 60-80 kgs/hectare
               Wheat: 48-72 kgs/hectare
Proportion of barley grown to wheat: 70 per cent
(From Adams, 1965:17)

B: Ancient yields from irrigation cultivation in southern Mesopotamia.

Time	Place	Yield (in liters per hectare)
2400 B.C.	Girsu (Lagash)	2537
2100 B.C.	Girsu (Lagash)	1460
1700 B.C.	Larsa	897

(From Jacobsen and Adams, 1958)

C: Proportion of wheat to barley grown at different periods.

Time	Place	Wheat to Barley Proportion of	Source
3500 B.C.	S. Iraq	1:1	grain impressions on pottery
2400 B.C.	S. Iraq	1:5	texts
2100 B.C.	Girsu (Lagash)	1:50	texts
1700 B.C.	S. Iraq	all barley	texts

(Source: Jacobsen and Adams, 1958)

Since it seems reasonable, on the evidence available, to suggest that irrigation was first used in marginal dry-farming areas to compensate for the fickle nature of the rains, the increased absolute yields available from irrigation may not at first have been consciously sought after. Another product of irrigation, which may not have been recognized immediately, is the increased size of individual seeds. Linseed (flax) serves as a good example. Seeds recovered from sites in dry-farming regions range from 3.84 to 4.03 mm. in length. Irrigation in warm areas, however, produced seeds from 4.39 to 4.94 mm. in length (Helbaek, 1969:418). Even larger seeds (up to 6 mm.) are reported from areas with improved irrigation farming (first millennium B.C., Iraq and Egypt). Lentils react similarly to cultivation in hot, dry areas where irrigation is a necessity.

With the availability of irrigation water in the summer, as well as in the winter, the extension of the humid habitat was accomplished. Such conditions probably already existed along the natural watercourses, and marsh resources certainly were used by the earliest inhabitants of southern Mesopotamia. Control of water, however, probably made the localized cultivation of date palms and onions feasible on a far larger scale than previously. Dates, especially, seem to have been an extremely important resource in Mesopotamia at least by the second millennium B.C.

IRRIGATION: LIABILITIES

For all its benefits, the liabilities of indiscriminate irrigation are and were severe. For one, the practice of irrigation in the alluvium seems to have altered and emphasized the process of alluviation and river course shifts. As long as he has inhabited the alluvium, man has widened, straightened, cleaned, or otherwise altered—on a greater or lesser scale —the channel of flow of the watercourses. As a result, there is a continuum of channels which runs from those which distribute most or all of their supplies for irrigation to those which yield little or no water to man. Shifts along the continuum are a characteristic of farming in the alluvium. Site surveys indicate that not until Partho-Sasanian times (300 B.C. to A.D. 600) was there major disregard for the prevailing 'natural' drainage patterns. Before that time most settlements seem to have been located near those channels which flowed with greater or lesser volumes of water at least since the beginning of cultivation in the plain. In the beginning, little more than breaching the levee and construction of small-scale feeder and field canals was necessary to obtain water. The construction of elaborate dams and the digging of major artificial canals was not attempted until there came into existence both political stability and a centralized authority to plan and control irrigation operations (Adams, 1960).

One of the greatest attractions of the Mesopotamian alluvium for the early settlers, then, was the ease of obtaining water for cultivation. Irrigation canals, however, also tend to form levees, although their buildup proceeds differently from that of a river in flood (see Adams, 1965). The silting up of ever increasing areas near major watercourses due to deposits from adjoining canal networks, combined with the breaching of major levees for irrigation water, gives major channels more impetus and opportunity to shift their beds into nearby lower lying areas.

Another, even more disastrous effect of irrigation as it has been practiced in the Mesopotamian and other (including the Indus and Helmand) flood plains is salination. The levees of smaller canals tend to isolate depressions and inhibit drainage of the wide, gently sloping levee backslopes of major watercourses built up by flooding and extended through irrigation. The result can be a rise in the ground water, bringing up with it salts present in the silt. As the surface water evaporates, these salts are precipitated out; the result has been the formation of uncultivable 'gilgai' soils in vast areas of the alluvial plain.

Ancient records suggest at least three major occurrences of soil salination in pre-modern Mesopotamia (Jacobsen and Adams, 1958). The earliest recorded and most serious of these affected the southern delta from about 2400 B.C. to at least 1700 B.C. A summary of Jacobsen and Adams's findings about this particular period is worthwhile here for the light it sheds on a number of seemingly disparate but actually closely interrelated factors. As a result of a dispute over land rights with the city-state of Lagash, the king of Umma breached and obstructed the feeder canals serving the border fields. (Umma is situated higher up on the watercourse which brought water to both cities from the Euphrates.) The king of Lagash, Entemena by name, after unsuccessfully protesting the impairment of flow, undertook to supply his city's fields with water from the Tigris. He succeeded so well that two things seem to have happened: (1) By 1700 B.C. the canal had become important enough to be called merely 'the Tigris'. This may indicate that, in fact, the main flow had gradually shifted to the artificially modified channel. (2) By the same date salinity had all but overwhelmed the region. What may have occurred is that a large area, formerly watered only by lesser amounts of Euphrates water, was drowned in huge amounts of Tigris water. Seepage, flooding, and over-irrigation probably all combined to create a decisive rise in ground water. This may have been compounded by the fact that Tigris water tends to be more alkaline than that from the Euphrates.

Quantitative as well as qualitative evidence for increasing salination of the lower Euphrates delta plain is also available. Not only is the presence of white, crusted salt on fields directly attested in contemporary texts, but a striking decrease in yields can also be demonstrated. Jacobsen and Adams (1958) suggest that the drop in fertility indicated by the figures in our Table IIB, can be attributed mainly to salination. This conclusion seems to be confirmed by a change in the types of cereals actually grown. One of the many factors that influence crop choice in any given area is the tolerance of a species to the salts present in the soil. Most cereals are considerably less salt-tolerant than six-rowed hulled barley. Therefore, the onset of salination should see, for instance, an increase in the proportion of barley to wheat grown in the affected areas. This does indeed seem to be the case (see Table IIC).

The significance of the preceding illustration is in demonstrating in an oversimplified fashion, how irrigation as practiced in this case, while a prerequisite for extensive settlement in the Mesopotamian alluvium, carried the germs of land destruction. After 1700 B.C. the center of settlement moved north from the delta to the river plain, an area which has a lower water table, but which requires more sophisticated techniques to irrigate.

THE SUBSISTENCE BASE

Throughout the preceding discussions of irrigation, mention has been made of specific plants and animals that formed the basis for subsistence in ancient Mesopotamia. It has long been known from third and second millennium B.C. textual materials that the basic agricultural staples of southern Mesopotamia were the irrigated cereals: wheat, millet, and especially barley; the wool, hair, meat, and milk yielders: sheep and goats; and the power producers: cattle and horses. It is only recently, however, that sixth millennium material from north and east of the delta has provided us with evidence of the presence, at that early time, of many of the resources and techniques attested as being so basic in later periods. Although Tepe Sabz, Choga Mami, and Tell as-Sawwan are all peripheral to the lower valleys of the twin rivers, their remains are important because so little of a comparable nature has been recovered from the area which later became the heartland of Sumerian civilization. A discussion, however brief, of the plant and animal remains, along with the evidence for irrigation from these three sites will not only serve to indicate the general similarity in subsistence base in three widely separated regions but, more important, will emphasize the individuality of adaptation in the different locations. In addition, some of the processes of socio-cultural development we believe should become evident, upon future research, in southern Mesopotamia are reflected in the remains of these peripheral sites.

Plants

The earliest of the sites is 2.5-hectare Tell as-Sawwan situated on a cliff above the Tigris River, north of Baghdad, on the dry side of the 200 mm.

isohyet. Three samples of carbonized vegetable matter were recovered from the 'defensive moat' partially surrounding this Samarra period site. Only one grain of six-rowed hulled barley (*Hordeum vulgare*) was identified from approximately 180 grains of the two-rowed hulled variety (*Hordeum distichon*). Other grains include hexaploid wheat (*Triticum aestivum*—3 grains), six-rowed naked barley (approx. 60 grains—*Hordeum vulgare*, var. *nudum*), and the earliest known domesticates: einkorn (*Triticum monococcum*—one grain) and emmer (*Triticum dicoccum*—approx. 20 grains). Four weeds: goat-face grass (*Aegilops crassa*—one grain), shok (*Prosopis stephaniana*—a great deal), caper (*Capparis spinosa*—approx. 300 seeds), and an unknown species of thistle (approx. 50 seeds) were also present. *Prosopis*, a non-competitive weed and the caper were probably gathered intentionally for their fruits. Significantly, three seeds of large linseed (*Linum usitatissimum*) were recovered. These suggest sophisticated irrigation near the site if they were not brought in from elsewhere. Most of the cereal grains, however, are comparatively small, suggesting that they were grown 'under rather unsuitable conditions, or that they were of races comparatively recently introduced in that environment and not quite adjusted' (Helbaek, 1964:46).

Irrigation direct from the Tigris above Baghdad today, requires some sort of lifting device. The same probably has been true at least since the sixth millennium B.C. Present evidence suggests that after the Samarra period, the area was only sparsely inhabited until large-scale lift irrigation became practicable. This dry area, difficult to irrigate, played a key role throughout history and pre-history as a buffer between the rain-fed north and the irrigated south. The two rivers, however, provided routes for communications, as well as water for small-scale farming, traveling armies, traders, and colonists. Through this desert area, too, the nomadic populations made their presence felt.

Helbaek suggests that at Tell as-Sawwan:

Most probably agriculture was conducted on the basis of the seasonal flood of the river, spill pools were exploited, run-off checked in favorable spots by primitive damming—and generally the activities which we may visualize as the forerunners of the later full-fledged canal irrigation. [1964:46]

If in Samarra times the Tigris did not flow immediately at the foot of the bluff upon which the settlement rests, there would have been flood plain available for cultivation (Adams, 1965:166). Water would have been the limiting commodity, whether it was lifted from the Tigris during the winter growing season or retained in spill pools for later use. Such a water supply would permit production for only a limited population and might promote differential control of productive resources by individual groups within the society. That social differentiation was a characteristic of the Tell as-Sawwan settlement is suggested by the range of wealth deposited with the burials in Period V, the earliest yet reported from the site.

The evidence for irrigation at Tepe Sabz is similar to that from Tell as-Sawwan (see Hole *et al.*, 1969), although the cultural content belongs to a different tradition—the Susiana (similar in style and comparable in date to the Mesopotamian Eridu/Hajji Mohammad tradition). Although the site lies below the 300 mm. isohyet, it is located where the inhabitants could have taken advantage of a small seasonal watercourse draining off of the hills to the north of the Deh Luran Plain. There were no ancient canal beds excavated at the site, but the botanical remains suggest that irrigation was practiced at least as a supplement to rainfall cultivation. That such was the case is underlined by the differences in the remains from Tepe Sabz and earlier Ali Kosh, which lies near the margins of the seasonally flooded central depression of the plain. Although the vegetable matter from Tepe Sabz has not yet been published in quantified form, Helbaek (1969:412ff) sees a marked increase in the abundance of both two and six-rowed hulled barley. Similarly, hexaploid wheat grains were identified at Tepe Sabz while they were not at the earlier and differently located Ali Kosh. Although both lentils and flax were recovered from Ali Kosh, the seeds were of a size to suggest that they were either small native highland varieties brought in, or that they represent unsuccessful attempts at growth in non-irrigated fields. At Tepe Sabz, however, in the lowest level, calcareous casts of what must have been fully irrigated flax (linseed) and lentil remains were recovered. The size range of the thirty-one examples of linseed leads Helbaek to conclude that '. . . linseed must have been grown by this technique [irrigation] for a long time to have developed such an impressive size' (1969:408).

Surveys in the Deh Luran Plain indicate that by the time of the first settlement at Tepe Sabz, many sites were located where the inhabitants might have made use of small channels descending from the mountains. Such sites were characterized not only by the distinctive 'Susiana a'-style painted ceramics, but also by 'polished celts,' possibly used as hoes to break the surface of fields and to construct and maintain small irrigation channels. It should be noted, however, that not all sites of the late sixth millennium in Khuzistan are located where water was readily available for irrigation. Therefore, the significance of the differences evident in the remains of the last phase at Ali Kosh and the first phase at Tepe Sabz may be debated. Whether the techno-economic complex of the Sabz phase was brought in by new people entering the Deh Luran area, or whether it merely represents different farming practices developed by the descendants of the same population in a different habitat is an interesting problem. A combination of both explanations would not be surprising.

The limited exposure of the Sabz phase at Tepe Sabz yielded no evidence of possible social differentiation such as that found at Tell as-Sawwan. A few settlements of this period from the Khuzistan area, however, may have been considerably larger than approximately one hectare characteristic of 'villages' like Tepe Sabz. Such variation may be significant as an indication of the initial growth of regional centers, perhaps as a result of the spotty distribution of scarce resources.

The environmental setting of the site of Choga Mami is similar to that of Tepe Sabz, lying as it does at the foot of the Zagros Mountains below the 300 mm. isohyet. Partially excavated by Joan Oates (1969), the remains of this late Samarran settlement comprise one of a number of early sites located near Mandali, Iraq, approximately 150 kilometers east-southeast of Tell as-Sawwan and 200 kilometers northwest of Tepe Sabz. The site is situated near a canal which is presently supplied from the Gangir River. Survey suggests that the alignment of this modern canal may have its origins in the Samarra Period, and excavation has provided a stratigraphically documented series of fossil channels (Oates, 1969:124-27). The earliest two watercourses seem to have been too far below the contemporary plain level to have been used for irrigation; they may have served as drainage or enclosing ditches as at Tell as-Sawwan. By the time that the last three channels were dug, however, their elevation exceeded that of the contemporary plain and were most likely used for irrigation. Indeed, the rise in ancient ground level which is evident near the site may be a result of the loosing of silt laden water onto fields.

That irrigation was indeed carried out in the area of Choga Mami during the Samarra period is supported by the botanical evidence. Over five thousand carbonized fruits and seeds have been recovered. Of the grasses, however, only one-tenth were cultivated cereals; these include equal proportions of emmer, hexaploid wheat, and six-rowed hulled barley, with lesser amounts of einkorn and oats (all domesticated; Field, 1969). Of the legume seeds, about one-thirtieth may have been cultivated: *Vicia* sp., lentils, and one or two others. Field comments that:

The greater proportion of both grasses and legumes were seeds so small that one is led to conclude that the plants may not have been collected for the seeds, but for the vegetative parts . . . such wild plants could perhaps have provided a source of animal fodder. [1969:140]

The linseed recovered from the site was wild, unlike that from both Tell as-Sawwan and Tepe Sabz. On the whole, however, the cultivated plants are remarkably similar at all three sites, the differences lying, where the samples permit distinctions, in the weeds and wild plant seeds recovered. It should be noted, however, that such statistical variation as is evident may be due as much to sample size and flotation method used for recovery as to different environmental situations and techno-economic practices!

As for interactions of irrigation agriculture and society in the Mandali area, Joan Oates notes (1969:143-44) that: 'The most probable motive for . . . strict adherence [of later house walls] to earlier boundaries would seem to lie in the existence of continuing and rigidly observed property rights.' Whether such rights did, in fact, exist during this early period and how they may have developed are intriguing questions. The hierarchy of land values which irrigation with a limited water supply underlines may have played a role in the development of a concept of land as property. Oates also notes a 'dramatic increase in the intensity of settlement, which is independently witnessed by our survey of the area and which we would attribute to the introduction of irrigated agriculture.' Such an increase in numbers of settlements is found at the same period of time in Khuzistan, but whether irrigation is to be seen as a cause or an effect of population increases in the two areas is debated. As noted previously, the widespread adoption of irrigation techniques can best be seen as a process, *interacting with* an increasing population in areas marginal to those where rainfall agriculture could be most securely practiced.

Animals

An increasing human population in any region tends to have an effect on the physical environment of that area. Such activities as irrigation tend to alter the natural drainage and may eventually lead to soil salination. Evidence for such a process is present in late fifth millennium botanical remains from Tepe Sabz (Hole *et al.*, 1969:363-66), and Joan Oates suggests a similar process may have taken place in the Mandali area of eastern Iraq during Samarra times (Oates, 1969:144). Fuel gathering and grazing of domestic flocks are two other activities which alter the distribution of wild flora and fauna. The cutting of large bushes and trees for fire-wood and the stripping of already poorly vegetated areas by wandering flocks destroy the habitat of the native wild fauna. When combined with hunting, such practices not only promote changes in the population size and types of wild animals but also reinforce dependence upon domestic species. Today, as in the past, sheep and goats especially are grazed on fallow fields, upon the stubble remaining after harvest, and upon the increasingly impoverished natural vegetation.

Animal bones are common finds in excavations of any site in the Near East. Great numbers of bones have been unearthed and then, except in unusual cases, laid aside and never comprehensively studied. This lack of interest may be due to the historical orientation of much of Mesopotamian archaeology; other topics, perhaps rightly, have been deemed more worthy of study. This is not to say that questions as to what animals the people of ancient Sumer utilized have been ignored. In most instances the presence of key faunal types has been noted, often from reliefs and fig-urines. These include sheep, goat, ox, and onager. The introduction of the horse and the camel have been speculated upon, but with very little basis in fact. Until very recently, little attempt has been made to quantify the total number of bones of different species, to determine the minimum number of individuals represented, and to question changing patterns over time and space.* With increasing interest in discerning regional proc-esses, internal differentiation, and specialization, cautious study of faunal remains can make an important contribution. For instance Kent Flannery (in Hole *et al.,* 1969) has suggested that in the early fifth millennium B.C., domestic cattle may have been more common than sheep and goats in parts of the Mesopotamian alluvium. Sites on the periphery of the allu-vium, however, usually yield a high proportion of sheep and goat bones. The evidence for this contrast in faunal distribution is slim, coming from only five sites: Tell as-Sawwan, Tepe Sabz, Choga Mami, Ras al Amiya, and Eridu.

The sample of animal bones from Tell as-Sawwan is too small to be treated statistically. Included in it, however, is a range of fauna typical of most excavated sites of the sixth millennium. Domestic goat (*Capra hircus hircus*) and sheep (*Ovis aries*) are represented along with some species of ox (*Bos primigenius*—wild, or *Bos taurus*—domestic). Large wild mammals include gazelle (*Gazella subgutturosa*), fallow deer (*Dama*

---

* One exception is the study by Max Hilzheimer, *Animal Remains from Tel Asmar* (1941).

mesopotamica), and some species of cat (*Felis* sp.) (Flannery and Wheeler, 1967). Wild goat is not native to the area around Tell as-Saw-wan; gazelle and fallow deer are still found in the nearby steppe. Bones of large fish (catfish?) probably pulled from the Tigris, are represented in the collection as are two kinds of mussel (*Unio tigridis* and *Pseudodon-topsis euphraticus*). Fish and mussel remains are also reported from Tepe Sabz, although the frequency of their appearance decreases drastically after the earliest phase.

Because the excavators were explicitly interested in the faunal assem-blage, the bones from Tepe Sabz and the earlier Tepe Ali Kosh are among the best-studied collections from the Near East. The total sample from the sixteen stratigraphic 'zones' defined at the two sites numbers nearly 13,600 identifiable fragments, or an average of 850 pieces per zone. This would constitute a reasonable sample, except that just over 12,500 of the bones come from the earliest six zones (Ali Kosh), leaving an average of only 109 bones per zone for the last ten (Tepe Sabz). If, however, the number of bones of each animal type in each zone is pre-sented as a percentage of the total bones found within that zone, the im-pression which numbers alone makes is modified.

Throughout the entire four-thousand-year sequence, caprine (sheep/goat) bones make up more than 50 per cent of the samples. Although it is only through analysis of the horn cores, metapodials, and third phalanges that the caprines can be distinguished with any certainty (Hole *et al.*, 1969:266-70), the proportion of sheep to goats does seem to have risen through time. By the Sabz phase (5500-5000 B.C.) not only are there esti-mated to be nearly as many sheep as goats represented in the sample, but also, the skeletal material of both caprines manifests fully modern char-acteristics.

Two new domesticates are represented in the earliest remains from Tepe Sabz; these are cattle and dogs. Throughout the sequence at Tepe Sabz (5500-4000 B.C.) bones from domestic cattle never make up more than 8 per cent of the samples, and although bones from the domestic dog make up more than 12 per cent of the sample from the Sabz phase, they drop by the following Khazineh phase to about 5 per cent. (It should be remembered that the size of the archaeological sounding and that of the sample from Tepe Sabz is small, and accidents of discovery could be criti-cal.) Cattle, of course, were to become important in the plowing of fields in wide areas of the Near East. As for dogs, although select breeds for war and hunting were developed, those whose remains are found at most sites were probably merely guard dogs and scavangers. Their presence may help to explain the almost total absence of 'chewable' bones (Hole *et al.*, 1969:314), and thus the small size of the Sabz sample.

Throughout the sequences from Ali Kosh and Tepe Sabz, hunting was important, although the appearance of domestic cattle and dog cut into the proportions of gazelle and onager (*Equus hemionus*) remains. Identified gazelle bones fluctuate between 10 and 20 per cent of the samples from Tepe Sabz, down from a high of about 30 per cent from the Mohammad Jaffar phase of Ali Kosh (6000-5600 B.C.) when sheep and goat remains are at a low. It should be noted at this point, however, that distinguishing gazelle teeth, ribs, and vertebrae from those of sheep/goat can be difficult, especially when the bones are in fragmentary condition. Onager remains make up a fairly constant 5 per cent of the bones from each phase of Tepe Sabz, also down from a high in the Mahammad Jaffar phase of about 10 per cent. Large herds of these asses until fairly recently roamed the desert and steppe of Mesopotamia and are the most common animal represented in the published faunal remains from early Eridu.

Besides onager and gazelle, wild goat (*Capra hircus aegagrus*) is thought to have been hunted throughout the sequence; its domicile was on the slopes of the Zagros Mountains. The herding of these animals during the tenth and ninth millennia (and perhaps before) in the highlands and their transferal into lowland habitats probably promoted domestication. Many of the forces described before as important in plant domestication can be seen to have played roles in the domestication of animals.

Flannery (1969:92) has emphasized the effect that a change in habitat may have had for the physiology of sheep. Quoting a study by Schmidt-Nielsen (1964), he suggests that the ability of sheep to 'survive high temperatures and desert conditions better than most other domestic animals' is due to a 'panting' mechanism and to their wool. The former device permits effective ventilation, the latter adaptation insulates the body from the heat. Sheep, however, require a more herbaceous type of vegetation upon which to feed than do goats. Since goats happily chew on bushy plants, one finds them herded not only in the mountains, but also in the desert, while sheep seem to thrive best in a lusher and more humid environment. Such generalizations, however, obscure the usually mixed character of herds in modern times, as well as, our evidence suggests, in ancient times. Goats today are herded primarily for their milk but also for their hair, while sheep supply in the first instance wool and milk only secondarily. Both animals are used for meat, as the butchered bones suggest they also were in the past. The importance of textiles in third millennium Mesopotamia is known from contemporary texts; made from wool, they comprised one of the primary exports of Sumer to the outside world. Used in exchange for such necessities as copper and wood, these textiles and the sheep from which they were derived formed an invaluable resource.

How early sheep were deliberately bred for their wool is unknown, just as it is uncertain how early milk production became important. It might be suggested that sheep were originally transferred into the lowland environment as a meat resource and only in later times were their other products fully developed and utilized. Suffice it to say that, as in the case of the cereals, there were multiple and complex pressures which led to the evolution of the domestic sheep and goat as they were known in Mesopotamia by at least 3000 B.C., if not earlier. Such pressures were undoubtedly derived from both Man and Nature.

Remains of other wild fauna, some fairly abundantly represented at Ali Kosh, make their last significant appearance in the earliest phases of Tepe Sabz. These include water birds, reptiles, fish, and mussels from aquatic habitats as well as the pig. Along with its domesticated counterpart, however, the remains of the wild pig (*Sus scrofa*) are rare throughout the Deh Luran sequence. This situation may be contrasted with both (a) highland villages, such as Jarmo, where domestic pig remains in considerable quantity are present in deposits from as early as 6000 B.C., and (b) later sites such as third millennium Tell Asmar, where more than 27 per cent of the 238 identified bones were identified as coming from pigs (Hilzheimer, 1941). Also represented at Tepe Sabz are rodents of at least three species and such small mammals as red fox (*Vulpes vulpes*) and wild cat (*Felis* sp.). The importance of these last in terms of nutrition, however, seems marginal. This minimal role may be contrasted with the important part played by the fauna gathered from aquatic habitats. Along with their terrestrial counterparts—almonds and pistachios—fish and mussels especially are concentrated sources of important vitamins and minerals. It may be hypothesized that 'all these calcium–Vitamin A sources probably became insignificant once the milking of domestic animals was established —an event for which we still have no archaeological evidence' (Flannery, 1969:86).

Turning now to Choga Mami, the preliminary list of faunal types represented at the site shows remarkable similarity to that already described for Tepe Sabz. Remains of domestic sheep, goat, pig, dog, and cattle are noted as present, but with the last found only rarely. Roe deer, fallow deer, fox, gazelle, pig, sheep, goat, wolf, onager, and cat are the wild animals listed (Oates, 1969:139-40). Future quantification of remains from Choga Mami seems promising. Oates (1969:144) notes that 'the faunal remains in the true Samarra levels show a great preponderance [of] gazelle over the larger deer . . . among the later 'Ubaid materials there is a further increase in the relative proportion of gazelle.' If such a change in the proportions of animals represented at Choga Mami is valid and can be attributed to a changing habitat, this evidence might suggest increasing steppe conditions possibly resulting from an increasing population causing deforestation. As Oates notes, however, a great deal more study of evidence of all sorts is necessary before any reasonably accurate picture of environmental change can be presented.

Unlike the situation for plant remains, there are presently available two published faunal collections from fifth millennium southern Mesopotamia. The largest is from Ras al Amiya, a site located near the ancient religious center of Nippur in the northern part of the delta. Discovered by accident during irrigation ditch excavations, the remains lie a meter below the present plain. The site seems to have been a village occupied for a limited span of time during the late Hajji Mohammad period. Almost two hundred bones from four levels were studied by Flannery and Cornwall (1969). Of these, only a little more than half were identified. Domesticated animals represented are cattle, sheep, and possibly goat. Wild fauna include wolf (or dog?), boar (or pig?), gazelle, onager, and mussels. All of these animals occurred also at Tepe Sabz but in different proportions. Cattle bones which never reach more than 8 per cent of the collection from Tepe Sabz, represent 45 per cent of the fragments from Ras al Amiya. Sheep/goat remains from the latter are about 37 per cent of the sample as compared with up to 80 per cent for Tepe Sabz at the comparable period. This pattern is in keeping with later economic texts from Nippur which indicate the importance of cattle herding in that area.

The possibility that caprines may initially have played only a secondary role in the economy of some areas of southern Mesopotamia is supported by a small sample from Eridu. Twenty-seven bones from this southernmost of the great Mesopotamian sites have been studied from photographs (Flannery and Wright, 1966). Of these bones twenty-two were identified as onager; also noted were teeth from domestic cattle and a single bone from what may have been a sheep, goat, or gazelle. This admittedly poor sample from level XIII of the 'Hut Sounding,' is of a date roughly comparable to that of the Ras al Amiya material (c 4500 B.C.). Much more excavation and analysis of fourth and fifth millennium material are necessary, however, before these crucial periods will be sufficiently well known for us to construct anything but the most general developmental framework.

If the faunal picture emerging for southern Mesopotamia in the fifth millennium has any over-all validity, it stands in striking contrast to that from the small third millennium site of Sakheri Sughir, located near Ur. Domestic sheep and goat bones outnumber cattle bones five to one, although identified individual caprines outnumber cattle only two to one. Since a cow may provide up to four times more meat than a sheep or a goat, 'it is probable that the ratio of sheep meat to cow meat in the diet was roughly one to one' (H. Wright, 1969:91). As indicated above, however, the main assets of the caprines are wool and milk while those of cattle are power and milk. Although both were perhaps more useful to mankind alive, the butchering of young male offspring for meat is attested in the archaeological record and is a well-known phenomenon from the area today. At Sakheri Sughir, bones from sheep are more common than those from goats, thus confirming our observations made previously.

More intriguing than the prevalence of caprines over cattle, however, is the obvious importance of fish at Sakheri Sughir. Fish bones comprise 72 per cent of the total sample, although they represent only 23 per cent of the total weight of the bones. Henry Wright points out that the latter proportion is perhaps 'more indicative of the importance of fish in the meat diet of rural Early Dynastic villagers' (1969:89). That fish were an important resource in the Ur/Eridu area is further underlined by the large number of fish bones found around the 'offering tables,' 'altars,' and in 'offering jars' from the late Ubaid temples at Eridu. Third millennium texts from Lagash mention what may have been a specialized section of society which derived its livelihood from fishing. Three categories of fish were noted for Sakheri Sughir: carp (Cyprinidae), drum (Otolithus sp.), and catfish (Silureus sp.). Other aquatic resources were mussels (Unionidae) and ducks. Large wild animals include onager, wild ox, and gazelle, the remains of which are few, however.

The point to be made here is that, in all probability, wild resources continued to be important, especially in rural life, well into the historical periods. The patterns of exploitation of wild fauna, however, undoubtedly differed from area to area, varying in relation to the productivity of the most easily reached habitats. In those habitats where sheep, goats, and/or cattle competed with the wild fauna for grazing, dependence upon domestic animals probably grew, although one can speculate, with some basis in fact, that the importance of the different domestic animals also varied from region to region. In the marshlands of the lower delta, however, fish and other aquatic resources retained a significant place both in the diet and in the culture. The use of rushes and reeds, attested by impressions left in the mud walls and floors of houses, and the apparent importance of fish in religion are cases in point.

TOOLS AND TECHNIQUES

The cultivation and preparation of plants and animals require tools and techniques. Tools are sometimes preserved in the archaeological record. Their use and significance, however, are understandable only through careful analysis of the artifacts themselves and the context of their discovery. The questions asked of such archaeological material must be derived either from present-day practices or more rarely from descriptions in ancient texts. Techniques, or more broadly—the state of knowledge, are among the most difficult aspects of ancient life to recover. The archaeologist is lucky when he has available to him ancient descriptions of farming or herding or metal-working such as exist for Mesopotamia. One of the most illuminating of these is the so-called Farmer's Almanac published by S. N. Kramer in *The Sumerians* (1963:105-9 and 340-42).

Of special interest is the use of shod oxen, the hoe, the drag, and the plow respectively during cultivation. According to Kramer's translation of the ancient instruction manual, shod oxen should be let loose on the water-soaked field after inundation in the spring. They both rip out the weeds and trample the surface, removing the vegetation presumably left after the preceding year's fallow. The field is then to be leveled and dressed with light narrow 'axes,' and the marks left by the oxen hoofs are to be removed. Finally, the field is dragged and the pick-axe wielder 'goes all around the four edges of the field,' perhaps preparing the ridges and channels for irrigation. At this point it is instructive to note not only that the oxen hoofs followed by the hoeing probably break up the sometimes extensive root systems of the weeds, but also that the final dragging operation seals the surface of the field, thereby reducing evaporation and keeping the water trapped in the ground during the long hot summer. [A similar process of field preparation is used in parts of modern Pakistani Baluchistan, but there all the water necessary for growing a year's crop may be derived from one flooding and stored in the silt of the field itself (Raikes, 1968).]

It is significant that, according to the Sumerian text, the plow is not to be used until it is time to prepare the field for sowing. Then, during a space of ten days, the ground is to be broken by two different types of plows, harrowed and raked three times, the soil pulverized with hammers, and a plough-seeder combination used to plant the grain. The field should be irrigated at least three times at different stages in the growth of the grain. Come harvest, the farmer is instructed to treat his workers well, presumably because it is at that time in the agricultural cycle that labor is at a premium. Finally the 'Farmer's Almanac' instructs that, at various times during the season, prayers be said to the appropriate deities in order to ensure a bounteous harvest.

In a text such as that just so briefly summarized, we can learn much that will put flesh on the meager archaeological skeleton. Without contemporary accounts, we would be forced to speculate even more than we do on the significance of such items as the stone hoes often found in archaeological sites. In fact other tools mentioned such as the plow and drag are usually not represented at all in the remains of ancient settlements. We presume that domestication of cattle was either accompanied or followed by the development of the plow and other power requiring implements. Such tools probably were originally made almost completely of wood, and only later tipped with the potentially more recoverable metal. The copper (later iron) in plow blades, ox-shoes, and other agricultural implements, however, was a valuable resource to ore-poor Mesopotamia. It was melted down and reused time and time again. Indeed much of the rural population probably did not have the use of metal until well into the third millennium. At that time, copper became more readily available (as did tin and therefore the strong alloy bronze) because of the growth of international trade, itself stimulated by the demand for this valuable resource. It is significant that most of the metal objects recovered are personal ornaments, weapons of the hunt and/or war, and vessels buried with the wealthy in their tombs. Not until the Jamdat Nasr period do graves at the great site of Ur contain any significant amounts of copper and even then lead objects are as common as those of the presumably more valuable copper. Household items of metal are occasionally found in the fill of domestic structures, but few non-lithic, non-ceramic agricultural implements have been recovered, perhaps partly because rural sites rarely have been investigated. Excavations at the rural third millennium settlement of Sakheri Sughir, however, indicate the almost total absence of metal and the continuing dependence on chipped stone for agricultural implements such as sickle blades and for what may have been butchering tools (H. Wright, 1969).

Metal does not seem to have been a necessity for agriculture in Mesopotamia until after the third millennium. Wood, reeds, stone, and clay, however, were always important, and although little if any of the first two are preserved except as impressions or as charcoal, lithic and ceramic artifacts are among the most common remains in sites of all periods. Clay is and was the one most useful and abundant resource of Mesopotamia. Houses are built of mud-brick today and have been at least since the sixth millennium. Tempered with chaff and sometimes reinforced with reeds or wood, mud bricks were used for the total range of structures from the poorest hovel to the greatest zigurrat. Larger and richer buildings such as temples, palaces, and town houses were often constructed with mud-brick baked in a kiln, sometimes founded on huge slabs of imported stone, and roofed with imported timbers. In contrast, the poorest shelters were constructed of reeds plastered over with mud or of mud alone with no reinforcement. Many of the earliest structures yet uncovered from Eridu, Ur, and Uruk are of this reed-with-mud construction used in conjunction with mud bricks. Construction with reeds and palm fronds with little use of mud is also known from the area today, but this would leave little trace in the archaeological record.

Besides helping provide shelter, clay was used for pottery and other useful items such as net sinkers, spindle whorls, sickles, drain-pipes, figurines, and architectural ornaments. Pots range in size from enormous storage vessels to miniature toy cups. They were used for everything from lamps to burial offerings and were made in a multitude of different shapes and designs. Initially pottery was completely hand-turned and uniquely decorated, but by the Uruk period the wheel had promoted increased standardization of both shape and decoration. Mould-made pots of standard size and shape also appear in the Early Uruk period and it has been suggested that these 'bevelled rim' bowls were used as standard measures for grain rations. They have been found in enormous numbers in areas presumed to have been used for storage.*

STORAGE

Storage of grain was one of the keystones of ancient Mesopotamian economy. The cultivation of crops on a yearly basis requires the avail-

* Proposal by Hans Nissen: see *Archaeology*, Vol. 23, No. 1, Jan. 1970, p. 50.

ability of seed saved from the previous harvest. In addition, the seeds of much of the flora exploited by man are used for food. Storage therefore may be considered a prerequisite for crop agriculture. Containers for grain such as large ceramic jars and plastered enclosures are well known from all periods. Until recently, however, evidence for the *large-scale* storage facilities always supposed to have existed has been wanting. Innumerable economic documents of the third and second millennia B.C. describe the distribution of cereal rations to dependents of both the temples and the large secular estates. How and where the large amounts of grain implied by such transactions were stored has never really been empirically investigated, although sections of both 'temples' and 'palaces' have been labeled as 'store rooms.'

The goddess of the storehouse was Inanna, whose main shrine was located at the city of Uruk, possibly the earliest 'urban' center in ancient Mesopotamia. Inanna's symbol was a bundle of reeds, sometimes depicted as sticking out from or forming the gate to what seems to be a predominantly reed structure, perhaps a silo. One seal impression from the site of Susa in Khuzistan, Iran, shows a man on a ladder with a basket of grain, perhaps an indication of storage on the second story of buildings. Oppenheim has recently underlined the significance of the discovery of texts relating to withdrawals from a public granary at early second millennium Sippar (1969:14-15). How characteristic such a locale for storage was is presently unknown; like a temple, a public granary would form a focal point and attraction for urban settlement.

What may very well be sixth millennium granaries have been found at Tell as-Sawwan; the remains within them suggest that storage and preparation of foodstuffs in a separate building may be almost as old as agriculture in the alluvium itself. Standing on the northeast side of the mound where the ground slopes away from the Tigris, the 'granaries' are described as 'T-shaped, consisting of rooms of different sizes, usually small, and with varying floor levels' (Wahida, 1967:171). The entrances to these buildings are 'usually narrow,' their floors, covered with gypsum plaster, were higher than their contemporary street levels, and the whole area was surrounded by a mud brick wall. Ghanim Wahida observes that:

Although very few seeds were found in these granaries, we did find a number of agricultural implements including querns, pestles, hoes and part of a sickle consisting of four flint-blades stuck together with bitumen. There were also flints, sling balls, unworked pebbles, etc. These are completely absent in the private houses. Moreover, the plain pottery was more common in the granaries than in the houses. [1967:171]

It is unknown whether the buildings so far published and called 'grana-ries' were communal or were the property of individual households or family groups who lived in the residential section of the settlement. Care-ful analysis of the ceramics according to find-spot and style may reveal patterns of distribution which might be helpful in determining the pat-terns of ownership and/or use. The presently available evidence, how-ever, does suggest segregation of activities into specific localities.

CEREAL PREPARATION

Preparation of hulled grains, which seem to have predominated at such sites as Tell as-Sawwan, includes a good deal of pounding in order to re-move the tough glumes. Whether further milling and grinding were un-dertaken at this early date to make flour for bread is unknown, however. What are sometimes called 'bread ovens' have been found in quantity at Ras al Amiya, Eridu, and other early Mesopotamian sites as well as at sites outside the delta such as Ali Kosh. Whether these open-topped, bell-shaped, and heavily fired enclosures were actually used for baking bread is unknown. Another suggestion for the function of such structures is their use as parching ovens to dry and crack the tough outer shells of some cereal grains as a preliminary to pounding (Hole *et al.,* 1969:349). No grains have been noted from any of the ovens so far investigated, how-ever, so the issue is unresolved. As for the use of cereals in the diet, Hole, Flannery, and Neely have suggested that a gruel of ground and roasted grains combined with water and perhaps also with vegetables and meat may have formed the mainstay of at least the early Deh Luran diet. They suggest that the hulled wheats and barleys are generally unsuited to mak-ing bread, although it does seem almost certain that six-rowed hulled barley was used to make the unleavened bread so characteristic of the Near East at least since the third millennium B.C. The preparation of barley after harvesting and before storing includes threshing, winnowing, washing, and drying. These many steps, all of which have to be under-taken immediately following the harvest, help explain why the demand for labor is and was so great at harvest time in Mesopotamia. As for the preparation of barley for consumption Oppenheim notes:

. . . the kernels may be husked by singeing ('parched grain'), soaked, or beaten with pestles into coarse groats . . . The kernels were sifted, pounded, or milled on a push quern, since no rotary quern was used before the Hellenis-tic period. [1964:315]

If push querns did provide the basis for food-grain preparation at least until the first millennium B.C., one wonders about their general scarcity particularly in third and late fourth millennium domestic structures but also in earlier remains as well. Two possible explanations for this state of affairs immediately come to mind. The first is that, following the pattern evident from sixth millennium Tell as-Sawwan, preparation of grains took place in communal, temple, or palace granaries with only the finished flour or groats being transported to the home for consumption. Central milling indeed may have been characteristic of certain quarters of cities and of large religious or secular establishments, but a more compelling reason for the scarcity of grinders may be that they were made of stone.

NEED FOR MATERIAL RESOURCES

In the Mesopotamian alluvium stone of the size to make a quern or grinding slab is a rare item, almost certainly imported from the Zagros to the east, from the stoney desert of Arabia to the west, or derived from localized outcrops in the alluvium. Rock from the areas around the Persian Gulf to the south and from the Mosul region in Assyria to the north might also have been used. With the growth of population, the demand for stone would increase, thus dictating both the careful removal of grinding slabs from houses about to be torn down and their reuse until broken. Most grinding stones recovered from sites located in the alluvium are indeed broken. Furthermore, at times clay had to replace stone, as in the case of the so-called bent clay nails which were common throughout Mesopotamia and which were perhaps used as mullers. Along the same line, the use of clay sickles in the place of wood has already been noted above. These, along with the mullers, are confined to Mesopotamian sites settled between the mid-sixth and the third millennium, as are the clay 'imitations' of stone hammers, hoes, and other implements of both metal and stone. The utility and toughness of a properly baked clay tool, however, should not be underrated, especially in an area with few rocks in the soil.

Other stone which had to be imported into Lower Mesopotamia includes: the flint and obsidian used for cutting tools until the end of the third millennium; the alabaster which was ground into bowls and statues and ornaments; the huge blocks of limestone used for building foundations such as those at al 'Ubaid, Uruk, Eridu, and other major cities of the Uruk and Jamdat Nasr periods; the diorite used for reliefs and statuary after the fourth millennium; and finally semi-precious stones such as lapis lazuli, carnelian, turquoise, agate, and steatite, some of which are in evidence as early as the sixth millennium and all of which were quite common by the Jamdat Nasr period. One may suggest that the long-distance trade evidently carried out to obtain such stones as lapis lazuli from Afghanistan, turquoise from Iran, and diorite from Oman grew out of a system already established for the obtaining and distribution of necessary grinding stones and flint from more nearby areas and reinforced by the demand for wood, and especially copper.

TRADE AND EXCHANGE

The whole subject of exchange, in which importation and trade are included, can be viewed at many different levels and from different vantage points depending upon the definitions used and the items involved. Basic to all types of exchange, however, is the yielding of goods and/or services by one party to another in return for recompense. With this broad definition even tribute paid by a town to a conquering king can be considered as an exchange for the fortunes and/or lives of the inhabitants. Trade and barter are more limited types of exchange. They presuppose recompense considered equivalent by both the parties to a transaction. Exchange usually takes place through the medium of individuals or through groups acting as units. Exchange in the archaeological record, however, is most often manifested only by the presence of non-locally available durable materials or products in a site, so that the identification of the parties involved in the exchange is a completely speculative task. Furthermore, the presence of say obsidian or lapis lazuli represents only one side of the exchange transaction. What flowed in the other direction? Was it goods or services or coercion or a combination of the three which brought such materials to Mesopotamia from such far away places as Anatolia and Afghanistan? On one level of analysis, we may ask what processes and mechanisms of exchange related Mesopotamia, viewed as a cultural unit, to a source area at any given period of time. On another, one can ask what was the place of a given settlement in the network of exchange within Mesopotamia, between Mesopotamia and a source area, or within the source area. And on a third level, what part did individuals, groups, or institutions play in the exchange network within the individual settlement as well as in the culture and society? Just as 'a culture' or 'a society,' however, is a conveniently but arbitrarily defined unit sharing many attributes with other equally fuzzy-edged units of the same or different magnitudes, so the boundaries of these different societal or organizational levels are unclear, grading imperceptibly into one another. While these questions cannot be answered in any detail here, they do, however, provide a framework for the discussion which follows.

The so-called 'obsidian trade' is perhaps the best-studied example of the long-distance movement of an exotic good to be found in the general area of our interest. Originating in the eighth millennium B.C., the flow of obsidian from Anatolia to sites in the Zagros and the Levant seems to have tapered off by the sixth millennium. Chunks of obsidian were able to reach Khuzistan, Iran, from a source in central Anatolia some 900 kilometers distant probably by being handed from settlement to settlement, perhaps through the medium of shepherds. According to some students, this 'trade' could have 'played a significant role in providing both the routes and the contacts for the movement of grains into new ecological habitats' (G. Wright, 1969:61). If obsidian is anything more than just the archaeologically recoverable manifestation of a broad network of long-distance contacts, however, is difficult to say. Whether obsidian was a major reason for the existence of the networks, as suggested by Gary Wright, is a question worth much further investigation.

Within Anatolia itself, studies undertaken by Renfrew, Dixon, and Cann (esp. 1966, 1968, and Renfrew, 1969) and Gary Wright (1969) indicate that the distribution of obsidian from specific sources more or less coincides with areas covered by typologically distinct assemblages. In other words, the use of trace-element analysis to pinpoint the location of different obsidian sources has allowed students to determine the existence of what seem to be networks of distribution—'supply zones'—surrounding the main sources. Outside of the Anatolian 'supply zones,' however, the amount of obsidian obtained in excavations drops quite sharply. The quantity of the black volcanic glass present seems to depend primarily upon distance from the edges of the 'supply zones,' but also upon the function of the individual sites, availability of other types of stone suitable for chipping and cultural affinities. What should be emphasized here is the role that the satisfaction of the demand for obsidian or other necessary resources may have played in promoting a certain degree of cultural uniformity within specific regions. Within each 'supply zone' the high proportion of obsidian at most sites indicates the presence of distribution mechanisms which must also have facilitated the dissemination of new ideas, techniques, and products as they become available.

The need for stone for tools within the Anatolian 'supply zones' was satisfied primarily by the locally available obsidian. Outside of Anatolia

the same need was filled by flints and cherts. Flint is a perfectly accept-
able substitute for obsidian in most instances and was widely used in
areas where obsidian was not readily available. But just as obsidian is
found in many predominantly flint-using areas, so flint tools are found
within the Anatolian obsidian 'supply zone.' This suggests the superiority
of each substance for particular types of tasks. Such a circumstance would
have promoted the trade of both materials into areas of need and outside
their respective 'supply zones.' In Anatolia, also, we find obsidian used for
items other than tools, such as pendants and mirrors. These secondary
uses are not evident outside of Anatolia until after the sixth millennium,
indicating that the value of obsidian as a raw material for tools out-
weighed its worth in other forms and/or that the accumulation of exotic
materials as a form of wealth had not yet come to play a significant role
in the structure of the various societies (see G. Wright, 1969). At sixth
millennium Tell as-Sawwan, however, one does begin to find evidence in
the form of grave goods, of the accumulation of products made from
exotic raw materials whose scarcity is increased by their removal from circulation.

Unlike Anatolia, where arable land, water, and resources for the manufacture of tools are in reasonably close proximity to one another and ac-
cessible, southern Mesopotamia is a region with potentially very productive soil—given proper water distribution—but with an almost complete
deficiency in many of the materials necessary for efficient agriculture,
even at a subsistance level (see Rathje, 1970 a and b for a similar situation in the lowlands of Middle America). As we have seen above, there
is a mosaic of micro-environments within the alluvium, but these generally lack stone for grinders and flint for tools. Copper and tin are completely absent from the alluvium as are other resources which became
necessary as early Mesopotamian society became increasingly elaborate.
This last category includes especially wood, but also gold, silver, semi-
precious stones, and spices. Bitumen was a resource used widely in the
alluvium. Sources of it are evident today all along the Assyrian Steppe
from Mosul to as far south as Deh Luran. As is the case with obsidian,
trace-element analysis may enable us, in the future, to say something
about the areas of distribution of this resource in relation to specific
sources. Henry Wright has begun to undertake such a study in southwest
Iran. We are singularly fortunate in being able to track down the source
areas and trace the distribution of obsidian and potentially bitumen. Generally, however, the student is totally unable to obtain information as to

the sources or even the nature of materials found in excavations. Not only is accurate information on possible source areas not available, but it is usually impossible to derive accurate description of materials used from the published reports of excavations.

If we accept the proposition that necessary raw materials had to be imported into the Mesopotamian alluvium, the question arises of how such materials were obtained and then distributed. It is possible that expeditions were either occasionally or regularly sent out to the most convenient source locations from the scattered communities which originally dotted the delta. Even on the small scale envisioned here, however, these early missions would have required both the accumulation of capital (in the form of produce) and some sort of organization and leadership which were beyond the potential of individual households to supply (again, see Rathje, 1970 a and b). They probably also would have utilized the special knowledge and kinship connections of certain members of the community to provide security and hospitality on the route.

A second method of acquiring resources, although not as direct as the first, would have been to arrange trading relationships with communities nearer to the sources. In this way a network of exchange could be established which would ensure both a more efficient utilization of the sources and the more immediate availability of the needed raw materials. Like the more direct method of resource exploitation, the trading network method requires the accumulation and administration of capital—in whatever form—in order to acquire the needed materials. It also is predicated upon the existence of a network of personal or political relationships throughout the trading area. Both methods of resource acquisition, however, are simplified outlines of what were, in all probability, much more complicated processes, involving aspects of each.

MECHANISMS OF SOCIAL DIFFERENTIATION

As the population of the alluvium increased over time, complicated mechanisms of resource acquisition and redistribution came into being. Centers grew up, some at least partly in response to a need for efficient distribution of raw and manufactured materials. Institutions in these centers exploited nearby sources both directly by using for labor personnel economically or socially bonded to them, and indirectly by obtaining the necessary raw materials from surrounding settlements in exchange for finished goods and/or services. The materials thus derived could be used in exchange for products and/or materials available from other centers both within and outside of the alluvium. According to Leemans (1950), contemporary economic texts indicate that most of the inland trade was carried out by boat and the chief medium of exchange, at least during much of the third millennium B.C., was barley. The main export of Mesopotamia, however, seems to have been handicrafts, which Diakanoff (1968b) believes were produced primarily in palace or temple workshops. In fact it seems likely that international exchange during the third millennium and perhaps before was based mainly on capital accumulated through the collection of a share of the goods produced on land or by flocks owned by the large secular and religious establishments. It is argued that, because production in Mesopotamia was so close to subsistence, only very large estates could mobilize the resources necessary to support both a battery of craft specialists to produce materials suitable for exchange and a group of administrative specialists to undertake acquisition of raw materials, the collection of foodstuffs, and the direction of economic efforts within the institution.

An argument such as that posed above finds support in a recently published study of a modern Iraqi community (Fernea, 1970). Fernea found that land registration imposed by the British led to the fixing of large holdings in the hands of a few families. This permitted the landowners to optimize the land per worker ratio, with the result that proper fallowing was achieved. Full fallow led not only to maximum crop productivity (low seeding rates, high yield) but also to an increase in the number of sheep and goats able to be supported on the greater amounts of fallow land. Land registration had the opposite effect on small holders. Both fragmentation of holdings at inheritance and the need for kin to share available land were accentuated. This led to an inability to fallow to the optimum extent with resulting decrease in both productivity and the size of flocks. An increase in salination also occurred which only aggravated the problem further. This situation promoted tenancy on the part of the small holder, out-migration, sale of land to the large landowners, an increase in pastoralism, and an increase in urban population. In sum, given the economic complex of grain/caprine within the environment of Mesopotamia, a specific intensity of land use is most productive. This situation, given an increasing population, tends to select for a particular type of land tenure (communal tenure with annual redistribution) and/or favors a particular size of land holding. The implications of this conclusion for the rise of a stratified society in ancient Mesopotamia will be outlined below.

The seasonal character of agricultural production in Mesopotamia seems to have led to a storage economy on the one hand and to the de-velopment of credit on the other. The basis for capital accumulation in the alluvium was primarily grain and secondarily herds, which are respec-tively harvested and sheared at well-defined times of the year. As already noted above, storage of seed, a type of capital investment, is a necessary prerequisite for agriculture. The care of sheep and goats as well as cattle is similarly an investment, even though these animals do yield products of one sort or another most of the year round. The need for manufactured goods, raw materials, and services is not confined to particular periods but is spread fairly evenly throughout the year. For the small farmer, the most efficient and certain way to obtain what was necessary was on credit, which in itself is a type of exchange. Goods and services are ex-changed for a promise of payment. Deferred payment is efficient because the farmer need not store any grain except that for his own consumption and use for planting. Theoretically this system could work even for full-time non-agricultural specialists, but in fact these individuals performed services not only for individual farmers but also for large establishments. Since full-time craft specialists are not farmers, there is little need for them to store grain in any amounts if they can be assured of supply upon demand. Furthermore, the mechanisms of accounting would have been so hectic and involved at harvest time that it was undoubtedly more efficient for the large establishments to distribute grain as it was needed and/or earned by institutional specialists. Even so, as these institutions grew in size, they required some sort of writing to permit accurate recording of transactions.

If indeed, as suggested above, most craft products were made in the essentially closed economic systems of large institutions, how did they reach individuals not connected with the establishments? Diakanoff (1968b) suggests that imported raw materials and products reached out-side economic units through the medium of state or temple trade agents. Not until the second millennium, however, did these men become private entrepreneurs (Leemans, 1950). In a similar vein, Oppenheim (1964:89) believes that the co-existence of storage and private economies may have promoted the use of surplus staples as money.

Evidence for most of the economic institutions and exchange mech-anisms described above comes from texts of the third millennium B.C. Until the 1950's, historians felt that most of ancient Mesopotamian econ-omy was based on a redistribution of goods and services by the temples which owned most of the land in any city state. Studies by Diakanoff, however, have shown that, in some cases, the majority of land was owned and exploited secularly both by large and small freeholders. By the middle of the third millennium some of these private establishments rivaled the temple in size of holdings although perhaps not in the production of craft products. Evidence for the existence of such social circumstances before the third millennium is, at best, indirect. Yet it seems possible to suggest the existence of some institutions and processes on the basis of the available archaeological data.

THE TEMPLE, THE PALACE, AND ENVIRONMENTAL PRESSURES

Among the earliest remains recovered from the alluvium is a 'temple.' Eridu level XVI (sixth millennium) has produced a small mud-brick structure, square in plan with a deep square recess on the northwest side. Within this recess was a small square pedestal, perhaps an altar, and in the center of the building was a second similar pedestal surrounded by ash and bearing other traces of fire. The remains of this building (a) are located in an area later occupied by temples; (b) contain two pedestals in locations similar to those found in later temples; and (c) seem unsuitable for use other than as a temple. This type of structure was repeated in somewhat different form in levels XV and XIV, but was absent in levels XIII and XII. Starting again in level XI, however, an unbroken even more elaborate series of temples follow one another on the same spot through the Middle Uruk period. The temple remains at the site of Uruk itself are spectacular indicators of the powerful place the temple had achieved in ancient Mesopotamia by the end of the fourth millennium. Another site of a Late Uruk temple is the small settlement of Uqair with its large plat-formed and painted shrine. Why man in ancient Mesopotamia built temples and how the institution grew to command such impressive efforts are basic questions upon which we can but speculate.

In most non-industrial societies, religion plays an important role in everyday life. Under such circumstances it can be viewed as an 'elaborate procedure to regulate the relationship between man and the gods, both before and after death. . . . [It is] a complicated and expensive technology designed to control man's environment or to influence it favorably' (Renfrew, 1969:159). According to Kramer, the most important ceremony in ancient Mesopotamia was the Year Renewal Rite (1963:140). In the late third millennium, this included a holy marriage 'between the king, who represented the god Dumuzi, and one of the priestesses, who represented the goddess Inanna, to ensure fecundity and prosperity of Sumer and its people.´ According to Jacobsen (1963), early Mesopotamian man believed that each natural force had a kind of will or spirit whose presence was solicited through (a) cult images, (b) temples, (c) services, and (d) ritual dance. Interpretations such as these are derived from the various myths and epics left to us in the Sumerian archives. Study of the religious literature from different periods of Mesopotamian history indicates that the foundations of belief underwent changes through time. These alterations in dogma, many scholars feel, reflect changes within ancient Mesopotamian society itself.

The Sumerian pantheon consisted of between 3000 and 4000 dieties. Most of these, of course, were local and personal gods, but each city was considered to be under the tutelage of a major diety. Thus Enki, god of the sweet waters of the rivers, lakes, and marshes, was the city god of Eridu. He appears mainly in creation and organization myths. Nanshe, the goddess of fish and fishing, held sway over the town of Nina (Sughul) in southeastern Lagash. Nanna, god of the Moon, was chief diety of Ur. Utu, god of the sun, bringer of justice and equity, was protector of Sippar in the northern delta. An, god of the sky and father of all gods, was worshipped in Uruk but was not a city god. As already noted, Inanna was goddess of the storehouse, of fertility and of the morning and evening stars. Her city was Uruk and she was depicted in many myths. Enlil, god of the wind, ruled over the religious city of Nippur, where temples to all the major dieties were located. In Nippur, according to the religious texts, the gods were supposed to join in assembly to undertake the business of running the Sumerian world. Ninlil, goddess of grain, oversaw affairs in Shuruppak (Fara). Ninurta (Ningirsu), the god of thunder the spring storms was the chief diety of Girsu (Tello) in Lagash. The list goes on, but it should be evident that the Sumerians believed that the affairs of each settlement were overseen if not actually directed, by a special god who had a shrine or temple in that settlement. More than one god, of course, could be worshipped in one village or town, and most of the larger cities had temples to many gods. The many alternate names of the gods make evident that the same forces originally were worshipped under different names in different parts of Sumer. Thorkild Jacobsen, has suggested, however, the importance of regional configurations of microenvironments in the rise of the peculiar Mesopotamian religious pantheon (1963). The nature of the chief god of any city, and often of the secondary deities, may have been a reflection of the dominant type of environmental exploitation in each region. This is inferred from the character of the earliest known non-human representations of these deities, as well as by their associated traits found in contemporary myths and epics. It should be noted, however, that most of our information comes from written documents of the third and second millennium B.C. By this time the nature of the Sumerian pantheon, as represented in the traditional literature, had solidified, although there seems to be basis for the claim that the myths are post hoc explanations and justifications for what was an already accomplished fact.

We have suggested above that, from the beginnings of settlement on the alluvium, environmental uncertainty played a major part in the affairs of men. The traditional system of irrigation used at least until the time of the Third Dynasty of Ur offered little assurance that enough water would be available during the winter growing season. Furthermore, flooding during harvest time was an ever present danger to both the existence and well being of the human population. In order to counter these and other threats, as well as to ensure good harvests and good health to both animals and man, the assistance and protection of the gods was sought. It seems reasonable to suppose that most settlements would include a shrine to one or another deity, and that certain persons in the settlement would have responsibility for the care of the shrine and for the performance of the appropriate rituals. In other words, among the first occupational specialists were the priests. Diakanoff has added further to the picture. He suggests that temple economies

arose on the basis of the communal reserve land fund and the land allotments made to community officials. Their original purpose was to secure the economic stability of the territorial community by the creation of a fund of agricultural and handicraft products for the needs of such a community as a whole (including cult needs), e.g. in cases of emergencies, and an export fund to secure imports of industrial raw materials not available in the home territory. [1968b:38]

From this point of view the rise of the temple in ancient Mesopotamia, while involving the relationship between man and the supernatural, was essentially an economic phenomenon. Its manifestation in both the archaeological and philological records is, for the most part, in terms of the exchange of goods and services on the estates of the gods. Goods were brought to the temples as offerings, i.e. in payment for religious services. While some were consumed by fire, others were redistributed both to temple and community personnel, or consigned to storage as capital accumulation. Members of the community would render services to the temple in return primarily for services but also for goods as well. Pressures arising from debt and/or environmental disaster would have been able to force dependence of some individuals on the temple, thus reinforcing trends toward a stratified and specialized society.

The accumulation of large amounts of land in private hands is another phenomenon of Mesopotamian history. The extent of such estates, at least by the Early Dynastic period, has only recently been recognized. The possessors of these estates, often feuding with the temple establishments, eventually became the secular leaders of Mesopotamian city states. By the Early Dynastic II period, what are presumably large secular 'palaces' are known from both Kish and Eridu. The so-called Royal Tombs of Ur are justly famous for their riches, although it is debated whether they represent the tombs of actual city rulers or merely members of extraordinarily rich families. Similar tombs have also been found at Kish and belong to the same Early Dynastic III period. In a most intriguing article, Bailkey (1967) has attempted to document the vicissitudes of the rise of secular power in historical Mesopotamia. Although the process seems to have varied from city to city, the major force favoring the establishment of a king was the need for leadership in war.

Increasing hostilities among the city-states, promoted by disputes over land (population pressure on existing resources), favored the centralization of coercive power in the hands of an accepted leader. The individual best able to mobilize the necessary force was one who had substantial leadership experience, a vast network of kinship ties, and a large stake in the survival of the community. The selection of such an individual inevitably ran against the vested interests of the religious oligarchy which tried to maintain control over such appointments and powers. Contemporary accounts indicate that in some cases they succeeded in retaining such control and in other cases they did not.

Land owned privately in ancient Mesopotamia was generally controlled by 'extended families.' According to Diakanoff (1968a:26), however, 'the break up of an agnatic household commune at the second or third generation did not necessarily involve the dissolution of cult and economic ties between newly formed families.' In fact the formation of agnatic groups of a higher order than the household might take place. As we have already seen the larger the land holding, the more productive it is, if the man-land ratio can be controlled. Rich owners could exploit the custom of mutual assistance within the agnatic group in order to secure the necessary labor for production, if they had leadership abilities, or if they were able to capitalize upon creditor-debtor relationships.

Such methods of mobilization of labor are in use in Mesopotamia today (Fernea, 1970).

Another method of gaining control over vast areas of land is documented for modern Iraq by Fernea (1970). The circumstances would equally well have obtained in ancient Mesopotamia. Due to a change in the course of a river channel, the flow of water in a major canal was drastically cut. This led to a decline in cultivatable area, and forced the outmigration of individuals and groups with poor locations *vis à vis* the remaining water. Control over the deserted lands fell to those who remained. When the water returned, those who stayed behind, if they were able to mobilize enough support, could retain control over concentrations of large and productive landholdings. Such a state of affairs can be stabilized by marriage alliances and kinship.

Water is a scarce and unpredictable commodity throughout the alluvium. As a result, only a small proportion of the land will produce crops year after year. The individuals who own such land will be better off in the long run than others who do not own land in such favorable locations. Individuals or groups owning the most productive land will be able to take advantage of their well-being by establishing debtor-creditor relations with the less fortunate members of the community. If population pressure or social constraints are such that individuals are forced to remain in their communities and if they cannot recoup their losses, then social differentiation and eventually stratification will result. Through such processes, not only can the consolidation of large estates proceed but the existence of a dependent labor force is ensured.

Before closing the discussion it is necessary to point out that much of what has been said above is predicated on the supposition that a concept of ownership of property existed in prehistoric Mesopotamia. Such a concept demonstrably existed in the third millennium, and the presence of seals used to mark goods suggests its existence as early as the late fifth millennium. Accumulation of large amounts of wealth with accompanying social differentiation may be witnessed for the same period in the large and evidently secular structure at Tell Uqair. If this structure was not a communal storehouse, it may be the earliest example yet reported of a type of structure which would be called a 'palace' in third millennium Mesopotamia.

Conclusion

Our discussion has concentrated mainly upon what might be called 'internal explanations' for the development of Sumerian society. We have postulated little population movement and have dealt only briefly with pressures originating outside the Mesopotamian alluvium. Both migration and external influences are attested in contemporary texts of the late third millennium. The constant arrival from the west of what are presumed to have been primarily nomadic peoples (the Akkadians) seems certain. Some students believe that it was not until an Akkadian usurper (Sargon of Akkad) placed himself on the throne of Sumer that the final step to true kingship was taken. Following the Sargonid kings, the Guti from the Zagros to the east are said to have ravaged Mesopotamia for nearly a century before the kings of Ur were able to recover the throne of Sumer and Akkad for the Sumerians.

The distinctions between Akkadians and Sumerians (and earlier 'Proto-Euphratians') are made primarily on the basis of the written language and secondarily on the basis of art styles. Whether it is really meaningful to distinguish two populations on the basis of elite-oriented characteristics is questionable. It seems probable that throughout history and prehistory, Mesopotamia was a melting pot with a more or less continuous in-flow of new peoples. At certain periods in the past, internal and external pressures built up to a point where those purporting to rule actually lost their legitimacy in the eyes of much of the population. The immediate cause for a change in ruler may have been seen by ancient chroniclers to have been an invasion by a nomadic tribe or neighboring state, a famine, or a court intrigue. With few exceptions, however, the reasons for political instability in Mesopotamia probably lay in the failure of an often despotic government to unite a heterogeneous population.

One way to rule a people of diverse origins is to play upon their prejudices against persons not of their own stock. In ancient Mesopotamia divisions could have been exploited along lines of language, ancestry, occupation, race, religion, class, and/or city of domicile. The last seems to have been particularly important.

The city-states of early historic Mesopotamia are known to have cherished their independence of one another. The earliest myths and epics are replete with references to skirmishes and battles between different cities, often over water and land. Later documents indicate that special privileges of taxation and citizenship were given to some cities by kings of Sumer and Akkad who did not wish to alienate their populations. Because a Sumerian king was thought of first as the ruler of a particular city and only second as the overlord of Sumer and Akkad, he was almost certainly suspect as favoring the fortunes of his city over those of the others. It is therefore significant perhaps, that with one exception, the longest periods of pan-Mesopotamian stability were initiated by kings with little identification with a particular existing city. The exception that seems to prove the rule, is the reign of the kings of the Third Dynasty of Ur. Not only did these kings reunite Mesopotamia after a period of disunity but they also undertook monumental building projects in all the major cities of the alluvium. They were also among the first to call themselves divine. Even though they seem to have been more even-handed than many of their predecessors, the downfall of Ur, overtly caused by Elamite invasions, was probably primarily the result of inter-city feuding.

Turning to prehistory, the individual nature of the development of the various cities in the alluvium is becoming apparent. Survey work undertaken by Thorkild Jacobsen and Robert McC. Adams (1958; and Adams, 1962 and 1965) and their students has turned up valuable data on changing population patterns. Although such surveys permit the location of major ancient canals and settlements, and a gross estimate of the size of ancient populations, there are serious difficulties in control over both time and space. The results of Adams's surveys around Warka are not yet available; nor have the surveys of McGuire Gibson around Kish or Henry Wright around Ur been published in any detail. Adams's work in the Diyala (1965) and in Susiana (1962) lead us to suspect, however, that the forthcoming studies will indicate the presence of regionally differentiated processes within over-all Mesopotamian trends. Except in the case of faunal and floral remains, however, little work has been done in defining and attempting to explain similarities and variation in the cultural remains at different sites and in different regions.

Efforts to formulate meaningful population figures for ancient settlements are complex indeed and the minimal amount of excavation undertaken in Mesopotamia makes such a task even more difficult. The area covered by the ancient city of Ur during the Ur III period was about eighty hectares. By analogy with modern Middle Eastern cities, one can count on between 125 and 250 persons per hectare (Adams, 1965:23-25). A population of between 10,000 and 20,000 people can thereby be postulated for Ur. For Uruk in the Early Dynastic period, a population of between 37,500 and 75,000 can be presumed. Such figures include only those persons living within the walls; they do not include the population of the hinterlands. To support such populations at subsistence levels Adams (ibid.) has estimated that optimally about 1.4 hectares of crop land per person is necessary. Such rough approximations result in between 14,000 and 28,000 hectares of irrigated land to support Ur, and from 42,500 to 85,000 hectares for Uruk (respectively about 140 to 280 square kilometers and 425 to 850 square kilometers). It has been estimated (Flannery, 1969:70) that the furthest natural flow irrigation could effectively serve before the widespread construction of water-lifting and storing devices was necessary was five kilometers on either side of a major watercourse. If such was the case Ur would have required minimally between 14 and 28 kilometers of major watercourses and Uruk between 42 and 85 kilometers.

On the basis of the evidence available, such speculations as these, while giving some idea of magnitude, have little meaning. It is not the situation at any one time but the change over time in settlement patterns and population size that is important to arguments utilizing population pressure as a mechanism for culture change. Surface surveys can give us some idea of the size of populations within broad archaeological periods. More exact estimates, if they are desirable, will come with further excavation of a wide range of sites in the continuum from urban to rural.

Finally, we wish to make a point about the general applicability of the arguments outlined above. Many of the forces and processes described as basic to the rise of civilization in Mesopotamia can be seen to have operated in other areas. Among these are Egypt, Sind, Turkmenistan, Seistan, Mesoamerica, Peru, China, and even Greece. The details of development in each of these different areas certainly varied according to local conditions and pressures. The big question, of course, is why civilization developed in some areas and not in others. We may suggest that an answer might be found by looking for clusters of pressures and not for single-factor explanations. We also suggest that in most cases, the primary pressures will be internal with diffusion of techniques and ideas from other 'centers' playing only a minimal role.

ACKNOWLEDGMENTS

The credit for anything right about this chapter should go to my colleagues in the Department of Anthropology, Harvard University and in the Near Eastern and South Asian sections of the University Museum, University of Pennsylvania. All mistakes are the responsibility of the author alone. To Professor J. O. Brew must go special thanks, for it was he who suggested that I rewrite his chapter: The Metal Ages: Copper, Bronze, and Iron; it was also he who kept me at the task when it threatened to overwhelm me. Special thanks must also be extended to Professors C. C. Lamberg-Karlovsky, Robert H. Dyson, Jr., and George F. Dales for their guidance in matters of Near Eastern Prehistory. The following individuals require acknowledgment and special credit for contributing significantly to many of the ideas contained herein: Peter Dane, Louis Flam, Carol and Christopher Hamlin, Jim Humphries, William Rathje, and Harvey Weiss. The chapter never would have appeared had it not been for the editing efforts of Henry C. Meadow, Deyne T. Meadow, and Harry L. Shapiro and the help provided by Dorothea Blizzard.

BIBLIOGRAPHY

Adams, Robert McC.
   'Factors Influencing the Rise of Civilization in the Alluvium: Illustrated by Mesopotamia' and 'Early Civilizations, Subsistence, and Environment' both in Carl H. Kraeling and Robert McC. Adams (eds.), *City Invincible*. University of Chicago Press, Chicago, 1960.
   'Agriculture and Urban Life in Early Southeastern Iran.' *Science,* 136 (1962): 109-122.
   Land Behind Baghdad, a History of Settlement on the Diyala Plains. University of Chicago Press, Chicago and London, 1965.
   The Evolution of Urban Society, Early Mesopotamia and Prehispanic Mexico. The Lewis Henry Morgan Lectures, 1965, presented at the University of Rochester, Aldine Publishing Co., Chicago, 1966.

Bailkey, Nels
   'Early Mesopotamian Constitutional Development.' *American Historical Review,* Vol. 72, No. 4, July 1967, 1211-1236.

Binford, L. R.
   'Post-Pleistocene Adaptations,' in S. R. and L. R. Binford (eds.), *New Perspectives in Archaeology.* Aldine Publishing Co., Chicago, 1968, 313-342.

Braidwood, Robert J., and Bruce Howe
   Prehistoric Investigations in Iraqi Kurdistan. The Oriental Institute of the University of Chicago, Studies in Ancient Oriental Civilization No. 31, University of Chicago Press, Chicago, 1960.

Buringh, P.
   'Living Conditions in the Lower Mesopotamian Plain in Ancient Times.' *Sumer,* 13 (1957):38ff.

Diakanoff, I. M.
   'Problems of Economics. The Structure of Near Eastern Society to the Middle of the Second Millennium B.C.,' *Journal of Ancient History* (in

Russian with English summaries), three parts: Nos. 102, 105 (= 1968a), 106 (= 1968b), Moscow.

Fernea, Robert A.
Shaykh and Effendi, Changing Patterns of Authority Among the El Shabana of Southern Iraq. Harvard University Press, Cambridge, 1970.

Field, Barbara S.
'Preliminary Report on Botanical Remains' (from Choga Mami). *Iraq*, Vol. 31, Pt. 2, Autumn 1969, 140-141.

Flannery, Kent V.
'The Ecology of Early Food Production in Mesopotamia.' *Science*, Vol. 147, No. 3663 (1965): 1247ff.
'Origins and Ecological Effects of Early Domestication in Iran and the Near East' in P. J. Ucko and G. W. Dimbleby (eds.), *The Domestication and Exploitation of Plants and Animals.* Duckworth and Co., London, 1969, 73-100.

Flannery, Kent V., and I. W. Cornwall
'The Fauna from Ras al Amiya, Iraq: A Comparison with the Deh Luran Sequence,' Appendix 4 in Hole, Flannery, and Neely, 1969 (see below).

Flannery, Kent V., and Jane C. Wheeler
'Animal Bones from Tell as-Sawwan, Level III (Samarran Period).' *Sumer*, 23 (1967):179ff.

Flannery, Kent V., and Henry T. Wright
'Faunal Remains from the "Hut Sounding" at Eridu, Iraq.' *Sumer*, 22 (1966):61ff.

Helbaek, Hans
'Early Hassunan Vegetable at es-Sawwan near Samarra.' *Sumer*, 20 (1964): 45ff.
'Plant Collecting, Dry-Farming, and Irrigation Agriculture in Prehistoric Deh Luran,' Appendix 1 in Hole, Flannery, and Neely, 1969 (see below).

Hilzheimer, Max
Animal Remains from Tell Asmar. The Oriental Institute of the University of Chicago, Studies in Ancient Oriental Civilization No. 20, University of Chicago Press, Chicago, 1941.

Hole, Frank, Kent V. Flannery, and James A. Neely
Prehistory and Human Ecology of the Deh Luran Plain. Memoirs of the Museum of Anthropology, University of Michigan, No. 1, Ann Arbor, 1969.

Jacobsen, Thorkild
'*Sumerian Mythology:* A Review Article.' *Journal of Near Eastern Studies*, 5 (1946):128ff.
'Religion' entry under *Assyria and Babylonia* in *The Encyclopedia Britannica*, 1963 and subsequent editions.

Jacobsen, Thorkild, and Robert McC. Adams
'Salt and Silt in Ancient Mesopotamian Agriculture.' *Science*, 128 (1958): 1251ff.

al-Khashab, Wafiq Hussain
The Water Budget of the Tigris and Euphrates Basin. University of Chicago Press, Chicago, 1958.

Kramer, Samuel Noah
The Sumerians: Their History, Culture and Character. University of Chicago Press, Chicago, 1963.

Leemans, W. F.
'The Old-Babylonian Merchant: His Business and His Social Position,' *Studia et Documenta*, Vol. 3. E. J. Brill, Leiden, 1950.

Lees, G. M. and N. L. Falcon
'The Geographical History of the Mesopotamian Plains.' *Geographical Journal*, 118 (1952):24ff.

Oates, Joan
'Choga Mami 1967-68: A Preliminary Report.' *Iraq*, Vol. 31, Pt. 2, Autumn 1969, 115ff.

Oppenheim, A. Leo
Ancient Mesopotamia, Portrait of a Dead Civilization. University of Chicago Press, Chicago, 1964.
'Mesopotamia—Land of Many Cities,' in I. M. Lapidus, (ed.), *Middle Eastern Cities*. University of California Press, Berkeley and Los Angeles, 1969, 3-18.

Porada, Edith
'The Relative Chronology of Mesopotamia. Part I. Seals and Trade (6000-1600 B.C.)' in Robert Ehrich (ed.), *Chronologies in Old World Archaeology*. University of Chicago Press, Chicago, 1965, 133-200.

Raikes, Robert
'Archaeological Explorations in Southern Jhalawan and Les Bela (Pakistan),' *Origini*, University of Rome, Vol. 2, 1968, 103-171.

Rathje, William L.
'Praise the Gods and Pass the Metates: A Tentative Hypothesis of the Development of Lowland Rainforest Civilization.' Rough draft prepared for Society for American Archaeology meetings in Mexico City, April 1970a.
'The Daily Grind.' Paper read by the author at the Society for American Archaeology meetings in Mexico City, April 20-May 2, 1970b.

Renfrew, Colin
'Trade and Culture Process in European Prehistory.' *Current Anthropology*, Vol. 10, Nos. 2-3, 151ff.

Renfrew, Colin, J. E. Dixon, and J. R. Cann
  'Obsidian and Early Cultural Contact in the Near East.' *Proceedings of the Prehistoric Society for 1966*, 32 (February 1967):30ff.
  'Patterns of Trade: Further Analyses of Near Eastern Obsidian.' *Proceedings of the Prehistoric Society for 1968*, 34 (February 1969):39ff.
Van Zeist, W.
  'Reflections of Prehistoric Environments in the Near East' in P. J. Ucko and G. W. Dimbleby (eds.), *The Domestication and Exploitation of Plants and Animals*. Duckworth, London, 1969, 35ff.
Vaumas, Étienne de
  'L'écoulement des Eaux en Mesopotamie et la Provenance des Eaux de Tello.' *Iraq*, Vol. 27, 1965.
Wahida, Ghanim
  'The Excavations of the Third Season at Tell as-Sawwan, 1966.' *Sumer*, 23 (1967):167ff.
Wright, Gary A.
  Obsisian Analyses and Prehistoric Near Eastern Trade: 7500 to 3500 B.C. Museum of Anthropology, University of Michigan, *Anthropological Paper* No. 37, Ann Arbor, 1969.
Wright, Henry T.
  The Administration of Rural Production in an Early Mesopotamian Town. Museum of Anthropology, University of Michigan, Anthropological Paper No. 38, Ann Arbor, 1969.
Wynne-Edwards, V. C.
  Animal Dispersion in Relation to Social Behaviour. Hafner, New York, 1962.
  'Self-Regulating Systems in Populations of Animals.' *Science*, Vol. 147, No. 3665 (1965):1545ff
The best general archaeological reference is still:
Perkins, Ann Louise
  The Comparative Archaeology of Early Mesopotamia. The Oriental Institute of the University of Chicago, Studies in Ancient Oriental Civilization, No. 25, University of Chicago Press, Chicago, 1949.
Supplement the above with the Eridu reports (preliminary) to be found in *Sumer* ,Vols. 3 (1947), 4 (1948), and 6 (1950), and:
el-Wailly, Faisal, and Behnan Abu es-Soof.
  'The Excavations at Tell es-Sawwan, First Preliminary Report (1964).' *Sumer*, 21 (1964):17ff.
al-A'dami, Khalid Ahmad
  'Excavations at Tell es-Sawwan (Second Season).' *Sumer*, 24 (1968): 57ff.

al-Soof, Behnam Abu

 'Tell es-Sawwan, Excavation of the Fourth Season (Spring, 1967).' *Sumer,* 24 (1968):3ff.

Further references can be found in Porada, 1965 (see above). A good general picture of the way of life, beliefs, etc., of the inhabitants of ancient Mesopotamia can be obtained by reading Kramer (1963) and Oppenheim (1964) in that order. For the most comprehensive bibliographies see the various fascicles of the *Cambridge Ancient History*, Vols. 1 and 2, Revised edition, Cambridge University Press.

L. S. CRESSMAN

VI

Man in the New World

PART I: THE EARLIEST POPULATIONS

Origins

IT IS A FIRMLY ESTABLISHED CONCLUSION of anthropology that the earliest population of the New World were in-migrants. The question is sometimes asked, How do we know that man did not evolve here? Briefly, the answer is, that there was no ancestral primate stock in the New World corresponding to that in the Old which lead to the ape and human evolutionary lines, both probably deriving from a common ancestral form in the Lower Miocene epoch or earlier in East Africa. The New World monkeys represent a more primitive and earlier stage of organization than the Old World variety. The evolutionary development runs from Old World monkeys (Anthropoidea) into the Hominoidea which in turn branched into the great apes (pongids) and Man (hominids). The evolu-

NOTE: Since the original publication of *Man, Culture, and Society* in 1956 the most significant developments in the study of Man in the New World have been, in the writer's opinion and allowing for an archaeological bias, in the area of the time of the earliest occupation of the New World and the culture of the in-migrants. I, therefore, have in general rewritten and enlarged that section. The constantly occurring new discoveries make it difficult to keep the subject up to date. I have emphasized the theoretical approach and discussed the empirical data in relation to theory. It is my belief that the student should be grounded in the theory or conceptual approach to the problem for then, and only then, can he adequately evaluate the observed data.

I have retained in Part II the same method of treatment as used earlier, recognizing quite clearly that it is but one of various possible methods. Pre-agricultural and incipient agricultural peoples are very closely dependent on their environment, a concept which I use freely in my discussion. Culture, however, as it becomes more complex with successful food production becomes itself a source of innovation apart from the environment. This theoretical position is illustrated in the brief discussions of religion and political organizations in the high cultures of Meso-America and Peru.

tionary history of the New World monkeys is obscure but two fossil genera from the Miocene of Colombia indicate they are closely related to certain modern varieties. At any rate the New World monkeys are not in the line of hominoid evolution. 'After the Eocene there were almost certainly no land-bridges between the Old and New Worlds which were favorable for the migration of animals adapted for life in tropical forests, and yet all the evidence at our disposal makes it reasonably certain that the early evolution of the Anthropoidea took place in such an environment,' (Le Gros Clark, 1959). The indigenous origin of New World population can thus be ruled out.

The homeland of the first humans to move into the New World must, therefore, be sought elsewhere. All the evidence from geology, physical anthropology, and archaeology indicates that the source area was in northeastern Asia. It is not firmly established whether the area bordering on the Pacific coast or the interior, eastern Siberia, was the source. In the writer's present opinion the former is the more likely source for the earliest people; later the Siberian people gradually merged into the movement, and from time to time both sources contributed. The population movements were probably intermittent on a small scale and non-directional except as guided by the search for food. The major problem now is the determination of the time of the earliest movements. The solution of the problem requires firm information from geology, physical anthropology, and archaeology.

Geological Factors

The Asiatic and North American land masses were at one time continuous across the area now broken by Bering Strait. Beringea is the name commonly used for this area of western Alaska, northeastern Siberia, and the shallow parts of the Bering and Chukchi Seas. This contact was broken and re-established various times. The minimum distance between the two areas is now about 52 miles although the open water is interrupted by Big Diomede and Little Diomede Islands. While uplift and depression of the earth's crust in the area occurred during the Pleistocene, but how often and to what extent is uncertain, the major cause of the appearance and disappearance of the land connection between the continents was the change in sea level associated with the periods of glaciation and deglaciation or melting of the glacial ice.

Certain terms should be defined at this point and I shall use those proposed by the American Commission on Stratigraphic Nomenclature in 1961 and now in general use.

(i) A glaciation was a climatic episode during which extensive glaciers developed, attained a maximum extent, and receded. (ii) An interglaciation was an episode during which the climate was incompatible with the wide extent of glaciers characterized by glaciation. (iii) A stade was a climatic episode within a glaciation during which a secondary advance of glaciers took place. (iv) An interstade was a climatic episode within a glaciation during which a secondary recession or a stillstand of glaciers took place [p. 660].

Glaciation and deglaciation are thus effects of climatic conditions, more moisture and greater cold for glaciation and warmth and decreased precipitation for deglaciation. Corresponding climatic conditions in general but on a reduced scale in each case accompanied a stade and an interstade respectively.

As glacial ice accumulated in great depth, in some areas well over a mile, over vast areas; for example, from the Atlantic to the Pacific Ocean and from the Arctic Ocean, except Alaska, south as far as the Columbia River in eastern Washington and east of the Rocky Mountains well into the United States the ice impounded the moisture which fell and did not return it to its source, the oceans. During an interglaciation or an interstade the melted or melting glaciers returned the resulting water to the seas. Thus glaciation gradually reduced the amount of water in the oceans and the sea level was lowered. The process was reversed during an interglaciation. Corresponding changes in sea level within a glaciation are associated with a stade and an interstade. Evidence at present indicates the probability that lowering of sea level follows closely the waxing of the glaciers while a rise of sea level begins well before there is any substantial reduction of the margins of the ice sheet. The latter condition is interpreted as due to the earlier melting of the ice at its center and drainage of meltwater to the sea.

The last of the four glaciations in North America is called the Wisconsin and it has been divided usually into Early and Late periods, or stades, and these are separated by a major interstade. The last major stade, or Late Wisconsin stade, is called the Vashon in reference to the Cordilleran ice sheet west of the Rocky Mountains and the Mankato in the rest of the continent.

The changes in sea level during the Wisconsin glaciation caused the land connection (the familiar Bering Land Bridge) to be exposed and submerged a number of times. Such a land connection had to exist to permit human predators and their prey to move back and forth between the continents. During the Vashon stade, approximately from 25,000 to 13,000 years ago, the land connection was about 1000 miles wide because sea level had been lowered by at least 100 meters. One must think of this land connection as building up gradually to a maximum extent and then after a period slowly being reduced in size until eventual submergence. The land surface was tundra, the climate arctic, and there was little relief. Pollen studies indicate that while the southern edge of the connection was somewhat warmer than the rest it was still arctic.

In Alaska this exposed land connection, in the main, lead into a vast unglaciated *refugium* of some 250,000 square miles. The glaciated Brooks Range in the north and the Aleutian and Alaskan ranges in the south acted like wings of a weir which directed humans and other animals into the *refugium*. Beyond the perimeter the ice stretched solidly as a barrier from coast to coast.

When so much accolade is now showered on the 'first,' it seems ironic that the first humans to set foot on the land of future Alaska were quite unaware of the fact that they had discovered a New World. As Hopkins writes, '. . . and found—quite unwittingly—a new world to conquer.'

The Alaskan *refugium* was an enormous cul-de-sac as long as it was bordered east and south by the ice sheet. Consequently, for passage to the interior to occur deglaciation had to take place. Since the continental (Laurentide) and Cordilleran ice of British Columbia grew from different centers, it is to be expected that with deglaciation, as the two sheets receded land would be exposed between them and an 'Ice-free Corridor' exposed through which movement into the interior could take place.

It is against this background of climatic change and its environmental accompaniment that the time and/or times of the entry of man into the New World must be visualized. Consequently the dates or time of land connections and their disappearance and of the presence of an ice-free route or routes into the interior are critical.

Briefly, what is the evidence—first, for land connections, and second, an ice-free corridor? While the model of land–glaciation–sea-level relations briefly sketched above is valid it must be remembered that the total picture is not that of the exact working of a piece of precision machinery. There are localized factors which modify the over-all situation. There are regional and localized disturbances in the earth's crust, localized differences in climate, regional differences in topography. Critical information is relatively scanty for the Late Wisconsin and nearly lacking for the Early. Detailed study of the glacial history of western Canada where the Laurentide and Cordilleran ice sheets met has barely begun.

Based on the model for glaciation–land-connection relations presented above, although the varying situations through the Wisconsin glaciation may be briefly summarized, it would be naïve to assume that it is as simple as this.

The Upper Pleistocene consists of the third interglacial and the fourth glacial usually but not always called the fourth glacial, commonly known is Europe as the Würm and in North America as the Wisconsin. The third interglacial is in New World terminology the Sangamon. Estimates suggest that the Wisconsin began at 50,000 to 70,000 years ago and at 40,-000 years the sea level was lowered by approximately 145 meters. This was followed by a warming trend, and by about 35,000 or 33,000 years ago sea level had risen so that it was about 40 meters below the present level, the minimum required to establish a land connection. This Mid-Wisconsin Transgression (rise of sea level or transgression of the sea on the land) also called Middle Wisconsin Interstade, lasted until 25,000 years ago. Then the Late Wisconsin Regression or Late stade followed, to end approximately 10,000 to 11,000 years ago; and by about 2,000 years ago the sea level attained its present position.

Since the climatic conditions which produced glaciation and the land connection also produced the continental and Cordilleran ice sheets, it is to be expected that during these periods when a land connection existed that an 'ice-free corridor' from Alaska to the interior of the continent was lacking. While this general principle is accepted, there are of course some differences of opinion on exact time of appearance and duration of such a corridor. Probably the best summary statement is that of Hopkins: 'One can state only that an ice-free corridor must have existed there [Yukon Territory, northeastern British Columbia, and northern Alberta] during the mid-Wisconsin episode of mild climate that took place between 35,000 and 25,000 years ago; that waxing glaciation probably closed the corridor again earlier than 20,000 years ago; and that the corridor must have remained closed until at least 14,000 years ago and *possibly almost 10,000 years ago*' (emphasis added (Hopkins (ed.), 1967, 467-68).

Table 1 summarizes the above discussion.

From this model and the chronological data one may deduce, for example, that if a valid archaeological site is located below the southern

TABLE 1

Depth in Meters Below Present Mean Sea-Level (MSL), Land
Connections, and Ice-free Corridors at Various Times

Years Before Present (B.P.)	M below MSL		Land Connection		Ice-free Corridor	
	A	B	Present (+) abs. (−)		(+)	(−)
7,500	−15			(−)	(+)	
8,500	−20			(−)	(+)	
9,000	−25	−39		(−)	(+)	
10,000	−35	−20		(−)	(+)	
11,000	−48	−65	(+)			(−)
12,000	−55	−40	(+)			(−)
15,000	−75	−90	(+)			(−)
18,000 to 20,000	−125		(+)			(−)
25,000	−40		(+?)			(−?)
30,000 to 31,000	−10			(−)	(+)	
33,000	−40		(+?)			(−?)
35,000	−75		(+)			(−?)
40,000	−145		(+)			(−?)

Col. A since 18,000 years ago represents the mean of approximately 150 dates. Earlier
than 18,000 dates are less reliable and are based on a limited number of dates and
correlation with continental Pleistocene events. Col. B is a series of late Pleistocene
dates for sea-level derived from the Gulf of Mexico and indicates the fluctuation in
late Pleistocene sea level observable there. Data derived from Curray, 1965. The
question mark following a plus (+) or minus (−) sign is intended to indicate that
the evidence is thought to be in favor of the sign but that there is uncertainty.

margins of the ice sheet and is firmly dated at 13,000 years ago that those
people who left their artifacts were a part of a population which had been
living south of the ice sheet since perhaps 25,000 years ago. From that
time to probably 11,000 years ago there was no ice-free corridor through
which to move south. One can go further and deduce that since there
was no land connection between 25,000 and 33,000 years ago, the time
when the ancestral population arrived in the Yukon cul-de-sac was *more
than 33,000 years ago*, or in the Early Wisconsin stade. Then during the
period from 33,000 to 25,000 years ago passage southward to the interior
was available. From then to 11,000 years ago this population developed
on its own lines.

Biological Factors: The Asiatic Population Reservoir

This subject need not detain us long. Fossil remains, although few in
number, of *H. sapiens,* apparently a protomongoloid stock, have been

found widely scattered in China. These date from the third interglacial period well into the Wisconsin glaciation. These fossil human remains indicate the presence of a population pool or reservoir, probably small hunting and gathering groups some of whose descendants might have pushed on eventually across the land connection to North America. In other words, during the late Pleistocene a population was available from which the New World population could have been derived. The evidence for man in the Lake Baikal region—and it is cultural—does not go beyond about 20,000 years ago. During the period of the land connection between 25,000 and 11,000 years ago there could have been groups derived from both northeastern China and Siberia contributing to the population movement, and in a vast area of land 1,000 miles in width, which the connection was, it is possible that various population groups never met and that different cultural traditions, known only to limited populations, existed contemporaneously.

This source Asiatic population, while having certain basic genetic traits in common, must have been highly diversified. It would probably have consisted of small nomadic predatory bands moving according to the availability of food. In this kind of human society the process of genetic drift is of the greatest importance in producing diversity. Hybridization is of limited importance. A small hunting band separating from a larger one may carry only a portion of the total gene pool, and that portion is what is carried on in the breeding population. In the vast areas of northeastern Asia there were undoubtedly many different minor gene pools contributing to the migrant population, and these diverse sources supplied the New World types. Genetic drift must have been a particularly important factor in producing further group differences between 25,000 and 11,000 years ago in the population south of the ice sheet in the highly differentiated environment of extreme western North America and Central America.

While the New World population would be expected to show similarities to the members of the source population, reservoir differences produced by genetic drift were added to by environmentally induced physical changes. Shapiro and others have demonstrated the effectiveness of the environment in influencing physical characteristics of a population, although the exact mechanisms are not yet fully understood.

No one should expect any New World group of 10,000 or more years ago to reproduce the physical likeness of some Asiatic ancestral pool beyond a limited sharing of basic genetic traits, those comprising the hypothetical genotype of the proto-mongoloid population. Physical anthropologists find suggestive likeness in some cranial traits of New World skeletal remains dated on the order of 10,000 years ago and those of the Late Pleistocene of China, but there are many differences. This is as it should be if the opinions expressed above are valid, as I think they are.

The Archaeological Evidence

I must discuss briefly certain methodological requirements because they are so critical in Early Man study.

The fundamental requirement for accepting a site as having archaeological validity is that it provide a record of distinctively human activity. It may be the remains of a long-ago campfire now but faintly marked in the surrounding earth. Bits of charcoal in the hearth, perhaps fragments of bones or of mollusc shell, flakes of stones found in the areas surrounding the hearth but not farther from the fire center are convincing evidence of human presence. A single tool or a cluster of them as long as they are surely the product of human manufacture is valid evidence of man's handiwork and presence. It is not always easy to be certain that the evidence is valid, and honest men disagree. These early men must many times have done what present 'stone age' people do as reported by anthropologists, that is, pick up a suitable stone when needed for some purpose and with a few blows from another make it into a simple but satisfactory tool for the purpose at hand, after which it is thrown aside. The archaeologist finding this tool many thousands of years later with no other tools near by cannot but be puzzled and hesitant to decide if he has found a tool or the product of some natural event. Very simple stone tools such as choppers or bone-smashing tools are often practically identical to some produced by natural forces, such as breakage the result of being struck by rocks falling from cliffs above, by gravel hurled about by a stream in flood or the pounding surf on an ocean beach, or thermal action.

The archaeologist likes to say, and generally he is correct, that the final test is this: Is the object in a cultural context? By this he means is there other evidence of related human activity at the site. The example given above—fire-hearth, charcoal, split or unsplit bones, and/or shell fragments and flakes of stone showing tool-making activity—is such a cultural context. Any honest archaeologist, however, will admit that artifacts, man-made objects, are found often isolated, in no cultural context, but there is no hesitancy in accepting the object as man-made. The archaeologist like any other scientist must deal with a world of probability, not certainty, for all the data are never known. His conclusions must, therefore, be subject to change as further evidence becomes available.

Among the non-cultural criteria which must be applied in assessing validity of archaeological evidence, two may be mentioned. Both have to do with the stratigraphic position of the find. First, is its position in the earth compatible with the potential time bracket of man's presence in the New World? The second, is the archaeological evidence in the stratum or bed that was being deposited when the human activity was taking place? If so then the cultural evidence is of the same age as the stratum of earth. The object may, however, be intrusive, that is, as in the case of a burial. Burrowing and digging animals may displace objects made by man, as will wounded mammals, birds, and even fish. Natural events which may cause earth slides or outwash of gravel may cover sites and change the normal geological order in which artifacts were deposited. Around the perimeters of glaciers, solifluxion, the 'flowing' of wet and slipping earth from the glacial meltwater, will change the original stratification of artifacts. An unconformity, a break in the natural sequence of deposits caused by a period of erosion which permits say, stratum 3 to rest on stratum 6 because 4 and 5 were eroded, unless observed and allowed for may confuse the stratigraphic record. The stratigraphic position of the cultural evidence must be correctly determined, and while this is not always easy it is usually possible.

If the population reservoir–land connection model used above is correct, then theoretically man *could* have been in the New World during nearly all of the Wisconsin glaciation. Firm knowledge for the Early Wisconsin stade on land connections and ice-free corridors is practically nonexistent. The evidence certainly indicates a land connection perhaps between 55,000 and 35,000 years ago but whether there were repeated connections is not known. Nor are we better informed on the availability of ice-free corridors.

What is the *observed* evidence?

The Valsequillo site in Mexico, south of the city of Puebla in the state of that name, is named for the Valsequillo gravels, a Pleistocene deposit famous for its numerous and varied fossil fauna. Over many years paleontologists have reported finding apparent stone artifacts in the gravels in association with the fossil fauna. Eventually in 1964 a field party of scientists from the United States and Mexico carried out a series of archaeological excavations to verify the reported associations. Carbon-14 dates derived from shells give an age of 21,850 ± 840 years ago (W-1895) for a midsection of the gravels, and more than 35,000 years ago for the base of the gravels. The section for analysis of the geological stratigraphy is apparently an unbroken sequence of the gravels. A scraper came from close to the location of the sample dated at 21,850 years ago. The oldest sites, those in the basal gravels, produced projectile points, scrapers and blades and flakes by edge trimming by both percussion and pressure, and burins. Prepared striking platforms were used. All artifacts are unifacial, that is, only one side is flaked. There is some improvement in stone-working during the early period. This period extends from 35,000 or more years ago through an unknown period for there is an unconformity or break in the section at this particular site. When the period of erosion represented by the unconformity began and how long it continued is not known but the overlying bed is dated at 21,850 years ago by identifying it with the same bed in the geological section. The upper bed (21,850 years ago) continues the artifact types found in the older beds but all artifacts are bifacial.

At Tlapacoya in the Valley of Mexico on the shoreline of ancient Lake Chalco hearths and artifacts have been found and dated from charcoal at 24,000 years ago. A date from each of two hearths gave approximately the same dates. Fossil remains of numerous Pleistocene animals are found in the area. The hearths had been dug into the gravel of the ancient shoreline. A 'true blade' and a variety of tools used in hunting and butchering activity are reported.

Wilson Butte Cave in the Snake River Valley of south-central Idaho, excavated by Ruth Gruhn, was occupied either at approximately 15,000 or 14,500 years ago. There is disagreement among archaeologists about the authenticity of the bone tool associated with the earlier date. I have examined it and think it is a true artifact. There is no doubt about the presence of stone artifacts in the 14,500-year-old level.

Excavation in the pluvial Fort Rock Lake Basin of south-central Oregon under my direction in 1967 produced an early occupation of Fort Rock Cave dated at 13,200 years ago. A hearth on the top of the gravels of the old lake shore provided the charcoal for the date. Definitely associated with the hearth were percussion flaked tools and surprisingly enough a mano (hand grinding stone). Two projectile points (one a Mohave type) scrapers, gravers, possibly burins, and a core and blade technique of stone- working. Two other shelters in the Basin produced artifacts dated at 11,200 and 11,950.

The Marmes Rockshelter in southeastern Washington on the Palouse

River above its confluence with the Snake has occupation dated by C-14 at 11,000, and at 13,000 by equating the containing bed with its appearance a short distance away where it has been shown to have the older date.

Ventana Cave in southwestern Arizona was excavated by Haury before C-14 dating had been developed and he had to rely on establishing dates by correlation of geological strata in the cave with known climatic sequences. The lowest level, the Conglomerate, contained tenuous evidence of human occupation: bits of charcoal, a stone flake, and a basalt hammerstone. The overlying stratum, the Volcanic Debris, containd two projectile points and hunting and butchering tools. Haury thought the same climatic conditions existed during the deposition of both strata, but it must be kept in mind that the Conglomerate is stratigraphically older than the superimposed Volcanic Debris. Some twenty years after the excavation the cave was revisited, and in a remnant portion of the Volcanic Debris stratum charcoal was painstakingly picked for a C-14 sample. This gave a date of 11,300 ± 1200 C-14 years ago. Obviously the Conglomerate is older but by how much is unknown, probably 1000 to 2000 years would not be out of line as an educated guess.

In southern Nevada a firm C-14 date of 13,500 years ago exists for human occupation at Tule Springs.

More than ten years ago, while looking for fossils in the face of the gravel in a borrow pit at the mouth of the John Day River in north-central Oregon, my attention was struck by an unusual stone in the gravel. I removed it with my hand-pick from the cemented gravel and was convinced by my examination that it was an artifact, a unifacial knife with one edge flaked by percussion in a zig-zag pattern. Three senior professional archaeologists examined this specimen independently at my request to check the identification as an artifact. Each identified it as such.

The artifact was imbedded in and cemented in the gravels deposited by the Spokane Flood, a natural disaster caused by the breaking of a glacial ice dam at glacial Lake Missoula in the western Rocky Mountains of Montana and Idaho. This flood was caused by the relatively sudden release of 500 cubic miles of water which piled gravel and other debris many hundreds of feet above the present level of the Columbia River.

The knife showed slight smoothing of its original surface either by sand blasting or water action carrying abrasive sand. Clearly, then, the knife had been in use before the flood to be incorporated some eight to ten feet below the surface of the deposit. Therefore the age of the gravel bed provides a limiting date before which the knife must be dated.

The date for the flood is uncertain but it occurred either about 18,000 to 20,000 or 32,000 to 35,000 years ago. The latter seems to me to be the preferable date, for it corresponds with the termination of the Early Wisconsin stade when the meltwater was heavy and the ice would have been rotten whereas the later date corresponds fairly closely with the major advances of the Vashon stade when the meltwater would have been less and the ice would have been stronger.

A series of reported sites in North America exist in the same time range as these just discussed but there is not general acceptance by archaeologists of their validity. I have personally examined some of them and am convinced of their validity. The series of accepted and firmly dated sites indicates that the questioned ones are in the possible time range, and they occur in appropriate geological settings. The major sites are in the Pleistocene alluvial fill along the coast north of La Jolla, California, in the same kind of fill on Santa Rosa Island off the Santa Barbara coast, at the Texas Street site in San Diego and in Lewisville, Texas.

In South America human occupations on the top Pedregal River terrace and on the shore of Lake Maracaibo in Venezuela are inferred to belong to the same time span as the North American sites and are called Camare and Manzanillo complexes, respectively. The assemblages consist of choppers and scraping and cutting tools, but projectile points seem to be lacking. Dates for the Camare manifestation range from 13,000 to 16,000 years ago and the Manzanillo is equated on the basis of cultural analogies. Carbon-14 dates were derived from samples of bone but this material is highly unreliable as a source material. The dates may be correct, however, and in view of the firm earlier dates from Central America there is every likelihood that they are.

Lanning and Patterson have reported a stratified site in Peru, about a mile from the coast in the lower Chillon valley. The two lower horizons are dated by reference to Scandinavian climatic sequences and are earlier than a C-14 date of approximately 10,000 years ago from a piece of wood in the top of the second layer. The estimated period of the two lower layers is from 14,000 to 11,500 years ago. While the estimated dates may be correct there are many difficulties in applying the Scandinavian sequence to the Peruvian sequence and any conclusion should be tentative. But again it must be kept in mind that the dates are well within the range of probability for the area. The tools in the earliest layers consist of small cutting tools, scrapers, perforators, a few burins and such, in contrast to the heavy working tools of the Venezuelan Camare assemblage.

It is worth noting that all the firm North American dates are for sites west of the Rocky Mountains in the intermontane region between the Rocky and the Cascade-Sierra Nevada ranges. Possibly, earlier sites along the Pacific coast in North America have been submerged by the rising sea level or washed away as the surf eroded the Pleistocene alluvium. This distribution of early sites is strongly suggestive of the thought that the earliest movements of population into the interior of the continent was by way of the intermontane corridor, and that groups fanned out to the Pacific coast from the southern terminus.

The Clovis fluted point is the diagnostic artifact of a culture between 11,000 and 11,500 years ago, represented mostly in the High Plains but extending as far east as Missouri and into the American Southwest. The point varies in size but whatever the size it is strong and well made on a blade detached from a prepared striking platform. Its distinguishing attribute is the removal of a number of flakes, usually three on each side from a slightly concave base toward the point. The lengths of the flakes on any point vary but generally do not extend beyond one-fourth to one-third of the total length. It is thought these flakes were removed to thin the base of the point for hafting to the shaft. These people hunted large Pleistocene mammals soon to become extinct and of course other animals, horse (*Equus*), camel, bison, wolf, etc., as well. They have been called Elephant Hunters because often their cultural remains have been found with mammoths they have killed and butchered, usually at a waterhole, bog, or spring where the animals would mire down when surprised by the hunters. Firm dates derived from numerous C-14 analyses of charcoal fix the time span of this culture. The number of points from any site is small.

Conventional archaeological opinion has argued that the Clovis point-makers represent a migration from Asia, carrying their technique into the New World. While it is true that a few Clovis points have been found in Canada and Alaska, their presence is best accounted for on the basis of northward diffusion since they are later than the southern ones. A bifacial industry found on the north side of the Brooks Range at Anaktuvuk Pass has been proposed as the ancestral source of the Clovis point. This argument does not hold up, for it has been shown by C-14 dating that the Brooks Range material is only about 7000 years old. Furthermore, even

if there was a developed Clovis industry in the southern part of the western United States by 11,500 years ago, on the basis of present evidence
there was no ice-free corridor available at the time period required. The
Clovis point, in my opinion, is most reasonably accounted for as an indigenous development.

Following the Clovis point, and in a somewhat more restricted territory,
comes the Folsom, dating from 11,000 to 10,000 years ago. This is the
point famous as the one first definitely recognized in 1926 as being associated with now extinct Pleistocene fauna. The point in general outline
resembles the Clovis but is more fragile and has a single long flake, fluting
flake, removed down each side from a slightly concave base. Sometimes the
fluting or channel extends to the tip but generally ends short of the point.
This is the classic or 'type' point. Agogino has pointed out, however, that
with the discovery of more Folsom sites that the classic type point is not
truly representative of those found in a tool assemblage. Some have only
one flake removed, others none, yet all occur together. Eventually the
technique of fluting ceased and the Folsom culture as a taxonomic unit
came to an end.

It is important for the student to understand clearly the following for
it has implications for human behavior through time far beyond its connection with the Folsom hunters. It is this. The people who made and
used the Folsom point in its varied form were primarily hunters of bison,
first *Bison antiquus* then others as that species became more scarce and
eventually extinct. The vast herds of bison provided the major economic
base for their society. In the process of improving these adaptive techniques to the postglacial environment experiments were undoubtedly
being made in the improvement of weapons and probably hunting, such
as developing the drive or stampede. The kind of social organization
necessary for exploiting the bison resource was quite different from that
required for hunting solitary or near-solitary animals, or the gathering of
seeds. In other words the basic life-way continued with little change
probably without anybody's being aware that no one was making or using
a fluted point any longer. Only a small aspect of life, one probably un-
noticed by the people, had changed. Because of our culture we have to
establish time units to define human experience, and this leads the
archaeologist to the search for distinctive attributes which he can recognize, often I am afraid without regard to whether they had significance in
the life of the people or not. The record of the prehistory of the Bison
Hunters of the Plains, from the Folsom hunters who learned to utilize

the bison for food to the introduction of the horse by Europeans, is a continuity of development with internal innovations supporting the increasing efficiency of their exploitative economy and acceptance of some cultural imports which were not detrimental to it. Prehistory as human experience is not as segmented as might be inferred from the sequences based on point types or some other artifact chosen by the archaeologist.

Fluted points, quite like the Folsom of the West, have been found in surface sites in Pennsylvania and a few Atlantic coast states. They have not been dated by C-14, and since there is no association with any faunal remains their chronological position is not clear; nor do we know what relation, if any, exists with the western manifestation.

In Nova Scotia at the Debert site, fluting, approximating somewhat that of the Clovis type, occurs along with unfluted points. Carbon-14 dates indicate this occupation occurred about 10,000 years ago. These people apparently came to the site during the reindeer migration to prey upon the migrating herds. For our purpose the important thing about the Debert site is that it shows that man had spread to the Atlantic coast by 10,000 years go. If his projectile points are to be considered a variant of the fluted tradition then his origins are probably to be found in some way, unexplained at present, with the earlier users of the same tradition west of the Mississippi River.

Mammoth bones brought up in trawlers' nets from the waters of the Atlantic continental shelf suggest the possibility of humans as hunters of these animals, as they were in the West, when the land surface with its rivers and estuaries extended much further because of the lowered sea level.

The Tonopah site in western Nevada and the Borax Lake site in Lake County, California, contain both fluted and unfluted points. Neither has been firmly dated. The Borax Lake site is tentatively dated at about 9000 years ago on the basis of hydration studies; but since the hydration rate for the area is unknown the date is tentative. Both sites, however, contain other artifacts similar to those distributed from southeastern Washington to San Diego County, California, through the northern Great Basin along the pluvial lakes of western Nevada and southeastern California. In addition to other shared artifacts, the Fort Rock collections of 1967 contain a basal fragment of a fluted point very similar to those from the two sites. The Fort Rock dates place this material between 11,000 and 8000 years ago, probably close to 10,000. The two sites do not fit into either the Clovis or the Folsom category.

SUMMARY

If the model I proposed at the beginning of this chapter is reasonably valid, then the earliest Asiatics came from that continent, probably from the Chinese sphere in the Early Wisconsin stade sometime between 40,000 and 70,000 years ago and had reached the state of Puebla by 35,-000 years ago. Progressively earlier dates should exist northward from the Valsequillo Gravels to the point or points of entry in Alaska, but any evidence north of the southern margin of the Cordilleran ice in Washington would have been obliterated. While this last statement is generally true it is not by any means always so. There are exceptions depending on the nature of the topography, the character of the sediments and their depth, and the character of the ice-flow. An ice-flow which overrides sediments and in its course deposits deep beds of glacial till may serve as a protective covering for the underlying sediments and their contents, much as a lava-flow protects underlying fossiliferous sedimentary beds. A striking example of the preservation by glacial overriding and deposition and later exposure of archaeological remains by gulley erosion is furnished by the Taber site in southern Alberta. Portions of the skeleton of a child under two years of age were found in 1961 by Stalker's field party, Geological Survey of Canada, but the possible significance of the bones was not recognized at the time. The bones were found in about the middle of a bed of alluvium and from 30 to 40 feet below the base of the overlying till approximately 60 feet thick. The glacial debris belongs to the Late Wisconsin stade and thus the bones are stratigraphically older than that period. The Taber site lacked dateable C-14 material but two similar geological sections in the same vicinity provided pieces of wood in closely similar stratigraphic positions. These were dated at more than 32,000 and 37,000 years ago, that is, beyond the limits of the C-14 range. How much earlier they are is unknown. Stalker writes, 'In the author's opinion, they are considerably older than that, and perhaps as old as 60,000 years. Determination of their exact age, however, must await discovery of material suitable for dating from the bone site itself' (Stalker, 1969, p. 428).

Remnant Pleistocene sediments south of the ice sheet are few as a result of erosion. The location of the earliest sites suggests that the intermontane area was the line the wanderers followed, spreading out to the broad alluvial coastal plain in the south. Possibly by 11,000 years ago and certainly by 10,000 the land connection between the continents was finally broken and the New World had to be peopled by the descendants of people already here. The routes and times of their dispersion are at present unknown. It is known that by 11,000 years ago contacts were established and developed for a long time between the Lower Snake River in southeastern Washington, south through the western part of the Northern Great Basin of south-central Oregon, through western Nevada in a corridor formed by the pluvial lakes and the Cascade-Sierra ranges through southeastern California and west to the southern California coast.

The ancestors of the Aleuts and Eskimos who are not American Indians are thought to have occupied the eastern part of the southern shore of the land connection, a climate somewhat less harsh than that of the area of the north but still arctic. The rising sea level interrupted the land connection—it is thought earlier near the Alaskan coast than further west—resulting eventually in a string of islands, the Aleutian chain. This population is thought to have been separated as the land connection was severed and the more easterly people remained on the mainland of what is now southwestern Alaska. Others held to the eastern islands in the chain and these gave rise to the Aleuts who gradually island-hopped westward. The former on the mainland became the Eskimos.

Two hypotheses are current, as is clear from the previous discussion, to explain the technological development in the New World before 10,000 years ago. The traditional one in simplified form is to derive practically everything, projectile points, bifacial tools, bone and antler instruments, etc., and the methods of their fabrication from the Old World through a series of migrations, each wave of which introduced a characteristic cultural contribution. The second hypothesis proposes a basic equipment of rather generalized hunting and gathering tools, such as choppers, hammerstones, and cutting tools. This has been called a 'pre-projectile point' stage but the validity of this concept is questionable. In my opinion the question is largely a semantic one, depending on the definition of 'projectile point.' It conceives of the cultural development of the early New World culture as essentially self-contained, growing out of the innovative and adaptive activities of these people cut off from Old World contacts for a period of probably 25,000 years. In my opinion, the firmly dated sites at 25,000 and more years ago with tools demonstrating the presence of developed technical skills of manufacture and the fracturing properties of various kinds of stone support the second hypothesis. There is no doubt that the boreal zone across Canada, Alaska, some of the Aleutian Islands, Japan, northeastern Asia, and the Lake Baikal region share common traditions, such as a microlithic technology. This is late, of the order of 10,000 years ago. Microliths are demonstrated for interior British Columbia, beginning about 7500 years ago with later spotty appearance in the Columbia River of central Washington. The rich archaeological sites of the Middle Columbia, extending from about 11,000 years ago to historic times, do not record the microlithic industry.

Hunting methods were adapted to the needs of the environment, that is, gregarious animals such as mammoth and bison could be hunted in appropriate ways and the solitary like the deer and mountain sheep by other means. As the larger Pleistocene fauna became extinct, methods were adjusted to exploit the remaining fauna with which the hunters were already familiar. No new genera of animals appear in the post-Pleistocene.

Along the Columbia River salmon were being taken at The Dalles, where the river begins its tumultuous course through the Cascade Mountains, at about 10,000 years ago and perhaps earlier. By 9000 years ago the same economy was established in the Fraser River canyon. Various sites in the Pacific Northwest as well as Clovis sites somewhat earlier record the use of bone for weapons. Along the south coast of California and on Santa Rosa Island by 10,000 and more years ago the people were exploiting the resources of the ocean shore line. In the Great Basin it is clear that the people had learned to use the rich plant resources by the same time. And in Nova Scotia the reindeer were then an important food animal. The South American evidence records analogous adaptive developments.

The contacts with southeast Asia and Japan, if they are eventually validated, are much too late to have influenced this basic pattern of environmental adaptive exploitation and adjustment.

The prehistory of the New World, south of Canada, from 10,000 years ago until the development of agriculture is to be understood as the carrying on of already established traditions, modifying these in response to natural changes, the innovative capacity of man, and changes brought about by the shifting of populations and contacts through trade or other means. Having excavated sites covering the long time-span of the last 13,000 years I am deeply impressed by the range and quality of the material culture of these very early inhabitants and their remarkable skill in learning to live with their environment.

PART II: CULTURAL ACHIEVEMENTS IN THE NEW WORLD

Hunting and Gathering Economies

Hunting, gathering, and fishing provided the economic basis of all populations before the development of agriculture and continued to do so until contact with the white man's culture except in those areas where agriculture eventually displaced it. In certain regions the basic patterns were established by 9000 years ago, for example, the taking of salmon as a major food source in the interior of the Pacific Northwest, the exploitation of the floral resources of the Great Basin, the shore line exploitation along the southern California coast, and the bison hunting of the western Plains. Agriculture, when it eventually spread from Meso-America to peripheral areas did not displace hunting and gathering in the marginal areas but served more as a hedge against hunger if the hunts were unsuccessful. North of Mexico groups engaged in agriculture to a greater or less extent lived at the time of contact generally east of a line drawn from the mouth of the Colorado River to the western part of the Great Lakes and down the Saint Lawrence River.

The cultural history of the hunting and gathering groups reflects a gradual improvement in the methods of exploitation of the particular environment. An example is the history of the major hunting and fighting weapons, the displacement of the *atlatl* and spear or dart by the bow and arrow.

The spearthrower is usually called 'atlatl,' a word derived from the Aztec language (Nahuatl). The thrower was a stick from eighteen inches to two feet long, with a grip for the hand on one end, and a hook or point on the other pointing forward toward the grip. The base of the spear was placed against the hook of the atlatl, steadied by the fingers of the throwing hand, and then thrown like a spear. The spearthrower, by lengthening the thrower's arm, provided greater leverage. It was better than just an arm but not as effective as the bow. Caves excavated in Oregon and Nevada show that the spearthrower was gradually replaced by the bow, but the period of overlap of the two weapons covered a span of probably not less than 250 years or more. In the southeastern United States, Mexico, and Peru it continued in use until the arrival of the Spaniards in the sixteenth century. An atlatl from north-central Oregon has been dated by Carbon-14 at A.D. 480, but it appears to have been more of a ceremonial than a utilitarian weapon.

No indications of the house types, costumes, or religious beliefs of these earliest people have come down to us; their weapons, tools, in some cases sandals and baskets, have been preserved. They used scrapers, knives, projectile points, and hammers of stone, and made some objects of bone. Perishable objects like basketry, if any, have rotted away in the open sites.

While these non-agricultural groups formed important, interesting societies, we cannot discuss them in detail here. It will be sufficient to point out that the economic and often the social life centered largely on the major type of food animal or other food source available in the area; bison in the Plains, fish and particularly the salmon in the Pacific Northwest, seal, walrus, and fish in the Arctic, and caribou in interior Canada. In California and parts of the arid region to the east, wild seeds were the main source of food supplemented by small rodents and occasionally antelope, deer, or mountain sheep. Settlement patterns, movement of population, ceremonies associated with the food quest, weapons, and tools all bore a definite adaptive relation to the natural resources of a particular environment.

In South America the main non-agricultural area was in the extreme south where the guanaco, a variety of small camel and a descendant from a large North American variety, was hunted. Along the coast, fishing was a mainstay.

No hunting and gathering society has ever developed a large population or a complex civilization. Complex civilization develops only when sedentary life, that is, life in a fixed place, is possible and man has the technical knowledge and skill to increase the amount of food production. This is dependent on agriculture, the domestication of plants and animals.

The Development of Sedentary Agricultural Life and Its Significance

A kind of semi-sedentary life did develop along the Pacific Northwest coast, where the ocean supplied vast quantities of food and the regular fish-runs up the rivers gave a certain economic security. But these settlements were usually only partly sedentary because the seasonal search for food—game in the mountains and berries during their seasons—would frequently take the whole group, or various parts of it, to different areas of natural abundance. The Chumash Indians of the California coast in the Santa Barbara region had large villages, some reported to have contained 1000 people at the time of the Spaniards' arrival. This density of population was achieved by a very high level of exploitation of shoreline foods, fishing, some nearby hunting, and a wide trade with the Channel Island people as well as those in the southern Interior Valley of California. They had probably reached maximum density of population for their life-way.

Advances in the arts and crafts and increase in population were brought about chiefly by the domestication of plants. No shaman, nor all the shamans in the world acting in concert, could affect the weather, increase the population of food animals or seeds, or change the salmon runs. Man, with agriculture, takes his destiny to some extent at least in his own hands. The main crop in the New World was maize, or corn, and it was intensively cultivated from the southern part of the United States to northern Chile. In South America the concentration on maize was limited to the area west of the Andean divide. East of the Andes there was a vast area from Venezuela to Argentina in which manioc, a root plant from which tapioca is made, was the main domesticated plant. Some maize was grown, however, in spite of not very favorable conditions.

In the northeastern part of the United States, maize was an important crop but was not as intensively cultivated as in the areas to the south. In the north Atlantic states it was grown with beans and squash, together making a diet generously supplemented with game. In the Gulf states game was less important as it was in the Southwest. In the Southeast sweet potatoes, melons, and gourds replaced the northern plants. In the Southwest the Pueblo peoples raised melons, beans, squash, and sunflowers in addition to maize, and added other plants to these after the coming of the Spaniards in the sixteenth century.

The earliest record of agriculture, as a basic economy, that we have is found in the area of later intensive cultivation; it is associated with small village populations in Mexico, Central America, and the Andes. In Mexico these cultures are sometimes called the 'Middle Cultures' because they came between the late high cultures and the earlier hunting and gathering type. However, the term 'archaic' is also used to designate this early culture. We do not know when agriculture began, but these Middle Cultures go back to the beginning of the Christian era and undoubtedly considerably earlier.

In many places, such as Guatemala, Honduras, southern Mexico, and much of Brazil, farming required clearing fields of brush and forest before planting. After four or five years of use the soil would no longer be as fertile as before, and would have to lie fallow (unplanted) for several years. This meant that other areas would have to be cleared in order to produce crops. When a village increased beyond the size that could be supported by the land available, a part of the population moved to a new locality and started again the process of land clearing. So, after a period of time, there would be scattered villages of related people throughout a large area.

In an agricultural society of this nature, religious ceremonies are usually held at various times during the year to make sure that the seeds will grow, that there will be good harvests, and to celebrate the gathering of the crops. Centers for religious purposes would be established; the people from the different villages would come to these centers at appropriate times for the ceremonies. The community would need priests, caretakers, and other functionaries not only during the ceremonies but also during the intervening periods. In this way it would seem that the start was given for the imposing religious centers that developed in the cities in Central America and, in a simpler form, in the southeastern United States.

The course of development of communities was often quite different. In some places in the Andean area and the American Southwest, where the inhabitants practiced irrigation and fertilization of the soil, or where the fields were constantly replenished by fresh soil brought down by rivers, intensive agriculture became possible.

When man engages in intensive agriculture, he is freed to a marked extent from dependence on nature. Both men and women work in the fields in intensive agriculture although often at different kinds of work. As their skill increases, a surplus of food beyond that needed for survival is produced. Then, as the food supply becomes greater, the population usually increases. A surplus of food also means that some classes can live without having to work in the fields; therefore, skills and crafts can develop because men and women can give their time to becoming specialists.

So in Central America and the Andes, where intensive agriculture was practiced, there were specialists in metallurgy, war, religion, statecraft, architecture, and weaving. These special crafts were developed only because those engaged in agriculture produced enough food for all.

Agriculture was developed in America quite independently of Europe or Asia, and there were probably different centers for different plants. Maize was domesticated from a wild variety but just where is uncertain.

All we can be sure of is that it was somewhere in the area of intensive agriculture between Mexico and Peru. Bat Cave in New Mexico produced a variety of domesticated maize, starting 2500 B.C. with a primitive form and showing an evolutionary sequence continuing to the top where we have essentially modern corn. Its domestication in the Tehuacan Valley of Puebla is earlier than 3000 B.C. Wheat was the great cereal crop of the western part of the Old World and millet of northern China, while rice was the chief cereal of southeastern Asia. Had the Indians brought a knowledge of agriculture with them, the chances are that they would have sought a wild seed similar to that in use in Asia, but this is not the case. The entire technique of maize cultivation is different from that of millet or wheat since the latter two are sowed and permitted to grow to harvest. Maize is planted in hills or holes and must be cultivated during growth to secure a crop. The similarity of methods of maize culture throughout the entire maize-growing area strongly suggests that it spread throughout the entire agricultural region from the one central point of development. Local species were gradually evolved to fit special environments, ranging from the Andean highlands to the northern area of the St. Lawrence River with its short growing season.

The only mammals domesticated in the New World were the dog, the guinea pig, the llama, and the alpaca. The two latter animals are small relatives of the camel and live in the Andes. The Americas lacked animals suitable for domestication. The meat of the llama was eaten but usually in connection with religious ceremonies. The llama and the alpaca were used largely as pack animals and for their wool. The turkey, bees, and perhaps the duck were also domesticated.

The American Indians have contributed enormously to our food supplies. Corn, white potato, sweet potato, bean, both kidney and lima, squash, melon, tomato, pumpkin, and pineapple were all native to the Americas. Corn made it possible for the New England colonists to survive. They took over almost all the details of corn raising, even to husking bees, from the Indians. We have continued to raise corn in much the same way, apart from the use of modern equipment.

In the New World, as in the Old, the earlier stages of agricultural society did not necessarily produce advanced civilizations, but only the seed from which they grew. Agricultural villages of the earlier stages were self-sufficient economically. But unless trade with other villages introduced new wares and new ideas, the earlier villages continued to remain provincial. As trade developed and new wares came to the attention of the people, new ideas developed. Along with them were introduced different ways of living. These tended to break down the isolation or provincialism of the village; they stimulated thought and ideas and made the whole related area interdependent, the beginning of One World.

This happened particularly in Central America and in the Andean area. At first there were many scattered, independent groups of agricultural peoples often mutually hostile. Then, as trade developed, their contacts increased and their frontiers were pushed back. Trade brought interdependence of communities and the extension of common features of living. On this basis political action then built up extensive power; and economic, religious, and political organization built rich civilizations.

Arts and Crafts

The arts and crafts did not develop uniformly throughout the hunting and gathering regions or the agricultural regions of North America.

Leather work was particularly well developed among the Plains Indians and those in the northeastern part of the United States. The skins of the bison, deer, elk, wolf, fox, and other animals were all used as articles of clothing for daily use as well as for ceremonial purposes. The men killed the animals and the women prepared the meat and the hides. Sometimes parts of the costumes were decorated with dyed porcupine quills or paint. Later, beads in geometric patterns served as adornments. Men's shields and buffalo robes were painted by the men with symbols which were supposed to confer supernatural power, and also with pictures of the owner's exploits in war and the hunt. The conical tents of the Plains Indians—the *tipis,* or *tepees*—were made of bison hide and when properly furnished with furs and hides were very comfortable.

The most efficient skin clothing was made by the Eskimo of the Arctic coast-line. The skins of seals were tanned and sewed together to form clothing so warm and efficient that Arctic explorers now use it in preference to our own products. American soldiers in the far north also use some articles of Eskimo clothing, especially the parka, or loose-fitting, shirt-like outer garment with a hood to pull over the head. While the costume looks bulky, it is extremely efficient and in some cases tastefully decorated by sewing pieces of different skins into it to make a colorful pattern. The Eskimo made a waterproof coat of seal intestines, and this he wore in his skin canoe, or kayak. Even if the kayak were turned over in the water the paddler would be quite dry when the craft was righted.

Bark was used in the birch forest areas of Canada for canoes and household articles and other utensils. This material was often decorated with carvings and porcupine quill ornamentation.

Wood carving was highly developed along the coast of the Pacific Northwest. The totem poles which displayed the family crest of the owner are the outstanding examples of the work. There were large houses of heavy cedar slabs, split with elk-horn wedges and cut with stone tools; a powerful chief's house was decorated with many carvings. Storage boxes, canoes, household utensils, and above all the masks used in dances gave the artist an opportunity to exercise his skill. The introduction of steel tools by white traders greatly stimulated the development of the art of wood carving by the northwestern artists.

Basketry was widely made and was probably universal, although with the development of pottery it tended to have a secondary value. Perhaps this is the reason why in some areas of high culture we hear little of basketry and much about pottery. Basketry falls into three main classes: plaited, twined, and coiled; each is found in the New World. Plaited baskets are made by interlacing the fibers as in a mat. Twined basketry is made with a series of warps radiating from the center of the bottom, with two weft rows passing over and under them and crossing over between warps thus reversing the order on the surface. Coiled basketry is built up with a coil starting from a bottom center and then as each layer is laid on the preceding one in a continuous spiral, it is sewed fast to the underlying coil by a splint which is inserted through holes punched with a bone awl.

The dry caves of the Great Basin have preserved many fragments of different kinds of basketry dating back as far as probably 11,000 years ago. In Fort Rock Cave in the northern Great Basin of south-central Oregon expertly made sagebrush bark sandals and twined basketry with false embroidery decoration have a Carbon-14 date of 9000 years ago. How far back the beginning of these kinds of fabrication goes is purely speculative but it must have been substantial.

A good deal of beautiful basketry, both coiled and twined, was produced in California. Especially fine pieces were made by the Pomo Indians in the Clear Lake district north of San Francisco Bay. In this area exquisitely beautiful patterns were applied to both coiled and twined baskets by using different colored bird feathers. In a culture otherwise very simple, we thus have an example of superb skill in a single craft.

The natives of the Canadian Northwest Coast, southern Alaska, and the western Aleutian Islands also made beautiful twined basketry. The coast

Indians used split spruce roots to secure a very fine material and their baskets were expertly made. The best baskets of Attu Island, in the Aleutians, are made from a fine grass; the workmanship on some is so expert that the baskets seem to be made of fine linen.

The Pima Indians of the Arizona desert also made beautiful baskets. They have been extraordinarily successful in their decoration by which they skillfully modify the lines, usually in black on a white background, to give the impression that they curve when they are straight, as all lines must be on a basket unless the design is painted.

The Indians of the southeastern states used strips of cane for their basket work; bark of other small bushes and trees were also used. Storage and carrying baskets and a wide variety of special types made for winnowing and sifting grain and flour and for other special uses show highly developed skill. Nests of baskets were also made, with a series of progressively smaller pieces in a large basket. Decorative patterns in geometric designs were produced by dyeing the strips of cane, usually black or red, before starting the basket. When these were woven into the basket, the designs appeared on both surfaces but in alternating spaces.

It is difficult to determine the antiquity of basketry techniques because of the highly perishable nature of baskets. Nevertheless, we know from specimens found with sandals in Fort Rock Cave, Oregon, that they go back nine thousand years and possibly were among the crafts brought into the New World by the earliest immigrants.

Cotton was cultivated in the area of intensive agriculture and provided the weaving material for most of the garments. It appeared in the American Southwest before A.D. 800. In the Andes and in Mexico, cotton was quilted and in Mexico it was soaked in brine to harden it for use as armor. This was so effective against arrows that the Spaniards came to use it instead of their heavy metal armor.

Wool was used in the Andes and to a limited extent along the southern Peruvian coast. It was secured from the llama for ordinary coarse garments, but the vicuna furnished the finest type which was used for the clothing of the ruling classes. In Peru we find the finest and most varied weaving in the New World. The highest development was reached along the south coast when both cotton and wool were used. In Alaska the Chilkat blanket was woven from the wool of the mountain goat. To give added body and strength, cedar bark was twisted into the wool as it was spun. Some coast Salish tribes of western Canada wove blankets from mountain goats' wool and adulterants, and from hair of white dogs with which adulterants were also mixed to increase the material.

It has usually been thought that the origin of pottery in the New World was to be found in Meso-America and attributed to a single invention. However, even though recent studies tend to show a distribution of pottery on the archaic time level from the Valley of Mexico to Peru in which there are certain elements of style of pot and techniques of decoration in common, we are not justified in assuming from this alone a single point of origin. There is also the possibility of independent invention of pottery-making among the late Basketmakers of the American Southwest. Strong evidence also exists now for the introduction from Asia of the basic type of pottery known as the Woodland in the northeastern United States.

Whatever the points and times of origin, pottery has provided in human history an important technological development as well as an important vehicle for the development of aesthetic expression. The basketmaker is limited in the type of art forms which may be created, since basketry is either woven or sewn and either form results in a series of rectilinear patterns since all lines must of necessity be straight. The most skilled weavers have learned to create the illusion of curvature but it is still illusion. Painting cannot be used on basketry with any success because of the rough surface.

Pottery provided the pot-maker with a product which could be modeled to a great variety of shapes, a smooth surface which could have the texture modified to produce designs or painted to express the aesthetic patterns of the people. In addition to these were the opportunities for the demonstration of skill in technical processes of construction and firing.

Once the basic techniques of pottery-making were mastered, regional differentiation quickly took place. Local styles both in shape and decoration are readily recognized. Pottery was something that could be traded and the distribution of sherds found by the archaeologist shows that some styles were more popular than others. Two or three examples will illustrate the point. In the Southwest a very attractive black-on-red ware called St. John's polychrome is very widely distributed from its point of origin in New Mexico. In Meso-America a fine orange ware was widely distributed and a glossy black ware known as plumbate was popular and widely traded from Central America, its point of origin.

Archaeologists who work in areas where pottery was made and used rely heavily on the changes in ceramic types as the basis for their chronological sequences and cultural relationships of their sites with those from other areas. Pottery does not disintegrate, although in the tropics color may be leached off, and the sherds show not only the method of manufacture but the change in styles of pots as well as the change in the art styles as reflected in this craft.

In North America pottery is found in Alaska and probably was derived from Siberia. Woodland pottery, found in central Canada, and in the United States in the north-central states and the northeastern states, is not painted but depends for its decoration on a modification of the surface texture by the use of a cord wrapped paddle, punctation, comb scoring, and other devices. To the south of the area occupied by the Woodland, where the culture is referred to as the Mississippi Pattern, we find that both surface-texture modification and painting occurred as decorative devices. In addition there was a great range of different-shaped pieces. Various kinds of animals served as models for the potter to add to the variety of more conventional forms. In the Southwest there are three generally recognized areas of pottery styles; the Puebloan or Anasazi in the Colorado Plateau and the Rio Grande, the Hohokam in the Salt River region of Arizona, and the Mogollon in southern and southwestern New Mexico. The Anasazi was in the main characterized by two principal styles: a black-on-white and a black-on-red. The Hohokam relied on a red or buff base with the designs in a contrasting red or brown color. Mogollon pottery was usually red with the use of a burnished black interior sometimes extending as a band part way down the outer surface. There also occurs a red-on-white type, and with the extension of Anasazi influence in classic Pueblo times the stimulus was given that produced the beautiful Mimbres ware.

I have not gone into the details of variation in styles for obvious reasons, nor have I discussed the utility wares of the areas as separated from the painted styles used for household purposes other than cooking and for ceremonial activities.

Pottery, but of a fairly simple kind, extended westward across California and up into Nevada. West of the Rocky Mountains and north of the southwestern influence true pottery does not occur, although some half dozen sherds were excavated by the writer in a cave in southeastern Oregon but so far it has been impossible to relate them to the ware of any other region.

Mexico saw a high regional development in pottery as did the other areas of high civilization. In the areas dominated by the great religious centers, as we would expect, there is a close connection between the fine pottery and the ceremonial activities. In the Nayarit part of the major Tarascan area of western Mexico, a great deal of attention was paid to the production of realistic works, dancing groups, family scenes, pets, and other objects and activities of daily life. Of course, the customary range of pots was also made. However, the realistic products of these people give one the impression that they had a certain gaiety and got a lot of fun out of the ordinary things of life. Here alone is this emphasis developed.

Polychrome ware is found throughout nuclear America. In Mexico perhaps its highest development was reached in the Puebla-Mixteca area where complicated designs were produced with fine clarity and control of the color and line work. A distinctive feature of the Zapotec area is the use of burial urns, or more correctly, urns used with burials in which the figure of some deity is represented in the conventional masked form. The color of the pieces is usually a dark grey.

Mayan pottery often uses both surface modification and painting in combination. Black, orange, and red pigments are effectively used in design patterns. Elements of ceremonial action or ritual designs in the Mayan style occur here as do characteristic, ritualistic, and symbolic designs in the Aztec, Zapotec, and other areas.

Peruvian pottery has been quite justifiably placed in a very high position of esteem. Here as elsewhere there are both regional differentiations and changes within each region through time. The Chimu pottery of the north coast is distinguished for the great skill shown in modeling by its makers. Characteristic features are pieces probably representing portrait modeling, representation of daily life scenes again in modeled form, stirrup spouted jars, et cetera. The high quality of this pottery declined from its former excellence in the period before the conquest.

Along the south coast the Nazca pottery is noted for the great skill in decoration in polychrome style with strong and vivid colors. The dominating design pattern is the conventionalized puma or feline design although, of course, many others are found. The design pattern shifted its incidence during the process of the development of the culture.

In the Highland area a series of styles developed with a high quality of art expressed in the Inca period in color techniques, design patterns, and shapes of the pots and jars.

Metallurgy, the process of removing metal from ore by the use of heat, and the reworking of the raw metal into various products, had been developed in the area from the Andes to Central Mexico. Copper, silver, gold, platinum, and tin were used. Bronze, usually a mixture of tin and copper, was made in the Andean region at the time of the conquest. Other metals were mixed with copper and the process of fusing them into an alloy was known. From South America it is thought that at least some of the metal-working techniques spread north to Mexico.

Metal was used mostly for ornamental and ceremonial objects; only a little of it served to make tools or weapons. All the great stone monuments and architectural masterpieces of Mexico, the Maya area, and South America were built with stone tools. What the future might have held for the Americas had there been no Spanish conquest we cannot say, but it is interesting to note that in the Old World the Bronze Age is one of the great stages in human progress.

Architecture, if we mean by the term substantial structures of stone, was limited primarily to the Andean-Mexican area, with some extension into the Pueblo area of our American Southwest. The Pacific Northwest produced impressive timbered houses. The southeastern area of North America developed a ceremonial town center for religious purposes by building earth pyramids to support timber and thatch sanctuaries or temples. Masonry, either with or without mortar, was limited to the Pueblos and to the peoples further southward, including the Incas.

The builder's skill outside of the present boundaries of the United States found expression almost entirely in designing temples, forts, tombs, and palaces for the nobles. In the Maya area and in Mexico, magnificent temples were built upon pyramids whose sides were faced with stucco-covered rock. Imposing stairways led to these temples; in some cases, the balustrades bore great stone sculptures of the god worshipped in the temple.

The temples were grouped with other public buildings and palaces in the center of the town and completely dominated the area. When Spanish soldiers saw the impressive massing of buildings with their color and ornamentation against the blue skys of Mexico and Yucatan, they could not hold back their admiration. One of a group of soldiers strolling in Mexico City wrote that not even his home city of Seville could boast of anything comparable to it.

In the Andean region, buildings were without mortar. The architects depended upon heavy, perfectly cut and fitted stones for stability. Or the stones were cut into irregular patterns, and these were fitted together accurately—a style called *polygonal*. In some cases the stones were held together with copper clamps for greater security. Andean architecture, despite its supreme excellence in stone fitting and its use of massive cut rock for building purposes, never approximated the variety or magnificence of the achievements in Central America.

In contrast with the elaborate religious, state, and palace buildings in Central and South America, the houses of the ordinary person were unimpressive affairs. The development of excellence in architecture seems to have closely followed upon the elaboration of systems of religious thought and development of a wealthy class in both the Old World and the New. Apart from religious buildings, the best architectural achievements in the New World are to be found in the Pueblo area of the Southwest. At Mesa Verde in southwestern Colorado and at Pueblo Bonito in the Chaco Canyon of north central New Mexico, extraordinarily beautiful buildings and groupings of them were made. These were dwellings for humans and not for gods. It is of some interest that pueblos of this kind are still used as dwellings, while the imposing temples farther south have been abandoned and lie in ruins.

Writing

Writing, which, is so important for communication of thought and develepment of scientific knowledge, made little progress in the New World. All over the continents there are paintings and carvings on rocks and cliffs that were probably intended to record some event or to recall some experience in the mind of the painter or carver. None of these approximate writing. The only place where writing did develop was in Mexico and Guatemala. The Aztecs and the Maya had manuscripts written on long, narrow sheets of paper, folded to make books. The Spanish priests destroyed all of these they could lay their hands on because they were mostly about religious rituals and the native religion they meant to stamp out. Deciphering these books is difficult. So far only the dates in the calendar system and some place names can be read in the Maya writing. We have a better knowledge of Aztec picture writing because the Spanish authorities in governing the conquered colonies used the native method of writing to compute tax lists, et cetera. These were often copies in Roman characters into both Nahuatl (the language of much of the conquered area) and Spanish.

No writing existed in the Andean region. Records were kept here by officials, such as tax collectors and census takers, by means of the quipu, a series of colored cords with knots to indicate numerical values. The colors of the cords had different meanings and could be interpreted by the trained officer.

Religion

Religious activities and beliefs varied extensively throughout the New World. One may naturally expect some differentiation between the religious expressions of people in a hunting and gathering economy, in an agricultural type, and those in a complex civilization even though the economic base is still agricultural. In this last case there may well be a distinction between the official ceremonial rituals carried out by the priesthood and the beliefs of the peasants, though it is more likely to be one of degree rather than of kind.

A large part of the northern part of North America was characterized in its religious activities by the quest for a supernatural guardian or helper, usually spoken of as a Guardian Spirit. Over a large part of the Plains area the Guardian Spirit was a pretty distinct object or being, while in the western area or the Pacific Northwest the concept was somewhat less definitely conceptualized. The Power Quest is the name frequently applied to the experience in this area although there were very frequently quite specific objects which became the source of power and thus corresponded to the Guardian Spirit.

Adolescent boys and sometimes girls had to go through the experience of securing a 'vision' and the success or failure of the quest was the proof of or lack of evidence of supernatural interest and assistance. The experience, when successfully carried out, was the positive proof or validation of the achievement of adulthood. Likewise when almost any kind of act beyond the ordinary day-to-day activities was planned, the individual tried to secure a vision as a proof of supernatural aid and success in the effort. A raid for horses, a war raid against an enemy party had to be validated by a 'vision' before anyone could secure the followers he needed.

Various methods were in use to secure a vision but most of them required the individual to expose himself to a lonely and dangerous vigil in some isolated spot. Here with fasting, prayer, and sometimes by sacrifice of a part of his body such as a finger joint, he sought the aid of the supernatural beings. In the area where four was the ritual number, it usually required four days to secure the vision. In the Pacific Northwest the seeker for aid usually went at night to the mountains or forest where he swam in the mountain streams or piled rocks into cairns, experiences which were sometimes accompanied by dreams in which a particular animal or object appeared to the dreamer and became his particular guardian. Sometimes power seems to have been derived from the sheer activity by which the individual had to go unarmed in an area dangerous because of wild beasts and possibly human enemies. It became a demonstration of the courage and the quality expected in adulthood.

Among the tribes of the Pacific Northwest Coast of Canada spirits were a property right and were inherited as any other form of property according to strict rules governed by kinship organization.

The property minded Yurok of northwestern California made a contract with the supernatural beings and both members were bound by its terms.

Among the agricultural pueblo dwellers of the Southwest, religious activity was communal in contrast to the individualistic character of that just described. The religous performances here were in the hands of various clans and the performances were carried out according to certain periods of the solar year. The main concern of the religion of these people was the promotion of the success of their crops. Much of the activity was concerned with production of rain so essential to farming in the dry country. The concept of fertility looms large in their thinking. In this communal activity we see the development of a somewhat more complex stage where certain specially prepared ministrants are responsible for the performance of the religious rituals which in turn benefit the whole community. However, the individuals of the community are not without their responsibility, for violation of the taboos which are imposed during the periods of religious dances may interfere with the success of the very performances. The religious rituals in this area are carried out after proper preparation in the plazas of the pueblos with the non-participants looking on and participating vicariously perhaps. The performances are ritual dances which are still very close to the people.

In the areas of high cultures in nuclear America we find a great elaboration of religious belief and ritual. There is quite clearly here (1) an official calendar of ritual performances of a very complex nature, and (2) the simpler level of belief and practice of the peasant peoples. The culture of this area was based on agriculture of a very efficient kind. It had to be to support the large populations and the classes of people engaged in the construction of the temples and public buildings and in public and administrative services. All our evidence indicates that the peasant religion was little different from what we infer it to have been all during the archaic period when it was a very simple nature religion concerned mainly with the success of agriculture at a simple level and essentially magical in nature. One of the basic concepts of this early religion must have been that of the renewal of life, reproduction and fertility, as expressed in the plants on which life depended. While the concepts went through amplification, redefinition, and refinement with the development of the priesthood and the division of labor derived from the richer economy, nevertheless these ideas are but the branches of the tree whose roots are to be found in the archaic fertility rituals and beliefs.

While differences of emphasis existed in the different regions of Mexico the period which we know best is the Aztec or last. The Aztecs had established their political authority over a vast area from the Gulf of Mexico to the Tarascan frontier in the west and to the Isthmus of Tehuantepec in the south. Consequently we would expect to find some of the concepts of the Aztecs gaining a foothold among the conquered peoples. To illustrate our point we shall briefly discuss certain of the Aztec beliefs and practices.

At the risk of oversimplifying our material, it may be said that the Aztec religion conceived of the world as a battlefield of pairs of conflicting forces. Day, presided over by the sun, was in conflict with the darkness of night. Each night the sun died or was sacrificed for man to overcome darkness and restore the life-giving light. Each morning the sun was reborn to make life again possible. This dichotomizing of life or dualistic principle made a world of sharp contrasts. The world was black and white, not shades of grey. Aztec architecture reflects, at least to this writer, the same sharpness of definition. Its angularity, precision, and organization seem to express in the stones of their temple structures this same military-like discipline and austerity.

There were many gods: the sun, the god of rain, the war god, and many others. The gods, like humans, had to be fed and gods were fed by sacrifices offered by specially trained servers, the priests. The favor of the gods could thus be secured. In Toltec times, several centuries before the Aztecs came into power, the idea of sacrifice had been amplified by the priests and the concepts defined concerning what kinds of offerings were best calculated to secure the favor of the gods. The Aztec priests developed these ideas still further. The sun had to be fed the life-giving qualities of man, and these resided in the heart. So human sacrifice came to hold an extremely important part in the Aztec religion. The sun was fed by the heart offered from the sacrificial victim. Human lives were offered also to the other gods as the most valuable sacrifice that could be made.

The performance of the official religion was carried out in the temple plazas and in front of the sanctuaries of the temple on top of the pyramid as well as within the sanctuaries. Many of these performances were highly dramatic in nature with each step of the ritual leading irresistibly to the sacrifice at the platform at the head of the long stairway of the temple. The common people did not participate in these rituals, but they were, of course, aware of them. This was an activity for trained and specially prepared people whose actions were carried out for the benefit of the whole people.

Not all rituals were of the same importance, nor were all social in nature. For example, a business man going on a trip to another area on business might offer a slave as a sacrifice to insure the success of his project. However, while this was an individual act, it was within the framework of the community's demands, for it was a priest who made the sacrifice and it was valuable in terms of the established system of values of the community.

The sacrificial victim became a god and the priests and the individuals who made the offering ceremonially ate parts of the body of the victim that they might share in his sacredness, a truly sacramental concept.

The temples were built on platforms made of rubble or adobe sometimes quite small at first. When a new god was introduced to replace an earlier one, he was usually honored with a temple built over that of the god whom he displaced. The earlier pyramid and temple were not destroyed, but simply served as a base over which a greater building was erected. By Aztec times, religious belief decreed that at the end of every fifty-two year cycle, the old life should be destroyed, at least symbolically, and a new cycle started. This meant that all fires had to be extinguished, all household pottery, et cetera, be destroyed, and all the temples had to be enlarged or renewed. The priests kindled fire anew and then it was distributed to the people. New articles for household use were made. New temples were built over the earlier ones. The excavations by the Mexican archaeologists have clearly demonstrated the sequence of temple building.

The calendar system of the Aztecs was closely related to the religious performances throughout the year. The rituals intended to influence nature and benefit the community by their effects on the crops had to be performed at stated times in the cycle of the year and so the calendar served both as a guide and a prescription for the performance of rituals on which the community welfare depended. Warfare, too, was integrated into the system of beliefs centering on religion. Some acts of war were for the sole purpose of taking prisoners to offer in sacrifice. Even where conquest was the object, it was preferable to take the enemy prisoner to offer later in sacrifice, rather than kill him in battle.

This brief description of some aspects of Aztec religion serves two purposes: first, to give a brief factual introduction to it, and second, to show how a system of values with certain dominating or integrating concepts organizes the fabric of a people's life.

In the Maya area we find again the great dependence of religion on agriculture, especially maize as the central concept. Here, too, we have the distinction between the official religion and that of the peasants, the close association with architectural achievements, and with the calendar to guide the ritual performances. Here, too, as in the Mexican area proper, the temples and associated wares, such as ceremonial pottery, provided the medium for the great development in the sculptor's and painter's art. Life among the Mayas depended upon the success of the farmers' efforts, as to be sure was the case among the Aztecs. Here, however, we find in some way a much more genial civilization developed. The development of the hieroglyphic system of writing with the calendar provided both a stimulus and a challenge to the artist in stone. The use of feathers and floral designs provided a freedom outside the conventionalized forms of masks and other ritual objects. In the temples on their platforms at Palenque and Piedras Negras the art of the sculptor reached perhaps its highest stage in the New World, and here it was in the service of religion. With Toltec influence entering northern Yucatan in the thirteenth century we find the introduction of Mexican religious ideas, carried on and developed by the refugees and their descendants from the great center of Tula when it was destroyed by the Chichimecs some two centuries earlier. At Chichen Itza we find not only architectural features of Toltec origin but human sacrifice on a scale entirely foreign to the limited practice of the Mayas. Contemporaneously at Uxmal approximately 100 kilometers distant we find no Toltec influence, but the whole atmosphere is Maya, with its emphasis on worship of the beings so useful to agriculture, and the architectural achievements reaching a stage of development unequaled in the New World. The balanced architecture with its religious symbolism and the superb Palace of the Governor indicate a well-defined value system and an almost unique capacity to express it in architectural form.

In Peru the official religion remained much closer to the original form of a nature religion than was the case with the Aztecs. However, the development of a class society and an autocratic state carried with it the necessity for appropriate elaboration of the religious concepts to explain and justify the socio-political system. By Inca times, the Inca who was the head of the state, was supposed to be descended from the sun. The sun was worshipped and the descendant of the sun shared the sacredness of his source. Human sacrifices were exceedingly rare from a comparative point of view. The llama was the chief sacrificial animal. There was a priesthood to perform the official rituals for the state. Throughout the year there were elaborate ceremonies, month by month, in which the Inca symbolically took part in person or through his priestly representative, thus indicating the concern of the entire state in the rituals. These were to insure a bountiful harvest and the harvests were followed by elaborate ceremonies of thanksgiving. In these planting and harvest rituals, there was wide participation by the people.

Religion does not appear to have assumed the same importance in the whole complex life of the Peruvians as was the case for the Mayas and Mexicans. Among the northern peoples, as has been pointed out elsewhere, their concept of life was determined by a vast number of supernatural beings or forces whose favor needed to be won or hostility averted and consequently the elaborate series of rituals and religious concepts developed to insure the well-being of the community. In Peru, on the other hand, the thinking was oriented much more toward a strong political and economic organization in which the welfare of the state was dependent to a large degree on the people themselves with religion playing an essential but minor role.

Political Organization

The only real political state to develop in the New World was that of the Incas of Peru. The Aztecs never went beyond the idea of a loose unity of conquered tribes based upon the lust for power and tribute. So when the Spanish attacked them, it was easy enough to win over allies from subject peoples who hated their conquerors.

The Incas, on the other hand, developed a very successful form of government and extended their state along the Andes and the coast from northern Chile well into Ecuador. If we can say the Inca state had but one dominant idea in its organization, it was to produce an efficient economic life and social security for all. The rulers progressively extended their power and incorporated conquered peoples into the Inca realm as full-fledged members. They explained their wars as an effort to carry the benefits of Inca civilization to the less fortunate who lacked it, a common justification for powerful aggressor states in all ages.

The Inca government extended the use of the Quechua language, the language of the ruling group, throughout the state. Roads were built to speed communication and aid in the administration. Careful censuses of the population were made and vital statistics were kept. Taxes were paid in the form of labor on the state fields or in some other activity, such as the army. Storage houses for food were maintained throughout the country so that in time of need, supplies could be sent from public warehouses to relieve local shortages. The Inca state, organized to provide economic security for its people eventually overreached itself, by extending its boundaries beyond its capacity for control, and the Spaniards found ready allies in disaffected peoples to bring to an end the Inca power.

RETROSPECT AND SUMMARY

In this brief survey of New World peoples and cultures, we have tried to present it in terms of functional developments and adaptation to habitats. In our discussion, we have had to choose from the vast body of information that describes the life of the New World peoples. We have tried to pick out those elements which seem most significant to us, through another author might well have chosen other topics for discussion. Not all subjects have been discussed with the same degree of fullness for not all are of the same importance. Pottery was discussed at some length because of its usefulness to the archaeologist and because of its significance in the technological and aesthetic developments of the life of a people. Religion, likewise, was discussed at length to illustrate the individual type of activity, the communal expression, and finally the complex type of an official religion with an organized priesthood associated with a class system. In addition, religion is of great importance in understanding a culture, for this can be done only if we can see the value systems which define the life of the people, their beliefs, and the resulting actions. Religion with its definition of the world and man's part in it becomes of extreme importance in this task.

Some inferences should be drawn from our discussion and made more explicit. It is clear that the simpler the culture of a people, the more closely are they a part of the ecological pattern of which their life is a part. With the improvements of economy from food-gathering to food-producing, men arrive at a position where they are able to exploit the environment to a greater extent. A necessity for any complex culture is an adequate food supply to produce an economic surplus which in turn makes possible a high degree of division of labor with development in the crafts and arts. The story in the New World is like that in the Old where, from a relatively undifferentiated base of simple economies, centers developed for one reason or another in which change occurred fairly rapidly according to different preferred patterns and regional differentiation in culture followed. Then trade occurred both in material objects and ideas and some of the regionalism broke down but not completely. If out of this regionalism warring rivalries arose then, unless they were halted, the development of the civilization tends to collapse as is shown by the Maya record. If a single power came to the fore as the Aztecs or the Incas, the patterns of this dominating group tended to establish a uniformity and the regional differences became less marked. Through the years the culture changed by innovation and diffusion to the distant areas from the more advanced centers.

A further point needs emphasis, namely, that no culture ever develops all its parts with the same degree of efficiency. Our discussion has illustrated this important general point about cultures, a point that is true of ours as it was true of those we have discussed.

One question which we should like to answer, but cannot and probably never shall, is what were the forces that brought about the development of the complex cultures or civilizations as some prefer to call them from the simple farming type. Economic efficiency, political organization, highly developed skills and knowledge are reflections of the development, not an explanation of how it took place. The archaeologist deals with mostly the bare bones of history, not the pulsing life of the living organism. He never digs up the ideas, the hopes, and aspirations of a people. In the story of development it is without doubt the ideas which make the difference but these unfortunately are probably forever beyond the reach of the archaeologists' tools.

By the study of living societies representing as closely as possible those whose fragmentary remains he digs up, the archaeologist tries to clothe the bare bones with flesh and create again the living society and the people in it whose life, long since gone, he is now attempting to understand.

BIBLIOGRAPHY

American Commission on Stratigraphic Nomenclature 'Code of Stratigraphic Nomenclature.' *Bulletin of the American Association of Petroleum Geologists,* Vol. 45, No. 5 (1961):645-665.

Curray, Joseph R.
'Late Quaternary History, Continental Shelves of the United States.' In H. E. Wright and David G. Frey (eds.), *The Quaternary of the United States.* Princeton University Press, Princeton, 1965, 723-433.

Hopkins, David M., editor
The Bering Land Bridge. Stanford University Press, Stanford, 1967.

Le Gros Clark, Sir Wilfrid E., F.R.S.
The Foundations of Human Evolution. Condon Lectures, Oregon State System of Higher Education, Eugene, 1959.

Stalker, A. MacS.
'Geology and Age of the Early Man Site at Taber, Alberta.' *American Antiquity,* 34 (1969):425-428.

E. ADAMSON HOEBEL

VII

The Nature of Culture

WHAT IS CULTURE?

HUMAN BEINGS are unique among all the creatures of the animal kingdom in their capacity to create and sustain culture. Each society of men possesses its own distinctive culture, so that the members of one society behave differently in some significant respects from the members of every other society. We observe, for instance, that the Andaman Islander from the Indian Ocean weeps with ceremonial copiousness when he greets a friend or relative after a long absence; a Frenchman kisses his comrade on both cheeks; while we content ourselves with seizing his right hand to agitate it with a pumping motion.

The situation is the same in each of these instances, as is the social function of the behavior; namely, to emphasize and reconstitute the special bond that exists between the two persons. But the cultures of the Andaman Islander, Frenchman, and American call for and produce different modes of action.

This is but a single instance of a culture pattern. However, culture is more than a collection of mere isolated bits of behavior. It is the integrated sum total of learned behavior traits which are manifest and shared by the members of a society.*

The factor of learned behavior is of crucial importance. It is essential to the concept of culture that instincts, innate reflexes, and any other biologically inherited forms of behavior be ruled out. Culture is, therefore, wholly the result of social invention, and it may be thought of as

---

* For another definition of culture with somewhat different emphases see Chapter 11.

social heritage for it is transmitted by precept to each new generation. What is more, its continuity is safeguarded by punishment of those members of a society who refuse to follow the patterns for behavior that are laid down for them in the culture.

Social life as such and cultural processes must not be confused. Many animals in addition to man experience social life and even possess social organization. The complex structure of ant society reveals an intriguing division of labor among queen, workers, fighters, and drones. The ingenious exploitation of captive aphids as food resources by some species of ants adds an auxiliary population to their social organization. Yet for all its complexity the social organization of ant society rests not in culture but upon instinct. There is no transmission, so far as we can tell, of behavior through learning. A set of ant eggs, properly incubated without the presence of any adult ants, will produce a host of ants, who on maturity will re-enact in every detail all of the behavior of the myriad generations of the species before them.

Would the same occur if a collection of human babies were cut off from all adult supervision, care, and training? Assuming that they could survive, which they could not, we would not expect them to manifest any of the special traits of behavior that characterized their parents. They would be devoid of language, complicated tools, utensils, fire, arts, religion, government, and all the other features of life that distinguish man among the animals. They would eat and drink, and they would mate as adults, and they would presumably find themselves shelter, for these would be direct responses to basic biological drives. Their behavior would be instinctive and, in large measure, random. But what they would eat and how they would eat would not be according to the specialized tastes and palates of men as we know them now. Nor would their mating conform to the limiting and channeling rules that give to each human society its present sexual characteristics. Left solely to their own instinctive devices, the children of men would appear as undeveloped brutes, although it is probable that they would soon standardize this behavior as they learned from each other what one or another had discovered. A rudimentary culture would soon take shape. The specific responses to the generalized drives of instinct would quickly become the specific patterns of culture.

The human capacity for culture is a consequence of man's complex and plastic nervous system. It enables man to make adjustments in behavior without going through a biological modification of his organism. As of this moment it is the end product of the whole process of inorganic and organic evolution which has moved in the direction of increasing complexity of the organism, including the nervous system. Only in man has the nervous system reached the stage of complexity and adaptability to make possible the creation *and* sustenance of culture through complex ratiocination, possession of a protracted span of memory for details, and the use of verbal symbols: language.

It would be an error born of self-adulation were we to think that no traces of the culture-creating capacity occur below the level of man. Our near relatives in the primate family are capable of inventing new forms of behavior in the solution of some of the simpler problems that are posed to them by experimental animal psychologists. They apparently can also reason on very elementary levels. The famous experiments of Wolfgang Köhler first demonstrated the ingenuity and intelligence of chimpanzees in joining sticks, piling boxes, and undoing locks in order to gain their goals—usually bananas. Further, it is now thoroughly established that chimpanzees can and do learn from each other the new discoveries and inventions of one of their numbers. The transmission of the discovery spreads by imitation. A new and learned pattern of behavior is temporarily shared by the society of chimpanzees. It is an element of nascent culture.

Post-World War II studies in Japan of semi-wild colonies of monkeys (*Macaca fuscata*) have even more convincingly demonstrated non-human primate cultural capabilities. The monkeys of one ravine have the custom of scratching away the earth to get at certain edible roots. Those of another area totally lack this habit. More significantly, the introduction and adoption of new food tastes have been carefully observed and documented. When candy was first introduced into the environment, two- and three-year-old juveniles were the first experimentally to taste it. Mothers learned to eat the candy from their offspring. Adult males then copied the females. But the young males, who have little to do with the juveniles, were the last of all to take it up—and some never did. A 'prestige factor' really seemed to be at work, for when in another colony an adult male introduced the practice of eating wheat for the first time, his example was followed by the 'chief' male of the group. From him it was passed on to the dominant female, who in turn transmitted it to her own offspring. Within four hours, wheat had been tried and accepted by the entire band!

Yet neither the chimpanzees, nor any other sub-human primates, are capable of more than the most rudimentary discoveries and inventions. What is more important, they are handicapped by their limited memory spans. Unless constantly re-directed by their human masters, they soon drop and forget their new activities which pass away as fads. The accumulation of inventions to build up a permanent body of culture materials is beyond their capacity. Of even more crucial significance, however, is the inability of all sub-human forms to develop speech. The bulk of culture is phrased in thought—sub-vocal speech—and transmitted by word of mouth. It is often said with only slight exaggeration that culture exists in and through communication. The lack of developed communication bars all speechless animals from real culture forever.

In the natural world, culture is a distinct type of phenomenon, which represents the highest level of evolutionary emergence. In the terminology of Herbert Spencer and A. L. Kroeber it is *superorganic*. It rests upon and emerges from the psychic organic mechanism of men, but it is not *in* the organic structure of men. The culture that is acquired by any individual is existent before his birth and persists after his death. Individuals and groups are the carriers and creators of culture, but culture has a quality of anonymity in that it is super-individual.

The levels of natural phenomena and their respective sciences.[1]

LEVEL OF PHENOMENA	TYPE OF PHENOMENA	HIERARCHY OF SCIENCES
IV. Superorganic	Culture	Anthropology, Sociology, Social Psychology, Political Science, Economics (History)
III. Psychic Organic	Sentient animals with highly developed nervous systems	Psychology and Neurology
		Physical Anthropology
II. Vital Organic	Protozoa, metazoa (plants and animals)	Organic Chemistry, Zoology, Biology, Anatomy, Physiology
		Biophysics
I. Inorganic	Earth and cosmic matter	Physical Chemistry, Physics, Geology, Astronomy

The relation of culture to society is often left ambiguous, although it is not difficult to distinguish the two. A society may be any animal ag-

---

[1] Adopted and modified from Herbert Spencer, *The Principles of Sociology* (1878), vol. 1, pp. 2-16; A. L. Kroeber, 'The Superorganic,' *Amer. Anthrop.*, vol. 19, 1917, pp. 163-213.

gregation, which holds together as an interacting group, and among the members of which exists an awareness of belonging together—the 'consciousness of kind.' A wild horse herd under the leadership of a dominant stallion is a society. So is the flock of barnyard pigeons wheeling in flight, and organized in nesting pairs.

A human society is also an animal aggregation with just these qualities. In the case of human beings, however, almost all social interrelations are dominated by existing culture. We do not know of any groups of cultureless men. Therefore, a human society is more than a mere aggregation expressing instinctive behavior. A human society is a permanently organized population acting in accordance with its culture. Human society = population + culture.

In its fullest sense, culture is a series of integrated patterns for behavior developed from mass habits. However a group of people may have arrived at their mass habits, and that is a subject for later chapters, habits once established tend to project themselves into future behavior. The habitual way sets the pattern for future action.

Statistically, a mass habit may be called a behavior norm. A norm would be that type of behavior which occurs with the greatest frequency (the mode) among the variable forms, or it may be that type which is closest to the average (the mean) among the variables, or it may represent the mid-point (the median) between the extreme poles of the range of variation.

In social life the norms, which are culture patterns, take on a compulsive, or normative, aspect. Norms as such consist merely of what is done. The normative consists in an additional element of *ought to be*. Patterns *of* behavior become patterns *for* behavior. 'The folkways,' wrote William Graham Sumner, 'are the "right" ways.' Deviations are frowned upon and socially discouraged. Conformity is nourished and rewarded. Each new individual as he is born into or enters the group is put through the process of child training or indoctrination now called *encultration*. Throughout life the deterrent, negative sanctions of society (scorn, ridicule, ostracism, deprivation, and punishment) serve to discourage and check deviation, and the positive sanctions of approbation (rewards and prestige) serve to induce conformity to the norms. Individuals are shaped more less uniformly to the common mold. A modicum of standardization is the common lot.

Not all norms apply to all of the members of a society. Culture does not spread itself evenly over the social loaf. Those norms which do apply to all members of the society and from which there is no permissible deviation are called *universals*. An example would be the prohibition of incest. All persons must refrain from sexual relations with brother, sister, parent, child in most societies. Universals are relatively rare within any given culture.

Much more numerous are the norms that are known as *alternatives*: the patterns that exist where several different norms apply to the same situation. A permissible range of choice and leeway is available. Neckties may be called for, but the choice may be between black, white, or colored four-in-hands or bows. Meat should be cooked, but the individual may choose between baking, boiling, roasting, broiling, rare, medium, well-done, seasoned, or unseasoned.

No society is wholly homogeneous. Differentiation based on sex and age is universal. There are distinct patterns of behavior for male and female, youth and adult, some of which are biologically founded and others not. Social differentiation between married and single persons is world-wide, and all societies have their religious specialists. This means that there are internal sub-groupings in every society. Each of these groups has its own behavior characteristics that are applicable only to its members. Such norms are known as *specialties*.

The specialties of one group may be known to the other members of the society and yet not be used by them, because they are not patterns for their behavior. Many American adult men know the Boy Scout salute, having once been Scouts, but they do not use it as a form of greeting once they have left scouting behind. In a complex society, however, most specialties remain unknown to most of the people. This may be because the specialties require unique aptitudes or a rigorous course of training undertaken only by a few. Or, it may be that the speicalties are the secret and hidden knowledge of a few, kept within their closed circle for the benefits that may be derived from secretiveness. The result is that no individual can ever acquire or manifest in himself all of the elements of his society's culture. It means, also, that no anthropologist, even the most assiduous, can ever make note of, to say nothing of record, all of the aspects of any culture, even the simplest known to man.

This, then, provides the answers to the oft-asked question, 'How can one speak of American culture when there are such divergencies in the cultures of New York City and the Kentucky Highlands? Between the Italians of Lower Manhattan and the Scandinavians of Minnesota?' The universals and alternatives shared by most Americans are the common binding and integrating elements of American culture and society. The specialties of the different regional groups and socio-economic classes are merely differentiating elements. Even within a quite homogeneous society, however, specialties will occur in connection with subgroup organization. Men have one set of functions to perform, women another. Married men behave differently from the unmarried, fathers from the childless. Uninitiated adolescents have different norms from those who have passed through to manhood. Medicine men have patterns not available to the laymen.

The cohesiveness of a society is in part an effect of the relative proportion of universals and alternatives to specialties.

To return to our consideration of norms and the normative aspect of norms, note should be taken of the difference between standards for behavior and real behavior. There are always some gaps between what a people say they do, or what they think they ought to do, and what they really do. We must not forget the old admonition, 'What you do speaks so loudly that I cannot hear what you say.' There is an inevitable conflict between the standards or ideals set up in a culture for control of behavior of persons as members of the social group and errant individual impulses. Cultural standards are selected and tested, on the whole, in terms of group benefit and group well-being. They call for the channeling and suppression of many possible lines of satisfaction of individual impulses.

Since every person is at one and the same time an individual and a group member, he wrestles constantly with the conflict of individual self-interest as against his obligations to the group interests. Thus it is that the members of a society, when thinking and acting as members of the group, express the cultural standards of the group. But when acting in response to dominant individual desires, they may be found consistently to contravene those group standards. They may create in their culture customary norms for violating the cultural standards.

An outstanding example is found in the behavior of the Trobriand Islanders with respect to incest. Clan incest is forbidden and believed to be supernaturally punished through the infliction of loathsome diseases and possibly death. Trobrianders in all seriousness 'show horror at the idea of violating the rules of exogamy . . . when judging the conduct of others or expressing an opinion about conduct in general.' Yet to commit clan incest is the great game played by the Trobriand Islanders. It is a custom that gratifies individual desires in defiance of their most highly valued standards. What is most striking is the occurrence of a highly developed body of customary techniques for thwarting the automatic effects of supernatural reaction. The natives possess a system of magic spells and rites performed over water, herbs, and stones, which when properly carried out is said to be completely efficient in undoing the painful supernatural results of clan incest. So strong is the acceptance of such actual behavior, that even when the incestuous activities of a pair are known, there is no social reaction beyond lascivious scandal mongering, unless someone for motives of personal antagonism undertakes to denounce the incestors publicly. Then and only then does the body politic become upset, for this act stimulates a public defense of the group standards. Then is the time for the incestor to commit suicide, blaming the public denouncer for his death—an onus that causes the public benefactor considerable discomfort.

The Comanche Indians of the Plains provide us with another example of such a social incongruity. Their ideal pattern of marriage is one in which a brother bestows his sister upon a man of his, not her, choosing. The groom is usually an older man. The girl is supposed to accept the match and learn to love and respect her husband. All Comanches sagely aver that this is the very best kind of marriage and most satisfactory in its results. Yet it was the regular thing in the old days for a young wife to abscond by joining an enterprising young brave on the war path. The members of the war party never objected to her presence, but aided the couple in their escape. Here was a customary pattern of group assistance in the violation of Comanche cultural standards and tribal law. For law it was, since the offended husband was forced by public opinion to prosecute the male absconder for damages and physically to punish his wife, unless the wife-stealer was powerful enough to protect her.

In these examples we see the existence of 'pretend rules': standards that are honored in spoken word, but breeched in customary behavior. Dry Oklahoma gives us a contemporary American example of what was a national exemplification of a similar situation in the days of federal prohibition of alcoholic beverages.

This sets the difference between *real culture,* what people actually do, and *ideal culture,* what they say (and believe) they should do. In awareness of this disparity no well-trained modern anthropologist is willing to take a people's word as full evidence of their real culture. He must observe their activity for himself. He insists on getting down to cases.

There is yet another aspect to this phase of culture that may be phrased in terms of *overt* and *covert* behavior. Overt behavior is that which is manifest in motor activity. It is externalized through movement and muscular action that may be directly observed. Covert behavior is that which goes on internally—thinking, dreaming, and the activity of the internal glands and organs.

The registry of sensory impressions in conscious awareness, is definitely influenced and often determined by culture. The sharp vision of the Indians on the plains is not the result of any superiority in actual visual acuity. It stems from their learned ability to read meaning in the way an animal or rider moves, the kind of dust he raises, and the lay of the land.

The moralistic story of the countryman and the cricket is a case in point. Walking down a busy city street one day, the countryman seized his city-bred friend by the arm, crying, 'Listen to the chirp of the cricket!'

The urbanite heard nothing until the bucolic friend led him to a crack in the face of a building where a cricket was proclaiming his presence unheard by the passing throngs.

'How can you hear such a little sound in the midst of all this noise?' the city man wondered.

'Watch!' his friend replied as he tossed a dime upon the sidewalk. Whereupon a dozen people turned at the faint click of the coin. 'It depends on the things you are taught to be interested in.'

The covert culture of a people forces them to perceive some facts and to fail to perceive others. Trobriand Islanders cannot recognize any physiological similarity between father and sons. We look for and often see similarities that are doubtful at best. We feel that similarities should exist. Trobrianders feel that there should be no similarities, because theirs is a matrilineal society in which the mother's brother rather than the father has the important social position with respect to boys, and in denial of the father's significance the Trobrianders hold to a belief in spirit conception of offspring. To recognize filial similarities might insinuate the falsity of the spirit conception doctrine and work to undermine a sacred Trobriand institution. It would be a subversive implication that the father was biologically connected with his sons' creation. The power of the covert culture is sufficient to blank out the Trobriand perceptive sense at this point.

We are familiar with this phenomenon in our own social life. We know how difficult it is for us to see those facts which would be upsetting to our deep-set beliefs.

Covert culture controls perception, because it sets attitudes and beliefs. These may be translated into overt action, but not necessarily so, or directly. There may be conflicts of standards in the covert culture which permit only one of the standards to be translated into action. Attitudes, too, may be verbalized into overt expression without attaining realization in full behavior.

Anthropologists also make a distinction between *material* and *non-material* culture. Material culture is always the direct product of overt action. It consists of tangible goods: the artifacts and paraphernalia a people possess as products of technology. Non-material culture consists of behavior per se, both overt and covert. Strictly speaking, material culture is really not culture at all. It is the product of culturally determined activity. Behind every artifact are the patterns of culture that give form to the idea for the artifact and the techniques of shaping and using it.

The study of material culture can contribute a good deal toward our knowledge of actual culture, but it is impossible to learn more than a little about the lives of a people from their material culture alone. Archaeology, which deals in a scientific manner with the recovery and study of the objects of material culture buried in the earth, is always limited in the results it can produce. The use and meaning of any object depends almost wholly upon non-material behavior patterns, and the objects derive their true significance from such patterns. A pointed stick may be a dibble, a weapon, a scepter, a stake, or a phallic symbol. This can be determined only through contact with the living culture.

Thus when the archaeologist uncovers a prehistoric culture, it is not really the culture that he unearths but merely the surviving products of that culture, tangible remnants of the intangible reality. The actual culture became extinct when the society that carried it passed out of existence. No culture can exist divorced from living beings.

A culture consists of elements or single traits, but the significance of a culture is less in its inventory of traits than the manner of integration of the traits. It is theoretically possible for two societies to possess identical inventories of culture elements, and yet so to arrange the relationships of these elements to each other that the complexes within the two cultures and the total forms of the two cultures will be quite unlike. By simple analogy, a mason may take two identical piles of bricks and equal quantities of mortar. Yet according to the manner in which he lays his bricks, he may produce a fireplace or a garden wall.

The configuration of a culture is its delineated contours as shaped by the interrelation of all of its parts. It presumes internal integration of all of its parts. It presumes internal integration in accordance with some basic and dominant principles or value systems underlying the whole scheme. These are the *existential postulates* set by the culture: propositions about the nature of things; and *normative postulates:* propositions about the desirability and undesirability of things. A clear and unambiguous configuration reflects the attainment of a high degree of integration through the selection of the numerous elements of the culture in terms of their consonance with the basic postulates.

In the anthropologists' discussion of the configuration of culture the Pueblo Indians of the American Southwest have been shown to possess a culture that stresses restraint and orderliness in behavior, avoidance of emotional excess and display in personal experience and ritual, rigorous suppression of individual initiative and innovation, with quiet co-operation in group endeavor. Pueblo culture presents to the individual the philosophy of a well-ordered universe in which man is but one harmonious part of a delicate balance involving all natural forces. As long as each man plays his ordained roles in the traditional manner, all people will prosper. The rain gods will provide the precious water, the gods of plants and fertility will mature adequate crops, the dancing gods will favor the village. All functions necessary to the good life and survival of the pueblo will be fulfilled. The failure of any person to perform his roles in the traditional and proper way is believed to upset the balance and bring down disaster upon the whole society. This is a cultural code that rests upon a maize-growing subsistence economy as practiced by a sedentary people, who build stone and adobe, multi-storied communal houses in a desert environment.

As a contrasting example we may briefly draw the outlines of configuration for the culture of the people of the island of Alor in Indonesia. Like the Pueblo Indians, the people of Alor are settled gardeners. But in their lives the dynamic principle of culture, which is of outstanding significance, is the continuing exchange of wealth. Striving for personal dominance over fellow tribesmen by means of financial activity, the making and collecting of loans is the chief adult activity, especially of men. It is apparently the consequence of notable individual insecurity caused by the peculiar and unsatisfactory relationships within the family as they affect the growing child. Money, which in Alor consists of pigs, Javanese bronze vessels, and gongs, is lent out as capital on which interest must be paid, so that the debtor is bound by tight bonds of obligation to the creditor. Marriage and death, in particular, call for extensive consumption of pigs in feasts, along with tremendous exchanges and payments in vessels and gongs. The burdens imposed on the participants are immense, for they must usually go into heavy debt to meet the demands of the occasion. Except as it stimulates the growing of pigs, all this heavy economic activity bears little or no relation to economic production or utilitarian needs.

War, until suppressed by the Dutch, did not rest on any military interest as such. Rather, it was expressed as a long, drawn out series of feuds marked by cowardly assaults on men and women, and carried out by trickery and stealth.

Illness is marked by a complete collapse of the will to live and an obsessive conviction of hopelessness.

The culture of Alor emphasizes non-utilitarian striving to best one's fellowmen, pushing the ego, to which it denies serenity and security, on to its final collapse in the illness that ultimately brings surcease in death.

In the Pueblos and Alor we have two kinds of culture configurations, which are reasonably clear-cut. This is not always the case, however, for many cultures do not attain concise integration in accord with a consistent set of basic principles. The nomadic buffalo-hunting Indians of the western American Plains had one line of integration of behavior traits that emphasized extravagant sensation seeking. One of the highlights of life was to bring oneself through fasting, thirsting, autosuggestion, and perhaps, self-torture to the phantasy state in which sensational visions would be encountered. Upon these visions, which were interpreted as supernatural visitations through which medicine power was bestowed, depended the successful outcome of any man's career. The purpose of the vision quest was to bring power and glory to the individual. Armed with such powers he could perform reckless deeds in battle. Armed with a record of such deeds, he could boastfully glorify himself, challenging other men to match their records of performance against his. This was but the central core of a whole series of culture traits glorifying rampant individualism and stimulating extreme sensate behavior.

Yet this is not *the* configuration of Plains culture, for equally strong, if not so spectacular, is another web of traits based on a contradictory set of basic principles. The first complex may be called the 'egotistical warrior' line. The second would be the 'considerate peace chief' line. This emphasized gentleness, generosity, reasonableness, and wisdom. Such virtues called for self-restraint, consideration of others, and a disposition to check the too quarrelsome assertiveness of the aggressive individualism called forth by the other line in the culture. Some men in the Plains tribes followed either one line or the other throughout their lives. In others, the incompatibilities of the two patterns set up an internal conflict for both individual and society. The restrained peace chief concept had its counterpart in important religious ceremonies as the extremely pious and sober ritual of the Medicine Arrow Renewal of the Cheyenne Indians. For this, all male members of the tribe, except murderers and their close kin, had to be present. When the sacred arrows were unwrapped from their protecting bundle not a cry or sound was permitted to disturb the holy atmosphere. Patroling soldiers clubbed any yelping dog into stunned silence or death.

Consistency in a culture is not, therefore, wholly to be expected. It is probably true, as Sumner maintained, that there is a strain towards consistency in the folkways of any culture: that contradictory elements tend to cancel one or the other out, or else to attain a synthesis in a new form. On the other hand, it is too much to expect a completion of this process in all aspects of any culture. Inconsistencies arise and persist because, in the first place, cultures are never consciously planned or directed in their general growth. In the second place, most cultural traits are acquired through borrowing. Not many human beings are originators. The sources of borrowing for any culture are diverse and unlike. While there is always a certain amount of selection (people do not borrow blindly), new elements may be taken up even though inconsistent with elements or principles already within the culture, because they appear to be desirable in themselves. Finally, there are almost always alternative possibilities among the answers to the problems that culture undertakes to solve. It may be a matter of simple accident that the first solution hit upon and adopted is not wholly consistent with pre-existing forms in the culture. Nevertheless, it may find its way into the cultural whole because it serves a need or interest satisfactorily. If it produces a conflict within the culture, that is a matter to be suffered.

Our discussion of the configuration of culture has indicated that the behavior of each individual is strongly influenced by the patterns of the culture with which he lives. The character of each individual is unique, for one individual's experiences never match those of another, nor is it probable that the constitutional components of any two persons are exactly identical. But the patterns and configurations of the cultures of different societies produce distinctive personality types that are generally characteristic of the members of those societies. In the personality and culture studies that have developed so fruitfully in recent years culturally determined personality configurations have come to be known as national (or tribal) character, ideal personality type, modal personality, and basic personality.

The ideal personality type is the abstract image of the 'good' man or the 'good' woman that is reflected from the moral standards set in the culture. Much psychopathology is the product of an unmastered conflict within the individual who is unable to assimilate the standards of the cultural ideal to the impulses of the self. It is the Freudian conflict of the super-ego and the id.

The basic personality structure is differently conceived. It exists not as an abstract image but rather as a modal core of attitudes produced in the average individual as a result of the patterns of childtraining characteristic of his culture. How is the infant fed, handled, bathed? What are adult reactions to infant defecation and urination? Does the child receive consistent loving attention? Or is it harshly rejected, or teased, or abused? How and in what ways does it suffer deprivation or enjoy gratification of its wants? In so far as the answers to these questions are found in consistent patterns of adult behavior, so will the basic personality structures of the children take form. The basic personality structure tends to persist throughout the life of the individual, coloring adult behavior and completing the cycle by influencing the configuration of adult culture. Thus the grown-up Alorese is 'anxious, suspicious, mistrustful, lacking in confidence, with no interest in the outer world. There is no capacity to idealize the parental image or deity. The personality is devoid of enterprise, is filled with repressed hatred and free floating aggression over which constant vigilance must be exercised. The personality is devoid of high aspirations and has no basis for the internalization of discipline.' [2] Such is the effect of Alorese infant and childhood experience on the personality of the grown-up native of Alor.

---

[2] A. Kardiner and associates, *The Psychological Frontiers of Society*, Columbia University Press, New York, 1945, p. 170.

In like manner, each culture puts *its* mark upon the individual who develops under its influence, whose personality is a blend resulting from his unique physical and nervous constitution, the patterns of his culture, and his individual experience in contact with the physical world and other people. Each man is a common type, molded by culture and society, and yet possessed of individuality that culture cannot submerge.

RUTH BENEDICT

VIII

The Growth of Culture

ALL BOOKS with such titles as *Progress*, or *The History of Civilization*, or *The Growth of the United States*, or *Modern Finance*, or *Modern Warfare* are books about some aspect of the growth of culture. When we talk about such subjects, they are parts of this great story, whether we are speaking about ancient Greece or contemporary Iowa. Even when we read about how the Romans destroyed Greece or the Goths destroyed Rome, we are learning about cultural growth. For destruction and growth go on together. As culture grows, it also destroys, and as it destroys, new growths appear.

The history of the human race is a wonderful story of progress. Archaeologists tell us that for thousands of years men made the same flint tools by striking stones together, took shelter in caves, and tied a skin around themselves for warmth. Only a few families could live near one another, for each grown man had to stalk wild animals to get food for his women and children. He could only accept nature's supplies as he found them; he knew no way to increase them. It was thousands of years later that his descendants discovered that plants could be sown and tended and harvested or that animals could be domesticated.

The human race is unique among all animal species because of the progress it has made from that day to this. Man alone has constantly enriched his way of life by invention and by complex learning. The fabulous growth of culture is his great achievement, and no other mammal has made this kind of progress. When we examine the growth of culture in human history, we are examining the basis for man's pre-eminence. Members of the human race have a right to just one great boast: that

223

they have an endless capacity to invent and learn. They can learn not merely as other mammals do, from imitation and from individual experience, but from experience passed down to a present generation from thousands of forebears now dead and gone.

The growth of culture in human history has created for the human race a man-made environment quite unlike the environment nature provided. Man took the wild grasses and developed them into wheat and barley and corn, which were productive enough to sustain his great cities. Even primitive people with no writing and no schools terraced mountains to make rice or corn fields and irrigated them by diverting water in regions where rainfall was not adequate.

Primitive tribes have invented tools and learned how to make pottery and baskets. They have fashioned elaborate traps and fish-weirs to make the food quest easier. They have made musical instruments to please their senses and lavished their craftsmanship on beautiful objects. Everywhere, also, among all races of men, they have expanded their world of known and seen human contacts to include also spirits and gods whom they call upon for help.

HUMAN BEGINNINGS

This long story of man's creativeness in the growth of culture begins far back with the first appearance of the human species. To us today Stone Age man seems culturally poverty-stricken because we have gone so far beyond him. But he had begun the distinctively human process of making inventions and transmitting them by teaching to his descendants. By the middle of the Stone Age, for instance, he had domesticated fire. No one will ever know what happened to make some men or women first put to domestic use that terrifying and destructive force. And what were the circumstances which led them to make water boil over a fire? They could hardly have seen in nature any boiling water. And how did they discover that they could kindle fire at will by rubbing two pieces of wood together? At any rate at least by the middle of the Stone Age in Europe man had not only learned these things; he had made them a part of his transmitted culture. He had learned ways of making and keeping fire and he could use it to warm himself when he was cold, and to cook and preserve his food. It was a complex invention which foreshadowed man's continuing career as a great inventor.

Perhaps even more significant was the gradual invention of language.

It involved arranging things in the environment in different categories or classes; it involved creating verbs to show how these things could act and be acted on. Originally it involved something else too: the long, slow development of the muscles used in articulation. Early Stone Age man had less specialized tongue muscles and his speech was certainly hampered by this fact. We cannot know when human speech first became a complex set of symbols; it was certainly a long slow process. Today, however, there is no primitive tribe, no matter how poor in material culture, which has not a complicated language and a vocabulary of words with fine shades of meaning.

Stone Age man was remarkable for his skill in making implements out of flint. By striking brittle stone he could fashion tools and weapons. Stone Age man in different areas and periods made different tools. Their shape was so standardized that experts can name the period and area from which most worked flints in a modern museum come. Although their stability over centuries reminds us of the distinctive nest a robin or a crow inevitably builds this distinctiveness depends on learning, not instinct. The human race, even at that early date, had to transmit even this basic industry by teaching each generation what man could learn by experience. When he had learned, he could transmit the new technique.

Stone Age man had begun the process of creating man-made cultural environments. Because nothing is left of his works except those made of durable materials, we do not know what he had invented in social organization, in rules of marriage, or in religion and folklore. It may have been much; it may have been surprisingly little. We do know that with his handling of fire, language, and flint implements he had adopted unique human methods of invention and learning. From that day to this, man has followed this path.

OBSTACLES TO THE ADOPTION OF NEW TRAITS

The growth of culture has not been as continuous and as purposeful, however, as we often imagine when we talk of progress. Our ideas of progress are themselves cultural inventions of restless modern man avid for improvements. In the modern world in one generation we adopt and learn to manipulate the automobile or the aeroplane or the telephone or the radio or the techniques of mass factory production. We do not pray: 'Oh Lord, keep us as our fathers were.' Even in finance or art, we invent freely, with our eyes on the future rather than on the past. We even create new religious cults by the dozen. It is easy, therefore, for us to picture human progress as if man had always reached out for a new idea or a new invention and had adopted it whenever he saw it.

History is full of examples of apparently simple discoveries that were not made even when they would be surpassingly useful in that culture. Necessity is not necessarily the mother of invention. Men in most of Europe and Asia had adopted the wheel during the Bronze Age. It was used for chariots, as a pulley wheel for raising weights, and as a potter's wheel for making clay vessels. But in the two Americas it was not known except as a toy in any pre-Columbian civilization. Even in Peru, where immense temples were built with blocks of stone that weighed up to ten tons, these huge weights were excavated, transported, and placed in buildings without any use of wheels.

The invention of the zero is another seemingly simple discovery which was not made even by classic Greek mathematicians or Roman engineers. Only by the use of some symbol for nothingness can the symbol 1 be used so that it can have the value either of 1 or 10 or 100 or 1000. It makes it possible to use a small number of symbols to represent such different values as 129 and 921. Without such inventions figures cannot be added or subtracted by writing them one above another, and multiplication and division are even more difficult. The Romans had to try to divide CCCLVIII by XXIV and the difficulty was immense. It was not the Egyptians or the Greeks or the Romans who first invented the zero, but the Maya Indians of Yucatán. It is known that they had a zero sign and positional values of numbers by the time of the birth of Christ. Quite independently the Hindus made these inventions in India some five to seven centuries later. Only gradually was it adopted in medieval Europe, where it was known as Arabic notation because it was introduced there by the Arabs.

Necessity is not only not the inevitable mother of invention; it is not possible to assume that a people will adopt new inventions or accept discoveries others make. The technique of making bronze was established in Europe and Asia a couple of thousand years before iron ores were worked, and even after ways of forging and tempering iron were known, bronze remained for centuries the favorite metal. It was prettier though not nearly so good for tools. Yet iron ores are abundant and not difficult to extract, and tools of iron can be readily made at little outdoor primitive forges, as they are among African tribes today.

Primitive tribes in the modern world often continued to practice some old and back-breaking custom even when they were in contact with some other primitive peoples who had admirably solved that particuar technological problem. The Chukchee, a reindeer herding tribe of eastern Siberia, carried on trade with Eskimo tribes who built themselves snow huts. These houses are dome-shaped; blocks of firm snow are cut out with knives and slanted inward until the final block at the top seals the dome. A single man can build one for himself in half-an-hour for a shelter, and large interconnecting ones are built for short-term winter dwellings. They can be heated with blubber lamps and can keep the inmates warm in Arctic winters. The Chukchee, however, stuck to their great skin tents, inside which they set up a smaller skin sleeping tent. Every morning the frost had to be beaten out of the skins, for the moisture from the breath and from perspiration froze, and, if left in, would make the skins crack. This daily beating of the tent covering was exhausting physical labor; in addition, the great bundle was heavy and cumbersome to transport, and erecting the tents on a new site was laborious. But the Chukchee never adopted the snow house of the Eskimo, no matter what difficulties they had with skin tents in the Arctic.

There was another side to this picture. The Chukchee were reindeer herders. They became rich through breeding and rearing these animals and they harnessed them to their sleds. The Eskimos, however, did not adopt reindeer herding. On the American continent, where the barren-ground caribou were available in large numbers and apparently might have been domesticated as the Siberian reindeer were, no domestication at all took place. The trait was not borrowed by American Eskimos or Indians, even though many other cultural inventions diffused across Bering Strait.

Even in modern western civilization, where we pride ourselves on our efficiency, each nation excludes some existing inventions. One might suppose that in great civilizations where counting and measurement are as important as they are in Europe and the United States, all nations would adopt systems with convenient units. The metric system, in which the integer is multiplied first by 10, then by 100 and 1000, can be applied to measurements of volume, of length, and of weight, and can be used to count money. In France the decimal system is used for every kind of counting and measuring. In the United States we use it to reckon money, but not volume, length, or weight. In England it is not even used in reckoning money and no measurements of length or weight or volume are reckoned by metric systems.

The growth of culture, therefore, has not had the kind of history an armchair student would imagine. It cannot be reconstructed logically and by deduction. Sometimes some obvious and simple thing was not discovered or accepted at all even when there was great logical need for it. Sometimes very complicated things were invented in the simplest primitive societies. This is true not merely in technology. It is true in social organization, in legal systems, in religion, and in folk philosophy. To understand the growth of culture in all these aspects, it is necessary to describe more fully how partial all men become to the special man-made environment they have created by their own cultural inventions and arrangements.

The habits of any culture fit the people who learn to use them like well-worn gloves. This fit goes very deep, for their ideas of right and wrong, their selection of human desires and passions, are part and parcel of their whole version of culture. They can react to another people's way of conducting life with a supreme lack of interest or at least of comprehension. Among civilized peoples this often appears in their depreciation of 'foreign ways'; it is easy to develop a blind spot where another people's cherished customs are concerned. Among primitive peoples this lack of interest in 'progress' has been proverbial. And for good reason. Every primitive tribe has its own elaborate cultural arrangements which ensure its survival, either technologically, or in their forms of social organization, or by ceremonies and offerings to the gods. Even though they may be eager for some things the white man brings—perhaps guns, perhaps beads, or whiskey, or empty tin cans out of which to make a knife— they do not generally look on the white man's culture as a solution of life's problems which is 'better' than the one they have. They may be culturally uninterested even in laborsaving devices. Often the value they put on time is extremely low and 'wisdom' is far more valued than efficiency. Our cultural system and theirs are oriented around different ideals.

Some primitive cultures have not been able to accommodate themselves to contact with the white man. Their whole way of living, when they were brought into contact with modern civilization, has fallen down like a house of cards. The Indians of the United States have most of them become simply men without a cultural country. They are unable to locate anything in the white man's way of life which is sufficiently congenial to their old culture. When the white man first came, the Plains tribes had a short-lived cultural upsurge when they enthusiastically incorporated the horse into their way of life, and the Northwest Coast Indians had a veritable renaissance of wood carving when they got metal. But closer contact laid bare the great gap between white and Indian values. The Indian cultures could not survive the white man's interference with their tribal war paths and the buffalo herds and salmon fisheries on which they depended. Acquaintance with the strange white customs of working for wages and paying for land and conducting private enterprise broke down their old social arrangements without putting anything intelligible in their place. The white man, for his part, was equally unable to see the cultural values which the Indian tribes cherished and which were being broken down and lost forever. Each side was blind to cultural ideals which to the other were the most real things in the universe.

In all such cases of contact between western civilization and other cultures, the white man is usually sure that he is of superior intelligence because he has the knives, the guns, the cigarettes, the metal skillets that the simpler people do not have. He judges that the others would have these things, along with reading, writing, and arithmetic, if they were not stupid. Actually careful observations and tests have shown that the matter is not so simple. Neither the intelligence nor the senses of primitive people need be inferior even when their manner of life is very simple. In western civilization we are heirs of inventions that have been made all over the face of the earth. All we have and know are items of our social inheritance. We were simply born into it by the accident of our birth. It is highly unlikely that any one of us has invented one single process. Just so, an American Indian was an heir of *his* culture. It was rather more likely than in the complex western civilization that he had individually had an opportunity to make some contribution to tribal ways or that he had had a chance to take leadership in some activities important to his people. His ways of life satisfied him because they solved human problems in ways he had been reared to understand. It had not crossed his mind to want the things the Europeans wanted. He had used his brains on a different set of activities that were more congenial.

No one has ever developed an objective scale of values according to which all different cultural goals may be graded as better or worse. Western civilization, for instance, is organized to extend its power widely over the earth. A valid case, however, can be made for the value of a cultural goal which has no place for conquest or financial domination. Every people value most the drives and emotions to which they are accustomed, and they usually condemn people who lack them. They are right in valuing their own way of life, but their depreciations of other cultures are often based on misunderstandings.

INTERNAL GROWTH OF CULTURE

Because all peoples defend their own way of life, it is easy to understand that one way in which cultures have grown richer and more complex has been by elaborating and multiplying their own most cherished customs. They carry further and further their favorite customs. Simple trading habits may be worked up into great tribal ceremonies. The potlatches of the Northwest Coast Indians were such ceremonies, in which chiefs tried to defeat other chiefs by giving them so many blankets and other goods that they would be unable to return the interest on them. Such tribes took the main theme of their cultural life from the situation of the creditor and the debtor, and they elaborated their ceremonies around this theme till their potlaches became systems of intricate cultural complexity.

In other tribes the most cherished observances are hospitable entertainments of the gods. In the Southwest pueblo of Zuñi, the spirits are thought to be happiest when they are given the opportunity to come to the world of the living and dance. Therefore men put on spirit masks and impersonate them. These Indians 'dance' their corn, too, to make it happy, and put on elaborate welcoming rites for the carcass of a deer after the hunt. They greet and honor even little pine branches they cut for their ceremonies. Since the sun, and spirits of rain, and spirits of animals, and spirits of enemies, and spirits of curing all have to be honored, Zuñi has a staggering mass of ceremonial addressed to this end. Both on the Northwest Coast and in Southwest pueblos, the local process of cultural growth has been, just as in other parts of the world, a kind of industrious weaving of a more and more complex cocoon. But the threads of this cocoon are still old, chosen, and simple habits, even when they are fashioned into such complex observances. They are valued in their congeniality.

Cultures tend to develop in this way, and it is therefore possible to understand the different lines along which, for instance, eastern civilizations like China and India have developed as contrasted to western civilizations. Unless one is to the manner born, the elaborations of another culture often seem superfluous. But the whole history of the growth of culture is full of superfluities to which people of that tribe or nation have displayed deep attachment and loyalty.

GROWTH OF CULTURE THROUGH DIFFUSION

Besides this kind of internal elaboration of preferred traits cultures have grown mightily by borrowing techniques and ideas from one another. This borrowing is technically called the diffusion of cultural traits. (See Plate IX.)

Western civilization itself is based on inventions which have been borrowed from every part of the world. Many of them were made by people of simple culture who did not share in western traditions. The alphabet was invented by Semitic peoples in the area north of the Red Sea and carried by Phoenicians to Greece and Rome. Over centuries it spread throughout Europe and into India. Paper—and gunpowder too—are old inventions made in China. The true arch, with its keystone, was a great architectural invention made in Babylonia thirty centuries before Christ; but ancient Greek architecture is not based on it. The great monuments and temples of Peru and Central America were built without any knowledge of it. Gradually, however, the Babylonian invention was adopted in ancient Etruria and in Rome, and became basic in Gothic cathedrals. Modified into a dome, it is used in modern public buildings.

Man has constantly enriched his food supply by introducing grains and fruits which were originally domesticated on the opposite side of the globe. Coffee was brought into cultivation in Abyssinia, but today we associate it particularly with Brazil and Java. Potatoes are roots first tended and harvested by South American Indians, and Bolivian Indians cultivated 240 varieties. But we call our white potatoes 'Irish.' Bananas come to us today from Central America, but wild varieties were first brought into cultivation in south Asia, and Polynesian peoples had carried them over immense areas of the Pacific before European navigators made their voyages of discovery. The banana in the New World is post-Columbian; it was borrowed from the Old World. Maize, an American Indian crop, is today a staple of many primitive tribes of Africa, and tobacco, also an American Indian crop, has been adopted in all parts of the world.

The diffusion of cultural traits from one people to another has constantly enriched human ways of life. Every little tribe is indebted to its neighbors for various inventions which the latter have borrowed farther afield and which they themselves modified after they copied it and perhaps improved.

RECASTING OF BORROWED TRAITS

Whatever traits tribes borrow from one another, they are likely to recast them to make them congenial to their own way of life. Sometimes this recasting has been drastic, sometimes not so drastic. But as a student follows any one cultural trait through tribe after tribe, he finds strange new meanings and uses given to it, or strange new combinations into which it has entered. The wheel, when it was invented in the Old World, spread rapidly in the period around 3000 B.C. into Assyria and Iran and India, and later into Egypt. These were regions of the world where pottery was at that time very important and when the wheel spread into Egypt, it was as a potter's wheel. Not until much later was it used as a chariot wheel. However, when after 200 B.C. the wheel was borrowed by peoples of northen Europe, they used it for wheeled vehicles for nearly a thousand years before they utilized it in pottery making. Tribes and nations could not put the wheel to use in a horse-drawn, wheeled chariot unless they had domesticated animals that could be trained to the harness, and they could not use it for pottery unless they had pottery industry and cared about making it more rapidly. So the wheel became a part of quite different arts of life as it diffused over the world.

New meanings are given to borrowed traits as they pass from area to area. This is just as conspicuous in traits of social organization, political arrangements, and religious practices as it is in traits of material culture. A religious ceremony, for instance, may be shared by all tribes over a great area. All may erect the same kind of house or enclosure on sacred ground, have the same kinds of torture or trance communication or order of march, and use the same insignia for officers and the same type of prayers. All these characteristics may have been spread from tribe to tribe in the area. Nevertheless, in spite of all these diffused traits, a widespread ceremony like the Sun Dance of the Plains Indians has been recast in tribe after tribe. In one tribe the whole ceremony is put on by someone who has had a vision of the Thundergod and desires to honor this spirit which has honored him; in another it is vowed by one man who proposes to avenge the death of a relative on the war path; in another it is a way of giving thanks for escape from danger or disease; in another it is a ceremony for the initiation of priests or shamans. These different meanings of the ceremony, of course, led to changes in the rites themselves and eventually the whole ceremony in one tribe comes to have its own special character, which it does not share with any other tribe.

This recasting of borrowed traits occurs in the same way in social organization and folklore and in any other field of life. A good example is the varied meaning of cannibalistic practices. Cannibalism did not occur in all parts of the world, but where it did it had the most contrasted meanings. It was used in some tribes as a way of ensuring the birth of children; only young children were eaten and only the immediate family participated; afterwards they believed that a child would be born again to the family. In other tribes, the hearts only of brave enemies were eaten; it was done in order to increase the bravery of the eaters. Sometimes cannibalism was a lusty enjoyment of good food; sometimes it was a proof that a man could face anything in the world if he could dare to swallow a portion of human flesh. Each tribe and area had taken this piece of behavior and used it in its own special way.

It is the same with adolescent ceremonies, with kinship systems, and with the institutions of kingship. People borrow, and, when they have adopted the trait, it has already become something else from the thing they borrowed. The process of diffusion has therefore not only allowed people all over the world to share in each others' creations and inventions; it has also increased the rich variety of human cultures.

EVOLUTION

The history of man from the Stone Age to the present is a wonderful story of cultural growth. The social inheritance of man has been enriched by multitudinous inventions and arts. In spite of terrible periods of devastation and destruction, the human race has built for itself a cultural environment which is capable of almost infinite richness.

Although a large part of the history of any given culture is due to accident, an evolutionary process may be traced. The growth of culture has not been haphazard. That is, certain earlier inventions, whether of tools or of institutions or of ideas, have been necessary before other inventions could take place. In primitive tribes courts which administered tribal justice could not evolve until there was some organization of the tribal state. Kingdoms could not arise till certain political inventions had been made which brought many neighboring communities into mutual relations with one another. Standing armies in the service of chiefs required a preceding elaborate division of labor and the existence of centralized power.

Evolution can be well illustrated in two fields, the technological and the political. In technology, modern man has built upon the unplanned discoveries of the human race which began with man-made flint tools and the utilization of fire and later the invention of agriculture and herding. Modern man, however, has not left his inventions to chance. At long last, with the modern growth of scientific knowledge, man has arrived at the point where he consciously invents. That is, he sets up for himself a problem he wants to solve and tries all sorts of experiments and combinations until he solves it. He tests and retests till he is sure his solution works.

We are so used to this kind of problem-solving that it is hard for us to realize that most cultural advances have been chance discoveries rather than conscious invention. These discoveries, made without benefit of a previously imagined goal, thus were, strictly speaking, accidental. Even today primitive tribes are found sometimes in regions that have no agriculture but who have nevertheless dumped their garbage near their homes until seeds have sprouted in the enriched earth close to their houses. They had not planned to fertilize these patches and plant seed within easy reach of their camp fires. When they saw what had happened they did not think about their discovery and go straightway and plant new plots. But they picked the seeds and vegetables which sprouted on their dump heaps, and found them handy. They had accidentally stumbled upon an experience out of which the practice of agriculture could grow—probably the same experience which men stumbled upon in the New Stone Age when the human race first began systematically to exploit the possibilities of purposeful cultivation and planting of the soil.

The great upward curve of progress in technology of which man can rightly boast, therefore, is an evolution from unplanned discovery to planned invention. Man has learned purposefully to set his goal and then to check and recheck the experiments that he sets up to achieve that goal. Methods of curing diseases are a good example of this change. During most of the history of the human race, men accepted their traditional curing practices on faith. To treat eye troubles some peoples chose plants which had an 'eye' on their fruit or blossom; 'like,' they said, 'cured like.' Some of these plants were actually beneficial, but others, we know by chemical analysis, could even cause blindness. Nevertheless the dangerous plant was used. Some tribes had cure-alls for the most unrelated human ailments. It might be 'baking,' which meant putting the sick person over a bed of buried hot stones and keeping him warm for days or weeks. This was good for certain aches and pains, but they used it also for broken bones without trying to reset them. Starving or bleeding might be their cure-all, but neither of these were good cures for tuberculosis. Nevertheless they did not experiment and they continued to use their cure-alls. In the practice of medicine we have come a long way.

In man's technological progress, therefore, it required tens of centuries to arrive at the idea of scientific planning and checking. Man made his latest great step forward when he said, 'Just what is it I want to do?' and then tested his results to see if he had attained his object. In this way he discovered that planning could unlock the previously unknown.

A second great evolution in human culture is man's increasing ability to live together in large numbers. In early times and among the simpler societies only a few hundred people, or at most, on special occasions, a few thousands could be organized into a community. Man had to make inventions in social organization and in distribution of goods and in the political field before large organized states were possible. As man made more and more of these inventions, he was able to live in larger communities and to achieve law and order over larger and larger areas. Trade and ceremonies brought people together peacefully, and ideas circulated. Men were stimulated to think and build and create.

The growth of greater human communities is, therefore, in spite of all the devastation these large groups have often visited upon one another, one of the major themes of human progress. It has changed the human topography of the modern world. In earlier times small communities of a few hundred souls might be the only 'in-group' these people knew; all the rest were 'out-groups.' An in-group is a group of people with loyalties and rights and obligations which they hold in common. Out-groups are all other communities. The primitive in-group might be an economically self-sufficient community within which each person was necessary to the livelihood and well-being of the tribe. Out-group people were annoyances or out-and-out enemies. Everywhere such tribes had one system of ethics to regulate their dealings with in-group members, and a different and often opposite one for out-group people. Stealing, for instance, was very frequently unknown within the in-group, but it was a virtue if a man stole from an out-group. Generosity was often a prime virtue within the tribe, but it did not extend to out-group people.

The advantages of extending the in-group to include millions of people who can profit by mutual security and mutual trade in material goods and mutual exchange of ideas is too obvious to need comment. Mankind has gone far in this kind of progress. We can project this upward curve into the future and recognize that some day mankind will organize the whole world so that he can reap the maximum benefits of security and commerce and exchange of ideas. We have not done it yet. We keep the old primitive contrast between in-group and out-group ethics in our distinction between killing a man of one's own country—which is murder and a major crime—and killing an enemy in war—which is a duty for which we honor the successful soldier. We keep the primitive contrast, too, in our hair-trigger suspiciousness of other sovereign nations—just as they keep them about us. We set up mechanisms of law and order within each nation, but, just as in primitive times, there are no such lawful mechanisms binding sovereign nations together. There is temporary alliance, but essentially there is still the old anarchy that has been traditional in the relations of out-groups to one another. In this world which has grown so small because of modern technological inventions in commerce and finance and armament and communication and transportation, it is just as necessary today to organize the world community for the secure enrichment of human life as it was in earlier times to organize a dozen little in-groups scattered a few miles from each other along a river course.

ROY A. RAPPAPORT

IX

Nature, Culture, and Ecological Anthropology

I

WE ARE CONCERNED in this chapter with the place of man in those larger systems that are called 'nature.' We are concerned, that is, with the ecology of men, and with the possible importance of a general ecological perspective in understanding and explaining human culture, and differences and similarities among the cultures of people living and dead.

Ecology is the science concerned with the relations between living organisms and their physical and biotic environments. It attends particularly to relations between unlike species, and to the ways in which members of particular species organize to maintain themselves in communities composed of many species. It is a holistic science, attempting to understand the lifeways of organisms by reference to their places in the larger systems of which they are parts.

The subject matter of ecology, transactions among living things and between living things and the non-living components of their habitats, implies behavior, and ecology is, in part, a behavioral science. But since ecology is also concerned with the biological effects of these transactions upon those who are party to them it is a biological science as well. Moreover, the natural world is nowhere a mere conglomeration, but everywhere forms associations composed of numbers of species which relate to each other in regular ways and whose members are organized in regular ways. Thus, ecology is also a social science; indeed, one general work in the field is entitled *The Sociology of Nature* (Reid: 1958).

It would be well to introduce here some of the general terms in which ecologists conceive the organization of nature. In addition to individual

237

organisms, ecologists are usually concerned with two more inclusive units. First, there is the ecosystem. An ecosystem may be defined as the total of living organisms and non-living substances bound together in material exchanges within some demarcated portion of the biosphere. The most important and typical of these exchanges are those of feeding. Basic to the ecosystem are plants, which, by photosynthesis, can produce living tissue out of inorganic materials in the presence of sunlight. Plants are the primary producers of living tissue in ecosystems, and material of plant origin is consumed by herbivores (primary consumers), who in turn may be fed upon by carnivores (secondary consumers). In some instances these carnivores themselves become the prey of yet other carnivores (tertiary consumers). Wastes, and the remains of dead plants and animals are reduced by decomposers, usually microscopic, into inorganic substances which can again be taken up by plants. Although most ecosystems are enormously complex their general scheme is roughly cyclical.

The groups of plants and animals of various kinds which form the living portion (or community) of an ecosystem are termed ecological populations. An ecological population is an aggregate of organisms having in common a set of distinctive means by which they maintain a common set of material relations within the ecosystem in which they participate. The position occupied by an ecological population in an ecosystem, a position defined by what it eats and what eats it, is sometimes called its 'ecological niche.' Usually, but not always, an ecological population consists of all of the representatives of one species to be found in a particular ecosystem. However, an aggregate of organisms is designated a species because its members may exchange genetic material, and ecosystems are not held together by genetic exchanges but by feeding relations. The material exchanged in a typical ecological transaction between members of unlike populations is not genetic material but living tissue: one eats the other. Species designations are useful in distinguishing ecological populations only insofar as they serve as a shorthand for positions in networks of feeding exchanges, that is for ecological niches, and it sometimes happens that two or more aggregates of the same species have different means for maintaining themselves in the same ecosystem. This is often so among men. For instance, herders and horticulturalists occupying the same area are as ecologically distinct from each other as two species (see, for example, Barth: 1956), and may be regarded as separate ecological populations.

Ecology, then, deals with transactions among all living systems—organisms, populations, and ecosystems—attempting to explain them in terms of a few general principles, notably those concerned with the conservation and dissipation of energy, with the maintenance of homeostasis and with adaptation. Like all physical systems living systems are subject to the second law of thermodynamics, and tend toward entropy—disorganization and dissolution. But they are open systems, and they maintain their structure and functioning, their organizations, by absorbing matter and energy from their environments. Living systems also tend to be cybernetic, regulating their functioning through the process known as 'negative feedback.' In response to system endangering changes in some aspect of the environment or themselves, living systems initiate processes which correct or compensate for such changes. For instance, in response to an uncomfortable increase in temperature, a human organism may perspire, diminish its physical activity, drink cool fluids, seek shade, undress, turn down the furnace, or turn on the air conditioner. These are all corrective responses to an environmental fluctuation that could produce an uncomfortable or even disastrous increase in the organism's internal temperature. Thanks to these and other self-regulatory responses, however, the organism is able to maintain homeostasis with respect to temperature. That is, it is able to maintain its internal temperature within a narrow range in the face of much wider fluctuations in the temperature of its environment. Similarly, populations of many species seem to regulate their own numbers through restrictions on breeding and feeding territories, through hierarchical social organizations, and perhaps through certain displays. The ethologist V. C. Wynne-Edwards (1962) has argued, for instance, that the flocking behavior of certain birds serves to impart information concerning the size and density of the population to its membership, and when their numbers threaten to violate the capacity of the region to feed them, some or all leave for more sparsely populated areas. Homeostasis with respect to population size thus seems to be maintained through the social conventions of a large number of species. When the regulation of its numbers by a population itself is ineffective, corrective processes take place on the ecosystemic level. For instance, in response to population increases among varying hares, there are increases in the populations of the lynx that prey upon them (Allee *et al.*, 1949: 323 Passim).

In addition to being homeostatic and self-regulating, some living systems, at least, are adaptive. That is, in response to enduring changes in their environments they change their very organization, their structure and functioning. Among populations of organisms adaptation is effected

by change in genetic composition in response to selective pressures in accordance with the principles of natural selection. Individual organisms,
although they cannot modify the genotypes with which they are born,
may be said to adapt to long-term environmental changes through the reorganization of their behavior. This is particularly true of men. Ecosystems also respond to changes in their physical setting—changes in available sunlight, moisture, temperature, or soil—through changes in their
species composition and their structure.

II

We have already implied that men may be brought within the purview
of a general ecological perspective. But men differ from other animals in
important respects. Although it is becoming increasingly apparent that
learning plays a significant role in the lifeways of many other animals, it
is also clear that their patterns of social organization and individual behavior are more narrowly specified genetically than is the case among
men. Moreover, this genetic specification is the outcome of selective pressures emanating from particular sorts of environments, and in the course
of evolution rather nice fits between the biological and social organization
of animal aggregates and the particulars of various sorts of ecosystems
have evolved.

The behavior and social organizations of men, on the other hand, are
almost completely unspecified by their genetic constitutions. While men
are born with needs comparable to those of other animals, they are not
born with genetically programmed ways of fulfilling them. They are born,
rather, with a capacity to acquire cultures, sets of beliefs, conventions,
knowledge, techniques, and artifacts dependent upon the invention and
use of symbols. Symbols are signals only conventionally related to their
referents and are capable of being combined into complex messages. Language is the fundamental symbolic system of the human species. Although
recent work in ethology has discovered limited symbolic ability among
some other species, the use of symbols has reached its fullest expression
among men.

Through symbols the subject matter of communication is freed from
what is immediate and present, and through symbols an enormous amount
of information can be stored and transmitted. The ability to invent and
employ symbols massively has obviously made a vast difference between
the modes of life of men and other species. Indeed, some anthropologists
have compared the emergence of the symbol to the emergence of life in

importance and novelty. It has been argued by both Kroeber (1917) and White (1949) that symbols, and the cultures synthesized from symbols and symbol use form a unique class of phenomena as different from the organic as the organic is from the inorganic, a class that is 'superorganic.'

While the existence of culture is, of course, considered by these writers to be contingent upon the existence of culture bearing organisms, i.e. men, once in existence cultures have 'lives' of their own. Levi-Strauss (1969:4) has written 'Culture is not merely juxtaposed to life nor superimposed upon it, but in one way serves as a substitute for life, and in the other, uses and transforms it, to bring about the syntheses of a new order.' Culture, in this view, is obviously subject to its own laws and cannot be explained by laws which govern biological and physical processes.

The concept of culture as autonomous superorganic, characteristic exclusively or almost exclusively, of *Homo,* has presented some obstacles to the assimilation of a general ecological perspective by anthropology. If culture is not organic and cannot be understood or explained in terms of the laws governing organic and inorganic phenomena, of what possible relevance to its elucidation can be general ecological theory, bound as it is to biological considerations? Further, how can ecology, which deals with that which is common to all species be of assistance in understanding culture which presumably occurs almost exclusively among men?

To circumvent such difficulties Julian Steward some years ago proposed a 'cultural ecology,' an approach based upon the special characteristics of *Homo sapiens* (1955: 30 pp.). The salient feature of this approach is that cultures, separated from the organisms bearing them, are seen to be participating in ecological systems. This separation seemed necessary to Steward because 'Man enters the ecological scene . . . not merely as another organism which is related to other organisms in terms of his physical characteristics. He introduces the super-organic factor of culture, which also affects and is affected by the total web of life (p. 31).' Moreover, the aim of cultural ecology, 'a determination of how culture is affected by its adaptation to the environment' is quite different from that of 'understanding . . . the organic functions and genetic variations of man as a purely biological species (p. 31).'

Several years ago (1967) Vayda and I argued that this strategy is unnecessary and perhaps misguided. We may grant that culture is ontologically distinct from organic phenomena, and may even grant that the laws (whatever they may be) that govern cultural processes are special to cultural phenomena. But ontological distinctiveness and special laws governing operation do not necessarily imply functional autonomy. Let us put this in simpler terms. To say that culture is 'made of' symbols and that organisms are 'made of' cells is hardly to say that they are not continuously interacting. It is, for instance, through a variety of cultural means that one provides the cells of his body with nutriment. To say that cultural processes are governed by laws of their own is not to say that culture does not play a role in yet larger systems subject to yet more general laws, larger systems that include in addition to human culture bearers, other species and non-living things. To employ a simple analogy, an automobile operates in accordance with certain physical laws, notably those of mechanics and thermodynamics. But the automobile also has a role in a larger social system. If we wish to understand how the automobile works, we go to physics. If, on the other hand, we wish to understand its uses and functions we go to economics, sociology, anthropology, and political science. If we wish to understand its effects upon the biosphere, we seek the insights of meteorology and ecology and other biological sciences. And so it is, I would suggest, with culture. While it may be that special laws (anthropologists have generally been unsuccessful in discovering them) govern the ways in which culture works, we must look to larger natural systems if we are to understand the functions and effects of cultural phenomena. In this regard we can do no better, at first, than to cite the sociologist Amos Hawley, who wrote over a quarter of a century ago:

> Culture is . . . a way of referring to the prevailing technique by which a [human] population maintains itself in its habitat. The component parts of culture are therefore identical in principle with the appetency of the bee for honey, the nest building activities of birds, and the hunting habits of carnivora. To argue that the latter are instinctive while the former are not is to beg the question. [1944: 404]

What interests Hawley are not the ontological differences which surely distinguish human culture, which is based upon symbol use, from the behavior of other animals which largely is not, but what is common to them: their functional equivalence. The slaughter and consumption of a deer by a lion armed only with his claws and by hunters armed with bows and arrows or shotguns and speaking to each other while they hunt are, ecologically speaking, transactions of the same general type. In both there is a material exchange between predator and prey populations. It does not, from the ecosystemic point of view, matter that the behavior of the men is cultural and the behavior of the lion is not, and we can surely say that cultures, or components of cultures, form major parts of the distinctive means employed by human populations in fulfilling their biological needs in the ecosystems in which they participate. As Vayda and I have argued, (1967) to so regard culture neither slights what may be its unique characteristics nor demands any sacrifice of anthropology's traditional goals. Indeed, it advances these goals by proposing additional questions to be asked about cultural phenomena. We may ask, for instance, what effects particular social conventions, such as rules of residence and group affiliation (Brookfield and Brown 1963, Leeds, 1965, Meggitt, 1965) or widespread cultural practices, such as warfare (Hickerson, 1965, Sahlins, 1961, Sweet, 1965, Vayda, 1961), have upon the dispersion of human and animal populations over available resources. We may inquire into the effects of religious concepts and rituals upon the birth and death rates and the nutritional status of those who perform them or believe in them (Aschmann, 1959, Freeman, 1970, Harris, 1965, Moore, 1957), and we may investigate the ways in which men regulate the ecosystems which they dominate (Rappaport, 1967, 1968).

In such questions as these we come to the significance of an ecological perspective for anthropology. It leads us to ask whether behavior undertaken with respect to social, economic, political, or religious conventions contributes to or threatens the survival and well-being of the actors, and whether this behavior maintains or degrades the ecological systems in which it occurs. *While the questions are asked about cultural phenomena, they are answered in terms of the effects of culturally informed behavior on biological systems: organisms, populations and ecosystems.* The distinctive characteristic of ecological anthropology is not simply that it takes environmental factors into consideration in its attempts to elucidate cultural phenomena, but that it gives biological meaning to the key terms—adaptation, homeostasis, adequate functioning, survival—of its formulations.

This procedure has certain advantages. First, let us note that the elucidation of 'functions,' the contributions made by items of culture to the survival or adequate functioning of the larger systems of which they are parts, is a long standing concern in the social sciences. Anthropologists have often proposed, as the larger units to which functions refer, cultures and societies. But cultures and societies are often difficult to bound, and it is difficult or impossible to define what is meant by their survival or adequate functioning, let alone to specify the conditions under which they may survive. Much less vagueness inheres in ecological definition. The biological systems to the survival of which cultural phenomena contribute (positively or negatively) may be demarcated in space and time, then counted, weighed and otherwise measured in a variety of ways. This permits us, among other things, to assess the impact of human groups and their technologies upon the ecosystems in which they participate (although measurement problems may be formidable.) Moreover, it is often possible to state at least some of the survival requirements of human groups and of the populations of other species in reasonably precise terms. Thus, we may be able to give empirical meaning to homeostasis by specifying the ranges within which such variables as man-land ratios, soil components or intakes of various nutrients must be held if the systems under study are to function adequately or even to survive.

While the procedures outlined here may be of assistance to anthropology in its efforts to rest its formulations on increasingly sound empirical bases, another aspect of ecological formulation is of greater importance. We approach here the second of the difficulties mentioned earlier, the matter of the relevance of general ecological theory to the elucidation of phenomena observed among the members of only one species.

All creatures, including men, must maintain their numbers within the capacities of their environments to support them. Men as well as other creatures are vulnerable to disease and thirst, parasites and predators. While ecological anthropology shares with the rest of cultural anthropology the aim of elucidating human culture, it differs from much of cultural anthropology in that it attempts to elucidate culture in terms of the part that it plays in those aspects of human existence which are common to all living things. Whereas cultural anthropology has generally taken as its starting point that which is uniquely human, an ecological perspective leads us to base our interpretations of human existence on that which is not uniquely human. As a general principle it may be asserted that the exposure of similarities among a class of phenomena, such as organisms, populations, or living systems in general, must precede any adequate understanding of whatever may distinguish the members of that class from one another. Unless underlying commonalities are recognized and understood the magnitude and significance of differences cannot be assessed. What the broader perspective would take to be relatively minor variations on a common theme may appear as contrasts of enormous magnitude to a narrower view. Moreover, to emphasize first man's status as an animal makes available to anthropological explanation the generalizations of ecology and other biological disciplines which, applying as they do to all of life, are of broader scope than any generalizations which anthropology may provide itself on the basis of its own observations, limited as they are to single species. Other things being equal, explanations of greater generality are to be preferred to those of narrower range because they allow us to introduce more order into our comprehension of the universe.

The strategy suggested to us by the ecological perspective, then, is to view man as a species whose populations live among other species, the better to understand that which distinguishes but does not separate him from the rest of nature, and the better to understand that which distinguishes one group of men from another. The starting point of ecological analysis in anthropology is the simplest and most unexceptionable of all possible assumptions. Men are animals, and like all animals they are bound indissoluably to environments composed of other organisms and non-living substances from which they must derive material and energy to sustain themselves and to which they must adapt if they are not to perish.

III

We have taken cultures to be the means by which human populations maintain themselves in ecological systems, and have thus placed culture in a category that also includes the equipment for survival of other species. But the differences between cultural and other mechanisms for survival are great, and neither these differences nor the difficulties they make for applying general ecological considerations to cultural phenomena should be underestimated.

Culture has provided man with an ecological flexibility far greater than that enjoyed by any other species. Whereas other species can, by and large, participate in only one or a few sorts of ecosystems—the reef, the temperate forest, the tropical savannah—and these only in ways narrowly defined by heredity, men have lived and made their livings everywhere, and in most of the ecological systems in which they are found they are not narrowly bound to particular subsistence techniques. Whereas members of most other species are restricted by their biology to the capture and ingestion of a limited range of foodstuffs, men, thanks partly to cultural means—weaponry, cooking, and cooperation contingent upon symbolic communication—utilize a wide range of plants and animals as food, and have available to them processes other than their own metabolisms by which they can convert material into energy. Moreover, to a much greater extent than other animals, men are able to modify their environments in ways which seem advantageous to them. And men, unlike other species, through reliance upon trade and other cultural conventions for redistributing resources, may inhabit regions which cannot provide them with all that is necessary to fulfill their biological needs. Thus, the problems associated with conceptualizing and studying the ecology of men are more complicated and ramifying than those associated with the study of other species, for they demand that we attend not only to relations between groups of men and the other species with which they are co-resident, but also to relations between groups of men occupying different regions. The study of human ecology cannot ignore such phenomena as warfare, trade, marriage conventions, political organization, or even religion.

A further complication should have now become apparent. The modification of cultures in response to changes in environments is not a simple process in which the features of culture are specified by the character of the environment. Adaptation to the environment through culture is not environmental determination of culture and we cannot predict from the geographical particulars alone of any region what will be the character of the culture prevailing there. How men will participate in any ecosystem depends not only on the structure and composition of that ecosystem, but also upon the cultural baggage of those who enter it, what they and their descendents subsequently receive by diffusion or invent themselves, the demands imposed on the local population from outside, and the needs which may be fulfilled by the local population from abroad. There is great variation in the cultures prevailing even in very similar environments, and it can be argued that cultures are imposed upon nature as well as nature imposed upon cultures.

We must consider the ideological aspects of culture in the light of this observation. Nature is seen by men through a screen composed of beliefs, knowledge, and purposes, and it is in terms of their cultural images of nature, rather than in terms of the actual structure of nature, that men act. Therefore, some anthropologists (Conklin, 1955, Frake, 1962, Rappaport, 1963, Vayda and Rappaport, 1967) have called our attention to the necessity, if we are to understand the environmental relations of men, to take into account their knowledge and beliefs concerning the world around them, and their culturally defined motives for acting as they do. But it should be kept in mind that although it is in terms of their conceptions and wishes that men act in nature it is upon nature herself that they do act, and it is nature herself that acts upon men, nurturing or destroying them. Disparities between men's images of nature and the actual structure of ecosystems are inevitable. Men are gifted learners and may continually enlarge and correct their knowledge of their environments. But their images of nature are always simpler than nature herself, and often incorrect, for the ecological systems in which men live are complex and subtle beyond their comprehension. (Only now is the science of ecology beginning to understand the principles of their operation.)

The discrepancy between cultural images of nature and the actual organization of nature is a critical problem for mankind and one of the central problems of ecological anthropology. To cope with this problem the ecological ethnographer must prepare two models of his subject matter. One, let us call it the 'cognized model,' is a description of the knowledge and beliefs concerning their environment entertained by a people. It is in terms of this model that they act. The second, we may call it 'operational model,' is a description of the same ecological system (including the people) in accordance with the assumptions and methods of the science of ecology. While many components of the physical world are likely to be included in both the cognized and operational models, their membership will seldom, if ever, be identical. The operational model includes those organisms, processes, and cultural practices which ecological theory and empirical observation suggest to the analyst affect the biological well-being of the organisms, populations, and ecosystems under consideration. It may include elements of which the actors may be unaware (such as microorganisms and trace elements) but which affect them in important ways. The cognized model, on the other hand, may well include components, such as supernaturals, whose existence cannot be demonstrated by empirical procedures, but whose putative existence moves the actors to behave in particular ways.

This does not mean, however, that a cognized model is merely a less accurate or more ignorant view of the world than is represented by an operational model written in accordance with the principles of ecology. A cognized model may be regarded as part of a population's distinctive means for maintaining itself in its environment. Since this is the case, the important question concerning a cognized model is not the extent to which it is identical with what the analyst takes to be reality, but the extent to which it elicits behavior appropriate to the biological well-being of the actors and the ecosystems in which they participate. The criterion of adequacy for a cognized model is not its accuracy, but its functional and adaptive effectiveness. Accordingly, the analysis of the ecological eth-

nographer consists of an integration of the cognized and operational models, an integration which permits him to describe the effects of behavior
undertaken with respect to the cognized model on the ecosystem as it is
represented in the operational model. In this way it becomes possible to
assess the adaptiveness not only of overt human behavior, but even of the
ideology which informs that behavior.

IV

It will have been noticed that we have been discussing nature and culture as, virtually, an opposition. This opposition seems to be at least implicit in much human thought. Culture is opposed to nature in the meta-
phors of myth, this dichotomy continues to be expressed in our everyday
use of such pairs as 'natural' versus 'artificial,' and even some anthropological theory, as we have seen, has embraced this distinction. A possible implication, perhaps unwitting, of the opposition of culture to nature in
some anthropological works is that through possessing or being possessed
by culture man has transcended nature, which is composed of organic and
inorganic phenomena. An enormous amount of intellectual effort and not
a little emotion has been expended by men on distinguishing themselves
from the other creatures with which they share the earth, and it may be
that some fundamental characteristic of human psychology lies beneath
this enterprise, for it seems to manifest itself in both science and religion
as well as in everyday thought. Be this as it may, the notion that through
culture man has transcended nature is perhaps reminiscent of certain religious notions. It can be argued that in its attempt to view man naturalis-
tically, anthopology unwittingly produced a conceptualization of man's
position in nature not unlike that of the theology with which it took issue.

The religious conception of man's unique creation only one step lower
than the angels was undermined in the eighteenth century when Linnaeus
classified men among the primates, and further imperiled a century later
when Darwin and his followers proposed that man emerged from a source
common to all of life through a process in no fundamental way different
from that which produced all other species. But his unique position was
restored in the twentieth century by those who have conceived culture
not simply as superorganic, but as autonomous and peculiar to man. Such
a concept of culture has come close to the concept of spirit in Judeo-
Christian thought. Neither culture nor spirit are subject to the laws of nature, but to their own laws which are 'above' or 'beyond' the natural. Both
spirit and culture are possessed by or possess men and not other creatures,

and insofar as man is cultural or spiritual he, and he alone among animals, is in nature but not entirely of it. Cultural evolution, in this view comes to have much in common with salvation, if not, indeed, apotheosis. Culture and spirit are logical equivalents in two bodies of thought which not only distinguish but separate man from the nature of which he is a part.

But superorganic or not, it must be kept in mind that culture is itself of nature. It emerged in the course of evolution through processes of natural selection different only in particulars from those that produced the lion's claws, the tentacles of the octopus, the social habits of the termites. Although culture is most highly developed among men, recent ethological studies have indicated some symbolic capacity among creatures, particularly other primates (Altmann, 1968). And while its operation may be subject to laws of its own, culture is not autonomous. Culture, through its relation to culture-bearing organisms, remains ultimately subservient to laws governing living things. Although cultures may be imposed upon ecological systems there are limits to such impositions, for cultures and components of culture are themselves subject to selective processes. In response to environmental changes cultures must transform themselves (in manners analogous to genetic transformation in response to changed environmental conditions) or the organisms bearing them will either perish or abandon them. Culture has evolved as a means by which certain populations maintain and transform themselves in changing environments, and ecological anthropologists generally hold the view that the survival and well-being of culture-bearing organisms remains the central role of culture to this day.

History and even our everyday experiences may require some justification of these last remarks. Although we may define adaptation and adequate functioning in terms of variables abstracted from living systems—organisms, populations, and ecosystems—it is clear that cultures sometimes serve their own components, such as economic or political institutions, at the expense of men and ecosystems. But, as we have already implied, cultural adaptations, like all adaptations can, and perhaps usually eventually do, become maladaptive (Sahlins, 1964), diminishing rather than enhancing the survival chances of the organisms bearing them. We shall return to the matter of cultural maladaptation later in the chapter.

V

Ecosystems may be of any size (Odum, 1959: 11), and so may ecological populations. A problem for the ecological anthropologist is to distinguish an aggregate which he can take to be an ecological population, and a portion of the biosphere that he may regard as an ecosystem. The matter of distinguishing such units is a complex one that can only be touched upon here. Among the criteria used to locate ecosystemic boundaries is the distribution of particular associations of plants, it being assumed that different animal communities will be found in different plant associations. But in continental areas particularly such a criterion is likely to yield units of such magnitude (e.g., the tundra) that detailed analysis would be very difficult or impossible. Moreover, the borders of systems defined by plant associations are highly permeable. Important material exchanges often flow across such borders. For instance, we can easily distinguish a coral atoll from the ocean which surrounds it. One is terrestrial, one is marine, and the species inhabiting each are different. But organic materials and minerals from the sea are crucial to the survival of the atoll flora and fauna. These are provided by birds who feed at sea but leave much of their droppings on land. Ecosystems, thus, are not sharply bounded and their discrimination rests to a considerable extent upon the goals of a particular analysis.

There are, however, some further leads. Among the food-collecting, horticultural, and peasant peoples traditionally studied by anthropologists it is often possible to distinguish groups exploiting resources (entering into trophic exchanges with other species) entirely, or almost entirely, within certain demarcated areas from which members of other human groups are excluded. It is both convenient and compatible with ecological theory to consider such groups ecological populations, and to regard the borders of the areas they exploit to be ecosystemic boundaries. Among horticulturalists and some peasant peoples, then, local territorial groups, often recognizable communities or kin groups, may be regarded as ecological populations and their territories as ecosystems. Hunters and gatherers, such as the Australian aborigines (Meggitt, 1962) and the Bushmen (Lee, 1968) are usually organized into local bands, but the memberships of these bands are highly transient and band territoriality is not strict. In such situations the ecological population probably must be defined to include all of the bands living in a particular region, and that region to be the ecosystem. Observations and measurements performed on one or a few bands possibly can be used as a statistical sample of the ecological relations of the entire population.

There are, of course, complications. As we have already noted two or more ecologically distinct populations may co-exist in what we may regard as one ecosystem, and one population of, for instance, transhumant pastoralist-farmers dwelling in mountains or gardener-fishermen occupying a coral atoll, many participate in two or more biotically distinct ecosystems in markedly different ways.

It must also be remembered that few human populations live in complete isolation from other groups living outside their territory (with whom they are likely to exchange women and goods, and against whom they may war). But the concept of the ecosystem, a system of feeding relations between ecologically dissimilar populations occupying the same area, can accommodate only awkwardly other kinds of relations between human groups, often ecologically similar, occupying separate localities. Instead of extending, and perhaps diluting, the concept of the ecosystem we may recognize that local ecological populations are also likely to participate in regional exchange systems composed of several or many local populations occupying wider geographical areas, and that their participation in these regional systems is likely to affect the biological variables with which ecological anthropology is concerned. For instance, the maintenance of an adequate birth rate within a local group is likely to depend upon spouses born in other local groups, and these spouses may be expected to labor in subsistence tasks. Death rates are affected by warfare, and warfare sometimes redisperses people over land or redistributes land among people, possibly affecting local population densities significantly. Crops raised by a local group may be dictated by demands from the outside, rather than by their own subsistence requirements. A full understanding of the environmental relations of human populations demands that we inquire into their intra-species regional relations as well as into their inter-species local relations.

VI

Let us now illustrate some of the points made in earlier sections by reference to the Tsembaga, one of about twenty local groups of Maring speakers living in the Bismarck Range in the Territory of New Guinea. In contrast to earlier analyses of this material, we shall pay particular attention here to their cognized model and to its place in their environmental relations.

The Tsembaga, who at the time of fieldwork in 1962-1963 numbered 200 people divided among five putatively patrilineal clans, may be considered an ecological population, and their territory, 3.2 square miles of forested land rising from 2700 to 7200 feet on the south wall of the Simbai

Valley, an ecosystem. About half of their land is arable, and the Tsembaga, who are slash and burn horticulturalists, cut new gardens in the secondary forest up to altitudes of 5000 to 5400 feet each year. Harvesting continues for a year or so to two years, after which the site must be allowed to lie fallow until the secodary forest developing upon it has reached a certain stage of maturity. This takes from seven to forty years, depending upon the site. Staples are root crops. Taro and sweet potatoes are most important, but yams, manioc, bananas, pandanus, and a great variety of greens are also grown. The Tsembaga also raise pigs which, although domiciled and fed in the women's houses, wander loose during the day and provide themselves with most of their diet. In addition to the rations of tubers given them (an adult pig is given about as much as a man) they consume garbage and human feces as well as what they can root up in abandoned gardens and secondary forest.

Immediately to the east of the Tsembaga, on the same valley wall, lies the territory of the Tuguma, a Maring local group with whom the Tsembaga are friendly. The land immediately to the west is occupied by the Kundagai, against whom the Tsembaga waged war four times in the half-century previous to 1962.

The Tsembaga, like all other Maring, are egalitarian. There are no chiefs or other authorities who can command or coerce the obedience of others. But relations between autonomous local populations such as the Tsembaga and the Kundagai, and between such populations and the other species with which they share their territories are regulated by protracted ritual cycles. Indeed, the operation of these cycles helps to maintain an undegraded biotic and physical environment, distributes local surpluses of pig throughout a region in the form of pork, and assures people high quality protein when they are most in need of it. The ritual cycles also limit warfare to frequencies that do not endanger the survival of the regional population but which allow occasional redispersion of people over land and land among people, thus, perhaps, tending to correct discrepancies between the population densities of different local groups. Yet other functions, for the description of which space here is insufficient, inhere in these cycles.[1]

While observations informed by general ecological and cybernetic principles indicate the regulatory functions of Maring ritual cycles, they are

[1] A more detailed description of ritual regulation among the Maring may be found in Rappaport 1968.

not so understood by the Tsembaga and other Maring, who perform them, they say, to maintain or transmute their relations with spirits.

In Maring cosmology there are two sets of spirits, those of the high ground and those of the low ground. The spirits of the high ground include two categories. There are, first, Red Spirits, the spirits of people killed in warfare. As they are said to dwell in the upper reaches of the territory, so are they concerned with the upper part of people's bodies, and the illnesses and cures thereof. The Red Spirits are also concerned with the rituals and taboos of warfare, and their characteristics correlate with this interest. They are said to be hot, like fire, and dry. Hotness and dryness are associated with hardness, strength, and anger, martial virtues which are said to be characteristic of men, and only men participate in most of the rituals addressed to them.

Red Spirits have almost nothing to do with subsistence, although marsupials, which are trapped and eaten (and which mainly inhabit the nonarable high altitude forest thought to be the home of the Red Spirits), are said to be their pigs. Red Spirits are also identified with and sometimes addressed as cassowaries, very large and fierce birds which also favor high altitude forests.

Dwelling with the Red Spirits is another supernatural called Smoke Woman. Unlike the Red Spirits, Smoke Woman was never human. It is through Smoke Woman that the living communicate with the deceased, the link being shamans who, after smoking extremely strong cigars of local tobacco, go into ecstasies during which Smoke Woman comes into their heads and speaks through their mouths, sometimes in tongues.

There are also two categories of spirits dwelling in the lower portion of the territory. First, there is Koipa Mangiang, who, like Smoke Woman, was never human, and who is said to reside in wide places in certain streams. As marsupials are the pigs of the Red Spirits, so eels are said to be the pigs of Koipa Mangiang.

Residing with Koipa in low ground are the Spirits of Rot, the spirits of local people whose deaths have not been the outcome of warfare. In contrast to the Red Spirits, the Spirits of Rot are concerned with the lower portion of the body and while the Red Spirits are hot, hard, and dry, the Spirits of Rot are said to be cold, soft, and wet. These are the soil characteristics that are said to favor plant growth and the Spirits of Rot, and Koipa Mangiang as well, are implicated in the fertility of gardens, pigs, and women. They are also (especially Koipa), associated with death, but death and fertility are seen to be processually related, for growth comes out of the decay, induced by coldness, softness, and wetness, of things once living. The spirits of the low ground, central to the rituals concerned with fertility, are only peripherally involved in warfare rituals.

The virtues of the two sets of spirits stand in clear contrast to each other, although we could, perhaps, note within the cosmology, as I have outlined it, some mediation between them. The Spirits of Rot and the Red Spirits were kinsmen in life, and thus, perhaps, stand, in some logical sense, between Smoke Woman and Koipa Mangiang. But of greater interest than this logical mediation is the dynamic mediation of the ritual cycles, for it is in terms of this mediation among supernatural entities that the actual material variables comprising the ecosystem are regulated.

The ritual cycle, the cognized model in terms of which it is performed, and its effects on both regional and local ecological events processes and variables are shown in the diagram on page 256. We may begin our description with the commencement of warfare. Warfare begins when a member of one local group (such as Tsembaga) inflicts an injury on the member of another local group of sufficient seriousness to demand homicidal vengeance. Such an injury is itself usually a homicide or attempted homicide undertaken as vengeance for a homicide suffered but unavenged in the previous round of warfare.

We have noted that the Red Spirits are primarily associated with warfare, and that their characteristics stand in opposition to those of the spirits of the low ground. Indeed, the virtues of the latter are thought to be inimical to those of the Red Spirits, and to the assistance that they might provide during warfare. It is therefore necessary, when warfare is initiated, to segregate the two sets of spirits and everything associated with them as much as possible, and to identify the community, especially the men, more closely with the Red Spirits. This is accomplished in an elaborate ritual during which certain objects called fighting stones are hung from the center post of a ritual house. This ritual converts the antagonists into the formal category of enemy (the Maring term is 'ax men') if they were not already such from earlier rounds of warfare. Henceforth their territory may not be entered except to despoil it, and they may not be touched or addressed except in anger. In the course of this ritual, in which only men participate, the Red Spirits are taken by the warriors into their heads, where they are said to burn like fire. Sexual intercourse is henceforth tabooed, of course, because contact with the cold, wet, soft women would put out the fires burning in the hot, hard, dry men's heads, and conversely women would be burned by contact with the men. For similar reasons food cooked by women, moist foods, soft foods, and foods identified with the lower altitudes become tabooed to the warriors, who also suffer a taboo on drinking any fluids while actually on the battle ground. The segregation of that associated with the high from that associated with the low, a segregation which is at its most extreme when warfare is initiated (indicated in the diagram by the greater number of x's between the spirits of high and low ground at this time), is suggested by these and other taboos. It is perhaps most clearly indicated by the prohibition against consuming marsupials, the pigs of the Red Spirits, together with the fruit of the marita pandanus, which is associated with the Spirits of Rot (parts of whose mortal remains are buried in pandanus groves). Marsupials and pandanus each may be cooked and consumed, but not in mixture or even at the same meal.

Not only are the two sets of supernaturals segregated from each other, but the living are separated from both by heavy obligations. These are owed even to the spirits of the low ground who are asked, when the stones are hung, to strengthen the warrior's legs. Because of these debts a taboo on the trapping of marsupials goes into effect, although they may be eaten if shot. Eels may neither be trapped nor eaten. Men cannot eat them because eels, being cold and wet, would be inimical to their strength. But they cannot be trapped even for consumption by women because they are the pigs of Koipa Mangiang, and while a debt to him remains his pigs may not be taken. The initiation of warfare, then, results in a maximal segregation of the elements composing the universe, a segregation expressed in taboos and in the debt of the living to the dead.

Fighting can go on for weeks. Sometimes it ended in the rout of one of the parties, and in such cases the victors despoiled the territory of their opponents, then retired to their own ground. Maring say they never seize the land of enemies because, even if they have driven off the living, their ancestors remain to guard it. Usually, however, warfare terminates by agreement between the antagonists that there has been enough fighting and injury and death for the time being.

With the termination of warfare reintegration of the universe commences. If a group remains on its land after the fighting, it ritually plants a sacred shrub called *rumbim*. Each man grasps the plant as it is placed in the ground, thus signifying his membership in the group and the connection of the group to the territory. With this ritual the taboos against sexual intercourse, against eating food cooked by women, and against

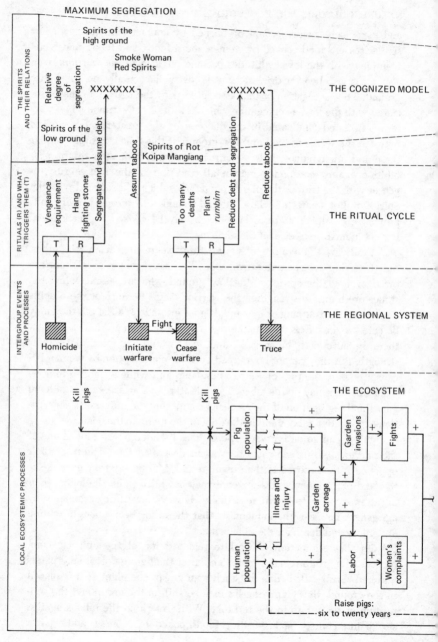

MAXIMUM SEGREGATION

THE SPIRITS AND THEIR RELATIONS

Spirits of the high ground

Smoke Woman
Red Spirits

Relative degree of segregation

XXXXXXX

XXXXXX

THE COGNIZED MODEL

Spirits of the low ground

Spirits of Rot
Koipa Mangiang

RITUALS (R) AND WHAT TRIGGERS THEM (T)

Vengeance requirement

Hang fighting stones

Segregate and assume debt

Assume taboos

Too many deaths

Plant *rumbim*

Reduce debt and segregation

Reduce taboos

THE RITUAL CYCLE

| T | R |

| T | R |

INTERGROUP EVENTS AND PROCESSES

THE REGIONAL SYSTEM

Homicide

Initiate warfare

Fight

Cease warfare

Truce

LOCAL ECOSYSTEMIC PROCESSES

THE ECOSYSTEM

Kill pigs

Kill pigs

Pig population

Garden invasions

+

+

Fights

+

–

Illness and injury

Garden acreage

+

Human population

+

Labor

+

Women's complaints

+

+

Raise pigs:
six to twenty years

256

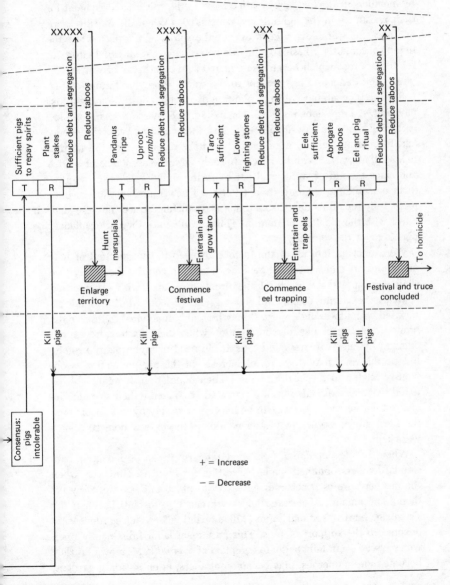

MAXIMUM INTEGRATION
(Koipa Mangiang and
Smoke Woman brought
together in the *tmbi ying*)

+ = Increase

− = Decrease

eating many other foodstuffs are lifted. There is a wholesale slaughter of
pigs when the *rumbin* is planted. All adult and adolescent animals owned
by members of the local group are offered to the spirits as a payment for
their assistance in the fighting just concluded. (When the Maring sacrifice pigs, the spirits are said to devour the spirits of the pigs, while the
living consume their flesh.) It may be noted here that all ritual efforts to
reintegrate that which became segregated at the outbreak of warfare require some reduction of the debt to the spirits through offerings of pig.

But the pigs offered with the planting of *rumbin* constitute only a first
payment. A large debt remains outstanding, and therefore many taboos,
including those on marsupials, eels, and those dealing with the enemy
and forbidding trespass upon enemy territory remain. Since the Maring
believe that warfare can be successful only with the assistance of spirits,
and since the aid of spirits will not be forthcoming if debts to them remain outstanding, a group cannot initiate a new round of warfare until
it has fully repaid its debts from the last. A sanctified truce thus goes into
effect with the planting of *rumbin*. This prevails until there are sufficient
pigs to repay the spirits.

We cannot go into all of the factors involved in the question of how
many pigs are sufficient and how long it takes to acquire them. Here we
shall only note that outside of the rituals associated with warfare and
festivals, the Maring usually kill and consume pigs only during rituals associated with illness and injury. It may be highly functional to reserve the
limited quantity of pig for consumption when their masters are experi-
encing physiological stress and thus are in need of high quality protein,
but be this as it may, the rate of increase of the pig population is obviously related to the health of the human population. It might also be
noted that since all male pigs are castrated (to increase their size and decrease their fierceness) sows can be impregnated only by feral boars, and
the herd grows more slowly than would be the case if domestic boars
were kept.

When the pig population is of moderate size it can be fed upon sub-
standard tubers obtained while harvesting for humans. However, when
the pig herd grows it becomes necessary to plant gardens especially for
them. The amount of acreage and work can be substantial. When the
Tsembaga herd was at maximum (170 animals) 36% of their gardens were
devoted to the support of pigs. This additional labor falls mainly upon
women, who eventually begin to complain of overwork. Moreover, as they
become more numerous, pigs become nuisances, often invading gardens,

and garden invasions cause trouble between pig owners and garden owners. In short, a large number of pigs becomes a burden and a nuisance, and when the pigs have become intolerable to a sufficient number of people to affect the consensus, there are sufficient pigs to repay the ancestors. It takes anywhere from six or seven to twenty years to accumulate this number, which is always likely to be below the carrying capacity of the territory for pigs.

When there are sufficient pigs, stakes marking the boundaries of the local population's territory are ritually planted. If the enemy remains on his territory, they are planted at the old border. If the enemy was driven out, however, the taboo on entering his land is abrogated and the stakes may be planted at new locations incorporating some or all of his land. It is assumed that by this time even the spirits of the enemy's ancestors have departed to take up residence with their living descendants, who, after they were routed, sought refuge with kinsmen living elsewhere. Erstwhile enemy land is thus considered unoccupied, and as such may be annexed.

Also abrogated at this time is the taboo on trapping marsupials, and a ritual trapping period, lasting for one or two months (until a certain variety of pandanus fruit ripens) commences. This culminates in an important ritual in which the *rumbin* planted after the last fight is uprooted. During this ritual there is further debt reduction and important reintegration of the cosmos. The beneficiaries of the slaughter of pigs at this time are mainly the Red Siprits. The pigs offered them are, in part, payment for their past assistance and in part in exchange for the marsupials (their pigs) that have recently been trapped and smoked and are now consumed. A relationship of equality with the Red Siprits, replacing the former indebtedness, is now being approached by the living. Correlated with this, the communion entered into years before by men when they took the Red Spirits into their heads is now concluded. The Red Spirits are asked to take the pig being offered them and leave.

It has already been mentioned that the cassowary is associated with the spirits of the high ground, the pandanus with the low, and from the point of view of reintegration perhaps the most interesting act in this elaborate ritual is the piercing, by a man dancing on hot stones, of a pandanus fruit with a cassowary bone. Then the pandanus is cooked with marsupials, and the mixture consumed. The spirits of the high and the low, long separated, are being drawn closer together, and the congregation, gradually absolving its debts, is drawing closer to both.

With the uprooting of the *rumbin* the taboo on beating drums is abrogated, and a *kaiko*, a year-long festival, culminating the entire ritual cycle, commences. During this festival other local populations are entertained from time to time at elaborate dances, and about six months after the up-rooting of the *rumbin*, when the taro has begun to open in the gardens, the fighting stones are finally lowered during a ritual called *kaiko nde*. With the lowering of the fighting stones, it becomes possible to trap eels, and one to three months later eel traps are placed in special places in var-ious streams. In the meantime friendly groups continue to be entertained, but taro is now the focus of the food presentations to the visitors. Taro is to the Maring the most important of foods; even sacrificial pig is called "taro" in addresses to spirits, and ritual presentations of taro to guests symbolize the ability of the hosts to maintain gardens on the one hand and social relations on the other. Among the Maring food sharing is syn-onymous with friendship; people will not eat food grown by enemies, and to eat a man's taro is to say that he is your friend.

The festival concludes in a series of rituals occurring on successive days and therefore represented together on the diagram. First there is the slaughter of a few pigs dedicated to the Red Spirits in rituals abrogating some residual taboos on relations with other groups arising out of warfare in earlier generations. At this time, too, inter-dining taboos among mem-bers of the local population assumed with respect to each other in mo-ments of anger are abrogated. The renunciation of these taboos permits the locals to perform the rituals which are the climax of the entire ritual cycle. Performed at sacred places in the middle altitudes, and accom-panied by the slaughter of great numbers of pigs, the rituals call to mind the sexual act.

The trapped eels, kept in cages in nearby streams, are carried by young men to the sacred sacrificial places (*raku*) up newly cut pathways, through frond bedecked arches, where they are joined by the women and young girls. The young men, women, and girls proceed together to the center of the *raku* where the eels are removed from their cages and, grasped by their tails, are flailed to death on the flank of a female pig, just slaughtered. The eel and the pig are then cooked together in the *tmbi ying*, a small circular house with a pole projecting through its roof. It is a house, moreover, into which on the previous night both Koipa Man-giang and Smoke Woman had been called and in which both had been present at the same time. The universe has finally been reintegrated.

The next day on the dance ground there is a massive distribution of pork to members of friendly groups through a window in a ceremonial fence especially constructed for the occasion. When the pork has been distributed the hosts, who have assembled behind the fence, crash through to join the throng dancing on the dance ground. Yesterday they reunited the high with the low and themselves with both in what might appear to the observer to have been a great procreative act. Today, in what may be a rebirth, they have broken through the restrictions separating them from their neighbors. Their debts to both the living and the dead have been repaid, and if the Australian government had not recently pacified the Maring area they would have been free to again initiate warfare, for the sanctified truce has ended.

The attempt here has been, first, to represent Maring cosmology, the cognized model associated with highest level regulation (there are also lower level cognized models dealing with the specifics of gardening, etc.), in dynamic structural terms. I have further attempted to relate Maring cosmology, by representing it structurally, to Maring material relations. On the basis of this illustration it may be suggested that the relationship of the cognized model to the operational model is similar to that of the 'memory' of an automated control device to the physical system it regulates. It is in terms of the understandings included in the cognized model that the ritual cycle is undertaken, but the ritual cycle in fact regulates material relations in the local ecological system and in the regional system. The operation of the entire cycle is cybernetic. In response to signals from the ecosystem (e.g. complaints of women concerning the burdens of pig husbandry) ritual actions are undertaken with respect to supernaturals (there are sufficient beasts to repay them, and sacrifices are made), but these actions have corrective effects upon the ecosystem (the pig population is reduced and women's labor in pig husbandry is reduced).

VII

How structures such as Maring cosmology develop remains a problem for which no satisfactory solution can yet be offered. Nevertheless, as bizarre as it may seem, it is not improper to regard this cosmology as a functional, perhaps even adaptive, codification of reality. We earlier argued that the criterion by which we assess the adequacy of a cognized model is not whether or not it conforms to our notions of the physical structure of nature, but whether or not it elicits behavior contributing to the well-being of the actors and to the maintenance of the ecosystem of which they are parts. It can only be suggested, in the absence of any studies, that to the extent that a cognized model fulfills this canon of adequacy it will be favored by selective forces.

But that the Maring cognized model and the rituals undertaken in accordance with it are adaptive or functional does not suggest that cognized models will always be so. Furthermore, it seems to become more apparent each day that there is no simple direct relationship between the amount of testable empirical knowledge included in a cognized model and the appropriateness of the behavior that it elicits. It is by no means certain that the representations of nature provided us by science are more adaptive or more functional than those images of the world, inhabited by spirits whom men respect, that guide the actions of the Maring and other 'primitives.' Indeed, they may be less so, for to drape nature in supernatural veils is perhaps to provide her with some protection against human parochialism and destructiveness, a parochialism and destructiveness that may be encouraged by a natural view of nature. It may be suggested, in light of our earlier discussions, that it is more adaptive to sanctify nature than culture. It also may be suggested that it is not yet clear whether civilization, the state, science, and mechanized technology are, in the long run, adaptive. And since civilization, state organization, science, and mechanized technology are recent developments in the evolution of culture, we may ask to what ends evolution might be leading us.

Anthropology has long been concerned with evolution, which it takes to be a set of processes producing either general increases in organization (advance or general evolution) or organizational changes enhancing survival chances in particular environments (adaptation). Adaptive studies in cultural anthropology are nicely exemplified by Sahlins' (1958) detailed investigation of traditional Polynesian societies, in which he argues cogently that important differences in social and political organization among those closely related peoples was a result of adaptation to islands differing in topography, area, and the location of resources. More recently Kottak (1971) has made a similar but less detailed analysis of cultural differences among related Madagascan groups. Works of Steward (1949), Wittfogel (1957), Wright (1969) and others on the emergence of state organization and civilization are among many concerned with evolutionary advance.

But adaptation and increase in organization do not exhaust the processes and results of evolution. As we noted earlier, evolution may also produce maladaptation, and maladaptation leads eventually to death. The very process of becoming organized to maintain itself under a particular set of environmental conditions may decrease the ability of a population to change its organization under changed conditions (Service, 1960), and what we call evolutionary advances may solve old problems by creating new ones. For instance, the development of the social differentiation, occupational specialization, and administrative hierarchies characteristic of the state surely made possible the existence of larger, denser populations living under more secure circumstances in organizations spanning wider and more diverse regions than had previously been the case. But these very features of state organization created ecological and social problems that have yet to be solved. For one thing, production goals set by supralocal authorities, or in light of supra-local considerations, are more likely to exceed the capacity of local ecological systems than are production goals set by local authorities or in terms of local requirements. The possibility of such violation is increased with increasing depth and complexity of administrative or economic structures because such increases in depth and complexity increase the likelihood of distortion, error, and tardiness in the communication of information, concerning environmental or other conditions, in response to which regulatory actions are taken. Further, when regulatory functions come to inhere in particular persons (bureaucrats, managers, or administrators) the misdirection of regulatory operations becomes more likely. The goal of regulation may no longer remain the well-being of men and the preservation of ecosystems, but may become the preservation of particular political, social, or economic institutions, perhaps at the expense of living systems. Moreover, when particular groups with special functions, like industrial firms or particular industries, become powerful they have a tendency to capture, or to attempt to capture, the agencies regulating them, and to elevate their own purposes to positions of pre-eminence in the larger living systems of which they are only parts. This process and the values rationalizing it were nicely summed up in the famous remark by Charles Wilson, an ex-president of General Motors, when he was Secretary of Defense of the United States. 'What is good for General Motors,' he said, 'is good for America.'

I would suggest that no matter how benign the purposes of General Motors may be, what is good for General Motors, or any such firm, cannot in the long run be good for America because for America to commit herself to what is good for General Motors is for America to sacrifice evolutionary flexibility, that is to say ability to adapt to circumstances continuously changing in ways that cannot be foreseen.

The purpose of modern industrial firms, as Galbraith (1967) and others before him have pointed out, is simply to perpetuate themselves. At their hearts are machines, and the perpetuation of industrial firms is a matter of keeping their machines running, much as the perpetuation of organisms is a matter of keeping their organs functioning. If this view is correct, the products of an industry—automobiles, deodorants, biological weapons, breakfast foods, pesticides, or whatever, are merely incidental to, even waste products of, 'industrial metabolism,' much as excreta is the waste of biological metabolism.

Because their machinery represents enormous investments, and because they employ very large numbers of people, industrial firms have become central to the economy of the modern world. As such, their perpetuation becomes the most compelling concern of the modern state. Thus, regulatory agencies, including the highest levels of government, come eventually to serve the interests of industries, which is to say the interests of vast complexes of machinery to which men have become subservient and for which ecosystems are nothing more than sources of raw material and dumping grounds.

Increasing industrialization has generally been regarded by members of western society to be virtually the *sine qua non* of progress, and increase in the amount of energy harnessed per capita of population has been proposed by an anthropologist (White, 1949: 368 pp, 1959: 144) as the most significant criterion of evolutionary advance. But the general ecological perspective that we have advocated here, which assigns biological meaning, and biological meaning only, to such terms as adaptation, adequate functioning, homeostasis and survival, at the very least suggests to us that some aspects of what we have called progress or evolutionary advance are, in fact, pathological or maladaptive. Perhaps it will be possible to build upon the foundation of general ecology a theory of cultural pathology and of the evolution of maladaptation in terms of which we might examine the institutions and ideology of our own as well as other societies. Such a theory could, perhaps, become part of our own adaptation, our own means for perpetuating ourselves and preserving those living systems to which we remain indissolubly bound and upon which we continue to be utterly dependent.

References Cited

Allee, W. C., A. E. Emerson, O. Park, T. Park, and K. P. Schmidt
  Principles of Animal Ecology. W. B. Saunders, Philadelphia and London, 1949.
Altmann, S. A.
  'The Structure of Primate Social Communication.' *in* S. A. Altmann (ed.), *Social Communication among the Primates.* Univ. of Chicago Press, Chicago, 1967, 325-362.
Aschmann, Homer
  'The Central Desert of Baja California: Demography and Ecology.' *Ibero-Americana,* 42 (1959).
Barth, Frederick
  'Ecologic Relationships of Ethnic Groups in Swat, North Pakistan,' *American Anthropologist,* 58 (1956):1079-1089.
Brookfield, Harold, and Paula Brown
  Struggle for Land. Melbourne, Oxford University Press, 1963.
Conklin, Harold C.
  'Hanunoo Agriculture in the Philippines.' *FAO Forestry Development Paper #12.* Food and Agriculture Organization of the United Nations, Rome, 1957.
Frake, Charles O.
  'Cultural Ecology and Ethnography.' *American Anthropologist,* 64 (1962): 53-59.
Freeman, M. M. R.
  'Not by Bread Alone: Anthropological Perspectives on Optimum Population' in F. R. Taylor, *The Optimum Population for Britain.* London, Academic Press, 1970, 139-149.
Galbraith, John Kenneth
  The New Industrial State. Houghton Mifflin, Boston, 1967.
Harris, Marvin
  'The Myth of the Sacred Cow' *in* Anthony Leeds and A. P. Vayda (eds.), *Man, Culture and Animals.* American Association for the Advancement of Science, Washington, 1965.
Hawley, Amos
  'Ecology and Human Ecology.' *Social Forces,* 22 (1944):308-405.
Hickerson, Harold
  'The Virginia Deer and Intertribal Buffer Zones in the Upper Mississippi Valley in Anthony Leeds and A. P. Vayda (eds.), *Man, Culture and Animals,* American Association for the Advancement of Science, 1965.
Kottak, Conrad
  'A Cultural Adaptive Approach to Malagasy Political Organization' in E.

Wilmsen (ed.), *Subsistence and Exchange Systems*. University of Michigan Museum Series in Anthropology, Ann Arbor, 1971.

Kroeber, A. L.
'The Superorganic.' *American Anthropologist* 19 (1917):163-213.

Lee, Richard
'What Hunters Do for a Living, or How To Make Out on Scarce Resources' in Richard Lee and Irven DeVore (eds.), *Man the Hunter*. Chicago, Aldine Publishing Co., 1968, 30-49.

Leeds, Anthony
'Reindeer Herding and Chukchi Social Institutions' in Anthony Leeds and A. P. Vayda (eds.), *Man, Culture and Animals*. American Association for the Advancement of Science, 1965, 87-128.

Levi-Strauss, Claude
The Elementary Structures of Kinship. Eyre and Spottiswoode London, 1969 (first published 1949 in French, under the title "Les Structures Elementaires de la Parante).

Meggitt, M. J.
The Desert People, Angus and Robertson, Sydney, 1962.
The Lineage System of the Mae Enga of New Guinea. Oliver and Boyd, Edinburg and London, 1965.

Moore, Omar Khayyam
'Divination—a New Perspective.' *American Anthropologist*, 59 (1957): 69-74.

Odum, Eugene P.
Fundamentals of Ecology. W. B. Saunders, Philadelphia and London. 1959.

Rappaport, Roy A.
'Aspects of Man's Influence on Island Ecosystems: Alteration and Control.' *In* F. R. Fosberg (ed.), *Man's Place in the Island Ecosystem*. Bishop Museum Press, Honolulu, 1963.
'Ritual Regulation of Environmental Relations Among a New Guinea People.' *Ethnology*, 6 (1967):17-31.
Pigs for the Ancestors. Yale University Press, New Haven, 1968.

Reid, Leslie
The Sociology of Nature, Pelican, New Orleans, 1958.

Sahlins, Marshall D.
Social Stratification in Polynesia. University of Washington Press, Seattle, 1958.
'The Segmentary Lineage: An Organization of Predatory Expansion.' *American Anthropologist*, 63 (1961):322-345.
'Culture and Environment' in Sol Tax (ed.), *Horizons of Anthropology*. Chicago, Aldine Publishing Co., 1964, 132-147.

Service, Elman
> The Law of Evolutionary Potential *in* Sahlins, Marshall and Elman Service (eds.) Evolution and Culture. University of Michigan Press, Ann Arbor, 1960, 99-122.

Steward, Julian
> 'Development of Complex Societies: Cultural Causality and Law: A Trial Formulation of the Development of Early Civilizations.' *American Anthropologist*, 51 (1949) reprinted in Julian Steward, *Theory of Culture Change*. University of Illinois Press, Urbana, 1955.

Sweet, Louise
> 'Camel Pastoralism in North Arabia and the Minimal Camping Unit' in Anthony Leeds and A. P. Vayda (eds.), *Man, Culture and Animals*. American Association for the Advancement of Science, 1965.

Vayda, Andrew P.
> 'Expansion and Warfare among Swidden Horticulturalists.' *American Anthropologist* 63 (1961):345-358.

Vayda, Andrew P., and Roy A. Rappaport
> 'Ecology, Cultural and Non-Cultural' *in* James Clifton (ed.), *Introduction to Cultural Anthropology*. Houghton-Mifflin, Boston, 1967.

White, Leslie
> *The Science of Culture.* Farrar and Strauss, New York, 1949.
> *The Evolution of Culture.* McGraw-Hill, New York, 1959.

Wittfogel, Karl
> *Oriental Despotism. A Comparative Study of Total Power.* Yale University Press, New Haven, 1957 .

Wright, Henry T.
> 'The Administration of Rural Porduction in an Early Mesopotamian Town.' *Anthropological Papers* #38. Museum of Anthropology, University of Michigan, Ann Arbor, 1969.

Wynne-Edwards, V. C.
> *Animal Dispersion in Relation to Social Behavior.* Oliver and Boyd, Edinburgh and London, 1962.

X

Language and Writing

LANGUAGE IS SO MUCH A PART of our daily activities that some of us may come to look upon it as a more or less automatic and natural act like breathing or winking. Of course, if we give the matter any thought at all, we must realize that there is nothing automatic about language. Children must be taught their native tongue and the necessary training takes a long time. Language is not something that is inherited; it is an art that can be passed on from one generation to the next only by intensive education.

It is difficult to realize the enormously important role that language plays in our social behavior. What would a society without language be like? It would of course have no writing or other means of communication by words, for all these are ultimately dependent on spoken speech. Our means of learning would therefore be greatly restricted. We should be obliged, like the animals, to learn by doing or by observing the actions of others. All of history would disappear, for without language there would be no way of re-creating past experiences and communicating them to others. We should have no means of expressing our thoughts and ideas to others or of sharing in the mental processes of our fellowmen. Indeed, it is very likely that we should not think at all. Many psychologists maintain that thought itself requires the use of language, that the process of thinking is really talking things over with ourselves.

A society lacking language would be incapable of engaging in any but the simplest of co-operative enterprises. An individual or group of individuals would have no way of planning such activities, of explaining them to others, or of directing the actions of the participants in co-operative enterprises toward the common goal. Each individual would

268

be to a large extent dependent on his own strength and ability since he would lack the means of securing the help of others.

Most important, a society lacking language would have no means of assuring the continuity of behavior and learning necessary to the creation of culture. Human society, without culture, would be reduced to the level of present-day ape societies. Apes have a bodily structure very like our own. Like humans, they learn readily from experience and by observing and imitating the actions of others. A number of experimenters have shown that apes not only learn to use tools but also invent them. Despite, however, the fact that individual apes learn easily and, as individuals, show remarkable progress in the acquisition of knowledge, apes as a species have never developed a culture.

There are two reasons for this. Lacking language, the apes have no way of continuing in word and thought their separate experiences in the use of tools and techniques. When an ape has disposed of a problem the knowledge he has derived from that experience remains static. He may remember it when and if another problem of the same sort arises, but he does not in between times mull over his knowledge and devise means of applying it to further problems. Man does. His overt experiences with practical problems are, like those of the ape, separate and distinct. But because man possesses language, he can continue his problem-solving activities beyond the actual physical experience and so develop, in thought and discussion, new applications of his knowledge and improved means of solving problems. In short, by reason of language, man's experiences are continuous, not discontinuous as among apes, and so show far more rapid development.

Secondly, man's possession of language enables him to share the experiences and thoughts of his fellows and to re-create his personal experiences for their benefit. An ape's knowledge, acquired through experience and observation, is his alone, except in so far as he can demonstrate it in physical activity so that it may be acquired by another ape. No matter how skillful an ape may become in the use of tools and techniques, his offspring will be obliged to begin their learning as he began his, by experience and observation. The learned ape cannot communicate his knowledge and so enable his successors to build upon it. Culture among men reveals progress. Each generation takes over, by word of mouth and tradition, the accumulated knowledge of their predecessors, add their own contributions as drawn from their experiences and observations, and pass the whole on to succeeding generations. This cumulative aspect, which differentiates human cultures from the kind of knowledge current in animal societies, is made possible by language.

THE ANTIQUITY OF LANGUAGE

Studies of the skeletal and cultural remains of ancient man have shown that the first human beings came into being about one million years ago. Man's early cultures were very simple and crude and we know only a portion of their material remains, the tools and implements made of materials tough enough to withstand the passage of time. It is highly significant, however, that these early traces of man's cultures reveal a cultural continuity through time. As we study the several chronological phases of culture in any given area of the world, there is revealed a slow but steady advance both in the number of tools made and in the complexity of their manufacture. The men of successive generations did not begin anew each generation to fashion their cultures but built upon the techniques which had been discovered in the past and transmitted to them by their ancestors.

The fact that the history of man's cultures shows a continuous and cumulative development extending from their earliest beginnings to the present means of course that man has possessed language as long as he has possessed culture. Language must be as old as the oldest of man's cultural artifacts; it began when culture began and has developed continuously ever since.

This inference as to the age of language is amply borne out by other observations which may be made on modern languages. First, it is clear that all human societies have possessed a language for as long as we have known them; there is no group of men anywhere, today or in the past, who lack this important aspect of culture. Secondly, we may also observe that modern languages are very numerous and exceedingly diverse. The precise number of distinct languages spoken today cannot even be estimated, but we know that there are several thousand. Some of these are historically related to one another; that is, they are clearly derived from a single earlier tongue. Languages so derived are said to belong to the same linguistic family or stock, and there are hundreds of such stocks in the world today. Most of these stocks show no resemblance whatsoever to each other, because, as we may almost certainly assume, all traces of common origin have long since disappeared.

The universality of language and the amazing diversity of modern idioms can only mean that language is very old. Studies of languages known for centuries through the medium of written records reveal that languages change with relative slowness. Thus, though English and German have certainly been separate languages for well over 2000 years, they still retain many obvious similarities in both vocabulary and grammar which point clearly to their common origin. The enormous diversity of modern languages, then, must have taken a very long time to achieve.

A third and final evidence as to the antiquity of language is found in the fact that known languages, ancient or modern, cannot be classed in terms of their level of development. There are neither primitive languages nor highly developed ones, if we take into account only their structural features.

Thus, all the languages we know possess a well-defined system of distinctive speech sounds. These are finite in number, are carefully distinguished from one another, and are put together to form words, phrases, and sentences in accordance with definite rules. In this respect, there is no real difference between the languages of people who possess very simple and crude cultures and those of the highly civilized peoples of Europe and America.

Similarly, all human groups, regardless of the crudity of their culture, have a vocabulary sufficiently detailed and comprehensive to meet every need likely to arise. Languages vary, of course, in the size of their vocabularies, but this variation is cultural, not linguistic. The language of a people having a relatively simple or undeveloped culture may have a smaller vocabulary than one belonging to a group with a relatively complex and highly developed culture. It is notable, however, that the vocabulary of any group, however simple its culture, appears to be indefinitely expansible. As new cultural items are invented or borrowed, the vocabulary increases or changes to meet the new requirements imposed upon it.

Finally, all languages possess a definite and clear-cut system of grammar. Grammar may briefly be defined as the meaningful arrangement of sounds or combinations of sounds to produce words, phrases, and sentences. Well-defined rules governing such arrangements are found in all languages, whether they are spoken by the pre-literate Pygmies of the Congo forest or the culturally advanced groups of modern Europe.

The basic similarities mean, of course, that language has so long been a human possession as to have developed to about the same level among peoples the world over. There remain today no traces of an earlier and cruder stage of linguistic development.

The Origin of Language

Spoken languages obviously leave no trace in the ancient deposits which mark the history of man's cultures. Written records of human languages began only a few thousand years ago; before that time no human group possessed the technique of writing. It is evident, then, that we have no direct evidence as to the origin of language or of the long period of history that elapsed between its beginnings and the first written records. The problem of the origin of language will never therefore be solved in the sense that we shall know directly the circumstances under which language arose or be able to trace in terms of specific historical events the course of its development.

Many theories have been advanced as to the origin of language. Most of these, however, are based on two central hypotheses: the interjectional and the sound imitative or onomatopoeic theory of the origin of language.

Interjectional theories maintain, in general, that interjections or involuntary cries, because these are a good deal alike in all modern tongues, form the earliest stratum of words used by man. All other forms, it follows, must have been derived from these in one or other manner. Sound imitative theories look to words like *bow wow, meow, choo choo,* or *ding dong,* and similar attempts by men to imitate animal cries and noises as marking the beginnings of language. From such imitations of sounds encountered in his environment, man formed the hundreds of languages we now find spoken.

Both hypotheses fail to solve our problem, however, largely because they fail to account for true linguistic forms. Neither involuntary cries nor sound imitative words are as such true linguistic forms. An involuntary cry is really part of an individual's response to strong stimuli. The involuntary ejaculation of surprise is not the same as the conventional word written *Oh!* because the former represents part of the response itself and does not, like the conventional *Oh!,* symbolize the response of surprise. True linguistic symbols, such as words, are all conventional and arbitrary, and their meanings must be learned by speakers. No one learns an involuntary cry; a baby may cry out long before it learns to speak.

Sound imitative words must similarly not be confused with attempts to reproduce sounds characteristic of man's environment. A word like *ding dong,* for example, is a conventionalized representation of the sound of a bell, not necessarily self-evident to anyone except a speaker of English who has learned to associate the sound *ding dong* with the ringing of bells. To understand how languages came into being we must know how man came to establish his arbitrary or conventional habits of associating speech sounds with experience. This is not explained by the sound imitative hypothesis which points out merely that men sometimes name things and actions by the noises they make and that on occasion such names become truly a part of language.

It follows, then, that a useful theory of linguistic origins must be based on a more careful analysis and study of modern tongues. Such studies, as we have suggested, reveal that the elements of speech, such as words, phrases, and sentences, are arbitrary symbols. By this we mean symbols which are themselves no part of the reality or experience symbolized. Thus, for example, the particular succession of sounds which make up the word *horse* have no necessary relation to the class of animals symbolized by it. There is, in short, nothing horse-like about the word *horse;* it is simply that speakers of English have learned to associate the sounds written *horse* with a given class of animal, just as they have learned to associate the forms *dog* and *cat* with wholly different groups of animals.

The fact that linguistic symbols are nearly all arbitrary in nature emphasizes the social aspect of language. Languages are always associated with groups of individuals; they never belong exclusively to a single individual. An individual acquires his language from the group with which he lives. If he deviates widely in speech from other members of the group, he runs the risk of being misunderstood or of not being understood at all. *Horse* is not just a word peculiar to an individual speaker of English, it is a word used and understood in much the same way by all English-speaking peoples.

Languages function in human societies primarily as a means of communication and co-operation. By means of language an individual is able not only to re-create his own personal experiences and so share them with others, but he is also able to co-ordinate his labors with those of others. A group of men can thus work together in a task too heavy or too complex to be undertaken by any one of them singly. To exemplify this point, let us imagine that a man, hunting alone, manages to kill an animal too large for him to handle. He leaves the dead animal and returns to his encampment or village. There he tells the others what he has done and secures their assistance. They return to his kill with him and assist him to skin the game, cut up the meat, and carry it back to camp.

During the whole of this procedure, one individual may take charge, indicating in words the task each is to perform, so that the separate acts of each man will assist rather than obstruct the total performance.

Contrast the action we have just described with a similar incident among, let us say, a pack of wolves. Here, too, we have a social group albeit one composed of animals who lack language. When one of the wolves makes a kill alone, he will eat as much as he can; he will not be concerned or able to inform the pack of his feat. But should the other wolves come upon him as he makes the kill or while he is eating the carcass, they will certainly join him uninvited. Each wolf will get as much as he can and if there is not enough to go around, the weaker wolves will get none at all. The actions of the wolves in disposing of the meat will be separate and individual, with no co-ordination or co-operation whatsoever.

It is probable that the ancient animals from whom man evolved lived in groups very similar to those of present-day animals. Their behavior was only in a small degree co-ordinated. Each worked for himself alone, with the exception that the very young had to be cared for by an adult. On occasion, however, necessity must have enforced some degree of co-operation and co-ordinated effort. Man's primitive ancestor was not a formidable animal in comparison with many others who shared his environment. He must often have had to defend himself against stronger predatory animals and he probably discovered very early that such defense was more effective if undertaken in co-operation with his fellows. When such co-operative enterprises increased in frequency, the habit pattern built up may easily have led to co-operation under other circumstances, such as, for example, the hunting of large animals for food. Even wolves hunt together and, while so doing, correlate their efforts, at least to some degree.

The development of co-operative labor did not alone bring about language, however. Many insect groups are effectively co-operative without language. But co-operation among insects is evidently on a different basis than among men. Unlike the social insects men are not born to a given role in their social groups. Men must learn to adapt their behavior to the roles provided by the society, and language provides a vital tool to this kind of learning.

How and in what way man's animal ancestors came to employ language as an aid in co-operative labor we shall never know. We may safely assume, however, that man's primitive ancestor could and did

make noises and perhaps the noises which accompanied the tasks undertaken together came slowly to symbolize the several actions and ends
involved in such tasks. In any case, it appears to be fairly certain that
language arose as a result of men learning to work together toward a
common end. For whatever reasons, man's primitive ancestors were
obliged to acquire such learning, and so they, alone of the animals,
stumbled upon the tool, language, which more than any other makes
co-operative and co-ordinated activity effective.

THE STRUCTURE OF LANGUAGE

Languages, like many other cultural phenomena, cannot be observed
or studied directly. Just as we can describe a method of making baskets
only by observing the actions of individuals who are weaving them, so
can we describe a language only by observing the speech behavior of
those who use the language.

Individual acts of speech are called utterances. These are complete
in themselves and consist of a flow of speech sounds uninterrupted by
the speech of another individual. Some utterances may be quite short,
like *Oh!, Come!, Who?*, or *John*. Others are longer: *John runs, I see a
man*, or *The man we saw yesterday is dead*. Still others may be very
long, examples of these are found in speeches, lectures, or sermons. A
first step in studying a language is then to collect utterances, as many
as possible, from native speakers of the language.

Once this has been done, it soon becomes obvious that utterances
differ not only in length but also in structure. Some of them consist of
a single unit which cannot be interrupted without considerable change
in meaning. If, for example, we say *John runs?*, it is evident that the
forms *John* and *runs* are interdependent. To stop after we have said
John is like playing an unresolved chord on the piano; the listener awaits
impatiently the completion of the utterance. We can of course say *John?
Runs?* but here we create a new meaning, quite different from that of
John runs?

Utterances consisting of a single unit are called constructions and the
interdependent parts of this unit are said to be united grammatically to
one another. An utterance like *John? Runs?*, on the other hand, is made
up of two units which are not held together grammatically but only follow one another without interruption.

Grammarians express the difference we have illustrated by comparing
John runs? with *John? Runs?* by saying that *John runs?* consists of one

sentence while *John? Runs?* is two sentences. A sentence, then, is an utterance the parts of which are united grammatically into a construction and which is not itself a part of some larger construction. All utterances, it is clear, must contain at least one sentence.

Sentences, like utterances, vary in length and complexity. Thus, all of the following are sentences, though from first to last they increase both in length and complexity. *John, John runs, Poor John runs fast, Poor John runs very fast, Poor John, the boy next door, is decidedly the best runner of the group.* These examples reveal that sentences may be divided into still smaller units called phrases and words. A word may be defined as the smallest portion of a sentence which can be pronounced alone and still retain meaning. All of the forms written separately in the examples cited above are words, since all of them, pronounced alone, have meaning to a speaker of English. Phrases consist of two or more words, not a sentence, which compose a construction. It is obvious that some combinations may function sometimes as sentences and at other times as phrases. Thus, the combination *Poor John,* taken alone, is a sentence, but as part of *Poor John runs fast,* it functions as a phrase.

All sentences, it is clear, must possess at least one word. Longer sentences may contain two or more phrases, but the limits of sentence length depend so much upon individual or social preferences as to defy accurate definition.

The total stock of words possessed by a language is called its vocabulary or dictionary. Languages differ as to the size of their vocabularies. In general the size of a vocabulary is directly related to the culture of a speech community. If the culture is complex, as among most English-speaking peoples, the vocabulary may be very large and contain numerous highly technical sub-divisions. In a simple and relatively uniform culture, such as that of the Polar Eskimo, the vocabulary will be correspondingly smaller and contain fewer technical aspects. It should not be assumed, however, that so-called primitive peoples have very small vocabularies. We frequently hear, for example, of very primitive folk whose languages possess at most only a few hundred words. This is obvious nonsense for even the simplest culture requires a far greater number of words merely to enumerate the many objects and acts dealt with in the course of every-day occupations.

When we examine the vocabulary of a language and compare the words it contains with one another we soon discover that words, like sentences and utterances, also vary in size and complexity. Take for example English pairs like *dog, dogs; work, worker; black, blackish; combine, recombine; do, undo*. *Dogs* is obviously derived from *dog* by the addition of *-s, worker* from *work* by adding *-er*, *blackish* from *black* by adding *-ish*, *recombine* from *combine* by adding *re-*, and *undo* from *do* by adding *un-*. Each of the added elements conveys meaning: *-s* denotes the plural, *-er* means 'one who,' *-ish* means 'something like' (that is, a blackish object is one which is colored something like one which is black), *re-* means 'to do something again' (in this case, to combine again), and *un-* conveys a negative or opposite meaning (to undo a knot is the opposite or negative of 'doing' or tying a knot). These added elements are not words, however, because they are never spoken alone but always in combination with some other form (either a whole word or part of a word). Some words may contain more than one such element, each adding a measure of meaning to the completed word. Thus, the word *ungentlemanly* is formed by adding *un-* (not) to *gentlemanly*. *Gentlemanly*, in turn, consists of *gentleman* plus the ending *-ly*, meaning 'in such and such a way or manner.' Finally, *gentleman* is itself composed of *gentle* plus *man* though the meaning of the combination is no longer the same as the sum of the meanings of its two constituent parts.

Words and parts of words like *dog, -s, work, -er, combine, re-, black, -ish, do,* and *un-* are called simple linguistic forms or morphemes. Some morphemes, like *dog* and *work*, may be pronounced alone; these are called free morphemes. Others, like *-ish* and *un-*, are never pronounced alone and are therefore called bound morphemes. Combinations containing more than one morpheme, such as *dogs* or *worker*, are complex linguistic forms. Complex linguistic forms also include phrases, sentences, and utterances, however. Words having more than one morpheme are usually described as derived words or derivations.

Languages differ greatly in word structure. In some of them, Chinese is a good example, most words have but one morpheme; derivations are extremely rare. In others, like English, there may be many single morpheme words plus a large number of words having two or three morphemes and a smaller number having more than three morphemes. Languages like Navaho or Eskimo are found at the opposite extreme in so far as word structure is concerned for here we may find large numbers of so-called polysynthetic words possessing as many as eight or ten or even more morphemes.

When morphemes are combined to form words and when words are combined into phrases and sentences, these combinations always follow definite rules of arrangement. Some morphemes, like *re-* and *un-* always precede the forms with which they are combined and so are called prefixes. Others, like *-er* and *-s,* follow the elements to which they are attached, these are suffixes. Rules of arrangement having to do with the structure of words in a language make up its morphology, one branch of grammar, which we may define as the meaningful arrangement of linguistic forms. The second branch of grammar is called syntax and has to do with the meaningful arrangement of words to form phrases and sentences.

Languages differ widely in grammar. In English sentences of the type *he runs,* for example, the verb *runs* has an ending *-s* because the pronoun is singular and third person. With pronouns like *I, you, we,* and *they,* we use *run,* not *runs.* Similarly, we say *a man runs* but *men run.* Grammarians express this rule of grammar by saying that third person forms of present tense verbs must agree in number with the pronoun or noun which precedes them. If the noun or pronoun is singular, the verb is also (as in *he runs, a man runs*) but when the noun or pronoun is plural, so also is the verb (*they run, men run*).

In German, however, the matter of grammatical agreement between pronoun and verb in the present tense is more complicated. Here, very often, we find a different verb form for every pronoun as in *ich laufe* 'I run,' *du läufst* 'you run,' *er läuft* 'he runs,' and *wir laufen* 'we run.'

Similar differences occur in English and German nouns. In English, the definite article *the* is used before almost any noun, as in *the man, the woman,* and *the maiden.* The German definite article, however, is different in each of these cases: *der Mann* 'the (masculine gender) man,' *die Frau* 'the (femine gender) woman,' and *das Mädschen* 'the (neuter gender) maiden.'

A final step in understanding linguistic structure is to compare morphemes with one another. Such comparison reveals that morphemes are composed of distinctive sounds called phonemes. Thus in English it is obvious that the morphemes *cat* and *pat* are alike except for the initial phoneme, that *cat* and *cot* differ only in their medial phoneme, and that *cat* and *cap* are distinguished by their final phonemes. *Cat,* then is composed of three phonemes and any change in any one of them will change *cat* to some other English morpheme or to an English-like nonsense word (for example *cet*).

The same thing is true of all other languages, that is, in all languages morphemes are built up of one or more phonemes. Languages vary greatly, however, in the complexity of their morphemes and in the kinds of phonemes they may employ. In some languages, morphemes may be very simple, in others the average morpheme may include a relatively large number of phonemes. Similarly, the kinds of phonemes employed, even in languages closely related may be quite different in pronunciation. Thus the German phoneme written *ch* (as in *buch* 'book,' or *lachen* 'to laugh') is quite unknown in English; our closest sound is *h*, a very weak imitation of the harsher German *ch*.

The number of phonemes employed in a language is usually quite small, rarely exceeding thirty. These are of course used over and over again to produce a great variety of morphemes. The following English morphemes illustrate this point; the eighteen morphemes listed employ only six phonemes: *man, map, mat, mass, nan, pan, tam, sam, pat, pap, gnat* (pronounced *nat*), *sap, tap, sat, nap, pass, tan, tat*.

It may be noted, however, that not all the possible combinations of the six phonemes are actually employed in English. Thus combinations like *san, tas,* and *nam* have no meaning in English; they are English-like nonsense words. Other combinations, like *psa, pnt, nmt,* or *psn,* however, are not at all like English words; indeed, all of them involve habits of pronunciation so different from those employed by a speaker of English that he would regard the forms as wholly unpronounceable.

It is clear, then, that the phonemes of a language must be combined according to definite rules. Each language has such rules of combination which are observed strictly by those who speak the language as a mother tongue, and which may differ markedly from the rules characteristic of other languages.

LINGUISTIC CHANGE

From what has been said about linguistic structure we might easily get the idea that the habits of speech characteristic of a given community always remain the same. This is not true, however. All languages are in reality undergoing constant change. We may demonstrate this in two ways: by studying the history of a single language or by comparing and classifying the many languages now spoken.

The history of a language can only be studied directly if the community which speaks it has possessed writing for a considerable period of time. The first written records in English, for example, appear about

A.D. 900 and continue in a more or less unbroken stream to the present day. Examination of these records reveals that from A.D. 900 to the present, a period of little more than 1000 years, English has changed radically in pronunciation, grammar, and vocabulary.

This change may be illustrated by comparing the word *acre* with two of its earlier forms, *acer* and *aecer*. *Acer* belongs to the Middle English period (about 1100-1500) while *aecer* is an Old English or Anglo-Saxon word (900-1100). The principal phonetic difference between *acre, acer,* and *aecer* is in the pronunciation of the initial vowel. In Middle English *acer,* the vowel *a* was pronounced somewhat as the *o* of *sot* while Old English *ae* has a pronunciation similar to that of the *a* in *man*.

The three words also differ in grammar and meaning. Old English *aecer* belongs to a category called 'strong nouns' and had several distinctive case forms, much like the strong nouns of modern German. These are distributed as follows:

	SINGULAR	PLURAL
Nominative	*aecer*	*aeceras*
Dative	*aecere*	*aecerum*
Genitive	*aeceres*	*aecera*

During the Middle English period the noun endings became more and more alike until today modern English *acre* has but one major variant, the plural *acres*.

Old English *aecer* referred primarily to a cultivated field; thus, in the Anglo-Saxon Bible, the passage describing Jesus and his disciples going on the Sabbath into a field of ripened wheat uses the form *aeceras* to mean a field on which a crop is growing. Later the term was also used to mean a measure of land. The Middle English *acer* came gradually to mean a field small enough to be plowed by a man with a yoke of oxen in a single day. Later in the Middle English period the term was a more accurate measure of land size though its application was still restricted to cultivated or cultivatable land. *Acre* now has a still more precise meaning (160 square rods or 1/640 of a square mile) and though it is most often used as a unit of measure for land it may apply to cultivated farm lands, wild land (such as forests or mountain areas), or to the land occupied by a city (as in the phrase, 'acres of houses, factories, and other habitations').

Since, however, only a few languages have been written for a considerable period it is not always possible to demonstrate linguistic change directly. In such cases we must resort to indirect evidences of change. These are found in the fact that all modern speech communities exhibit geographical differences in pronunciation, grammar, and vocabulary. English, for example, is not the same everywhere that it is spoken. The English of England has a number of major dialects as we go from one part of the island to another and all of them differ from the English spoken in Canada, the United States, Australia, and South Africa. In the United States, too, English is not everywhere the same; differences in pronunciation and vocabulary are found between the English spoken in New York and that of New England, the south, the midwest, and the far west. This can only mean that English has changed and furthermore that change has taken different directions in different regions of the English-speaking world. What was once one more or less uniform language has divided into a large number of mutually distinct dialects.

THE CLASSIFICATION OF LANGUAGES

The discovery that languages change led to a method of classifying languages. English, as we have seen, does not really refer to only one language but to a whole group of languages or dialects broadly alike but differing in many details of pronunciation, grammar, and vocabulary. Linguists express this by saying that the modern English languages are descendants of a single common ancestral English and so belong to a single 'family' of languages. Each of the modern idioms is the ancestral English plus those changes in pronunciation, grammar, and vocabulary peculiar to the area in which it is spoken. Actually, of course, this statement is not precisely accurate historically for we know that the older forms of English were also dialectically divided. Some of the modern dialects may have developed from one dialect of the early period, others from quite a different one.

The modern dialects of English do not of course differ very greatly from one another. Much more marked differences are found between English, German, Dutch, Swedish, Danish, and Norwegian. Most of these are mutually unintelligible; that is, a native speaker of English cannot, without special instruction, either speak or understand the other languages. Despite this, however, it is evident that these languages do have many features in common; they are not so markedly different as, for example, Chinese is from English. To illustrate this let us compare the words from one to ten in English, German, and Swedish by putting these in parallel columns as follows:

ENGLISH	GERMAN	SWEDISH
one	ein	en
two	zwei	två
three	drei	tre
four	vier	fyra
five	fünf	fem
six	sechs	sex
seven	sieben	sju
eight	acht	åtta
nine	neun	nio
ten	zehn	tio

Here, it is evident, there are both differences and similarities. The differences are often marked but in only a few cases are the words unrecognizably different. Many other examples would reveal that these differences and similarities pervade the entire vocabularies of the three languages. The similarities are indeed so marked and so frequent that they cannot be due wholly to chance nor to mutual borrowings. Indeed, the latter possibility is largely ruled out by the fact that the three languages have for centuries been spoken in quite separate areas.

It follows, then, that these languages resemble each other because, like the separate dialects of English, they are descendants of a common earlier tongue. We have no record of this early ancestral language; as far back as our records go, the three languages are recognizably distinct. But, on the basis of the numerous and far-reaching similarities which today exist between these languages we can and do class them together as members of the same linguistic stock or family.

A linguistic stock, then, is a group of modern and ancient tongues between which there exist a large number of similarities and systematic differences in pronunciation, grammar, and vocabulary, too great to be explained by chance or borrowing. The member languages of such a stock are said to be derived from a single ancestral form, usually called the prototype language of the group. Thus, the languages of the Germanic stock, such as English, German, Dutch, Swedish, Norwegian, Danish, and a number of less important idioms, are modern descendants of a theoretical or assumed language called Proto-Germanic. We have no records of Proto-Germanic for our written records do not go back far enough in time.

In a few rare instances, however, we may verify an historical classification of this type. Thus, for example, we note that French, Spanish, Italian, Roumanian, and a number of other languages exhibit the same kind of similarities and systematic differences found in the Germanic group. They are for that reason classed as members of the Romance stock and are said to to be derived from a language called Proto-Romanic.

But here we have historical records which confirm, in part at least, the inferences drawn from our comparison of the modern languages. These reveal that Latin, once spoken only in the city of Rome and its environs, was spread throughout much of southern and western Europe by the developing Roman Empire. When first established, these outlying colonies spoke much the same language as Rome. Each of the colonies and Rome, however, modified their Latin in the course of time and since they were more or less isolated from one another these changes were largely independent of each other. As time went on, the changes became progressively greater until today the modern Romance tongues are not only different from Latin but also differ markedly from each other. Such resemblances as still exist between the Romance languages are due to the fact that all of them are connected by a continuous tradition to Latin. Spanish, Italian, French, Portuguese, Roumanian, and the other Romance languages are, then, modern versions of Latin, each characteristic of the population of a particular region in Europe.

How Languages Change

When we compare the several stages in the history of a given language we may note not only that the language changes in pronunciation, grammar, and vocabulary but also that changes take place in accordance with three major processes. Some of the words of modern English, for example, are direct descendants of Old English words having the same or similar meanings. Thus, modern English *cow, house, mouse,* and *louse* are directly derived by change of vowel from Old English *cū, hūs, mūs,* and *lūs,* where the vowel *ū* had approximately the sound of the vowel of *soothe.* Similarly, *why, bride, mice,* and *fire* come from Old English *hwȳ, brȳd, mȳs,* and *fȳr* (*ȳ* pronounced as in German *grün* 'green' or French *rue* 'street'), while *stone, boat, bone,* and *go* are derived from Old English *stān, bāt, bān,* and *gān* (*ā* pronounced somewhat as in *calm*). A goodly portion of our modern English vocabulary, then, existed in Old English as well, the modern forms as we have seen differing from those of the early period in pronunciation, grammar, and meaning.

We also find, however, that Old English possessed a number of forms no longer used in modern English, forms which have been replaced by modern words of different origin. Similarly, there are large numbers of words which have been added to the English vocabulary since the Old English period; words which had no counterparts at all in the earlier language. Words of this type illustrate the two remaining processes of change: analogic change and borrowing.

Analogic change takes place when the speakers of a language create new words by combining older materials on the pattern of already existing forms. In Old English, for example, the plural of *cū* 'cow' was *cȳ*. As we have seen, Old English *cȳ*, had it persisted to modern times, would have given some such form as *°kye*, a word we mark with an asterisk to denote that it does not actually exist. But while we do not use *°kye* as the plural of *cow*, we have a form *cows* which has this meaning. *Cows* is made up of two elements; *cow-* from Old English *cū* and *-s* from Old English *-as* (compare Old English *stān* 'stone'; *stān-as* 'stone-s'). The combination *°cū-as* never existed in Old English; it was created much later on the analogy of *stone, stones; book, books;* and other similar singular-plural alternates. In brief, *cows*, though it is made up of two linguistic elements (*cow* and *-s*) which go back to Old English, is a new creation made by combining two forms not hitherto joined. Modern English has lost *cȳ* but has added *cows*.

Analogic forms are very numerous and mark every stage in the history of language. Also numerous in English and in other language are words taken over by one speech community from another; so-called borrowed forms. Take note, for example, of the following Biblical passage in Old English, its literal translation, and its form in modern English.

Se Haeland for on reste-daeg ofer aeceras; sothlice his leorning-chihtas hyngrede . . .

The / Healing one / fared / on / rest-day / over / (the)acres; / soothly / his / learning-knights / hungered / . . .

Jesus went on the Sabbath day through the corn; and his disciples were a hungered . . .

Note in particular the Old English words *Haeland, reste-daeg,* and *leorning-chihtas*, replaced in the modern English text by *Jesus, Sabbath,* and *disciples*. *Haeland* is derived from *haelan* 'to make well, to make whole' by adding *-end* to the stem *hael-*. *Hael-* is today found in the phrase *hale and hearty* (*hale* in the sense of healthy is no longer freely used) and in the word *heal* and its derivatives. The ending *-end*, which in Old English made the noun 'the healing one' from the verb *haelan* 'to heal, make whole,' no longer is used in modern English. It survives un-recognized, however, in such words as *fiend* and *friend* from Old English *feond* 'one who hates' and *freond* 'one who loves.' *Haeland* too has been lost and replaced, in this Biblical sense at least, by the proper name *Jesus*.

Reste-daeg is of course an obvious compound, the elements of which still exist in modern English. But the compound does not; we may say *day of rest*, but we oftener use *Sabbath*, borrowed ultimately from the Hebrew *Shabbath*, or *Sunday* from quite a different Old English word *sunnan-daeg* 'sun's day.' Similarly, *leorning-chihtas* 'learning-knights' has been replaced by *disciples*, borrowed from the Old French *disciple*, ultimately from Latin *discipulus*. Here are exemplified three instances in which Old English words have been replaced in modern English by words borrowed from other languages. In addition of course there are a large number of modern English borrowings for things, sections, and concepts which were not expressed in Old English. Professor Jespersen, an authority on the English language, estimates that nearly two-thirds of our modern English vocabulary is made up of words borrowed from the Scandinavian languages, French, Latin, Greek, and other sources.

PHONETIC CORRESPONDENCES

The method we have described for the classification of languages is called by linguists the comparative method. It results, as we have seen, in a division of the world's languages into historically distinct groups, called linguistic stocks or families. Within any stock there are certain words common to most or all of the languages of that stock and these words are presumed to have existed in the prototype languages as well. Thus, for example, we find that French *coeur* (earlier *cor* and *cuer*) 'heart' is paralleled in the Romance stock by such forms as Italian *cuore*, Provençal *cor*, Spanish *corazon* (from Old Spanish *cuer*), and Portuguese *coração* (from Old Portuguese *cor*). From these similarities we may infer that Proto-Romanic had a word pronounced something like *cor* which also meant 'heart,' an inference which is borne out when we actually find in Latin the form *cor* 'heart.'

When the words common to most or all the language of a given stock are examined we find that their similarities and systematic differences in sound can be summarized in a series of descriptive statements called phonetic correspondences. Such statements deal with sounds or phonemes rather than words. Properly constructed, a statement of phonetic correspondences between two or more languages will concisely describe all the phonemic differences and identities that exist between them.

A good example of a phonetic correspondence, and one which also illustrates how such descriptive statements are formulated, is found when we compare the Germanic languages with Latin and Greek and their modern descendants. The oldest known Germanic language, Gothic, had, among others, the consonants *f*, as in *fadar* 'father,' *þ* (pronounced as the *th* of thick), as in *þreis* 'three,' and *h*, as *haírto* 'heart.' These correspond to Latin *p*, as in *pater* 'father,' *t*, as in *tres* 'three,' and *k*, as in *cor* 'heart.' Initially, then, we may proceed on the hypothesis that Latin *p*, *t*, and *k* (written *c*) correspond always to Gothic *f*, *þ*, and *h*, respectively.

This hypothesis is not entirely valid, however. First, we discover that Gothic *speiwan* 'spew' corresponds to Latin *spuere*. Gothic *gasts* 'guest' to Latin *hostis* 'enemy,' and Gothic *fisks* 'fish' to Latin *piscis*. Here it is evident that a Gothic *p*, *t*, and *k* correspond to Latin *p*, *t*, and *k*. Further examples of a like nature disclose that whenever Latin *p*, *t*, and *k* are preceded by an *s* (as in *spuere*, *hostis*, and *piscis*) the corresponding sounds in Gothic are not *f*, *þ*, and *h* but *p*, *t*, and *k*.

Were we to develop this rule still further, other exceptional instances might be found until ultimately our statement of correspondences could be so formed as to cover all or nearly all of the forms in which the sounds in question occur.

Phonetic correspondences, properly stated, give the ultimate proof of relationship between languages of the same stock or family. For such relationship is never to be demonstrated by random similarities; any two languages, related or not, will reveal some unsystematic resemblances. It is only when two or more languages can be connected by regular sound correspondences, demonstrably linking forms in terms of systematic identities and divergencies in sound feature, that we may legitimately conclude that they have a common historical origin.

WHY LANGUAGES CHANGE

Many reasons have been advanced to account for linguistic change. Most of these, however, scarcely bear repetition for they are in general based upon incomplete or premature analysis. Indeed it may well be said that linguists even today know too little of linguistic change to be able to account for it.

One reason why we know so little about the actual circumstances under which languages change is that we have so far been concerned primarily with the results of change and not enough with the functional relation between language and other aspects of man's cultures. Languages are obviously and clearly related to cultures through vocabulary; as a culture increases in complexity so does the vocabulary of the language which is associated with it. English, which is associated with a highly complex series of cultures, has a far larger and more complicated vocabulary today than it had in the Old English period, when the culture of its speakers was considerably simpler than it is today. Furthermore, we can show that English changed more rapidly during the Middle and modern English period than in the Old English period. Very possibly, then, the series of extremely rapid changes which marked the shift from Old English to modern English were, directly and indirectly, associated with the accompanying shift from the relatively simple rural and isolated culture of the speakers of Old English to the highly industrialized world culture of the speakers of modern English.

It is also significant that some European languages have changed much less than English. An outstanding example is found in Lithuanian, which has changed so little that it today retains scores of older traits which have long since disappeared from English. The significance of this lies in the fact that Lithuania has also been less affected by cultural changes than the English-speaking regions of the world. It has remained very largely a rural and isolated region, participating much less in modern world cultures than the English-speaking areas.

These facts suggest that linguistic change is part and parcel of cultural change taken as a whole. The difficulty in demonstrating this hypothesis lies in the nature of language itself. For though there is an obvious relation between vocabulary and culture, the precise effect of vocabulary changes upon the sounds and grammatical processes of language is far from being clear. Is it true, for example, that large and rapidly accumulating additions to the vocabulary of a language actually results in sound changes and changes in grammatical structure? And if this is so, precisely how are such results brought about? We do not possess the data with which to answer these questions and until we can acquire such data it would appear that the factors responsible for linguistic change must remain unknown.

LANGUAGE AND WRITING

Most of us have learned so well to translate spoken words to writing and writing back into speech that we think of writing itself as a form of language. This, of course, is not so; writing, like the phonograph, is only an external device by means of which we made a more or less permanent record of speech. Many languages even today remain unwritten and the fact that a language may be written does not in itself change it in any important particular.

Writing, then, is an item of culture quite distinct from language and has a different origin and history. To begin with, writing is far more recent than language. As we have seen, man probably acquired language about one million years ago, at the same time that he acquired the first rudiments of culture. Writing, however, does not appear anywhere until the Bronze Age and even then is found in only a very few societies. For a long time the knowledge of writing was limited only to a few individuals in the societies which knew the technique; the bulk of the people neither wrote nor read. It is only since the invention of printing that such knowledge became truly widespread.

Writing was probably invented at least three times in world history. One occurrence took place somewhere in the Near East, probably among the Bronze Age Egyptians. This writing eventually spread to Europe and much of Asia in many different systems as each of the groups who took it over adapted it to the requirements of their own language. Chinese writing may well represent a second invention, taking place very soon after that of the Near East. Some scholars, however, hold that Chinese writing may be derived from some one of the earlier Near Eastern forms. Today, the Chinese system of writing is employed by only a few other groups found in the immediate environs of China.

A third invention of writing occurred somewhat later among the Maya Indians of Guatemala. Maya writing spread northward to the Aztecs of Mexico who did not, however, take over the complete Maya system but only a somewhat modified version of it. Knowledge of Maya writing died with much of the rest of their early culture; the few surviving documents cannot today be read. Aztec writing has also gone out of use though we still preserve and can read many of the older Aztec records.

PICTURES AND WRITING

There can be little doubt that writing developed from the technique of drawing pictures. All the earlier forms of writing suggest this, for all of them include characters which either are themselves pictures or are clearly derived from pictures.

Drawing and painting, incidentally, are very old techniques. As early as the Middle Paleolithic (Old Stone Age) man made crude drawings; a little later in the same period there developed in Europe at least a highly competent art, expressed not only in drawings and paintings but also in sculptures, modelings, and engravings.

Pictures are not themselves a form of writing, however, though they may serve occasionally as reminders or memoranda of past events. In some societies pictures were specifically used, not only as memoranda, but also as a means of communication between one group and another.

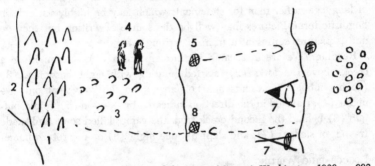

From Ernest T. Denig, Tribes of the Upper Missouri, Washington, 1930, p. 603. Courtesy of Bureau of American Ethnology, Smithsonian Institution.

Fig. 1. 'Picture Writing.'

Since such pictures served as means of communication rather than art forms and were often drawn hastily, they soon became highly conventionalized and abbreviated. The objects pictured were not drawn in detail but symbolized by some arbitrarily chosen mark. Thus, for example, a horse might be indicated by a horseshoe-like mark, a buffalo with a small circular mark, and a camp or stopping place by a shaded circle (See Figure 1). Such symbols were then arranged to describe an event or depict a narrative.

In Figure 1 a drawing of this sort is illustrated. Note the crudity and bareness of the pictorial style; the draughtsman was clearly not concerned with accurate or realistic representation. All he really wanted to do was to communicate as briefly as possible the experience encountered by his group.

Such narrative drawings are often described as a kind of writing, called pictographic writing, or picture writing. This, however, is not quite accurate. Narrative drawings are not tied to particular words, phrases, or sentences; they may be interpreted by a variety of speech forms. Thus, item (1) of Figure 1 need not be interpreted 'we are in a camp of 13 lodges'; any statement similar in meaning will do as well. Narrative drawings in brief may be described or interpreted in words but they do not stand for or symbolize any specific word or combination of words.

True writing, on the other hand, is distinctly tied to particular words or word combinations. The written form *horse,* for example, can only be read as the word *horse,* no form of similar meaning will do. A true writing, then, does not exist until the symbols used stand for specific items of language rather than for statements which may be highly variable in linguistic form. Pictures may well be the source of writing but they do not as pictures represent a form of writing.

Reading: 'We are in a camp of thirteen lodges (1); encamped on a creek above the forks (2); started hunting with eight horsemen (3) (each symbol ɔ represents one horseman); on the way slept out two nights (4); traveled in the direction indicated by – – – ɔ (5); found buffalo (6) behind the second creek from the camp; killed some and made travois, or sledges (7); and slept but one night (8) on our return home.'

Logographic Writing

We do not know just how the transition from narrative pictures to true writing took place; the earliest forms of writing on record have already made the change. It is probable, however, that it came about through the rebus method. A rebus, or a picture puzzle, consists of drawings meant to be interpreted in terms of the names of the objects represented rather than in terms of the objects themselves. A very simple rebus is composed of a picture of a mill plus a stone or cement walk and a key. Taking each picture as the symbol of a syllable, we see that the three together stand for the name *Milwaukee.*

Narrative pictures become true writing, when the pictures no longer serve to remind the beholder of some event but stand as symbols for the name of the object represented. As long as the Plains Indians interpreted the picture ∧ as a dwelling, encampment, or some similar notion however it might be expressed in words, it remained a narrative drawing. Had they begun to interpret ∧ as a symbol standing for the word *tipi* and never any other word, then they would have possessed a true writing.

When pictures begin to symbolize the name of the object represented we speak of them as characters associated directly with a linguistic form. The reader reacts to a character just as he reacts to the speech form represented by it. Words were probably the first linguistic forms symbolized in this way. A writing which so symbolizes words is called logographic and the symbols, each of which symbolizes a particular word, are logograms. Many of the characters used in the early Egyptian and Maya writing, as well as many of those employed today in Chinese writing, are logograms. (See Plate X.)

Pictures which become logograms are soon rigidly conventionalized; that is, they are always drawn in the same way and they are always associated with the same meaning. When this happens, the character may change without regard for the original picture from which it was derived. Examples may be found by contrasting early and modern Chinese characters. Thus *fire* was originally depicted as flames moving upward (a); the modern character (b) is not so expressive. The same is true of the old and new characters for *water* (c and d): (representing water flowing).

(a)   (b)   (c)   (d)

Fɪɢ. 2. The pictorial origin of Chinese ideograms is evident in their early stages of development. Conventionalization has obscured this in the recent characters.

The main difficulty with a logograph is to find a way of representing words the meanings of which are not easily pictured. This problem may be solved in a variety of ways. The Egyptians, for example, used the picture of a tadpole to represent the word meaning 100,000, presumably because tadpoles always occur in great numbers. In Chinese writing, many techniques are used. Thus, the character picturing the meaning woman (wife) is combined with that for child to express the meaning good or happy, presumably, because one who has a wife and child is happy. Similarly, the character for sun and that for moon combined symbolized the word meaning bright, a common characteristic of these two heavenly bodies.

The most common device, however, is to use a character for a word the meaning of which is easily picturable to stand also for words similarly pronounced. Thus, if English were written in logograms, we might symbolize the word *pear* by the picture of the fruit and use this picture also to symbolize the word *pare*. In Egyptian a conventionalized goose is used not only for that word but also for son, identical in pronunciation with goose. And in Chinese the word *wan* 'scorpion' is represented by the same character as the similarly pronounced word *wan* meaning 10,000.

This technique may of course lead to ambiguities; the reader may be uncertain sometimes as to which words is to be read. The Chinese solve this problem by adding a character, called a determinant, to the base character, called a phonetic, to distinguish the symbols for identically pronounced forms. Thus, the meaning of the word *fang* 'square' is easily pictured and its character then becomes the phonetic for *fang* 'district,' *fang* 'spin,' *fang* 'ask,' *fang* 'kettle,' and *fang* 'board,' all of which are similarly pronounced. The last five words are distinguished in writing by different determinants. So, *fang* 'district' is written with the character for *fang* 'square' plus that for the word meaning 'earth,' and the combined characters are read 'that word which sounds like *fang* "square" but has reference to earth.' Similarly, the character for *fang* 'spin' is that for 'square' plus that for 'silk,' *fang* 'ask' is 'square' plus 'talk,' *fang* 'kettle' is 'square' plus 'metal,' and *fang* 'board' is 'square' plus 'wood.'

It is obvious, however, that logographic writing is cumbersome; it usually requires a large number of different characters. In modern Chinees writing, for example, all symbols can only be reduced to 214 basic constituents. These and all their commonly used combinations must be memorized by one who wishes to read and write Chinese fluently.

SYLLABARIES

It is clear, of course, that no system of writing can be strictly logographic in the sense that each word is represented by a wholly distinctive character. Even Chinese writing, which employs logograms exclusively, uses only 214 basic characters which, combined in various ways, furnish enough logograms adequately to write the language without ambiguity. In so doing, it is evident that a phonetic factor is recognized: words similarly pronounced but different in meaning are represented by characters wholly or in part the same.

In Chinese writing this principle could be applied to words because of the fact that most Chinese words are uniformly one syllable in length. But in languages in which words vary in length, the principle must be applied to syllables rather than words. Thus, if English used a single character to represent not only the word *sun* but also the first syllable of *sundry,* this character would be associated directly with a phonetic form (the syllable *sun-* regardless of its meaning) rather than a linguistic form (a series of sounds plus their meaning). Such characters, like the phonetic characters of Chinese writing, take on a constant phonographic (sound representative) value and may be called phonograms.

When phonograms are used they seem most often to be symbols of syllables rather than whole words, as in Chinese writing, or single sounds as in alphabetic writing. Each phonogram in a system of syllabic writing or syllabary denotes one syllable.

Syllabaries are widespread in both ancient and modern speech communities. The ancient languages of Mesopotamia (Iraq), such as Babylonia and Sumerian, were written largely by means of a syllabary though logograms were also used. These peoples wrote on clay tablets with a stylus having a wedge-shaped end. Because the characters were different combinations of wedge-shaped impressions, the writing is called cuneiform, from the Latin word *cuneus* 'wedge.' Old Persian and the Greek of Cyprus were also written in syllabic characters. Today we find the most important syllabaries in Japan (the Japanese use two syllabaries as well as Chinese logograms) and India. Recent systems of writing, devised by missionaries for non-literate peoples, often take form as syllabaries, and among the Cherokee we find syllabary invented by Sequoyah to write his language. (See Fig. 1, Ch. XI.)

Syllabaries are, of course, far simpler than logographic systems if only because they require fewer characters. This is clearly evidenced by Japanese writing, which employs both techniques. Japanese logograms are quite as complicated and require as many characters as Chinese writing but the Japanese syllabary, quite as efficient as the logographic system, needs only 65 characters.

Alphabetic Writing

Only once in human history has an alphabetic system of writing developed from the syllabary. This important event took place around 1800 B.C. when a Semitic-speaking peoples, probably living on the Sinai Peninsula, took over an Egyptian syllabary of some 24 characters and transformed these into consonant symbols. We do not know precisely who these people were but we do know that the system of writing they initiated spread rapidly to all the other Semitic-speaking peoples of the same region. Two distinct styles of writing emerged: the South Semitic which today is used, in somewhat modified form, by the Ethiopians and the North Semitic (Phoenician, Hebrew, and Aramean) which is today the basis of the modern writing of Hebrew, Syrian, and Arabic. The North Semitic style, in its Phoenician and Aramean varieties, spread also to Asia and Europe giving rise to the modern Indian writing and ultimately to the several alphabets used during the historical period and today among the Europeans.

The Egyptian syllabary from which our alphabets sprang consisted of 24 hieroglyphic (the older logograms; literally a hieroglyph is a sacred mark or carving) and hieratic (later abbreviated hieroglyphs) characters. These stood for syllables having only a consonant and a vowel. In using them, however, the Egyptians paid attention only to the consonant ignoring the fact that a given consonant might be followed by any one of several vowels. Any ambiguities resulting were removed by the use of determinants and logograms.

When these characters were taken over by the Semites, they used them only for the consonants in their languages; the vowels were simply not represented. It was up to the reader to add the vowels from the context in which the word was used. This of course would be impossible in English or other European languages but it did work in the Semitic languages by reason of the fact that if the consonants belonging to a word are written and indication is made of where the vowels fit in, the reader can easily guess the vowels which are to be supplied. Semitic writing is then alphabetic in that each character symbolizes a single sound but it is incompletely formed, since it does not clearly symbolize all the distinctive sounds of the language being written.

The Greeks learned the Semitic alphabet from the Phoenicians. We know this not only because the fact is recorded but also because the Greek word *alpha* means only the first letter in the alphabet and is probably borrowed from Semitic *aleph* 'head of an ox,' descriptive of the picture from which the characters *alpha*, *aleph*, and our modern A were ultimately derived. Similarly, Greek *beta*, *gamma*, and the names for many other characters are derived from Semitic words having a meaning referring back to the older pictures from which the characters developed.

Unlike the Semitic language, Greek cannot be written adequately without vowel signs. In taking over the Semitic alphabet, which had symbols for consonants unknown to Greek, the Greeks used these superfluous characters to represent vowels. Semitic *aleph*, originally a consonant, became in Greek the character for the vowel *alpha*, Semitic O, a guttural consonant became the Greek vowel O, and the ambiguous *I-J* of Semitic became the vowel *I* in Greek. With these and other changes the Greeks made over the Semitic alphabet to suit the writing of their language, so devising a fairly good phonemic writing in which nearly every distinctive sound of Greek was represented by a single character.

From the Greeks this now relatively complete alphabet spread in two directions: through the Etruscans to Rome and north to the Bulgars, Serbs, and Russians. Rome in turn gave the alphabet to most of the rest of the peoples of Europe. In each of these groups to which the alphabet spread innovations arose as the people fitted the borrowed characters to the peculiarities of their own speech. The details of the spread of the alphabet and its many forms are far too complex to describe here; indeed, we have still to learn many of these historical details.

Today, however, man possesses wholly the techniques necessary to record, as accurately and efficiently as possible, any and all of the languages he speaks. This invention, the complex product of many peoples at different periods of time, is one of man's most useful and productive possessions. Without it, there could be no wide-spread communication, historical records, or education in the modern sense of the word. It is not surprising, then, that many scientists date the beginnings of true civilization from the invention of writing.

LESLIE SPIER

XI

Inventions and Human Society

LIKE ALL ANIMALS man has had to adapt himself to his environment. In lesser part this has been physiological adaptation, in much larger measure a change of habits to meet new conditions. This great capacity for adaptations, directed by intelligence—inventing new devices and procedures— sets man apart from other animals.

Tool-nimble fingers, a flexible memory, ability to see and solve problems has made it possible for man to manipulate his environment. Man's life has not been wholly shaped by environment: on the contrary, he has selected from its resources and reshaped it to his desires. Where in simpler societies he was more or less a victim of his surroundings, through the ages he has increasingly created methods and contrivances to change its nature—planted groves, irrigated arid lands, brought materials from afar, air-conditioned his home.

Each device or idea that entered into this adaptation or modification was a specific invention. Inventions are not in mechanical devices alone, for we may legitimately speak of the invention of an idea. Indeed, the machine itself is part of the physical world, so much steel or wood: the essence of invention lies in a new idea.

The development of all civilizations has been the accumulation of mechanisms and ideas. In simpler societies of primitive peoples and in the ancient past their number was few; in the great civilizations accumulation and elaboration proceeded with ever-increasing speed.

All tools—the product of invention—are essentially extensions of the body: a crowbar lends greater leverage to the hands alone; a rifle gives striking power at a distance. As such, many tools depend on man's bodily structure; even their ultimate derivatives, automatic power machinery,

296

had their inception in these bodily-determined forms. The rotary motions of a twirled spindle or a screw depend on the outward rotation at the wrist of the two bones of the forearm. Since the world over the majority of people are right-handed, these twists are overwhelmingly clockwise, that is right-handed, as in screws and most machinery. A left-handed individual does not invent a parallel device; he is forced to make his bodily movements conform to the established pattern. With the right-handedness of machine parts standardized, it is taken for granted as part of our thought habits that substitute parts or added appliances will be of the same kind. Again, typewriter and piano keys are fitted to our ability to move the fingers individually. But the position of letters on a standard typewriter keyboard bears little relation to the relative strength of the fingers, the most frequent letters of written English being allotted to the weaker digits of the left hand. This arbitrary arrangement of keys was a matter of chance on the part of the inventors of the first practical typewriter in mid-nineteenth century. The convention they established has had to be learned by all typists; hence a reversal of relations has come about: bodily structure is ruled by a culturally determined factor. Both the invention of tools and their conventions of use show at the same time the great flexibility of human physique and mind and their channeling into cultural molds.

Invention has other roots than adaptation or exploiting environment. Sheer novelty, display of ingenuity, variations of a perfectly learned technique, purposeful improvement, aesthetic expression, and other inner urges are equally sources. Further, the new construct is as often as not the result of chance variation or combination.

Inventiveness is not confined by mental superiority to certain races as against others. Every trait of human life (culture) was invented, and all peoples have their culture. The Eskimo, like the Yankee, displays ingenuity in solving his problems; where they differ is in the Yankee's richer experience with mechanical devices and in the demands of his society for such contrivances. Again, smaller communities, where each man must attend his every need, lack the specialization of labor of larger groups whereby skill in craftsmanship is attained and attention given to particular problems. On the whole inventiveness is a rare trait: few of us invent anything quite new and at best make only minor modifications in what we have. A class of men dedicated to producing novelties—our inventors—is a specific feature of our civilization and of very recent date.

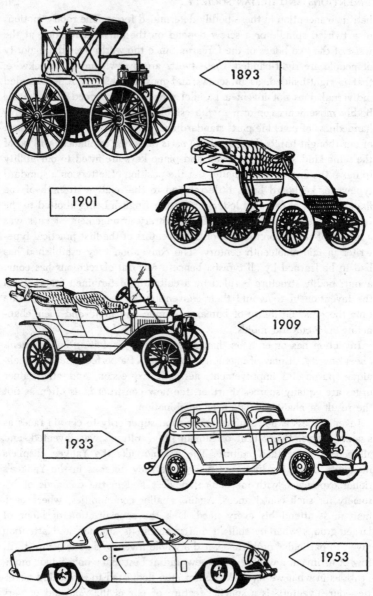

1893

1901

1909

1933

1953

Courtesy of Mr. Philip Van Doren Stern and the Viking Press, New York.
Adapted from A Pictorial History of the Automobile.

Certain primary inventions have profoundly affected the course of civilization. Some solved problems of physical need, others regulated conduct or served aesthetic and intellectual ends. Among those deserving special consideration are developments in clothing, housing, pottery, basketry, cloth-weaving, the wheel, and time-reckoning.

Little is known of the origin of the great inventions that have given direction to civilizations. Their roots are lost in dim antiquity and the record is obscure. But more significant for the understanding of cultural development is the fact that, strictly speaking, there were no 'first origins.' As the typewriter, for example, was a new combination of the alphabet, moveable type, lever action, familiarity with metals—and only as a new combination a 'new invention'—every invention was a development out of pre-existing knowledge of devices and materials.

The social consequences of inventions have been very great. In our own day, for instance, the automobile markedly changed the character of American life. Yet the automobile as a 'new invention' is no more than the adaptation of a powerful, compact, power plant to the age-old cart. (See Fig. 1.) Its impact on our social life has been great, providing convenient flexible transport, freedom of settlement and movement, and annihilation of time. It brought a move toward suburban and country living, arresting to a considerable extent the tendency for families to concentrate in large cities; factories were free to locate away from railroads and rivers; motor transport became a successful competitor of railroads as well as providing a feeder system for them; mechanization gave speed and impact to our army; ease of travel not only speeded up the tempo of business but provided pleasure and a fuller acquaintance with our country to the many. Good roads extending into the remotest sections destroyed isolation. A whole series of new industries arose—manufacture of automobiles and their accessory parts, garages, gas stations—and a new craft of repairmen. It has been said that the automobile turned us into a nation of mechanics—true in the sense that knowledge of mechanical devices and some ability to work with them is common to most men. As a consequence of these changes, there is more uniformity of custom,

---

FIG. 1. Inventions are frequently new combinations of older elements or the application of new devices to older mechanisms. The earliest automobiles (see top figure) clearly reveal their origin from a horse-drawn vehicle equipped with an engine. The subsequent developments illustrate the effect of the new principle on the design of the vehicle.

habit, and outlook over the country, and at the same time an interdependence and mutual interest in all sections. On the reverse side must be reckoned new dangers to life and limb, new fire hazards, and greater mobility for criminal activity. But good or bad, the changes in our social life effected by this invention have been profound.

It is difficult for us to envisage comparable effects of inventions in the past. Yet the case of the wheel and cart is clear: it provided transport utilizing the draft power of animals and effected a greater mobility of life. Pottery and the potter's wheel, basketry, and cloth-weaving changed the nature of domestic life and ultimately led to the development of great industries. Clothing made possible life in any climate at will and gave an outlet for the expression of social and aesthetic values. The social consequences of the other great inventions were comparable. What must be considered is that relative to the simplicity of life in earlier communities even the first forms of these inventions markedly changed daily habits, social relations, and modes of thought.

Clothing

The impulses toward clothing the body are compounded of protection against the weather, gratification of display and adornment, indications of social distinction, and a sense of shame. It is uncertain which one can be credited with first bringing clothing into being, but once clothing was in use these impulses have dominated in varying degrees. Man's hairlessness would seem to have called for some covering from earliest times, yet it is far from certain clothing was in use even by Paleolithic times. By the Neolithic Period, however, clothing may have been in general use, but we have every reason to believe that factors other than natural protection were at work to stimulate the use of apparel even then.

Complete covering is a characteristic of modern civilization, but this is exceptional. Among most peoples clothing for constant wear is quite scanty, extra garments being worn only when needed. Constant covering is usually confined to wrapping the loins or covering the private parts, but not always.

Clothing is often enough so ill-adapted to climatic needs that protection cannot be claimed as the prime or universal impulse. Clothing is so much a matter of habit that we who are fully clad fail to understand that the unclad are quite inured to climatic extremes. The Indians of the Nevada deserts, men and women, went completely naked for the most part in spite of sub-zero weather and excessive heat. Nor where clothing is worn for protection is it always well adapted for that purpose.

With the exception of the Arctic regions, where complete covering is worn, paradoxically full-body clothing is, in general, characteristic of temperate and hot climates. It is prevalent through a wide central area of the Old World from Japan, China, and Mongolia to western Europe. In parts of this area full covering would seem to be dictated as protection against extremes of cold and heat—as in north China, mountainous Balkans, northwestern Europe, the deserts of Arabia and North Africa—but it seems evident that in earlier times the inhabitants of these districts were relatively unclad. In general full-body clothing for the purpose of protection develops in regions of extreme dry cold or heat and is absent in hot moist regions (as tropical Africa). Where the human body can physiologically adapt itself to lesser extremes, even with some discomfort, the amount of clothing appears to bear little relation to climatic circumstances. Full clothing in the continuous zone of the central Old World argues, however, for the imitation and spread of a habit rather than repeated protective adaptations invented in each adverse region. The common lack of correspondence between full clothing and extreme climates is evidence against protection as a prime consideration in the use of clothing and suggests that other impulses were commonly dominant.

Adornment, display, and social distinction are obvious even where clothing is simple and scant. One nearly universal distinction is between men's and women's costume. Yet the marked distinctiveness of men's suits and women's dresses among ourselves is not common: we may be said to underline sex. But even where covering is minimal distinctions are made in clothing for the sexes, and these slight differences bulk large in the minds of the users. Other social distinctions are symbolized in attire: special costumes for soldiers, priests, the wealthy, slaves. While the infinite gradations of social position are markedly shown among ourselves by differences in cloth, its cut and color, and the manner dress is worn, parallel though minor differences appear in the quality and adornment of primitive clothing. Everywhere even minute differences in dress, posture, and bearing unconsciously give stamp to the social relations between individuals.

Dress is most commonly a vehicle for display and self-adornment. In most primitive communities exaggerated display in dress is characteristic of men, not women. Among ourselves (but only in recent generations) this has been reversed, a soberness of color, cut, and tendency to uniformity marking men's attire in contrast to women's.

Fashion is a concept most often associated with clothing alone, but erroneously, for there is just as much of fashion displayed in the realm of ideas, economic views, and even in science. In small primitive groups a new fashion may come from the imitation of the dress of a neighboring people. On the whole such communities are static, little interested in the foreign and in novelty. In larger communities such as ours social specialization calls constantly, not only for new appropriate symbols of dress, but for new forms and ornament for prestige sake and for sheer novelty. The new fashion spreads by imitation, wanes in its turn before the next novelty, and thus fashions have a fictitious appearance of being cyclic. Fashions are ordinarily but variations, while the fundamental contours, materials, and symbolic values of the dress remain constant, short of a complete cultural change.

Concealment may not have been an original factor in the development of clothing, but, rather, a derived attitude: concealment actually emphasizes sex and is reinforced by embarrassment and shame of nakedness among the habitually clothed. Where little or no clothing is worn, as in the tropics, or is stripped off, as inside an Eskimo igloo, exposure is a matter of course and evokes no particular response. Strikingly, the parts of the body which must be hidden at all costs (not always the sex organs) varies among peoples habituated to concealment.

The kinds of costuming that have developed in the various regions are obviously dictated by cultural considerations. In each area a specific type of dress has come to prevail and has been imitated throughout that region. Polynesia is characterized everywhere by loin 'cloths' of beaten bark (tapa), often added as an upper garment, with less common use of aprons or skirts of pendant fibers. Plains Indian men wear a poncho-like shirt, breechclout, long leggings, and moccasins, all of skin; their women a skin dress hanging to mid-calf, short leggings, and moccasins. While there are tribal, local, and individual differences the fundamental pattern is uniform.

Full-body clothing (of fur or skin) is characteristic of the Arctic and sub-Arctic. Further, this is tailored to fit the body—provided with sleeves and legs. Dress of woven cloth is characteristic of southern civilizations—ancient America from Chile to our Southwest and in the Old World from the Mediterranean to China. This was not tailored: in both regions squares of cloth were utilized just as they came from the loom, without cutting. Pueblo Indian dress, for instance, was a square wrapped around the waist by men, folded vertically around the body by women. In Mediterranean lands were the familiar uncut, draped cloth garments of classical Greece, Rome, and Egypt. This use of the uncut product of the loom as clothing in the central areas of Old and New Worlds was a parallel and independent invention. The parallel went farther. It has been shown that in North America full body clothing of skin, tailored to the limbs, spread southward into the Plains area; the use of cloth squares, for ponchos for instance, spread northward to the same region; here in the Plains a combination was made of the two—full-body clothing of skin, somewhat tailored, partially made over to the shape patterns of woven cloth. In Asia a similar combination was made: tailored skin clothing of northern Europe and Siberia coalesced in central and eastern Asia with the uncut cloth squares whose manufacture had spread from the south, giving the tailored cloth garments of Chinese men and women, for example: trousers for both, shirts and coats with sleeves. Here, in contrast to the New World, the form concept of the north prevailed but new material was substituted. In both cases invention, as usual, was essentially a recombination of things already familiar.

Houses and the Arch

Man lives in more varied climates than any other species, partly because of the adaptability of his physique, more by reason of cultural factors, the devices he created: clothing and shelter. It must be assumed that the earliest humans, lacking a thick covering of body hair, sought and constructed simple shelters. Paleolithic men are known to have used caverns and undoubtedly made shelters in the open. From Neolithic times onward true houses have been built.

Houses are adapted to the environment, but their kind is not dictated by it. Eskimo snow houses and Central African structures of light palm thatch make use of available materials. But only Eskimos on the central Arctic shore make houses of snow; other Eskimos east and west, with quite as much snow, build of driftwood timbers and sod in the same domed shape. Quite different adaptations exist side-by-side, as in the mud-walled houses and thatched dwellings of the western Sudan. In general houses are more substantial where climate is rigorous, but there are striking exceptions. Indians of Nevada made use of a mere ring of brush even through sub-zero winters, and in central Canada the crude Indian houses are more deficient for shelter progressively north to the Arctic.

Even though shelter is the primary impulse, houses from earliest times on show convention of materials, form, and style—a definite architecture, no matter how simple. Among the items setting off the culture of one area from another is a style of building peculiar to it: the flat-roofed adobe (clay) rectangular buildings throughout the Mediterranean, the skin-covered conical Plains Indian tipi, our gable-roofed frame house and brick or stone, flat-roofed buildings. In each area specialization and elaboration of houses generally appears near its center, simpler or cruder copies near the margins (large decorated tipis in the central Plains, small crude ones at its peripheries).

Principles of house construction vary greatly. In contrast to our frame-house construction, the coastal Indians of Alaska set huge split planks upright, edge to edge, for the walls, without inner framework, resting the gable roof on their upper ends. The Hausa (northern Nigeria) first make a conical roof on the ground, lift it bodily onto supporting posts, and build a cylindrical wall of thatch around these.

Houses of early times and among primitive peoples are small, usually one-room domiciles. The small size and often roving nature of these communities inhibited large constructions. Only after large communities appeared in the ancient worlds of the Mediterranean, Mesopotamia, India, China, and in Middle America, was monumental construction attempted.

A limitation to building larger structures lay in structural principles: houses with flat roofs were limited in size by the length of their roof timbers. Greater span could be had only by introducing interior columns or walls to support series of short beams. The great architectural monuments of ancient Egypt and Greece are impressive in their massiveness or grace of line, but were hampered in development by the continued use of beam and column alone.

A new principle came with the invention of the arch, known in Sumeria six thousand or more years ago. It had its rudimentary beginnings in the tombs of still earlier date in which great slabs were leaned together to meet at the apex or with corbelled stone roofs, where the stones of the walls protruded, one above another, to meet finally at the top. The true arch is formed of wedge-shaped stones set in an arc above the opening. It can carry a disproportionally heavy superstructure, since the load is thrust sideways toward the walls by the wedging of the stones. The walls must be massive to bear the sideways thrust, but this is obviated when arches are placed side by side (as in the Roman aqueducts), each arch countering the thrust of its neighbors.

First developed in ancient Mesopotamia, the principle of the arch spread slowly westward through the Mediterranean world and eastward to India. Early uses were primarily for short spans in the interior of buildings and for bridging low places. Its use to arch over doorways, supporting upper walls, at the hands of the Etruscans (sixth to four centuries B.C.) brought recognition of its utility for embellishing the faces of buildings. The cultural heirs of the Etruscans, the classical Romans, so extended this use for triumphal gateways, aqueducts, arcades—sometimes tier above tier of arches—that it became the pattern of Roman architecture. Like other fundamental inventions of early days such uses spread only slowly from this center.

For many centuries it made no impress on the lesser-developed peoples of western and northern Europe. When in the twelfth century, western Europeans (particularly in northern France) adopted the arch, they gave it a new form, pointed at the apex (Gothic arch). In this they were influenced by their older house construction of crooked timbers meeting at the ridge. The new 'invention' was, as usual, a recombination of older elements.

Eastward also the arch took on new form. The Byzantine world, which, continuing in the Graeco-Roman tradition, had long made use of the round (Roman) arch, developed a form with incurving sides about the time of the Mohammedan Arab expansion in the seventh century. Arabic-speaking peoples ultimately carried this form west through North Africa into Spain. As Mohammedan influence penetrated, the Byzantine arch (and the Byzantine dome) spread to the Balkans, even beyond to south Germany and Russia, and eastward, by the sixteenth century, to India.

The arch itself was capable of expansion by inventiveness. Its span is normally in a flat plane, but given depth it becomes a vaulted ceiling. One of the earliest uses of the round (barrel) vault was in the Cloaca Maxima, the great sewer of Rome. A further elaboration lay in the crossing of vaults whose lines of intersection (groins) produce effects of great beauty. High pointed arches and intersecting vaults became the dominant theme in cathedral building in the Renaissance, a type ultimately carried in college and church building over the world.

A second noteworthy development was the dome; structurally this is a series of arches intersecting at their apexes. The fully developed dome seems to have been an invention of classical Rome, and, like the arch, was imitated in all lands under Roman influence. Romanesque architecture, with round arch and dome, reached into the New World with the settling of the Spaniards (as in the Mission architecture of southern California). In Byzantine incurved form it reached eastward as far as central Asia and India.

The arch and dome were invented independently elsewhere, but these few beginnings never went beyond rudimentary forms and were never applied to architectural purposes beyond the simplest. The Maya of Yucatan made use of corbeled arches, anchored by massive walls, but were limited to narrow vaulted rooms. Domed structures appeared early in Mesopotamia. The central Eskimo also achieved a small domed house of snow blocks, but their culture presented no need for other use. Arch and dome as principles of construction remained Old World devices until recent times; they spread over the area of the higher civilizations, developing new forms and purposes which, in their turn, spread over much the same regions. They became basic elements in our engineering.

POTTERY AND THE POTTER'S WHEEL

Simple as molding a vessel of clay may seem, pottery manufacture may have had but few independent beginnings. It is by no means a universal art, for it is absent among natives of peripheral regions of Old and New Worlds—Australia, Polynesia, much of Siberia, and the northern and southern extremities of the Americas. Its fundamental types are few (only two in the Americas, for example), which, with their restricted areas of occurrence, suggests spread by imitation rather than repeated invention.

A factor inhibiting its invention was common use of other containers. Often these were less fragile, more easily transported, and quite as serviceable (for cooking, for example). California Indians used baskets for all domestic purposes, Plains Indians skin receptacles, Australians folded bark vessels. Cooking in these was usually by dropping in hot stones, replacing them as they cooled—a reasonably efficient method. Pottery, which can be set directly on the fire, is a convenience, not a necessity. Yet this may well have allowed preparation of a wider variety of foods and thus changed eating habits.

Pottery-making peoples utilize the wares for many purposes other than cooking—for storage of foodstuffs and other articles, even as 'coffins.' This exemplifies the tendency in each culture area to specialize in one craft—basketry, pottery, wood or skin working—and to use it almost to the exclusion of others. Technical skills acquired in that craft and habitual familiarity with it tend to inhibit other developments.

Two levels of pottery development are distinguishable in time and area of occurrence. Vessels shaped by the hand alone appeared in the Old World in the Neolithic Period and in the Americas at some unknown but early date. Modeling by hand is still in vogue among outlying primitive groups of the Old World and was the only method known in the New. Over a more restricted, centrally located region of the Old World (China-Egypt-Europe) this was superseded in the Bronze Age by pottery spun on a wheel.

Hand-shaped pottery is commonly wide-mouthed and globular, but remarkably symmetrical and smooth. Shaping with the hands inside and out means avoiding constricted necks but does encourage surface modeling. Spinning on a horizontal wheel, with fingers lightly forming the walls, encourages graceful incurving forms (like Greek vases), with small necks more common. Wheel-made pottery is not more perfect but is produced in quantity more swiftly.

The two modes of manufacture are coupled with a social distinction. Hand-modeling is usually woman's work, a domestic product for home use. But men are the potters where the wheel is employed. The change may have come originally from the prior association of men with wheels, as wheelwrights and carters, reinforced by the possibilities of quantity production for livelihood.

The most common method of manufacture of hand-shaped wares is by coiling: adding strips of clay to the growing edge of the vessel, smoothing them down until they adhere firmly. A variant involves the use of a stone or clay 'anvil' held inside while the clay is compacted by beating the exterior with a paddle—a method invented at least twice: in North America and in the regions of southeast Asia. Molding over a form is less common and often no more than a rude substitute method in imitation of coil-made pottery.

The introduction of the potter's wheel or disc in the Bronze Age was the earliest adaptation to other mechanical purposes of the wheel, by origin a cart wheel. It serves as no more than a horizontal fly-wheel for the lump of clay set spinning at its hub. A complete invention in itself, more recent changes have been simply the use of a treadle, later power machinery, to turn it in place of the hand.

The potter's wheel is an Old World device of considerable antiquity whose point of origin is unknown. It was in use in Egypt and Mesopotamia by early Bronze Age (at least by 3000 B.C.), in Crete by 2500 B.C., in Troy before 2000 B.C. It spread slowly from this general region: north-ward to Britain in the Iron Age (where hand-shaped pottery persisted until Anglo-Saxon days), eastward to southern Siberia and China 2000 years ago. Three subsidiary focal points figured in this spread: (a) Egypt to the Mediterranean, northward through Europe, (b) China to its cul-tural dependencies Korea and Japan, (c) India to Sumatra and Java.

Decoration of the two classes of wares differs little, though there is more incising and stamping of lines and added modeled ornament on hand-shaped wares. Both varieties bear painted designs, usually on a base coat of colored clay applied to the outer surface. It is noteworthy that both incised and painted designs are more commonly geometric forms than realistic floral or human figures: these were geometric designs developed in basketry and weaving, transferred to quite another field, the vessel surface. The finest examples of native pottery—all hand-shaped—both in quality and decoration are those of the western Americas, where the modeled portrait jars of ancient Trujillo (Peru) are unexcelled.

The preparation of a surface coat led to the invention of glazes, coat-ings which when baked (fired) are glossy and render the vessels water-tight. Glass-like coatings were known in ancient Babylonia and Egypt. An opaque glaze (tin enamel) was also known in Mesopotamia: brought to Spain by Moorish conquerors about A.D. 1000 it was copied through-out western Europe. A special derivative of this was majolica ware of Italy (sixteenth century), from which Delft ware of Holland and Eng-land was further derived to imitate porcelain. An independent origin of a glaze took place in southwestern United States some 600-700 years ago; but its use for designs alone, not as a surface coat, shows only par-tial parallel to the Old World development.

Porcelain, the highest type of pottery, is a Chinese invention. Its essen-tial quality is given by a special glaze which fuses to a transparent coat adhering closely to a fine-grained core of clay. The old Mesopotamian glazing practices began to affect China, via the Iranian (Persian) lands, about 2000 years ago. By the third century of the Christian era these were being transformed; full-fledged porcelains appeared by the sixth and seventh centuries; and the art reached its pinnacle in the eighteenth, at which time European potters began to imitate it.

The sequence of developments in pottery shows that the normal course of invention is that of budding-off of specialized forms, recombination of bits of older knowledge and experience, and the spread of the arts by imitation rather than the re-invention of solutions to the common problems.

WEAVING AND THE LOOM

Woven fabrics have probably been repeatedly invented, unlike the few beginnings of pottery. Interlacing of cords occurs among all peoples and probably dates from remotest antiquity. Certainly by Neolithic times men were well equipped with specialized forms of nets, mats, baskets, and cloth to serve varied purposes.

Inventiveness in this field rests on skillful and accurate movements of the fingers. Fingering dexterity is a learned skill: the smooth sequence of thumb and finger movements, when automatic and habitual, becomes a basis for variant manipulations. All this rests on two fundamental and peculiarly human traits: the ability to move thumb and fingers in varying co-ordination and the tendency to vary the uses of acquired habits, largely in the spirit of play and discovery.

From this point of view distinctions between baskets, bags, nets, and cloth are somewhat fictitious—distinctions based rather on shape, use, or flexibility. It is reasonably clear that the several types were not outright new inventions but flowed one from another as new manipulations and new materials were tried.

Baskets serve as containers for storage, carrying, or cooking and especially in the last capacity substitute for pottery or wood or stone vessels. Even poorly constructed baskets are effective for holding liquids as the strands soon swell tightly closed.

Baskets occur in all parts of the world, but not among all peoples. The extent of use and craftsmanship varies. For example, among Indians in North America baskets were extensively made west of the Rockies only and were almost wholly lacking in the north; within the western area, their maximum development in use, perfection, decoration, and variety of form was in north central California. Here baskets served every domestic purpose from cooking to women's caps to cradles. These are the world's finest baskets. Outwardly from this center these features appear in progressively diminishing degree—a characteristic of culture traits in general.

Three fundamentally different techniques are employed in basket construction: (a) simple checkerboard weave, where semi-rigid split canes are interwoven at right angles; (b) twining, by twisting together two flexible strands (wefts) around a series of parallel warp rods (c) coiling, where a flexible strand is sewn over and over a coiled rod which forms the foundation in bottom and sides of the basket. The three have separate areas of occurrence as a rule: Philippine basketry is almost all checkerboard, central Californian coiled, on the Alaskan-west Canadian coast twined, for example. Their mutual exclusiveness derives from the circumstance that skills developed in each distinctive technique tend to inhibit the origin or imitation of the others.

Twining is akin to true weaving. Where very flexible warps are used, baskets are woven upside down with the warps hanging free, as in the Aleutian Islands. Immediately south of this, on the southern Alaskan coast, cloaks are woven in precisely this fashion using mountain goat wool. Incipient looms of this suspended warp type are known from various parts of the world.

True weaving of cloth involves four primary elements: fine spun yarns, a frame (loom) on which to stretch the limber warp yarns, a device (heddle) for separating and lifting alternate warps at one time for the insertion of the weft, the interlacing of weft yarns directly across the warps without twining.

Yarns for cloth are both more flexible and longer than basket strands. Where short cotton and wool fibers are used, they are spun into continuous cord. The age-old method for cordage, used throughout the world, is to roll the fibers together on the bare thigh under the palm. But wherever cloth is made, a spindle is employed for speed and quantity production—a slim stick set spinning by the fingers so that an attached bundle of fibers is twisted together at its tip. Spinning in this fashion, like the loom, dates from Neolithic times and is still used by outlying peoples over the world. The spinning wheel is simply a spindle turned by a belt from a large wheel flipped by hand. It is an Old World contrivance of restricted distribution which appeared in Europe about the fourteenth century, probably derived from India or adjacent territory. A smaller ('Saxon') wheel, invented in Europe in the sixteenth century, works with a treadle, performs spinning and reeling-in operations simultaneously, and thus permits continuous operation. Power-spinners (nineteenth century) are merely motor-driven forms of this.

Loom weaving was invented and used only in two well-defined areas: in the New World from Chile to southwestern United States, in the Old in the area from the Far East through southern Asia to Europe and

North Africa. The American loom represents the simpler older form of both areas. In this two sticks serve as heddles; to one are attached loops to lift every other warp, the other (without loops) shoved behind the remaining warps raises them in turn for the passing of the weft yarn. On such looms the unrivaled fabrics of ancient Peru, ancient Egypt, and India were woven. An improvement for speed and convenience was the frame heddle, but it involved no new principle. This is a frame carrying cords or wires with a loop or eye at the middle of each through which alternate warps pass; set vertically across the horizontally placed warps of the loom, they are raised by treadles. The loom with frame heddles was in use throughout the area from Europe (where it appeared by sixteenth century) to eastern Asia, but was unknown in the New World. A further improvement was the flying-shuttle (invented in 1733) by which the bobbin of weft yarn was mechanically thrown from side to side. The weaving of more complex designs calls for more numerous heddles, each holding its appropriate group of warps. Where too many heddles would have been awkward, groups of warps are linked by cords which are pulled by an assistant in memorized sequence, a European practice alone which prevailed for several centuries until replaced by the Jacquard loom in which a mechanical selector operates. But even the most complicated power-driven looms of today are basically little more than the primitive loom where the dividing of the warps in groups and the passing of the weft yarn between them is carried on by finger play.

An accidental outgrowth of interlacing warp and weft at right angles was the development in all weaving areas of straight line geometric designs. The difficulty of producing curves—which must proceed by minute steps diagonally across the rectangular web—inhibited decoration with floral or other curved figures unless fine threads were used. It is clear that the early development of geometric forms in cloth and basketry fixed the decorative style of many regions, where it was transferred bodily to other media, such as pottery, whose techniques and surfaces would have permitted free use of other designs.

Basketmaking, spinning, and loom-weaving are most commonly women's occupations—stay-at-home activities—among primitive peoples and, by inference, in ancient communities. Only where weaving became a gainful pursuit, as in the 'cottage-industry' of eighteenth-century Europe, were spinning and weaving taken over by men.

PLOW, WHEEL, AND POWER-PRODUCING DEVICES

The wheel, plow, and potter's wheel form a group of fundamentally important inventions which, with identical cultivated grains, shows the linkage of the early civilizations of the Old World from the Mediterranean and Europe to China. From this common basis, established in the Bronze Age of 5000 to 3000 years ago, divergent specialization produced the distinctive features of the historic civilizations: Egypt differentiated from Greece, China from India, Mesopotamia and Iran from both west and east. This whole area was set off by the sharing of these fundamental traits from the outer Old World (northern Asia, the Oceanic islands, Africa south of its Mediterranean fringe) and from the New, where they were wholly absent. All these inventions produced great changes in social life and habits from those of preceding Neolithic times.

In the Neolithic Period and among outlying primitive peoples of our day cultivation of the soil was small scale, hardly more than garden cultivation, carried on by laborious hand digging and hoeing. As a more or less incidental occupation close to home it was normally woman's work, while men were engaged in more arduous food quests by hunting and fishing. With the introduction of the plow, harnessed to draft animals, the scene changed: cultivation on a broad scale (agriculture) as a means of livelihood became a man's occupation. And with this came a shift in the products from emphasis on root crops and vegetables to broadcast cereals: wheat, barley, millet primarily.

The point of invention of the plow is unknown, save that it was somewhere in this area of Old World higher civilizations. The plow itself is no more than a digging stick, set crosswise as a plowshare to furrow the soil on a shaft to which oxen were harnessed. It is probable that men as handlers of the unruly beasts now substituted for women in cultivation—a somewhat accidental cause of a gross social change, but one furthered by the new possibilities for making a living. Except for substituting a metal share, and much later adding a mold-board to turn the furrow, the plow retained its form unchanged for centuries. Mechanical improvements, with the use of power devices, and the addition of mechanical drills and harvesters are developments of the nineteenth century.

The origin of the wheel—in the same region—is quite as obscure. It is by far the most significant of the early inventions, for the wheel lies at the basis of all our mechanical development and without it power-producing devices would probably never have come into existence.

It is clear, however, that the wheel was first devised for vehicles, for moving heavy loads other than by sheer muscular power. While there is some speculation that vehicles had their origin in certain wheeled toys and the discs of spindles known in antiquity, it is likely that these provided no more than some familiarity with wheel-like forms. The evidence favors, rather, the use of rollers under the dragging ends of poles which were attached to the shoulders of ox or horse, or even man. This 'dragcart' or 'travois' (which had even until recently a distribution over a vast area from peasant Europe eastward to the Plains of America) was often furnished with sledge runners where the load came on the dragging ends of the poles. When logs were pinned under the runners, so that they moved along with the vehicle, a cart was formed. Cutting away the unneeded central part of the roller or providing two solid discs fastened on a moveable axle were refinements. There were other problems involved—mounting moveable wheels on fixed axles, a pivoted front axle or separately pivoted front wheels to steer a four-wheeled wagon—which were, in fact, solved only well along in the historic period. This sequence in development is far from conjectural; there are many evidences supporting it in survivals of the rudimentary forms in backward communities.

The oldest form was clearly a two-wheeled cart, originally for farm use. Transport of goods in trade for any distance long awaited the building of roads. (Even as late as the eighteenth century in England rural transport by cart was suspended during winter and pack train substituted, because roads became impassable.) There is reason to think that the cart had its origin in interior Asia, spreading to southern Asia, thence, via the Mediterranean, into Europe. The earliest wheeled vehicle yet unearthed is from ancient Kish in Sumeria. The two-wheeled conveyance (a chariot) was derived by the Egyptians from the Asiatic Hyksos in the seventeenth century B.C. but only later spread through the Mediterranean world. By the Hallstatt Period (earlier Iron Age, 900-500 B.C.) ox-carts with solid wooden wheels were in use in central Europe, but did not reach distant Scandinavia until much later. In China the device was copied some time in the Bronze Age, certainly before the ninth century B.C.

The four-wheeled wagon was a development of the Near East in later Bronze Age, confined for a long time to Mediterranean lands as a vehicle for state occasions. It made no progress northward through Europe until the Middle Ages and was never in common use there until recent centuries. It is far more dependent on good roadways than the cart.

The earliest mechanical adaptation of the wheel seems to have been the potter's wheel. Cog-wheels (intermeshing forms of toothed wheels) are known from the Classical Period, as were pulleys and belted drive wheels. But there was little application of wheels to machinery until the advent of steam power made machine appliances possible on a large scale.

Most power-producing devices are relatively late in the world's history. Water-driven wheels for lifting irrigating water from low canals are very ancient in the arid lands of the Near East. Wind mills, a power substitute where flowing streams were lacking, were invented only in the Middle Ages (by twelfth century) in western Europe. While the Romans knew the expansive power of steam, their devices served merely as toys and curiosities. The effective use of this source of power came only with the invention of the steam engine in England toward the close of the eighteenth century. Applied first to pumping collieries and hauling out the mined coal, the inter-stimulus of the engine on the coal industry with the increased quantity of coal available to produce steam brought mechanical appliances in ever increasing number through the nineteenth century. Devices for generating electric power, inventions of the second half of the nineteenth century, provided a further source of power less fettered to locality than water, wind, and even steam. It has the obvious advantage of providing energy for power and light in convenient form at great distances from the source of supply. The invention of internal combustion engines (gasoline and diesel) in our own day offered compact mobile power units for ship, automobile, and plane, quite changing our social and economic life. The latest power-producing inventions, rockets and atom-smashing mechanisms, hold vast possibilities of further social change.

In the long range view the most noteworthy characteristics of these inventions have been: first, the accumulation of experiences; second, the acceleration in their appearance—few at first, at long intervals; coming with a rush in recent centuries, generations, years; third, the marked social changes they wrought in the societies that utilized them.

TIME-RECKONING AND THE CALENDAR

Time is man-made; nature knows only change. We are so much the victims of time in our culture, subject to self-imposed and unconscious routining by the hour and the day, the 'pressure of time,' 'the need for speed,' that we blindly assume the inevitability and naturalness of time-reckoning. Man is aware of changes in his body and in the outer world—changes through day and night, the succession of the seasons, and their recurrent nature. But the reckoning of periods of change, by hour, day, or year, is a human concept, projected on the world, and known to no other animal.

The reckoning of time in some fashion is universal among all peoples and probably has great antiquity. This is warranted by its unconscious and automatic character, and as such has been ingrained in all languages. In no known language is it possible to form a sentence without indicating time (tense) though the speakers are unaware of this requirement. The system of tense employed, however, often differs appreciably from a simple past, present, and future.

At the outset it must be explained that some of our units of time are based on the recurrence of changes in the outer world, others are wholly artificial. Changes through the day, the succession of days, the apparent movement of sun, moon, and stars, the phases of the moon, the cyclic change of the seasons, the succession of the years, all are easily recognized natural events. But there are no natural counterparts to the division of time by hour, minute, or second, to the grouping of days by weeks or by calendar (as opposed to lunar) months.

A number of quite different calendric systems have been invented; common to all is a count by years and lunar months, less frequently by seasons. The 'year,' however, may not be a solar year, a full circuit of the earth around the sun. Indians of southern Arizona, for example, reckon doubly: a record of events runs by solar years, but the 'year' that controls everyday life is six months long, with six named months repeated—this because there are two complete cycles of planting and harvesting in a solar year. The point at which a year begins must be arbitrary unless it be one of the solstices, which is quite rare as an initial point. The same Indians reckon their new solar year from the first appearance of cottonwood leaves, early February. The arbitrary initial point of our own calendar shows a chain of cultural inheritance: our calendar is that of the Romans who had adopted the Egyptian system with a solar year fixed by the rising of the star Sirius.

The month is ordinarily a more important grouping of days. This is almost universally the lunar month, the period of waxing and waning of the moon. To refer to particular periods—that is, to reckon time—the months must be named: the pattern of naming varies, but most commonly has reference to natural phenomena of the period (snow falls, corn ripens, et cetera). Types of name show systematic occurrence; while in general North American Indians used such descriptive designations, in the coastal strip from Alaska to northern California the pattern was one of numbering the months.

Unless something of great social significance hangs on it, primitive people are little concerned with the exact duration of these periods and the relation of one to another. The dark phase of the moon may be ignored in the reckoning. As there are twelve and a fraction lunar months in a solar year, a count by months can never agree with the year. Primitive peoples are little concerned with this discrepancy; continuing the count of month names with seasonal reference over the years, the name soon becomes inappropriate to the season, so, while they argue over it, they make a practical adjustment, beginning anew. The problem of adjusting the lunar month (29 days) and the solar year, which does not end evenly with a completed day (365 days, 6 hours, 48 minutes, 46 seconds), awaited more precise astronomical knowledge and in every case represented an intellectual achievement.

The origin of more precise reckoning lay in priestly observation of the solstices and the movements of the stars, coupled with month and day counts, for the purpose of regulating rituals. The time for a certain ceremony (of Pueblo Indians, for example) was fixed by one of the solstices (the moment of most northern or southern position of the sun); other rites followed by day count. The 'moveable' and 'fixed feasts' of our ecclesiastical calendars are such because they depend, one on astronomical events, the other on day and month count. Where it was assumed that the stars affected man's fate, as in the ancient Near East, very accurate reckoning was made of the movements of the planets among the fixed stars.

European peoples all use a twelve-month calendar derived from the Romans (as indicated by our Latin-based month names). Its history shows both the artificial nature of any calendar and the adjustments made as astronomical knowledge grew. Prior to Julius Caesar the Romans had attempted to fix ceremonials simultaneously by lunar and solar counts, which cannot be reconciled. In 46 B.C. Caesar (on the advice of a Greek astronomer, Sosigenes) ended the confusion by imperial decree, establishing arbitrary months of 30 and 31 days alternately, a short month to fill the gap, and decreed each fourth year should be reckoned with an extra day to absorb the accumulated quarter-days of the solar round. The extra 48 minutes 46 seconds was unknown to the Romans; its accumulation through the centuries again brought confusion. Since the Roman Catholic Church had an interest in keeping its ceremonials in proper relation to the sun's progress, Pope Gregory XIII, on the advice of his astronomers, in 1582 ordered 10 days dropped to restore the relation and directed that the added leap-day be omitted in all years beginning a century except those divisable by 400. (Actually the Gregorian year, which we now use, leaves a very small error between the reckoning by completed days and the completed earth's circuit around the sun.) As the principal international organization of the time, the Church's edict established the system throughout Europe.

Any day is designated in our calendar by assigning the proper one of 7 day names, 30, 31, 28 (or 29) number names in the month, and the year count from the birth of Christ. The Chinese calendar count is on a basis of a cycle of 60 days (without reference to beginning and end of the solar year) and one of 60 moons; thus reference is by naming the day of its cycle, the moon, and the year of the emperor's reign. The Maya of Yucatan devised a calendar based on a 'month' of 20 days, eighteen of which, with five days inserted, made a 365 day year; and a second cycle comprising thirteen groups of these 20 days which yielded another period, 260 days, the 'Sacred Year.' These two cycles, running concurrently, brought together the same named day in both cycles after 52 years had elapsed; hence a dating also in terms of 52 year periods. Their sequence of years was also reckoned in units of 20 years and units of 400 years. In addition, their long continued observations showed them that five apparent revolutions of the planet Venus equaled eight solar years, and 65 Venus 'years' the span of two 52 year periods.

The week is a short group of days on which intimate social activities are patterned (church, wash day, business, and domestic pursuits). Having no counterpart in nature, weeks can vary from two days (the minimum) to our seven, or more. West Africa, for example, has weeks of three, four, and five days, each with appropriate rites and activities. The origin of the week was in recurrent marketdays or ceremonial rites at fixed intervals. The many bases for weeks show the repeated invention of this reckoning. It is noteworthy that the week is Old World in occurrence, such short clusters of days hardly appearing in native America.

Like the patterning by the week, our activities through the day are regimented by its divisions. The day has no such natural units as hours, minutes, seconds: our '24' and '60' divisions are artificialities derived ultimately from Babylonia. They remain characteristic of the higher civilizations that have use and feel need for minor divisions of time, never having spread to the simpler societies of the outlying parts of the Old World. Our own civilization, with its insistence on routining activities by the clock and crowding each minute, has developed as one of its outstanding characteristics an almost hysterical attitude with respect to time.

GEORGE PETER MURDOCK

XII

How Culture Changes

IT IS A FUNDAMENTAL CHARACTERISTIC of culture that, despite its essentially conservative nature, it does change over time and from place to place. Herein it differs strikingly from the social behavior of animals other than man. Among ants, for example, colonies of the same species differ little in behavior from one another and even, so far as we can judge from specimens embedded in amber, from their ancestors of fifty million years ago. In less than one million years man, by contrast, has advanced from the rawest savagery to civilization and has proliferated at least three thousand distinctive cultures.

The processes by which culture changes are by now reasonably well known to science. They cannot be understood, however, without a clear comprehension of the nature of culture, and this must be summarized here even at the risk of some repetition of material in earlier chapters.

Culture is the product of learning, rather than of heredity. The cultures of the world are systems of collective habits. The differences observable among them are the cumulative product of mass learning under diverse geographic and social conditions. Race and other biological factors influence culture only in so far as they affect the conditions under which learning occurs, as when the presence of people of markedly different physique operates as a factor in the development of race prejudice.

Culture is learned through precisely the same mechanism as that involved in all habit formation. Hunger, sex, fear, and other basic drives, as well as acquired motivations, impel human beings to act. Actions encounter either success or failure. With failure, especially when accompanied by pain or punishment, an action tends to be replaced by other behavior, and its probability of recurring under similar conditions is

319

diminished. Success, on the other hand, increases the tendency of responses to occur when the same drive is again aroused in a like situation. With repeated success, responses are established as habits, and are progressively adapted to the situations in which they are appropriate.

A culture consists of habits that are shared by members of a society, whether this be a primitive tribe or a civilized nation. The sharing may be general throughout the society, as is normally the case with language habits. Often, however, it is limited to particular categories of people within the society. Thus persons of the same sex or age group, members of the same social class, association, or occupational group, and persons interacting with others in similar relationships commonly resemble one another in their social habits, though diverging behaviorally from persons in other categories.

The social sharing of habits has several causes. The fact that the situations under which behavior is acquired are similar for many individuals conduces in itself to parallel learning. Even more important is the fact that each generation inculcates in the next, through education, the cultural habits which it has found satisfying and adaptive. Finally, the members of any society exercise pressure upon one another, through formal and informal means of social control, to conform to standards of behavior which are considered right and appropriate. This is particularly true of behavior in interpersonal relationships, where the success or failure of an action depends upon the reaction of another person to it, rather than, for example, upon its adaptiveness to the innate qualities of natural objects. Once one has acquired a limited number of stereotyped patterns of social behavior one is equipped to cope successfully with widely diversified social situations, and one is also provided with a body of reliable expectations regarding the probable responses of others to one's own behavior. This gives confidence and spares the individual an immense amount of individualized learning, which is ever a painful process. It is with good reason, therefore, that every society lays great stress on social conformity.

The habits that are variously shared within a society, and which constitute its culture, fall into two major classes, namely, habits of action and habits of thought. These may be termed, respectively, 'customs' and 'collective ideas.' Customs include such readily observable modes of behavior as etiquette, ceremonial, and the techniques of manipulating material objects. Collective ideas are not directly observable but must be inferred from their expression in language and other overt behavior.

They include such things as practical knowledge, religious beliefs, and social values. Moreover, they embrace a mass of rules or definitions, which specify for each custom the persons who may and may not observe it, the circumstances in which it is and is not appropriate, and the limits and permissible variations of the behavior itself. Collective ideas also include a body of social expectations—anticipations of how others will respond to one's own behavior, especially of the sanctions, i.e. social rewards and punishments, that can be expected from conformity and deviation. With every custom and with every organized cluster of customs, such as a 'culture complex' or 'institution,' there is ordinarily associated a mass of collective ideas.

Actual social behavior, as it is observed in real life, must be carefully distinguished from culture, which consists of habits or tendencies to act and not of actions themselves. Though largely determined by habits, actual behavior is also affected by the physiological and emotional state of the individual, the intensity of his drives, and the particular external circumstances. Since no two situations are ever exactly alike, actual behavior fluctuates considerably, even when springing from the same habit. A description of a culture is consequently never an account of actual social behavior but is rather a reconstruction nf the collective habits which underlie it.

From the point of view of cultural change, however, actual or observable behavior is of primary importance. Whenever social behavior persistently deviates from established cultural habits in any direction, it results in modifications first in social expectations, and then in customs, beliefs, and rules. Gradually, in this way, collective habits are altered and the culture comes to accord better with the new norms of actual behavior.

Changes in social behavior, and hence in culture, normally have their origin in some significant alteration in the life conditions of a society. Any event which changes the situations under which collective behavior occurs, so that habitual actions are discouraged and new responses are favored, may lead to cultural innovations. Among the classes of events that are known to be especially influential in producing cultural change are increases or decreases in population, changes in the geographical environment, migrations into new environments, contacts with peoples of differing culture, natural and social catastrophes such as floods, crop failures, epidemics, wars, and economic depressions, accidental discoveries, and even such biographical events as the death or rise to power of a strong political leader.

The events which produce cultural change by altering the conditions under which social behavior proves adaptive, i.e. is or is not rewarded, are invariably historical, i.e. specific with respect to time and place. Events occurring at different places and times may resemble one another, however, and exert parallel influences upon different cultures. It is thus possible to view changes in culture either in relation to their spatial and temporal setting or in relation to comparable events wherever and whenever they have occurred. The former or 'historical' approach answers such questions as what? when? and where? The latter or 'scientific' approach, by illuminating the processes by which change occurs, answers the question how? Both approaches are valid and completely complementary.

Historical anthropologists commonly discuss particular traits of culture, such as the use of tobacco, the wheel, the domesticated horse, the alphabet, or money, treating of their 'invention' at specific times and places and of their 'diffusion' from the points of origin to other parts of the world. Since our problem is to describe *how* culture changes, we must abandon the bird's-eye view of the historian and examine the processes within societies by which all changes, and not merely particular ones, take place. These processes may be conveniently grouped under the terms 'innovation,' 'social acceptance,' 'selective elimination,' and 'integration.'

Cultural change begins with the process of *innovation*, the formation of a new habit by a single individual which is subsequently accepted or learned by other members of his society. An innovation originates through the ordinary psychological mechanism of learning, and differs from purely individual habits only in the fact that it comes to be socially shared. It is nevertheless useful to distinguish several important variants of the process.

An innovation may be called a *variation* when it represents a slight modification of pre-existing habitual behavior under the pressure of gradually changing circumstances. The slow evolution in the forms of manufactured objects over time usually represents an accumulation of variations. In the same manner, tattooing can be extended over a wider area of the body, additional barbs may be added to a harpoon, skirts may be lengthened or shortened, folk tales may grow by accretion, or ceremonial may become increasingly elaborate and formalized. Variation occurs in all cultures at all times. The individual increments of change are often so slight as to be almost imperceptible, but their cumulative effect over long periods may be immense.

When innovation involves the transfer of elements of habitual behavior from one situational context to another, or their combination into new syntheses, it is called *invention*. At least some degree of creativeness is always present. Most of the important technological innovations are of this type. Thus the invention of the airplane involved the synthesis of such elements as the wings of a glider, an internal-combustion engine from an automobile, and an adaptation of a ship's propeller. Though less well known, inventions are equally common in the non-material aspects of culture. The city-manager plan, for example, represents an obvious transfer of techniques of business management to the sphere of local government, and most forms of religious worship are modeled on behavior toward persons of high social status, e.g. sacrifice upon bribery, prayer upon petitions, laudation upon flattery, ritual upon etiquette.

Since invention always involves a new synthesis of old habits, it is dependent upon the existing content of the culture. A synthesis cannot occur if the elements which it combines are not present in the culture. It is for this reason that parallel inventions so rarely occur among unconnected peoples of differing culture. With the exception of such simple and obvious combinations as the hafting of tools, anthropologists know of only a handful of genuine inventions that have been arrived at independently by historically unrelated peoples. Among them perhaps the most famous are the fire piston, invented by the Malays and a French physicist, and the dome, developed by the ancient Romans from the arch and independently invented by the Eskimos for their snow igloos.

Among peoples of the same or related cultures, on the other hand, parallel inventions are extraordinarily common. The culture provides the same constituent elements to many people, and if one person does not achieve the synthesis others are likely to do so. The Patent Office furnishes thousands of examples. In one famous instance, the telephone, applications for a patent were received on the same day from two independent inventors, Bell and Gray. Another noted case is the independent formulation of the theory of natural selection by Darwin and Wallace. So common is this phenomenon that scientists often live in dread of the anticipation of their discoveries by rivals. Parallel invention thus appears to be frequent and almost inevitable among peoples of similar culture, though so rare as to be almost non-existent among peoples of different culture.

A third type of innovation may be called *tentation*. Unlike the previous types, which merely modify or recombine elements of habit already in existence, tentation may give rise to elements that show little or no continuity with the past. The mechanism by which these are acquired is that which psychologists call 'trial-and-error learning.' Tentation may occur in any situation in which established habits prove ineffective and individuals are so strongly motivated that they try out other modes of behavior in a search for an adequate solution to their problems. They will ordinarily try out first a number of variations and recombinations of existing habitual responses, but if all of these fail they will resort to 'random behavior,' in the course of which they may accidentally hit upon some novel response which solves the problem and thereby becomes established as a new cultural element.

Crises are particularly conducive to tentation. In a famine, for instance, people try out all sorts of things that they have never eaten before, and if some of them prove nutritious and tasty they may be added to the normal diet. An epidemic similarly leads to a search for new medicines, and both primitive and civilized peoples have discovered useful remedies in this way. War also leads to improvisation, as do economic crises. Scientific experimentation, it should be pointed out, is often a form of controlled tentation, as when a new series of chemical compounds are systematically put to test. The saying that 'necessity is the mother of invention' applies more forcefully to tentation than to invention proper.

When accidental discoveries lead to cultural innovations, the process is commonly that of tentation. The origin of the boomerang in aboriginal Australia will serve as an example. Over much of that continent the natives used curved throwing sticks to kill or stun small animals, and in a limited part of the area the true boomerang was used for this purpose. Almost certainly the first boomerang was produced by sheer accident in the attempt to fashion an ordinary throwing stick. Observing the unique behavior of the particular stick in flight, the maker and his fellows doubtless attempted to duplicate it. They must have resorted to tentation, or trial-and-error behavior, until they eventually succeeded, and thereby established boomerang manufacture as a habit. The history of modern 'inventions' is full of such instances, the discovery of the photographic plate by Daguerre being one of the most familiar examples.

Tentation also accounts for a type of cultural parallel which is distinct from genuine independent invention. There are certain universal problems which every people must solve and for which there are a limited number of easy and obvious solutions, so that peoples in different parts of the world have often hit upon the same solution quite independently. Rules of descent provide a good illustration. In all societies, each individual must be affiliated with a group of relatives to whom he regards himself as most closely akin and to whom he can turn for aid in time of need. There are only four possibilities: partrilineal descent, which relates an individual to kinsmen in the male line; matrilineal descent, which affiliates him with relatives through females; ambilineal descent, which aligns him with other individuals who are descended from a particular common ancestor in any line; and bilateral descent, which associates him with a group of his very closest relatives irrespective of the mode of their connection. Every society must choose one of these alternatives or some combination thereof, and, since the possibilities are limited to four, many peoples have, of necessity, arrived independently at the same cultural solution. Funeral customs present another example, since there are only a limited number of feasible ways of disposing of a dead body. In all such instances, if a society is compelled for any reason to abandon its previous custom it will inevitably, through tentation, arrive at an alternative solution which other peoples have independently adopted.

The fourth and last type of innovation is *cultural borrowing*, which is what the historical anthropologist, with his bird's-eye view, calls 'diffusion.' In this case the innovator is not the originator of a new habit, but its introducer. The habit has previously been part of the culture of another society; the innovator is merely the first member of his social group to adopt it. From the point of view of psychology, cultural borrowing is merely a special case of the learning process known as 'imitation.' The innovator, faced with a situation in which the shared habits of his own society are not fully satisfactory, copies behavior which he has observed in members of another society, instead of resorting to variation, invention, or tentation to solve his problem.

Of all forms of innovation, cultural borrowing is by far the most common and important. The overwhelming majority of the elements in any culture are the result of borrowing. Modern American culture provides a good illustration, as can be shown by a few random examples. Our language comes from England, our alphabet from the Phoenicians, our numerical system from India, and paper and printing from China. Our family organization and system of real property derive from medieval

Europe. Our religion is a composite of elements largely assembled from the ancient Hebrews, Egyptians, Babylonians, and Persians. Metal coinage comes from Lydia, paper money from China, checks from Persia. Our system of banking, credit, loans, discounts, mortgages, et cetera, is derived in its essentials from ancient Babylonia, with modern elaborations from Italy and England. Our architecture is still largely Greek, Gothic, Georgian, et cetera. Our favorite flavors in ice creams, vanilla and chocolate, are both borrowed from the Aztecs of Mexico and were unknown to Europeans before the conquest by Cortez. Tea comes from China, coffee from Ethiopia, tobacco from the American Indians. Our domesticated animals and plants, virtually without exception, are borrowed. If the reader were to make a list of absolutely everything he eats during the next week, analysis would probably show that one third are products that were already cultivated in Neolithic times and that at least two thirds were being raised at the time of Christ, and it would be surprising if the list contained any item that was not cultivated for food somewhere in the world when Columbus sailed for America.

Our own culture is not unique in this respect, for it is doubtful whether there is a single culture known to history or anthropology that has not owed at least ninety per cent of its constituent elements to cultural borrowing. The reason is not far to seek. Any habit that has become established in a culture has been tried out by many people and found satisfactory. When a society finds itself in a dilemma, therefore, the chances that an element already present in the culture of another people will turn out to be an adequate solution to its own problem are vastly greater than those of any random and untested innovation of another type. Cultural borrowing is thus highly economical, and most peoples tend to ransack the cultural resources of their neighbors for adaptive practices before they resort to invention or tentation.

Cultural borrowing depends upon contact. Obviously the opportunity for borrowing is lacking in the case of a completely isolated society. Other factors being equal, the extent to which one culture will borrow from another is proportionate to the intensity and duration of the social intercourse between their bearers. Contact need not always be face-to-face, however, for there are numerous instances of cultural borrowing at a distance through the medium of written language or through copying of articles received by trade. By and large, however, societies borrow mainly from their immediate neighbors, with the result that the products of diffusion are ordinarily clustered in geographically contiguous areas.

Trade, missionary enterprise, and political conquest create conditions conducive to cultural borrowing. Peculiarly important, however, is inter-marriage, for this brings individuals of differing culture together within the family, where children can learn from both parents. Diffusion then proceeds through the socialization process, which produces far more perfect copying than does cultural borrowing on the adult level. The American 'melting pot' operates largely through this mechanism. Primitive peoples practicing local exogamy, i.e. requiring individuals to obtain spouses from another village or band, commonly reveal considerable cultural uniformity over wide areas, as in aboriginal Australia and among the Indians of the Northwest Coast. By contrast, in areas like Melanesia and Central California where marriage normally takes place within the community, even villages a few miles apart may differ strikingly in dialect and customs. In the one case culture is diffused through the same process by which it is transmitted; in the other, even adult contacts tend to be restricted to a minimum.

Incentive—a need or drive—is as essential in cultural borrowing as in other types of innovation. A people rarely borrows an alien cultural element when they already possess a trait which satisfactorily fills the same need. Thus the blubber lamp of the Eskimos was not borrowed by the Indians to the south, who had plenty of wood for fires to heat and light their dwellings. On the other hand, the extraordinarily rapid diffusion of tobacco over the earth after the discovery of America reflected the general absence of competing traits. It has been observed that the first individuals in a society to borrow alien customs are likely to be the discontented, underprivileged, and maladjusted. Thus in India Christian missionaries have made many more converts among the 'untouchables' than in the higher strata of society, and in our own country new political movements on both the extreme right and the extreme left attract an unduly high proportion of unsuccessful and neurotic people.

The presence in a receiving society of some of the habit elements involved in a new trait greatly facilitates borrowing. It is for this reason that diffusion occurs most readily among peoples of similar culture, who already share many elements of habit. Thus Englishmen and Americans borrow more frequently and easily from each other than from Russians, Chinese, or Hottentots. Conversely, aboriginal peoples are greatly handicapped in taking over the complex technology of modern civilization. They cannot, for example, begin to manufacture the steel products which they want without also taking over such things as blast furnaces and rolling mills.

Cultural borrowing will occur only if the new habit is demonstrably rewarding. The native quickly adopts steel knives and axes from the white man because their superiority to his former stone implements becomes immediately apparent. On the other hand, Europeans were slow to borrow paper manufacture from the Chinese because the advantages of paper over parchment appeared very slight at first. The Chinese and Japanese have not yet adopted the alphabet from western civilization because, however great its ultimate advantages, it would impose heavy burdens and discomforts upon all literate persons during the necessary period of readjustment. Geographic and climatic factors may prevent diffusion by withholding or reducing the possibilities of reward, and social prejudices such as ingrained conservatism may counterbalance potential advantages by inflicting disapprobation upon innovators.

Borrowing need not be exact. Oftentimes, indeed, all that is borrowed is the external 'form' of a custom and not its 'meaning,' i.e. the collective ideas associated with it. The familiar caricature of the cannibal chief wearing a silk hat provides a good illustration. Frequently an imperfect copy is quite adequate. Thus when the Plain Indians took over horses and riding equipment from the Spaniards they omitted the horseshoe, which was quite unnecessary on the prairie. Sometimes changes are imposed by the conditions of the geographical environment. When the Iroquois Indians adopted the birchbark canoe from their Algonkian neighbors, for example, they altered the material to elm bark because of the scarcity of birch trees in their habitat. Frequently cultural factors favor a modification. The original Phoenician alphabet lacked characters for vowels, the nature of their language being such that consonant signs sufficed for the identification of words. Since this was not true of the Greek language, when the Greeks borrowed the Phoenician alphabet they converted characters for which they had no need into symbols for vowels.

Modifications are so common in cultural borrowing that authorities like Malinowski have regarded the process as scarcely less creative than other forms of innovation. Often, indeed, it is inextricably blended with invention or tentation. This is well illustrated in instances of 'stimulus diffusion,' in which only the general idea of an alien cultural trait is borrowed, the specific form being supplied by improvisation. Thus a famous Cherokee chief named Sequoyah, though an illiterate man, had noticed that white men could somehow understand messages from pieces of paper on which peculiar marks were inscribed, and he came to the conclusion that this would be a useful skill for his own people to acquire. He therefore set himself the task of devising a system of marks by which the Cherokee language could be written. Inventing some signs of his own and copying some from pieces of printed matter—numbers and punctuation marks as well as letters, upside down or on their sides as often as upright—he produced a novel form of writing, a syllabary rather than an alphabet, which his tribesmen learned and continued to use for many years. (See Fig. 1.)

Courtesy of Mr. Tom B. Underwood,
Museum of The Cherokee Indian, and The Stephens Press.

FIG. 1. Sequoyah, the famous Cherokee Indian chief, invented this syllabary for recording his native language by giving syllabic values to alphabetic letters and typographical signs arbitrarily chosen and arranged from English and German type.

The second major process in cultural change is *social acceptance*. So long as an innovation, whether original or borrowed, is practiced by the innovator alone in his society, it is an individual habit and not an element of culture. To become the latter it must be accepted by others; it must be socially shared. Social acceptance begins with the adoption of a new habit by a small number of individuals. From this point it may spread until it becomes part of the sub-culture of a family, clan, local community, or other sub-group, or until it becomes a 'specialty' characteristic of persons belonging to a particular occupational, kinship, age-graded, or other status

category, or until it becomes an 'alternative' widely but optionally practiced. Eventually it may even become a 'universal,' shared by all members of the society. The term 'degrees of cultural saturation' has been
proposed for the various steps in social acceptance.

The learning mechanism involved in social acceptance is imitation, as
in the case of cultural borrowing, but the model whose behavior is copied
is a member of one's own rather than another society. So similar are the
two processes that the term 'diffusion' is often applied to both; social acceptance is called 'internal' or 'vertical' diffusion to differentiate it from
cultural borrowing, which is termed 'external' or 'horizontal' diffusion.
With minor exceptions, most of what has previously been stated about the
latter process applies equally to the former. Since close contact and similarity of culture can be taken for granted, however, copying is usually far
more exact, and this is accentuated by social control.

A factor of considerable importance in social acceptance is the prestige
of the innovator and of the group who are first to imitate him. Changes
advocated by an admired political or religious leader are readily adopted,
whereas few will follow an unpopular or despised innovator. Clothing
styles accepted by 'the four hundred' quickly diffuse throughout the
masses, but the garb of a Harlem gang does not spread to Park Avenue.
Women imitate men more readily than *vice versa*. In our own society, for
example, many women have adopted masculine garments, smoking and
drinking habits, and occupations, but there appears to be no concerted
movement among men to wear skirts, use cosmetics, or apply for positions
as nurses, governesses, or baby-sitters.

Selective elimination constitutes a third major process of cultural
change. Every innovation that has been socially accepted enters, as it
were, into a competition for survival. So long as it proves more rewarding
than its alternatives a cultural habit will endure, but when it ceases to
bring comparable satisfactions it dwindles and eventually disappears. The
process superficially resembles that of natural selection in organic evolution. It should be noted, however, that cultural traits do not compete directly with one another but are competitively tested in the experience of
those who practice them. Oftentimes the competition is carried on between organized groups of people with contrasting customs and beliefs,
as between nations, political parties, religious sects, or social and economic classes, and the issue is decided indirectly by the victory of one
group over the other. By and large, the cultural elements that are eliminated through trial and error or social competition are the less adaptive

ones, so that the process is as definitely one of the survival of the fittest as is that of natural selection.

Few of the genuine gains of culture history—the achievements of technology, of science, of man's control over nature—have ever been lost. The so-called 'lost arts of antiquity' are largely mythical. To be sure, particular peoples have declined in civilization, but not until they have passed on their contributions to others. What man has lost, in the main, is a mass of maladaptive and barbarous practices, inefficient techniques, and outworn superstitions. New errors arise, of course, in each generation, but it is comforting to realize that the mortality of error is vastly greater than that of truth.

It is the genuine achievements of man that anthropologists have in mind when they say that culture is cumulative, comparing culture history to the growth of a snowball as it is rolled down a hill. Even achievements that are superseded rarely disappear. Today the electric light has proved superior to earlier methods of lighting, but the gas mantle, the kerosene lamp, and the tallow candle still survive in out-of-the-way places or under special conditions. Survival is often assured through a change in function. The use of outmoded weapons has been preserved, for example, in athletic sports like fencing and archery and in boyhood toys such as the sling and the peashooter. Other ancient usages survive in legal, religious, and academic ceremonial. Written records, of course, preserve much of the culture of the past from oblivion. Our libraries bulge with the puerilities as well as the achievements of history.

The fourth and last important process of cultural change is that of *integration*. The shared habits that constitute a culture not only fluctuate in their degree of social acceptance, and compete for survival, but they also become progressively adapted to one another so that they tend to form an integrated whole. They exhibit what Sumner has called 'a strain toward consistency.' Every innovation alters in some respect the situations under which certain other forms of habitual behavior occur, and leads to adaptive changes in the latter. Similarly it must, in its turn, be adjusted to modifications elsewhere in the culture. While each such change is in itself, of course, an innovation, their reciprocal interaction and cumulative effect deserve special recognition as an integrative process.

The history of the automobile during the present century in our own culture provides an excellent example. The changes brought about by this technological invention are described by Professor Leslie Spier in Chapter X. A similar story could be told for other modern innovations such as the telephone, the airplane, the radio, and electrical household gadgets, and all of them pale before the potentialities of atomic energy.

Certain anthropologists have erroneously assumed that the elements of any culture are in a state of nearly perfect integration, or equilibrium, at all times. Actually, however, perfect equilibrium is never achieved or even approached. The adjustment of other elements of culture to an innovation, and of it to them, requires time—often years or even generations. In the meantime other innovations have appeared and set in motion new processes of integration. At any given time, therefore, a culture exhibits numerous instances of uncompleted integrative processes as well as examples of others which have been carried through to relatively satisfactory completion. What we always encounter is a strain toward internal adaptation, never its full realization.

The period of time which must elapse between the acceptance of an innovation and the completion of the integrative readjustments which follow in its train Ogburn has aptly called 'cultural lag.' During such a period of lag people attempt, through variation, invention, tentation, and cultural borrowing, to modify old customs and ideas to accord with the new, and to adjust the new to the old, so as to eliminate inconsistencies and sources of friction and irritation. In a modern democratic society, politics is a major scene of such efforts.

The net effect of the various processes of cultural change is to adapt the collective habits of human societies progressively over time to the changing conditions of existence. Change is always uncomfortable and often painful, and people frequently become discouraged with its slowness or even despair of achieving any genuine improvement. Neither history nor anthropology, however, gives grounds for pessimism. However halting or harsh it may appear to participants, cultural change is always adaptive and usually progressive. It is also inevitable, and will endure as long as the earth can support human life. Nothing—not even a nuclear war—can destroy civilization.

XIII

The Family

THE WORD FAMILY is so plain, the kind of reality to which it refers is so close to daily experience that one may expect to be confronted in this chapter with a simple situation. Anthropologists, however, are a strange breed; they like to make even the 'familiar' look mysterious and complicated. As a matter of fact, the comparative study of the family among many different peoples has given rise to some of the most bitter arguments in the whole history of anthropological thought and probably to its more spectacular reversal.

During the second half of the nineteenth century and the beginning of the twentieth, anthropologists were working under the influence of biological evolutionism. They were trying to organize their data so that the institutions of the simpler people would correspond to an early stage of the evolution of mankind, while our own institutions were related to the more advanced or developed forms. And since, among ourselves, the family founded on monogamic marriage was considered as the most praiseworthy and cherished institution, it was immediately inferred that savage societies—equated for the purpose with the societies of man at the beginning of its existence—could only have something of a different type. Therefore, facts were distorted and misinterpreted; even more, fanciful 'early' stages of evolution were invented, such as 'group marriage' and 'promiscuity' to account for the period when man was still so barbarous that he could not possibly conceive of the niceties of the social life it is the privilege of civilized man to enjoy. Every custom different from our own was carefully selected as a vestige of an older type of social organization.

This way of approaching the problem became obsolete when the accumulation of data made obvious the following fact: the kind of family featured in modern civilization by monogamous marriage, independent establishment of the young couple, warm relationship between parents and offspring, et cetera, while not always easy to recognize behind the complicated network of strange customs and institutions of savage peoples, is at least conspicuous among those which seem to have remained on—or returned to—the simplest cultural level. Tribes like the Andamanese of the Indian Ocean Andaman Islands, the Fuegians of the southernmost tip of South America, the Nambikwara of central Brazil, and the Bushmen of South Africa—to quote only a few examples—live in small, semi-nomadic bands; they have little or no political organization and their technological level is very low since, in some of them at least, there is no knowledge of weaving, pot-making, and even sometimes hut-building. Thus, the only social structure worth speaking of among them is the family, mostly monogamous. The observer working in the field has no trouble identifying the married couples, closely associated by sentimental bonds and economic co-operation as well as by the rearing of children born from their union.

There are two ways of interpreting this pre-eminence of the family at both ends of the scale of development of human societies. Some writers have claimed that the simpler peoples may be considered as a remnant of what can be looked at as a 'golden age,' prior to the submission of mankind to the hardships and perversities of civilization; thus, man would have known in that early stage the bliss of monogamic family only to forego it later until its more recent Christian rediscovery. The general trend, however, except for the so-called Vienna school, has been that more and more anthropologists have become convinced that familial life is present practically everywhere in human societies, even in those with sexual and educational customs very remote from our own. Thus, after they had claimed for about fifty years that the family, as modern societies know it, could only be a recent development and the outcome of a slow and long-lasting evolution, anthropologists now lean toward the opposite conviction, i.e. that the family, consisting of a more or less durable union, socially approved, of a man, a woman, and their children, is a universal phenomenon, present in each and every type of society.

These extreme positions, however, suffer equally from over-simplification. It is well known that, in very rare cases, family bonds cannot be claimed to exist. A telling example comes from the Nayar, a very large group living on the Malabar coast of India. In former times, the warlike type of life of the Nayar men did not allow them to found a family. Marriage was a purely symbolical ceremony which did not result in a permanent tie between a man and a woman. As a matter of fact, married women were permitted to have as many lovers as they wished. Children belonged exclusively to the mother line, and familial as well as land authority was exercised, not by the ephemeral husband but by the wife's brothers. Since land was cultivated by an inferior caste, subservient to the Nayar, a woman's brothers were as completely free as their sister's temporary husband or lovers to devote themselves to military activities.

Now, the case of the Nayar has been frequently misunderstood. In the first place, they cannot be considered as a vestige of a primitive kind of social organization which could have been very general, in the past, among mankind. Quite to the contrary: the Nayar exhibit an extremely specialized and elaborate type of social structure and, from that point of view, they do not prove very much.

On the other hand, there is little doubt that the Nayar represent an extreme form of a tendency which is far more frequent in human societies than is generally acknowledged.

There are a large number of human societies which, although they did not go quite as far as the Nayar in denying recognition to the family as a social unit, have nevertheless limited this recognition by their simultaneous admission of patterns of a different type. For instance, the Masai and the Chagga, both of them African tribes, did recognize the family as a social unit. However, and for the same reason as among the Nayar, this was not true for the younger class of adult men who were dedicated to warlike activities and consequently were not allowed to marry and found a family. They used to live in regimental organizations and were permitted, during that period, to have promiscuous relations with the younger class of adult girls. Thus, among these peoples, the family did exist side by side with a promiscuous, non-familial type of relations between the sexes.

For different reasons, the same type of dual pattern prevailed among the Boróro and several other tribes of central Brazil, the Muria, and other tribes of India and Assam, et cetera. All the known instances could be arranged in such a way as to make the Nayar appear only as the more consistent, systematic and logically extreme case of a situation which may eventually reappear, at least in embryonic form, in modern society.

This was well shown in the case of Nazi Germany, where a similar cleavage was beginning to appear in the family unit: on the one hand, the men dedicated to political and warlike activities, with a great deal of freedom resulting from their exalted position; and on the other hand, women with their '3K' functional assignment: *Küche, Kirche, Kinder,* i.e. kitchen, church and children. One might very well conceive that, had the same trend been maintained for several centuries, this clear-cut division of functions between men and women, together with the accompanying differentiation of their respective status, could very well have led to a type of social organization where the family unit would receive as little recognition as among the Nayar.

During recent years anthropologists have taken great pains to show that, even among people who practice wife-lending, either periodically in religious ceremonies or on a statutory basis (as where men are permitted to enter into a kind of institutional friendship entailing wifelending among members), these customs should not be interpreted as survivals of 'group marriage' since they exist side by side, and even imply, recognition of the family. It is true enough that, in order to be allowed to lend one's wife, one should first get one. However, if we consider the case of some Australian tribes as the Wunambal of the northwestern part of the continent, a man who would not lend his wife to her other potential husbands during ceremonies would be considered as 'very greedy,' i.e. trying to keep for himself a privilege intended by the social group to be shared between numerous persons equally entitled to it. And since that attitude toward sexual access to a woman existed along with the official dogma that men have no part in physiological procreation (therefore doubly denying any kind of bond between the husband and his wife's children), the family becomes an economic grouping where man brings the products of his hunt and the woman those of her collecting and gathering. Anthropologists, who claim that this economic unit built up on a 'give and take' principle is a proof of the existence of the family even among the lowest savages, are certainly on no sounder basis than those who maintain that such a kind of family has little else in common than the word used to designate it with the family as it has been observed elsewhere.

The same relativistic approach is advisable in respect to the polygamous family. The word polygamy, it should be recalled, refers to polygyny, that is, a system where a man is entitled to several wives, as well as to polyandry, which is the complementary system where several husbands share one wife.

Now it is true that in many observed cases, polygamous families are nothing else than a combination of several monogamous families, although the same person plays the part of several spouses. For instance, in some tribes of Bantu Africa, each wife lives in a separate hut with her children, and the only difference with the monogamous family results from the fact that the same man plays the part of husband to all his wives. There are other instances, however, where the situation is not so clear. Among the Tupi-Kawahib of central Brazil, a chief may marry several women who may be sisters, or even a mother and her daughters by former marriage; the children are raised together by the women who do not seem to mind very much whether they nurse their own children or not; also, the chief willingly lends his wives to his younger brothers, his court officers, or to visitors. Here we have not only a combination of polygyny and polyandry, but the mix-up is increased even more by the fact that the co-wives may be united by close consanguineous ties prior to their marrying the same man. In a case which this writer witnessed, a mother and daughter, married to one man, were together taking care of children who were, at the same time, stepchildren to one woman and, according to case, either grandchild or stepbrother to the other.

As to polyandry proper, it may sometimes take extreme forms, as among the Toda where several men, usually brothers, share one wife, the legitimate father of the children being the one who has performed a special ceremony and who remains legal father of all the children to be born until another husband decides to assume the right of fathership by the same process. In Tibet and Nepal, polyandry seems to be explained by occupational factors of the same type as those already stated for the Nayar: for men living a semi-nomadic existence as guides and bearers, polyandry provides a good chance that there will be, at all times, at least one husband at hand to take care of the homestead.

If the legal, economic, and sentimental identity of the family can be maintained even in a polygynous or a polyandrous set-up, it is not sure that the same would be true when polyandry exists side by side with polygamy. As we have already seen, this was to some extent the case among the Tupi-Kawahib since polygynous marriages existed, at least as a chief's privilege, in combination with an elaborate system of wife-lending to younger brothers, helpers, and visitors from different tribes. Here one might argue that the bond between a woman and her legal husband was more different in degree than in kind from a gamut of other bonds which could be arranged in order of decreasing strength: from rightful, semi-permanent lovers to occasional ones. However, even in that case, the children's status was defined by the legal marriage, not by the other types of unions.

We come closer to the so-called 'group marriage' when we consider the modern evolution of the Toda during the nineteenth century. They had originally a polyandrous system, which was made possible through the custom of female infanticide. When this was prohibited by the British administration, thus restoring the natural sex-ratio, the Toda continued to practice polyandry; but now instead of several brothers sharing one wife, it became possible for them to marry several. As in the case of the Nayar, the types of organization which seem remotest to the conjugal family do not occur in the more savage and archaic societies but in the relatively recent and extremely sophisticated forms of social development.

Therefore, it becomes apparent why the problem of the family should not be approached in a dogmatic way. As a matter of fact, this is one of the more elusive questions in the whole field of social organization. Of the type of organization which prevailed in the early stages of mankind, we know very little, since the remnants of man during the Upper Paleolithic Period of about 50,000 years ago consist principally of skeletal fragments and stone implements which provide only a minimum of information on social customs and laws. On the other hand, when we consider the wide diversity of human societies which have been observed since, let us say, Herodotus' time until present days, the only thing which can be said is as follows: monogamic, conjugal family is fairly frequent. Wherever it seems to be superseded by different types of organizations, this generally happens in very specialized and sophisticated societies and not, as was previously expected, in the crudest and simplest types. Moreover, the few instances of non-conjugal family (even in its polygamous form) establish beyond doubt that the high frequency of the conjugal type of social grouping does not derive from a universal necessity. It is at least conceivable that a perfectly stable and durable society could exist without it. Hence the difficult problem: if there is no natural law making the family universal, how can we explain why it is found practically everywhere?

In order to try to solve the problem, let us try first to define the family, not by integrating the numerous factual observations made in different societies nor even by limiting ourselves to the prevailing situation among us, but by building up an ideal model of what we have in mind when we use the word family. It would then seem that this word serves to designate a social group offering at least three characteristics: (1) it finds its origin in marriage; (2) it consists in husband, wife, and children born out of their wedlock, though it can be conceived that other relatives may find their place close to that nuclear group; and (3) the family members are united together by a) legal bonds, b) economic, religious, and other kinds of rights and obligations, c) a precise network of sexual rights and prohibitions, and a varying and diversified amount of psychological feelings such as love, affection, respect, awe, et cetera. We will now proceed to a close examination of these several aspects in the light of the available data.

MARRIAGE AND THE FAMILY

As we have already noticed, marriage may be monogamous or polygamous. It should be pointed out imr..ediately that the first kind is not only more frequently found than the second, but even much more than a cursory inventory of human societies would lead to believe. Among the so-called polygamous societies, there are undoubtedly a substantial number which are authentically so; but many others make a strong difference between the 'first' wife who is the only true one, endowed with the full rights attached to the marital status, while the other ones are sometimes little more than official concubines. Besides, in all polygamous societies, the privilege of having several wives is actually enjoyed by a small minority only. This is easily understandable since the number of men and women in any random grouping is approximately the same with a normal balance of about 110 to 100 to the advantage of either sex. In order to make polygamy possible, there are definite conditions which have to be met: either children of a given sex are voluntarily destroyed (a custom known to exist in a few rare cases, such as female infanticide among the Toda already referred to), or special circumstances account for a different life expectancy for members of both sexes, as among the Eskimo and some Australian tribes where many men used to die young because their occupations—whale-hunting in one case, warfare in the other—were especially dangerous. Or else we have to look for a strongly hierarchical social system, where a given class: ancients, priests and sorcerers, rich men, et cetera is powerful enough to monopolize with impunity more than their share of the womenfolk at the expense of the younger or the poorer people. As a matter of fact, we know of societies—mostly in Africa—where one has to be rich to get many wives (since there is a bride-price to pay), but where at the same time the increase in wives is a means to increase wealth, since female work has a definite economic value. However, it is clear that the systematic practice of polygamy is automatically limited by the change of structure it is likely to bring up in the society.

Therefore, it is not necessary to wonder a great deal about the predominance of monogamic marriage in human societies. That monogamy is not inscribed in the nature of man is sufficiently evidenced by the fact that polygamy exists in widely different forms and in many types of societies; on the other hand, the prevalence of monogamy results from the fact that, unless special conditions are voluntarily or involuntarily brought about, there is normally, about just one woman available for each man. In modern societies, moral, religious, and economic reasons have officialized monogamous marriage (a rule which is in actual practice breached by such different means as premarital freedom, prostitution, and adultery). But in societies which are on a much lower cultural level and where there is no prejudice against polygamy, and even where polygamy may be actually permitted or desired, the same result can be brought about by the lack of social or economic differentiation, so that each man has neither the means, nor the power, to obtain more than one wife and where, consequently, everybody is obliged to make a virtue of necessity.

If there are many different types of marriage to be observed in human societies—whether monogamous or polygamous, and in the last case, polygynous, polyandrous, or both; and whether by exchange, purchase, free-choice or imposed by the family, et cetera—the striking fact is that everywhere a distinction exists between marriage, i.e. a legal, group-sanctioned bond between a man and a woman, and the type of permanent or temporary union resulting either from violence or consent alone. This group intervention may be a notable or a slight one, it does not matter. The important thing is that every society has some way to operate a distinction between free unions and legitimate ones. There are several levels at which that distinction is made.

In the first place, nearly all societies grant a very high rating to the married status. Wherever age-grades exist, either in an institutional way or as non-crystallized forms of grouping, some connection is established between the younger adolescent group and bachelorhood, less young and married without children, and adulthood with full rights, the latter going usually on par with the birth of the first child. This threefold distinction was recognized not only among many primitive tribes but also in peasant western Europe, if only for the purpose of feasts and ceremonies, as late as the early twentieth century.

What is even more striking is the true feeling of repulsion which most societies have toward bachelorhood. Generally speaking it can be said that, among the so-called primitive tribes, there are no bachelors, simply for the reason that they could not survive. One of the strongest field recollections of this writer was his meeting, among the Boróro of central Brazil, of a man about thirty years old: unclean, ill-fed, sad, and lonesome. When asked if the man were seriously ill, the natives' answer came as a shock: what was wrong with him?—nothing at all, he was just a bachelor. And true enough, in a society where labor is systematically shared between man and woman and where only the married status permits the man to benefit from the fruits of woman's work, including delousing, body painting, and hair-plucking as well as vegetable food and cooked food (since the Boróro woman tills the soil and makes pots), a bachelor is really only half a human being.

This is true of the bachelor and also, to a lesser extent, of a couple without children. Indeed they can make a living, but there are many societies where a childless man (or woman) never reaches full status within the group, or else, beyond the group, in this all important society which is made up of dead relatives and where one can only expect recognition as ancestor through the cult, rendered to him or her by one's descendants. Conversely, an orphan finds himself in the same dejected condition as a bachelor. As a matter of fact, both terms provide sometimes the strongest insults existing in the native vocabulary. Bachelors and orphans can even be merged together with cripples and witches, as if their conditions were the outcome of some kind of supernatural malediction.

The interest shown by the group in the marriage of its members can be directly expressed, as it is the case among us where prospective spouses, if they are of marriageable age, have first to get a license and then to secure the services of an acknowledged representative of the group to celebrate their union. Although this direct relationship between the individuals, on the one hand, and the group as a whole, on the other, is known at least sporadically in other societies, it is by no means a frequent case. It is almost a universal feature of marriage that it is originated, not by the individuals but by the groups concerned (families, lineages, clans, et cetera), and that it binds the groups before and above the individuals. Two kinds of reasons bring about this result: on the one hand, the paramount importance of being married tends to make parents, even in very simple societies, start early to worry about obtaining a suitable mate for their offspring and this, accordingly, may lead to children being promised to each other from infancy. But above all, we are confronted here with that strange paradox to which we shall have to return later on, namely, that although marriage gives birth to the family, it is the family, or rather families, which produce marriage as the main legal device at their disposal to establish an alliance between themselves. As New Guinea natives put it, the real purpose of getting married is not so much to obtain a wife but to secure brothers-in-law. If marriage takes place between groups rather than individuals, a large number of strange customs become immediately clearer. For instance, we understand why in some parts of Africa, where descent follows the father's line, marriage becomes only final when the woman has given birth to a male child, thus fulfilling its function of maintaining her husband's lineage. The so-called *levirate* and *sororate* should be explained in the light of the same principle: if marriage is binding between two groups to which the spouses belong there can be without contradiction a replacement of one spouse by his brothers or by her sisters. When the husband dies, the levirate provides that his unmarried brothers have a preferential claim on his widow (or, as it is sometimes differently put, share in their deceased brother's duty to support his wife and children), while the sororate permits a man to marry preferentially in polygamous marriage his wife's sisters, or—when marriage is monogamous—to get a sister to replace the wife in case the latter remains childless, has to be divorced on account of bad conduct, or dies. But whatever the way in which the collectivity expresses its interest in the marriage of its members, whether through the authority vested in strong consanguineous groups, or more directly, through the intervention of the State, it remains true that marriage is not, is never, and cannot be a private business.

FORMS OF FAMILY

We have to look for cases as extreme as the Nayar, already described, to find societies where there is not, at least, a temporary *de facto* union of the husband, wife, and their children. But we should be careful to note that, while such a group among us constitutes the family and is given legal recognition, this is by no means the case in a large number of human societies. Indeed, there is a maternal instinct which compels the mother to care for her children and makes her find a deep satisfaction in exercising those activities, and there are also psychological drives which explain that a man may feel warmly toward the offspring of a woman with whom he is living, and the development of which he is witnessing step by step, even if he does not believe (as is the case among the tribes who are said to disclaim physiological paternity) that he had any actual part in their procreation. Some societies strive to reinforce these convergent feelings: the famous *couvade,* the custom according to which a man is made to share in the inabilities (either natural or socially imposed) of the woman in confinement, has been explained by some as an attempt to build up a welded unit out of these otherwise not too homogeneous materials.

The great majority of societies, however, do not show a very active interest in a kind of grouping which, to some of them at least (including our own), appears so important. Here too, it is the groups which are important, not the temporary aggregate of the individual representatives of the group. For instance, many societies are interested in clearly establishing the relations of the offspring with the father's group on the one hand, and with the mother's group on the other, but they do it by differentiating strongly the two kinds of relationships. Territorial rights may be inherited through one line, and religious privileges and obligations through the other. Or else, status from one side, magical techniques from the other. Innumerable examples could be given from Africa, Australia, America, et cetera. To limit oneself to just one, it is striking to compare the minute care with which the Hopi Indians of Arizona traced different types of legal and religious rights to the father's and to the mother's lines, while the frequency of divorce made the family so unstable that many fathers did not actually share the same house as their children, since houses were women's properties and, from the legal point of view, children followed the mother's line.

This brittleness of the conjugal family, which is so common among the so-called primitive peoples, does not prevent them from giving some value to conjugal faithfulness and parental attachment. However, these are moral norms and they should be contrasted strongly with the legal rules which in many cases only acknowledge formally the relationship of the children with either the father's or the mother's lines or, when both lines are formally recognized, do so for wholly different types of rights and/or obligations. Extreme cases have been recorded such as the Emerillon, a small tribe of French Guiana now reduced to about 50 persons. Here, according to recent informants, marriage is so unstable that, during a lifetime, everybody has a good chance to get married to everybody of the opposite sex and the tribe is said to use special names for children, showing from which one of at least 8 consecutive marriages they may be the offspring. This is probably a recent development which should be explained on the one hand by the smallness of the tribe and, on the other, by the unstable conditions under which it has lived for the past century. However, it shows that conditions may exist where the conjugal family is hardly recognizable.

Instability accounts for the above examples; but some others may stem from quite opposite considerations. In most of contemporary India and in many parts of western and eastern Europe, sometimes as late as the nineteenth century, the basic social unit was constituted by a type of family which should be described as *domestic* rather than *conjugal*: ownership of the land and of the homestead, parental authority and economic leadership were vested in the eldest living ascendant, or in the community of brothers issued from the same ascendant. In the Russian *bratsvo*, the south-Slavic *zadruga*, the French *maisnie*, the family actually consisted of the elder or the surviving brothers, together with their wives, married sons with their wives and unmarried daughters, and so on down to the great grandchildren. Such large groups, which could sometimes include several dozen persons living and working under a common authority, have been designated as *joint families* or *extended families*. Both terms are useful but misleading since they imply that these large units are made up of small conjugal families. As we have already seen, while it is true that the conjugal family limited to mother and children is practically universal since it is based on the physiological and psychological dependency which exists between them at least for a certain time, and that the conjugal family consisting of husband, wife, and children is almost as frequent for psychological and economical reasons which should be added to those previously mentioned, the historical process which has led among ourselves to the legal recognition of the conjugal family is a very complex one: it has been brought about only in part through an increasing awareness of a natural situation. But there is little doubt that, to a very large extent, it has resulted from the narrowing down to a group, as small as can be, the legal standing of which, in the past of our institutions, was vested for centuries on very large groups. In the last instance, one would not be wrong in disallowing the terms joint family and extended family. Indeed, it is rather the conjugal family which deserves the name of: *restricted family*.

We have just seen that, when the family is given a small functional value, it tends to disappear even below the level of the conjugal type. On the contrary, when the family has a great functional value, it becomes actualized much above that level. Our would-be universal conjugal family, then, corresponds more to an unstable equilibrium between extremes than to a permanent and everlasting need coming from the deepest requirements of human nature.

To complete the picture, we have finally to consider cases where the conjugal family differs from our own, not so much on account of a different amount of functional value, but rather because its functional value is conceived in a way qualitatively different from our own conceptions.

As will be seen later on, there are many peoples for whom the kind of spouse one should marry is much more important than the kind of match they will make together. These people are ready to accept unions which to us would seem not only unbelievable, but in direct contradiction with the aims and purposes of setting up a family. For instance, the Siberian Chukchee were not in the least abhorrent to the marriage of a mature girl of let us say about twenty, with a baby-husband two or three years old. Then, the young woman, herself a mother by an authorized lover, would nurse together her own child and her little husband. Like the North American Mohave, who had the opposite custom of a man marrying a baby girl and caring for her until she became old enough to fulfill her conjugal duties, such marriages were thought of as very strong ones, since the natural feelings between husband and wife would be reinforced by the recollection of the parental care bestowed by one of the spouses on the other. These are by no means exceptional cases to be explained by extraordinary mental abnormalities. Examples could be brought together from other parts of the world: South America, both highland and tropical, New Guinea, et cetera.

As a matter of fact, the examples just given still respect, to some extent, the duality of sexes which we feel is a requirement of marriage and raising a family. But in several parts of Africa, women of high rank were allowed to marry other women and have them bear children through the services of unacknowledged male lovers, the noble woman being then entitled to become the 'father' of her children and to transmit to them, according to the prevalent father's right, her own name, status, and wealth. Finally, there are the cases, certainly less striking, where the conjugal family was considered necessary to procreate the children but not to raise them, since each family did endeavor to retain somebody else's children (if possible of a higher status) to raise them while their own children were similarly retained (sometimes before they were born) by another family. This happened in some parts of Polynesia, while 'fosterage,' i.e. the custom whereby a son was sent to be raised by his mother's brother, was a common practice on the Northwest Coast of America as well as in European feudal society.

The Family Bonds

During the course of centuries we have become accustomed to Christian morality which considers marriage and setting up a family as the only way to prevent sexual gratification from being sinful. That connection has been shown to exist elsewhere in a few scattered instances; but it is by no means frequent. Among most people, marriage has very little to do with the satisfaction of the sexual urge, since the social set-up provides for many opportunities which can be not only external to marriage, but even contradictory to it. For instance, among the Muria of Bastar, in central India, when puberty comes, boys and girls are sent to live together in communal huts where they enjoy a great deal of sexual freedom, but after a few years of such leeway they get married according to the rule that no former adolescent lovers should be permitted to unite. Then, in a rather small village, each man is married to a wife whom he has known during his younger years as his present neighbor's (or neighbors') lover.

On the other hand, and if sexual considerations are not paramount for marriage purposes, economic necessities are found everywhere in the first place. We have already shown that what makes marriage a fundamental need in tribal societies is the division of labor between the sexes.

Like the form of the family, the division of labor stems more from social and cultural considerations than from natural ones. Truly, in every human group, women give birth to children and take care of them, and men rather have as their specialty hunting and warlike activities. Even there, though, we have ambiguous cases: of course men never give birth to babies, but in many societies, as we have seen with the couvade, they are made to act as if they did. And there is a great deal of difference between the Nambikwara father nursing his baby and cleaning it when it soils itself, and the European nobleman of not long ago to whom his children were formally presented from time to time, being otherwise confined to the women's quarters until the boys were old enough to be taught riding and fencing. Conversely, the young concubines of the Nambikwara chieftain disdain domestic activities and prefer to share in their husband's adventurous expeditions. It is by no means unlikely that a similar custom, prevailing among other South American tribes, where a special class of women, half wantons and half helpers, did not marry, but accompanied the men on the warpath, is at the origin of the famous legend of the Amazons.

When we turn to activities less basic than child-rearing and war-making, it becomes still more difficult to discern rules governing the division of labor between the sexes. The Boróro women till the soil while among the Zuñi this is a man's work; according to tribe, hut building, pot making, weaving, may be incumbent upon either sex. Therefore, we should be careful to distinguish the *fact* of the division of labor between the sexes which is practically universal, from the *way* according to which different tasks are attributed to one or the other sex, where we should recognize the same paramount influence of cultural factors, let us say the same *artificiality* which presides over the organization of the family itself.

Here, again, we are confronted with the same question we have already met with: if the natural reasons which could explain the division of labor between the sexes do not seem to play a decisive part, as soon as we leave the solid ground of women's biological specialization in the production of children, why does it exist at all? The very fact that it varies endlessly according to the society selected for consideration shows that, as for the family itself, it is the mere fact of its existence which is mysteriously required, the form under which it comes to exist being utterly irrelevant, at least from the point of view of any natural necessity. However, after having considered the different aspects of the problem, we are now in a position to perceive some common features which may bring us nearer to an answer than we were at the beginning of this chapter. Since family appears to us as a positive social reality, perhaps the only positive social reality, we are prone to define it exclusively by its positive characteristics. Now it should be pointed out that whenever we have tried to show what the family is, at the same time we were implying what it is not, and the negative aspects may be as important as the others. To return to the division of labor we were just discussing, when it is stated that one sex must perform certain tasks, this also means

348 MAN, CULTURE, AND SOCIETY

that the other sex is forbidden to do them. In that light, the sexual division of labor is nothing else than a device to institute a reciprocal state of dependency between the sexes.

The same thing may be said of the sexual side of the family life. Even if it is not true, as we have shown, that the family can be explained on sexual grounds, since for many tribes, sexual life and the family are by no means as closely connected as our moral norms would make them, there is a negative aspect which is much more important: the structure of the family, always and everywhere, makes certain types of sexual connections impossible, or at least wrong.

Indeed, the limitations may vary to a great extent according to the culture under consideration. In ancient Russia, there was a custom known as *snokatchestvo* whereby a father was entitled to a sexual privilege over his son's young wife; a symmetrical custom has been mentioned in some part of southeastern Asia where the persons implied are the sister's son and his mother's brother's wife. We ourselves do not object to a man marrying his wife's sister, a practice which English law still considered incestuous in the mid-nineteenth century. What remains true is that every known society, past or present, proclaims that if the husband-wife relationship, to which, as just seen, some others may eventually be added, implies sexual rights, there are other relationships equally derived from the familial structure, which make sexual connections inconceivable, sinful, or legally punishable. The universal prohibition of incest specifies, as a general rule, that people considered as parents and children, or brother and sister, even if only by name, cannot have sexual relations and even less marry each other. In some recorded instances—such as ancient Egypt, pre-Columbian Peru, also some African, southeast Asian, and Polynesian kingdoms—incest was defined far less strictly than elsewhere. Even there, however, the rule existed since incest was limited to a minority group, the ruling class (with the exception of perhaps, ancient Egypt where it may have been more common); on the other hand, not every kind of close relatives were permitted as spouse: for instance it was the half-sister, the full-one being excluded; or, if the full-sister was allowed, then it should be the elder sister, the younger one remaining incestuous.

The space at our disposal is too short to demonstrate that, in this case as previously, there is no natural ground for the custom. Geneticists have shown that while consanguineous marriages are likely to bring ill effects in a society which has consistently avoided them in the past, the danger would be much smaller if the prohibition had never existed, since this would have given ample opportunity for the harmful hereditary characters to become apparent and be automatically eliminated through selection: as a matter of fact this is the way breeders improve the quality of their subjects. Therefore, the dangers of consanguineous marriages are the outcome of the incest prohibition rather than actually explaining it. Furthermore, since very many primitive peoples do not share our belief in biological harm resulting from consanguineous marriages, but have entirely different theories, the reason should be sought elsewhere, in a way more consistent with the opinions generally held by mankind as a whole.

The true explanation should be looked for in a completely opposite direction, and what has been said concerning the sexual division of labor may help us to grasp it. This has been explained as a device to make the sexes mutually dependent on social and economic grounds, thus establishing clearly that marriage is better than celibacy. Now, exactly in the same way that the principle of sexual division of labor establishes a mutual dependency between the sexes, compelling them thereby to perpetuate themselves and to found a family, the prohibition of incest establishes a mutual dependency between families, compelling them, in order to perpetuate themselves, to give rise to new families. It is through a strange oversight that the similarity of the two processes is generally overlooked on account of the use of terms as dissimilar as *division,* on the one hand, and *prohibition* on the other. We could easily have emphasized only the negative aspect of the division of labor by calling it a prohibition of tasks; and conversely, outlined the positive aspect of incest-prohibition by calling it the principle of division of marriageable rights between families. For incest-prohibition simply states that families (however they should be defined) can only marry between each other and that they cannot marry inside themselves.

We now understand why it is so wrong to try to explain the family on the purely natural grounds of procreation, motherly instinct, and psychological feelings between man and woman and between father and children. None of these would be sufficient to give rise to a family, and for a reason simple enough: for the whole of mankind, the absolute requirement for the creation of a family is the previous existence of two other families, one ready to provide a man, the other one a woman, who will through their marriage start a third one, and so on indefinitely. To put it in other words: what makes man really different from the animal is that, in mankind, a family could not exist if there were no society: i.e. a plurality of families ready to acknowledge that there are other links than consanguineous ones, and that the natural process of filiation can only be carried on through the social process of affinity.

How this interdependency of families has become recognized is another problem which we are in no position to solve because there is no reason to believe that man, since he emerged from his animal state, has not enjoyed a basic form of social organization, which, as regards the fundamental principles, could not be essentially different from our own. Indeed, it will never be sufficiently emphasized that, if social organization had a beginning, this could only have consisted in the incest prohibition since, as we have just shown, the incest prohibition is, in fact, a kind of remodeling of the biological conditions of mating and procreation (which know no rule, as can be seen from observing animal life) compelling them to become perpetuated only in an artificial framework of taboos and obligations. It is there, and only there, that we find a passage from nature to culture, from animal to human life, and that we are in a position to understand the very essence of their articulation.

As Tylor has shown almost a century ago, the ultimate explanation is probably that mankind has understood very early that, in order to free itself from a wild struggle for existence, it was confronted with the very simple choice of 'either marrying-out or being killed-out.' The alternative was between biological families living in juxtaposition and endeavoring to remain closed, self-perpetuating units, over-ridden by their fears, hatreds, and ignorances, and the systematic establishment, through the incest prohibition, of links of intermarriage between them, thus succeeding to build, out of the artificial bonds of affinity, a true human society, despite, and even in contradiction with, the isolating influence of consanguinity. Therefore we may better understand how it came to be that, while we still do not know exactly what the family is, we are well aware of the prerequisites and the practical rules which define its conditions of perpetuation.

The so-called primitive peoples have, for that purpose, very simple and clever rules which the tremendous increase in size and fluidity of modern society makes it sometimes difficult for us to understand.

In order to insure that families will not become closed and that they will not constitute progressively as many self-sufficient units, we satisfy ourselves with forbidding marriage between near relatives. The amount of social contacts which any given individual is likely to maintain outside his or her own restricted family is great enough to afford a good probability that, on the average, the hundreds of thousands of families constituting at any given moment a modern society will not be permitted to 'freeze' if one may say so. On the contrary, the greatest possible freedom for the choice of a mate (submitted to the only condition that the choice has to be made outside the restricted family) insures that these families will be kept in a continuous flow and that a satisfactory process of continuous 'mix-up' through intermarriage will prevail among them, thus making for a homogeneous and well-blended social fabric.

Conditions are quite different in the so-called primitive societies: there, the global figure of the population is a small one, although it may vary from a few dozen up to several thousands. Besides, social fluidity is low and it is not likely that many people will have a chance to get acquainted with others, during their lifetime, except within the limits of the village, hunting territory, et cetera, though it is true that many tribes have tried to organize occasions for wider contacts, for instance during feasts, tribal ceremonies, et cetera. Even in such cases, however, the chances are limited to the tribal group since most primitive peoples consider that the tribe is a kind of wide family, and that the frontiers of mankind stop together with the tribal bonds themselves.

Given such conditions, it is still possible to insure the blending of families into a well-united society by using procedures similar to our own, i.e. a mere prohibition of marriage between relatives without any kind of positive prescriptions as to where and whom one should correctly marry. Experience shows, however, that this is only possible in small societies under the condition that the diminutive size of the group and the lack of social mobility be compensated by widening to a considerable extent the range of prohibited degrees. It is not only one's own sister or daughter that, under such circumstances, one should not marry, but any women with whom blood relationship may be traced, even in the remotest possible way. Very small groups with a low cultural level and a loose political and social organization, such as some desert tribes of North and South America, provide us with examples of that solution.

However, the great majority of primitive peoples have devised another method to solve the problem. Instead of confining themselves to a statistical process, relying on the probability that certain interdictions being set up, a satisfactory equilibrium of exchanges between the biological families will spontaneously result, they have preferred to invent rules which every individual and family should follow carefully, and from which a given form of blending, experimentally conceived of as satisfactory, is bound to arise.

Whenever this takes place, the entire field of kinship becomes a kind of complicated game, the kinship terminology being used to distribute all the members of the group into different categories, the rule being that the category of the parents defines either directly or indirectly the category of the children, and that, according to the categories in which they are placed, the members of the group may or may not get married. The study of these rules of kinship and marriage has provided modern anthropology with one of its more difficult and complicated chapters. Apparently ignorant and savage peoples have been able to devise fantastically clever codes which sometimes request, in order to understand their workings and effects, some of the best logical and even mathematical minds available in modern civilization. Therefore, we will limit ourselves to explaining the crudest principles which are the more frequently met with.

One of these is, undoubtedly, the so-called rule of cross-cousin marriage, which has been taken up by innumerable tribes all over the world. This is a complex system according to which collateral relatives are divided into two basic categories: 'parallel' collaterals, when the relationship can be traced through two siblings of the same sex, and 'cross' collaterals, when the relationship is traced through two siblings of opposite sex. For instance, my paternal uncle is a parallel relative and so is my maternal aunt; while the maternal uncle on the one hand, the paternal aunt on the other, are cross-relatives. In the same way, cousins who trace their relationship through two brothers or two sisters, are parallel-cousins; and those who are connected through a brother and a sister are cross-cousins. In the generation of the nephews, if I am a man, my brother's children will be my parallel-nephews while my sister's children are my cross-nephews.

Now, the startling fact about this distinction is that practically all the tribes which make it claim that parallel relatives are the same thing as the closest ones on the same generation level: my father's brother is a 'father,' my mother's sister a 'mother'; my parallel-cousins are like brothers and sisters to me; and my parallel-nephews like children. Marriage with any of these would be incestuous and is consequently forbidden. On the other hand, cross-relatives are designated by special terms of their own, and it is among them that one should preferably find a mate. This is true to the extent that quite frequently, there is only one word to mean both 'cross-cousin' and 'spouse.' What can be the reason for this claim, exactly similar among hundreds of different tribes in Africa, America, Asia, Oceania, that one should not marry, under any pretence, a father's brother's daughter, since that would amount to marrying one's sister, while the best conceivable spouse consists of a mother's brother's daughter, namely a relative, who on purely biological grounds, is exactly as close as the former?

There are even tribes which go a step further in these refinements. Some think that it is not cross-cousins who should marry, but only cross-cousins once removed (i.e. children of cross-cousins); others, and this is by far the most frequent case, are not satisfied with the simple distinction between cross- and parallel-cousins; they subdivide the cross-cousins themselves into marriageable and non-marriageable ones. For instance, although a mother's brother's daughter is, according to the above definitions, a cross-cousin in the same sense as a father's sister's daughter, there are in India, living side by side, tribes which believe that one of them, only different according to case, make a suitable spouse, death being preferable to the sin of marrying the other.

All these distinctions (to which others could be added) are fantastic at first sight because they cannot be explained on biological or psychological grounds. But, if we keep in mind what has been explained in the preceding section, i.e. that all the marriage prohibitions have as their only purpose to establish a mutual dependency between the biological families, or, to put it in stronger terms, that marriage rules express the refusal, on the part of society, to admit the exclusive existence of the biological family, then everything becomes clear. For all these complicated sets of rules and distinctions are nothing but the outcome of the processes according to which, in a given society, families are set up against each other for the purpose of playing the game of matrimony.

Let us consider briefly the rules of the game. Since societies try to maintain their identity in the course of time, there should be first a rule fixing the status of the children in respect to that of their parents. The simplest possible rule to that end, and by far the most frequently adopted, is the generally called rule of *unilineal descent,* namely that children get the same status of either their father (patrilineal descent) or their mother (matrilineal descent). It can also be decided that the status of both the father and the mother are taken into consideration, and that they should be combined to define a third category in which the children will be put. For instance, a child of a father belonging to the status A and of a mother belonging to the status B, would himself belong to a status C; and the status will be D if it is the father who is B and the mother who is A. Then, C and D will marry together and procreate children either A or B according to the sex orientation, and so on indefinitely. Everybody with some leisure time may devise rules of this kind, and it will be surprising indeed if some tribe, at least, cannot be found where each rule is actually being applied.

The rule of descent being defined, the second question is to know in how many exogamous groups the society in consideration is being divided. An exogamous group is one inside of which intermarriage is forbidden and which, consequently, requires at least another exogamous group with whom it may exchange its sons and/or daughters for marriage purposes. Among ourselves, there are as many exogamous groups as restricted families, that is an extremely high number, and it is this high number which allows us to rely on probability. In primitive societies, however, the figure is usually much smaller, on the one hand because the group itself is a small one, and on the other hand because the familial ties go much further than it is the case among us.

Our first hypothesis will be the simpler one: that of unilineal descent and of two exogamous groups, A and B. Then, the only solution will be that men of A marry women of B, and men of B marry women of A. A typical case will be that of two men, respectively A and B, exchanging their sisters so that each one may get a wife. The reader has just to take a pencil and a sheet of paper to build up the theoretical genealogy which will be the outcome of such a set-up. Whatever the rule of descent, siblings and parallel-cousins will always fall in the same category, while cross-cousins of whatever kind will fall in opposite categories. Therefore, only cross-cousins (if we are playing the game with 2 to 4 groups) or children of cross-cousins (if we are playing with 8 groups, for 6 provide an intermediary case) will meet the initial rule that spouses should belong to opposite groups.

So far, we have considered groups tied up in pairs: 2, 4, 6, 8. They can only come in even numbers. What, now, if the society is made up of an odd number of exchanging groups? With the preceding rule, there will be a group which will remain alone by itself, without a partner with whom to set up an exchange relationship. Hence, the need for additional rules which can be of use whatever the number of elements, either even or odd.

There are two ways to meet the difficulty. Exchange can either remain simultaneous and become indirect, or remain direct at the expense of becoming consecutive. The first type will be when group A gives its daughters as wives to group B, B to C, C to D, D to $n \cdot \cdot \cdot$ and finally n to A. When the cycle is completed, every group has given a woman and has received one, though it has not given to the same group as that from which it has received. In that case, pencil and paper will show that parallel-cousins always fall in one's own group, same as brothers and sisters, and cannot consequently be married according to rule. As to cross-cousins, a new distinction will appear: the female cross-cousin on the mother's side (i.e. the mother's brother's daughter) will always fall in the marriageable group (A to B, B to C, et cetera) while that on the father's side (father's sister's daughter) will fall in the opposite group (that is, the one to which my group gives wives, but from which it does not receive any: B to A, C to B, etc.).

The alternative would be to keep the exchange direct, though in consecutive generations: for instance, A receives a wife from B, and returns to A the daughter born from that marriage to become the spouse of a man A of the following generation. If we keep our groups arranged in a series: A, B, C, D, $n \cdot \cdot \cdot$, the general set-up will be, then, that any group, let us say C, at one generation gives to D and receives from B; at the following generation, C repays B and gets its own return from D, and so on indefinitely. Here again the patient reader will find out that cross-cousins are being distinguished in two categories, but this time in a reverse way: for a man, the correct mate will always be the father's sister's daughter, the mother's brother's daughter being always in the 'wrong' category.

These are the simplest cases. All over the world there are still kinship systems and marriage rules for which no satisfactory interpretation has as yet been brought forward; such are the Ambrym system in the New Hebrides, the Murngin of northwestern Australia, and the whole North American complex known as the Crow-Omaha kinship system. It is fairly certain that to explain these and other sets of rules, however, one will have to proceed as we have shown here, namely to interpret kinship systems and marriage rules as embodying the rule of that very special kind of game which consists, for consanguineous groups of men, in exchanging women among themselves, that is building up new families with the pieces of earlier ones, which should be shattered for that purpose.

The female reader, who may be shocked to see womankind treated as a commodity submitted to transactions between male operators, can easily find comfort in the assurance that the rules of the game would remain unchanged should it be decided to consider the men as being exchanged by women's groups. As a matter of fact, some very few societies, of a highly developed matrilineal type, have to a limited extent attempted to express things that way. And both sexes can be comforted from a still different (but in that case slightly more complicated) formulation of the game, whereby it would be said that consanguineous groups consisting of both men and women are engaged in exchanging together bonds of relationships.

The important conclusion to be kept in mind is that the restricted family can neither be said to be the element of the social group, nor can it be claimed to result from it. Rather, the social group can only become established in contradistinction, and to some extent in compliance, with the family, since in order to maintain the society through time, women should procreate children, benefit from male protection while they are engaged in confinement and nursing, and, since precise sets of rules are needed, to perpetuate throughout the generations the basic pattern of the social fabric. However, the primary social concern regarding the family is not to protect or enhance it: it is rather an attitude of diffidence, a denial of its right to exist either in isolation or permanently; restricted families are only permitted to live for a limited period of time, either long or short according to case, but under the strict condition that their component parts be ceaselessly displaced, loaned, borrowed, given away, or returned, so that new restricted families may be endlessly created or made to vanish. Thus, the relation between the social group as a whole and the restricted families which seem to constitute it is not a static one, like that of a wall to the bricks it is built with. It is rather a dynamic process of tension and opposition with an equilibrium point extremely difficult to find, its exact position being submitted to endless variations from time to time and from society to society. But the word of the Scriptures: 'You will leave your father and mother' provides the iron rule for the establishment and functioning of any society.

Society belongs to the realm of culture while the family is the emanation, on the social level, of those natural requirements without which there could be no society, and indeed no mankind. As a philosopher of the sixteenth century has said, man can only overcome nature by complying with its laws. Therefore, society has to give the family some amount of recognition. And it is not so surprising that, as geographers have also noticed with respect to the use of natural land resources, the greatest amount of compliance with the natural laws is likely to be found at both extremes of the cultural scale: among the simpler peoples as well as among the more highly civilized. Indeed, the first ones are not in a position to afford paying the price of too great a departure, while the second have already suffered from enough mistakes to understand that compliance is the best policy. This explains why, as we have already noticed, the small, relatively stable, monogamic restricted family seems to be given greater recognition, both among the more primitive peoples and in modern societies, than in what may be called (for the sake of the argument), the intermediate levels. However, this is nothing more than a slight shift of the equilibrium point between nature and culture, and does not affect the general picture given in this chapter. When one travels slowly and with great effort, halts should be long and frequent. And when one is given the possibility to travel often and fast, he or she should also, though for different reasons, expect to stop and rest frequently. The more roads there are, the more crossings there are likely to be. Social life imposes on the consanguineous stocks of mankind an incessant traveling back and forth, and family life is little else than the expression of the need to slacken the pace at the crossroads and to take a chance to rest. But the orders are to keep on marching. And society can no more be said to consist of families than a journey is made up of the stopovers which break it down into discontinuous stages. They are at the same time its condition and its negation.

DAVID G. MANDELBAUM

XIV

Social Groupings

THERE ARE MANY WAYS in which people get themselves organized to live and work together. Every one of us belongs to a number of different social groups. Each group consists of a set of people who co-operate for some purpose. Sometimes the membership of the group is small and its purpose is very specific, as in the case of a baseball club or the workers in the corner market. Sometimes the membership of the group is very large and its purpose more general, as in the case of a large school or the national government.

For the most part, the groups to which a person belongs were there before he participated in them and will continue to exist after he leaves them. These established units of society are, in a way, like a college football team; individual players join the squad and then leave it, but the team goes on.

The nature of the groups to which an individual will normally belong varies among the different peoples of the world. An Australian tribesman, one of the aboriginal inhabitants of that island-continent, is concerned about the grouping and subgrouping of the fellow tribesmen he considers to be his relatives. His own place in these intricate groups of relatives determines whom he can marry and what ceremonies he may perform. A villager in south India is aware, from his childhood days, of his membership in a group called a caste. His hereditary membership in that group not only determines whom he may marry, but also regulates such diverse matters as the trade or profession he may follow, the kinds of food he may take, and in whose company he may eat.

EVERYONE BELONGS TO A FAMILY AND TO A COMMUNITY

Whatever diversity there may be among social groupings the world over, there are at least two types which are found in every human society. The family is one of them, as has been noted in the preceding chapter. In every land, among every people, the child is ordinarily raised and nurtured within a family. And the family is the first social group that the child comes to know.

The other type of group which is universal to humanity—and frequently enough the second group which the child begins to recognize—is the local community. Just as no person normally lives all his life alone, devoid of any family, so does no family normally live entirely alone, apart from any local group. All of us, you and I and the Australian tribesman and the villager of India, have neighbors.

We behave toward these neighbors according to the rules and notions of proper neighborly behavior of our respective societies. And our neighbors have similar, reciprocal behavior toward us. These rules and notions, patterns of behavior they may be called, are almost never consciously recognized or written out. It is only the anthropologist and other students of society who attempt to analyze and catalogue the patterns of local group behavior. Nevertheless, the patterns are fixed and effective, even though they are not neatly listed in a rule book. In parts of Australia, each Bushman is expected to, and does, defend the hunting territory he shares with his neighbors against any trespassers who do not belong to his local group. In many sections of India, a villager is obligated to help his neighbors on the occasions when offerings are made to the local deity and when celebrations are staged in its honor. In India, as indeed is true in the farming communities of western countries, a villager often helps his neighbors at harvest time and in turn receives help from them in ways which are regularly repeated every year.

HORDE, VILLAGE, AND NEIGHBORHOOD

The local group is known by various names. It is called a *horde* in the descriptions of the social organization of the Australian tribesmen. The term *band* is frequently used to denote the local group, especially in books about American Indians. Among the old civilizations of Europe and the Orient, the local community is best known as the *village*. In our own country, we often speak of the local community as a *neigh-borhood*.

The essential idea, no matter which particular term is used, is that of a group of people, all of whom live within a limited area and co-operate to some extent. The area may be a valley or the shores of a lake or a city block, but the families within the area usually know each other, or at least recognize enough common interests so that they can act together in certain ways to meet mutual problems. This mutual action to meet common problems accomplishes more than just the attainment of some specific goals. It renews the solidarity of the people of the group, preparing them for more action together. Because in acting together they feel rewarded for so doing, they are ready and willing to work together in the future.

Each family within the local group will have some different customs from those of its neighbors, but all will have certain common ways, especially in relation to each other. Similarly in a set of local groups, any one group will have some peculiarities of its own but all in the set will act alike in some important ways, particularly in those ways which govern the relations among the local groups. The size of the local group and the extent of the area it occupies depend in large part on how the community makes its living. A band of Plains Cree Indians in western Canada needed a large territory in which to pursue the migratory buffalo. A village in the more fertile tracts of India will need only a few square miles in which to grow enough rice to support its population.

How New Communities Are Founded

New local groups usually come into being when some families feel that they can make a better living by moving to some richer and more promising territory. But this is not the only way in which new communities may arise. When I lived among the Plains Cree I found that one of the eight bands of the tribe, the group called the 'Parklands People,' had had a curious history. Its story began in 1790 when one George Sutherland arrived in Saskatchewan from Scotland as a trader in the employ of the Hudson's Bay Company. He was evidently a rest-less kind of person who did not take kindly to the restricted life of a storekeeper. So he took a Cree wife and left the Hudson's Bay Company to live on the prairie in the native style. Subsequently he took two more Indian wives and begot twenty-seven children who grew to adulthood. All the children married with the neighboring Cree but always returned to live with the old man. So George Sutherland came to be the first chief of a band which he had himself engendered and the band became one of the recognized communities of the tribe.

Another way in which new communities may be founded stems from the factions within a local group. It is extremely common to find two factions within a local group in any society. The differences of opinion between the factions may be centered on religious matters or political ideas or claims to land and property. In any one culture, the causes of these quarrels and the means of settling them tend to be alike in all the local groups. Usually these arguments do not prevent the families of each faction from co-operating in matters of general community concern. But occasionally the rifts become so bitter that one faction may just up and leave the local area to settle in another place.

One such incident occurred not many years ago in a village of the Hopi Indians, the agricultural tribe of Arizona which is widely known for its Snake Dance ceremony. For many years there had been antagonism in the village between the faction which believed in taking over a few of the ways of the white man, especially in the matter of sending the village children to the government school, and the more conservative faction which wanted to have nothing whatever to do with the whites or any of their ways. At last matters came to a head and it was decided to settle the argument once and for all. The men of the two factions met in a field facing each other. A line was drawn at each end of the field and the two sides began pushing, one against the other. After much heaving and straining, the conservative side slowly began to give ground, and with a final shove the pro-school side pushed them back across the line. That was the Hopi way of settling a dispute that had become too bitter to be borne any longer. The losing side packed up and went off to found a new village where they still live.

All these reasons for the founding of new local communities have been at the root of great historic movements in the past and are still operating today. In the history of the United States, religious reasons led to the founding of the Pilgrim communities in New England; later, political reasons led some Tory groups to move to Canada after the Revolutionary War and to establish new settlements there; still later, economic motives made for the westward migration and the founding of new communities in the western states; more recently, the operation of wartime industries, such as the atomic energy establishments, have attracted thousands of workers to sites where new communities have come into being.

Home Is Where Your Neighbors Live

The local group is so important to men the world over not only because it marks off the area within which the family lives and works, but because it is home for every one of its members. Within the territory of his local community a person knows the lay of the land, he knows the hills and the paths, he is familiar with the plants and animals and can recognize which are useful and which are dangerous. In urban life, the member of the local group knows the streets and stores of his home neighborhood and is familiar with the good places and with those that are to be avoided. Moreover, he knows the people and knows their ways. In his relations with neighbors whom he does not like, he knows in what manner they are apt to be disagreeable. His friends are there and he knows their gestures and speech; in central Australia, he can even recognize their footprints. It is there that he is usually most comfortable, most secure. There he is at home.

This feeling is shared by tribes which have been called wild savages. Even the people with the simplest and crudest ways of life do not wander aimlessly through the forest or across the plain. The Australian tribesmen have as little in the way of tools and possessions as any primitive folk. Yet they have strong and clear notions about the territory of a local group and the families which rightfully belong to it. For the Australian natives, as for most of humanity, the local community contains practically all of his society and his culture. Most of the people he knows and cherishes, all the customs, beliefs, and manners which he follows, exist within his local community.

As a matter of fact, it is only in the great new cities of our civilization that the local group has lost some of its importance. A city dweller may not know who lives in the next house or apartment and so can have little feeling for, or participation in, a neighborhood. Perhaps for that very reason there are many efforts, in the form of community centers, local clubs, regional associations, to re-establish the friendly neighborly spirit that was lost in the course of the swift growth of a large city. Many people who now live in cities grew up in congenial, long established neighborhoods, and they miss the loyalties of the local group. Often they transfer their loyalty to the next larger group, the city itself. And they tend to be great boosters for the city and fanatically devoted to such a symbol of the city as, for example, a baseball team like the Brooklyn Dodgers.

RELATIVES OF THE CLAN

In many parts of the world there is yet another way in which people group themselves. A person will consider himself related by bonds of kinship to certain people within the local group and often to certain people in other local communities as well. All the individuals with whom he has this special relationship form his clan.

Some of these individuals are really his blood relatives whom we would call by such terms as uncle and cousin. Others have no kinship that would be considered close in our society except that they belong to a clan of the same name and so must treat each other as though they all actually were blood relatives. It is as though all the people with the same last name in our society, say MacDonald, considered themselves to be relatives, treated each other as relatives, and were considered by their fellow citizens to be a distinct group of relatives.

Indeed it was not so many centuries ago that the MacDonalds did form a clan in Scotland. And the men of the clan MacDonald worked together and fought together. The Scottish clans were defeated in 1746 and their clan solidarity was dispersed forever. But on that battlefield is the last evidence of the old clan unity. The slain Scottish soldiers were not placed in individual graves; all the dead of one clan were buried in a common grave and on the tombstones which now mark each place can still be read 'the MacDonalds,' 'the Mackintoshes,' and so on down the roster of Scottish clans whose members and whose very existence as functioning social units were wiped out on that field. For after that day in 1746 the clans were not even permitted the symbols of clan membership, such as the distinctive kilts. It was not until later, when the unity and the pride of each clan had been thoroughly broken, that the wearing of the MacDonald tartan and the piping of clan tunes were again allowed. That clan pride had something to do with the defeat, because the MacDonalds had been placed to the left of the line of battle, not in the place of honor at the right which they believed was their due. And so historians tell us that the clan MacDonald did not fight as well that day as they might have done if they had not been angry about this affront to the honor of their group.

Clan Membership through the Father . . . and through the Mother

The Scottish clans traced descent through the father, and so were of the type called patrilineal clans. That is, all the children of the family, both boys and girls, were members of the MacDonald clan if their father was a MacDonald. If a MacDonald girl married a man of the clan Gordon, she still was accounted a MacDonald, although her children were Gordons and stood by the Gordons in time of clan need.

In some areas, the clans are matrilineal, and the children of a family belong only to the clan of their mother. That is the case in the former native state of Travancore at the southernmost tip of India. The ruler of the state, the Maharaja, must come from the royal clan. Here, as among every people who have clans, a man must not marry a woman of his own clan. Hence the Maharaja's wife is not of the royal clan and his children, who belong to the clan of their mother, are therefore not of the royal lineage. When a Maharaja dies, not his own son, but his sister's son—who does belong to the royal clan—succeeds to the throne.

Clan Functions: Social Insurance and Regulation of Marriage

The clan, whether matrilineal or patrilineal, is in many ways simply an expansion of the family. It frequently happens that all clan members who are about the same age call each other brother and sister. And a fellow clansman of one's father's age, in a patrilineal clan society, will often be called 'father'; a clanswoman of that generation will be called by the term for father's sister. Of course, a person always knows the difference between his real brother and a clan-mate whom he calls 'brother.' But he will share with the clan-mate something of the pattern of mutual helpfulness that he has with his real brother. Thus the individual is strengthened by his relationship with a group much larger than the immediate family.

Just as a person's family helps him and stands by him in case of need, so does his clan support him when he needs its aid. This support may range from helping him collect the price of a bride to protecting his life should he incur the wrath of other clansmen bent on blood-vengeance. This very collective responsibility of the clan for the deeds and demeanor of its individual members makes it a strong force for social order. Since all the clansmen know that they will bear a share of the trouble if one of their clan-mates goes astray, they try to see to it that a potentially erring member is kept within socially approved limits.

Both the clan and the family are important in regulating the choice of a partner in marriage. Apart from a very few, highly exceptional instances, marriage within the family, of brother and sister, is everywhere prohibited and regarded as incest. Similarly, marriage within the clan is prohibited. As we have noted in regard to the marriage of the Maharaja of Travancore, a man can never marry a woman of his own clan. This clan exogamy, as the rule of marrying outside the clan is called, occurs wherever there are clan groupings.

There is this important difference between the functioning of a family and that of a clan. In every form of the family, the relationship of the children to both the father and the mother is recognized. But a clan stresses the relationships through one side of the family only. In a matrilineal clan, only your mother's kinsmen and her mother's kinsmen are considered close relatives, while your father's uncles and cousins may hardly be considered as related to you at all. In one matrilineal society, among those Nayar of south India who still carry on the traditional ways, the matrilineal principle is developed to such a degree that the father comes to the house of his wife and his children only as a visitor; his real home and his place is with the household of his mother and her brothers. However, the bonds of the family, the emotional ties among father and mother and children, are universally present, and so the emotional and social relationship between father and children are not completely obliterated even by extreme emphasis of the mother's kin.

Public Service by the Clan

Another difference between the family and the clan is that the simple family of parents and children has a relatively short duration in time. When the children grow up, they may found families of their own and the former family group breaks up. The clan is more stable through the passage of years. It is a corporation which outlasts any of the individuals in it. True, a clan may die out, or may amalgamate with other clans, or may split into several different clans, but generally a clan exists through many generations. For that reason, it is often the responsibility of the clan to perform certain services for the public good, services which the clan can always perform since it is a social unit which continues to exist beyond the lifetime of any individual in it.

One such function of a clan has already been mentioned, that of providing the chiefs of a state, as has been the case in Travancore. Among the Hopi Indians, certain clans provide priests for the performance of religious ceremonies. Among some of the Australian tribes, each clan is responsible for the religious propitiation of an animal or plant which is useful to the tribe. The members of the Kangaroo clan, for example, must perform the ceremonies which are believed to be necssary for the continued appearance of kangaroo in the tribal territory. Usually clan members may not eat the animal with which they have a special relationship. So the Kangaroo clan gets no economic benefit from performing the rituals, but assures the supply of that animal for the rest of the tribe.

TOTEMISM AND SOME TECHNICAL TERMS

This special relationship between a clan and some animal or object, is known as *totemism*. Sometimes, as in Australia, clan totemism is important in many aspects of the tribal culture. In other cases, clan totemism amounts to no more than the animal name by which a clan is known. It must be noted that clans always have distinctive names; these are labels by which all the members of a clan can be referred to and by which co-membership can easily be recognized. Frequently the members of a clan will wear a special symbol or have similar dress as was true of the Scottish clans.

In some societies, two or more clans may be grouped together in a section which is technically known as a *phratry*. The members of each clan in the phratry consider themselves more closely related to the other clans in their phratry than to the rest of the clans in the tribe. Where the whole tribe is divided into two divisions, whether matrilineal or patrilineal, each division is called, in anthropological terminology, a *moiety*. A few more technical terms may be noted for those who will want to read further on the subject of social organization. The term *sib* is used in the same sense as we have used the more popular term, clan. A patrilineal clan may be referred to as a *gens* or a *father-sib*. A matrilineal clan is also known as a *mother-sib,* or simply as a clan.

STRENGTH AND IMPORTANCE OF THE CLAN

Clans are found at various levels of human life, from relatively crude hunting and gathering cultures, such as those of the Australian tribes, to high civilizations of ancient tradition, such as those of India and China. Conversely, peoples who do not have clans are found at all social and economic levels, from the hunting Eskimo to ourselves.

Generally the clan is most important in those societies where the clan members live together in the same local community. When I first visited the Kota of South India, I noticed that each tribal village was arranged in three rows of houses, or streets. The houses of each street were inhabited by men of a single patrilineal clan. When the girls of a clan grow up, they marry and move to another village or to another street in the same village. But the men of the clan stay together and live together all their lives and their clan solidarity is strong. The sense of unity and the mutual co-operation of any social group, whether clan, club, or army company, is strengthened by common residence. If its members live together, they inevitably come to know each other better, and come to rely on each other more than if the group is scattered and its members rarely meet.

This consideration has much to do with the weakening of clans in many parts of the world. When people stay put for most of their lives, co-operation within a clan is feasible and advantageous. Even in the great populations of north China, clans have been, until recently, live social groupings. Although a clan might have hundreds of thousands of members, it did have its home territory where a great many clansmen lived together, it had its ancestral temple, and there were lands owned as clan property. The poorer members were helped by funds donated by the richer families. To this day, no intermarriage is permitted within the clan. In India, also, the clan remains effective as a means of regulating marriages.

However, when economic and social conditions change rapidly, and when there is much shifting of population, clan members become scattered, they lose touch with each other, and forget their consciousness of clan. Clan functions are apt to be taken over by other social groupings. In the villages of India and China, where conditions of life have remained fairly stable, the clan still functions, at least in regulating marriages. But among the people of the large cities in both countries, the function of the clans and their very memory is fast passing away.

What Makes a Tribe

The families of a local community, both in societies that have clans and in those that do not, almost always have a sense of belonging to a social unit larger than the local group, one that includes a number of different communities. Among most primitive people, this larger unit of society is the tribe.

The communities that make up a tribe usually occupy the same general territory, commonly speak the same language, and follow the same way of life. But neither mutual territory, common language, nor similar culture can alone account for the existence of any tribe. Often enough two primitive groups have occupied adjoining country and have been mortal enemies. Some peoples who speak the same language consider themselves to belong to utterly different social groups. In fact, sharing the same manners and customs may only increase the frequency of disagreements between two tribes.

The important basis for the existence of a tribe is not any one of those factors, but the combination of them that gives every person in the tribe a feeling of belonging with the other men and women of the tribe. The real bonds which hold any group together, whether it be tribe, clan, or state, are the attitudes which the individuals in that group have toward each other, and the behavior patterns of reciprocal help, of co-operation, which are the tangible demonstrations of those attitudes. Formal patterns of organization, like tribal councils or annual conventions, contribute much to the feeling of unity and to the united action of a group, but they are not absolutely essential for its functioning.

As the children of the tribe grow up, they learn the formal patterns of organization—how to take part in a tribal council—and the informal ways of co-operating with fellow tribesmen—how to recognize them, what to expect of and from them, when to give them hospitality and support. Thus the tribe perpetuates itself from generation to generation. In modern times, many tribes have been shattered and scattered because alien peoples and cultures disrupted the tribal way of life. In much of Africa, this has been so recent and so unnerving a process that the very term 'detribalized' native has come to mean a person who represents great social and personal problems. He has lost the traditional standards by which his forefathers guided their lives and he has not been able to adopt other patterns adequate for the new conditions in which he must live. In the face of the disrupting influences, many tribesmen, in various continents and conditions of life, try to keep their tribal identity and to build a new way of existence which will preserve something of their traditional tribal identity.

THE MEANING OF TRIBAL MEMBERSHIP AMONG THE PLAINS CREE

The tribal grouping of the Plains Cree Indians of western Canada will illustrate these ideas about the nature of a tribe. The eight bands of the Plains Cree, as they existed just before the buffalo vanished from the Canadian prairies, ranged over a vast territory that was some six hundred miles from one end to the other, from the Qu'Appelle valley near the present Manitoba-Saskatchewan line to the region where Edmonton now stands. Several of the bands would come together once a year to participate in the Sun Dance, the great ceremonial event of this and of other Plains tribes. But there was never any occasion on which all of the bands met together. And there was no tribal council or any meeting of representatives from all the sections of the tribe.

Nonetheless there never was any doubt as to who was a member of the tribe and who was not. When a young man of the tribe reached an age when he began to feel restless and wanted to see a bit of the world beyond the terrain of his own band, he would commonly go to visit the other Plains Cree bands. If he was from one of the easternmost communities, he would travel westward, staying a while with one encampment of the tribe and then going on to another, until he reached the westernmost bands, those whose territory adjoined the habitat of the Blackfoot Indians, the constant enemies of the Plains Cree.

As he came into a new band encampment, he would seek out those who were related to his family (the Plains Cree did not have clans) or were relatives of relatives of his. Some kinship connection could always be found because there was frequent intermarriage among the various bands. In one of the tipis of his relatives he would first be fed, and then he would be asked to tell the news and gossip of his own community.

The young man might be a total stranger to the band he was visiting, in that no one there had ever seen him before or perhaps had ever heard of him, but he was never a stranger socially. He always could be placed as a member of a group that was known to the host, and as such, he was accorded the same hospitality that his host would receive were he visiting a family in the young man's community. Gossip about people known to both the host and the visitor always helped establish the social relationship between the two on a firm footing. Though gossip may sometimes seem to be mean and unnecessary, it is, in all human societies, one of the best ways of reaffirming friendly relations—between the gossipers at least.

It not infrequently happened that the young man would take a fancy to one of the girls of the community he was visiting, and when he returned to the encampment of his parents, he would come with a bride. Plains Cree parents generally preferred that their sons marry girls from their own community, girls whom they knew and whose family they knew. But the young men themselves often found the girls of distant bands of the tribe more attractive than the girls they had seen and known since childhood. This, of course, is not a kind of happening restricted to the Plains Cree; among the young men of any people, the young women of other communities tend to seem more glamorous than those from the home group.

Occasionally visitors from other tribes would come to an encampment, usually for purposes of trade. But there was a great difference between the attitude toward a fellow tribesman, even if he were a young fellow whose name was unknown, and the attitude toward a familiar and respected man from another tribe. Both would be given food and shelter, but there could not be the intimacy and the exchange of greetings and gossip with a member of another tribe that there was with a fellow tribesman. This was true even with the northern neighbors of the tribe, the Wood Cree, who spoke the same language, and from whom the Plains Cree had descended. But the Wood Cree lived in the forests, they were not buffalo hunters and warriors, and their whole way of life and their world view was different from that of the Plains Cree. Despite the bond of language the disparities of culture were so great that the Plains Cree did not like to have much to do with the forest dwellers.

With the tribe's southern neighbors, the Assiniboine, there were more close and cordial relations, even though the two languages were completely different. There was even some intermarriage between Plains Cree and Assiniboine. But even the best known Assiniboine was felt to be more of a stranger, in some ways, than a fresh young tribesman newly arrived from a distant band. There was always something of an unknown quantity about a person from another tribe, while one knew pretty much what to expect of a fellow tribesman, just as one knew what to expect of one's neighbor in the band.

Blackfoot Indians sometimes came on trading missions, but their visits had to be well prepared and announced, because they came much more often to raid the encampments and steal the horses. A party of Blackfoot seen lurking about the camp would be liable to be shot on sight. The Plains Cree did their share of raiding in return, usually in small war parties recruited within a single band. If a young man from another band should be visiting at the time a raiding party was setting out, he would be quite likely to join the raiders and attempt to make a name for himself. Such mutual participation in arms would further strengthen the bonds of tribal unity among the bands of the tribe.

Indeed the main occasion on which the members of several, perhaps all, of the bands of the tribe would deliberately come together for a common purpose, was related to warfare. Sometimes when a dearly loved son or daughter had been killed in an enemy raid, the parents would make the circuit of the various bands, bewailing their child and asking the warriors to join a vengeance party. They usually would have no trouble in recruiting young men from every band they visited, and when the party was complete, it would penetrate enemy territory until an encampment of the enemy tribe was found and wiped out.

TRIBAL WAR AND PEACE

It is in making war that a tribe most commonly functions as a unified social group. Because the tribesmen feel themselves to be related, they react to an attack against one part of the tribe as though it were an attack on all, and they quickly rally to concerted defense and counterattack. Moreover, outsiders are usually not considered to be human beings in the same sense that fellow tribesmen are human. Hence it is no crime or sin to treat outsiders as hunted animals. A tribesman who is always kind and considerate toward persons in his own group, can therefore be completely cruel and callous when dealing with those outside his tribe. There is a feeling, even among the most advanced nations, that the consideration and proper behavior shown toward a person of one's own kind need not be used when dealing with a person of another race, or belief, or country. The Plains Cree, like most tribesmen of the primitive world, felt that theirs was the only way of life fit for real men, that the manners and customs of other people were somehow degraded just because they were different. This tribal attitude, too, is not unknown among the citizens of modern states.

Making peace and keeping the peace are much more difficult for a tribe to accomplish than is making war. Matters of social control, of education, of the punishment of transgressions are usually carried out by the family and the local community in a tribal society. It often happened in the history of the Plains Cree that a famous and respected Plains Cree chief would agree to a peace, smoke the pipe of peace, and even while he was so doing, a party of warriors from one of the bands of his tribe would be out raiding an encampment of the other group. Tribes usually have only meager means of preventing the individuals of the separate bands from behaving in this fashion.

From Tribe to State

The state is the grouping which does have the means of controlling such behavior. Basically a state consists of a set of local communities which are so organized that certain men of the group have the power to act for all in making the people of the several communities do certain things and seeing to it that they refrain from doing other things. Among all the communities of a state there is general agreement as to who shall act for them and according to what patterns such action should be taken. It must be noted that this agreement does not always spring up voluntarily, because many of the states that have grown to be great arose when a tribe went on a military rampage, subdued other peoples, and kept them in subjugation for long periods. In that case, the agreement among the communities of the subjugated people was an enforced agreement, just as the Anglo-Saxon groups agreed to pay tribute and to be ruled by the Norman overlords after the Norman conquest of Britain.

A good many tribal societies show the beginnings of the functions of a state. Among the Plains Cree, for example, each band had a kind of club to which most of the warriors belonged. This club, though it is usually called the Warrior Society, did no military duties. Its main task was to regulate the buffalo hunt.

When the tribesmen were gathered in a large encampment, individual hunting could not be tolerated because all the game would be driven away from the vicinity in a short time, and the encampment then would have to break up. So when a buffalo herd was sighted, the Warrior Society members stood guard to see that no one disturbed the buffalo before proper preparations had been made. When all the hunters were ready, a signal was given and the tribesmen charged into the herd.

If any man tried to make a kill before that signal was given, or scared off the herd because he could not control his horse, the Warriors immediately rode up to that man's tipi. They slashed it to ribbons, broke his bows and guns, destroyed all that he possessed, as punishment for his offense. Ordinarily a man's relatives would immediately come to his support to prevent such harm from befalling him. But in this case, no one would try to stop the Warriors; one of the Society members who was busily tearing up the guilty man's blankets might be his own brother.

In this latter instance the obligations of kinship that the Warrior would normally act upon, were subordinated to his obligations to all the people of the encampment. In like manner, a Warrior carried out his obligations to the group as a whole, rather than to the narrow circle of his own kin, when the family of a murdered man was seeking blood vengeance. Then a Warrior related to that family, instead of joining them in the hunt for the murderer, would forcibly take them into a meeting with the relatives of the murderer. He would help restrain them from violence until some payment was arranged which would settle the feud. Here again, the welfare of the whole community was the guide to a Warrior's action, rather than the usual demands of kinship.

But among the Plains Cree, as in other tribal societies, the occasions on which certain men had the right and the duty to act for the several communities were few and infrequent. Those few occasions did form the beginnings of true government but never went beyond these mere beginnings. The obligations to one's relatives, and the action patterns based on blood relationships were much more important than any obligation to a set of local groups, from which develop the patterns essential to the existence of a state.

CONFEDERATION AND CONQUEST IN THE MAKING OF A STATE

There have been times when a number of tribes would get together to fight off a common enemy and, in order to do so effectively, would adopt patterns of mutual aid and follow leaders who would act in the interests of the whole confederation of tribes. The League of the Iroquois, in what is now upstate New York, was an example of such a confederation which developed in the direction of becoming a state. These confederations worked very well as long as the common danger was great. But as soon as the common enemy was defeated, each tribe and the local communities within a tribe would forget about co-operating and drift back to the condition in which each local group followed its own sweet way without consideration of the interests of the former confederation as a whole.

States more often have come into being through conquest rather than through confederation. The members of a conquering tribe sometimes discover that they can get a good steady income from keeping the conquered people under their rule, that it is more profitable to turn a beaten enemy into a subject than into a corpse. Then the victorious group has to develop some kind of system whereby certain of the tribesmen have the job of acting for all of the overlords in keeping the subjects subdued and the income from them flowing to the victorious tribesmen. This process has frequently led to the rise of a new state.

When tribesmen overrun an established state, they usually take over much of the established system of government. This happened when the Mongol tribes conquered the Chinese kingdoms and when the Vandals and other tribes defeated Rome. But in the modern world, subject peoples have a way of remembering their old independence and of overthrowing the conquerors sooner or later. Hence some nations have pretty much given up the idea of keeping other nations permanently under their rule. Defeated peoples are dealt with so that they supposedly will never be a threat to the victors again, and independent government, real or presumed, is returned to a conquered nation.

FROM NATION TO CONFEDERATION OF NATIONS

The very term nation implies a group of people who not only are organized into a state, but also have a common way of life. Thus the French state includes under its authority such diverse peoples as North African Arabs and the folk of tropical Madagascar. But when we speak of the French nation we mean those peoples mainly of France proper who (despite all political differences) have certain manners and customs and linguistic habits in common.

Those men who are now trying to set up an effective confederation of nations are faced with problems that were familiar to those who tried to bring about a permanent confederation of tribes. After the common danger is over, each group tends to go its own way and to place its own interests above the mutual welfare of the whole set of communities. Because a lasting confederation of nations has never been set up effectively before, the task is difficult. But it is not at all impossible. In fact, the development of human social organization toward a real confederation of nations promises to be faster and possibly smoother than the earlier development from tribe to state.

AGE GROUPS

Local community, tribe, state—all are groupings which arise from the universal situation that people who live in the same locality have similar interests and problems. There are also other types of social groups based on mutual interests and problems. Among the most common of such types are those based on age.

Persons of the same age, in any community, tend to congregate and co-operate. In some societies, groupings according to age are very important. Among the Masai tribe of east Africa, for example, there is an initiation ceremony held once every four years for the boys who have reached puberty since the previous ceremony was given. In the course of the ceremony the boys are circumcised and thereafter may live in the bachelors' dormitory and assume the duties and privileges of a warrior. Each initiation class becomes an age-class, and the youths of the age-class live together in the same dormitory, earn a distinctive name for their class, and get a distinctive design for their shields.

The exact groupings according to age vary among different peoples, but all societies recognize at least three divisions in the life of the individual as a basis for social organization. The distinctions always made are: children, adults, and aged. Though children often have their own social groupings, such as the Cub Scouts in our society, these units are not usually of any great influence on the community as a whole.

However, children may occupy a very important place in a society. Dr. Ralph Linton tells the story of visiting the chief of a tribe on one of the Marquesan islands in the South Seas. The chief's wife was of royal blood and so the chief's son was even more royal than his father. Since the son, then aged nine, was so full of the supernatural power called *mana* because of his extremely royal blood, any attempt to discipline him would have been sacrilege. The boy had had an argument with his father a few days before Dr. Linton's visit, and had made the house taboo for the others by naming it after his own head. So the family had to move out and could not use the house again until the boy lifted the taboo. The nine-year-old was getting along very well because he could use the house himself and could eat anywhere in the village. He was enjoying the situation thoroughly.

RITES OF PASSAGE

The passage of an individual from the social status of a child to that of an adult does not always coincide with his physical maturation. Thus a person is legally a child in our society for a number of years after he has become an adult physically. Among many primitive peoples, as among the Masai, an individual's transfer from childhood to adulthood is marked by the celebration of a ceremony. Such ceremonies, and others which similarly mark a person's change of status, are called rites of passage. These rites of passage occur not only in relation to entering adulthood, but also in relation to birth, marriage, and death. Our own society observes a number of such rites of passage, baptisms, weddings, and, among the wealthier classes, coming-out parties for debutantes.

The passage of an individual from the adult group to that of the aged is hardly ever marked by one of the rites of passage. This is partly because it is difficult to tell just when a man enters old age, and even more because men rarely like to think of themselves as old. It is true that in many regions, the aged are given a great deal of respect and are highly honored. This was true in China; among some Australian tribes, the old men were so important that these societies are characterized by the term *gerontocracy*, the rule of the aged. This is in marked contrast with the situation in our culture, especially for women. In certain parts of our society, it is very difficult for a woman to admit that she is more than relatively few years beyond puberty. At least, it is difficult for her to do so until she is far enough beyond puberty to be a grandmother.

STATUS AND ROLE

The importance of social status becomes especially apparent when we see a person changing from one status position to another. In the everyday behavior of people, status is no less important. Within every social group, from the smallest to the largest, there are different status positions. The individuals do not have the same parts to play in the functioning of the group; they perform and are expected to perform different parts. Each status position requires the individual who holds it to perform certain obligations in respect to others in the group and it entitles him to receive certain rights from the others.

Thus in a family of our society, or of any society, there are such status positions as husband, wife, father, mother, daughter, brother, sister. The husband and father in your family is the same person, but he has different rights and obligations when he is acting in the status of *father* in regard to his children than when he is acting as *husband* in regard to—perhaps it is better put, in respect to—his wife. In the family in which he was born (his family of 'orientation') he had other status positions, that of son and perhaps that of brother. These required still different kinds of behavior than the kinds he is expected to follow in his statuses of husband and father in his later family (of 'procreation').

In a large, highly formalized social organization such as an army, the rights and obligations of each status position are carefully spelled out in numbered paragraphs. The requirements of the status of private or colonel are defined in the manuals and regulations. Even more, the specific rights and duties of such a particular status as captain of the chemical warfare company in an armored division are meticulously detailed in the army's regulations.

In such large formal establishments, there are usually informal status positions as well, which are not part of the official table of organization. Usually a soldier is not only a member of his platoon but he is also one of an informal group of buddies (a 'primary group') with whom he spends his leisure hours and whose members help each other in many ways. Within this informal group, there often are status positions of leaders and followers, and these positions may not be in accord with the official rank, since a corporal may be the leader there and his sergeant one of the followers.

The corporal who is a leader among his buddies although of lower official rank than some of them exemplifies another aspect of status. Within the requirements of a status position, its duties and prerogatives will be differently enacted by different kinds of persons. One captain may be content merely to carry out the minimal requirements of his status while another may spend long hours in looking after the welfare of the men of his company and perfecting himself and them in the skills expected of the unit. Or one may concentrate on perfecting the internal, technical, spit-and-polish details while another may concern himself mainly with the relations of his unit to the others in the outfit and to the larger tasks of the division.

Role is the manner in which different personalities carry out the status requirements. It refers to the fact that some captains are diligent and others are dilatory in the fulfillment of the expectations of their status, yet both fulfill the requirements of the position. Some are usually temperate and others are usually short-tempered in their relations with the men of their command; both kinds of captain have the same status but perform different roles within the status.

Role also refers to the fact that a person tends to show similar behavior in his several status positions. The intemperate captain may also be a short-tempered husband, an impatient father, an impulsive partner at bridge. He plays a similar role in these statuses. Lest this example seem too invidious, it is well to add that the very quality which may make him an uncomfortable bridge partner may qualify him as a superb combat leader. Moreover, most people do not show a patently consistent role in their various statuses. The overbearing boss may come home to act as a tender and thoughtful father. It is one of the intriguing problems for future research to ascertain whatever personal and social consistencies underlie such apparently inconsistent roles.

Certain roles are approved by the group, others are disapproved or indifferently regarded, yet in every society there is a range of role enactment. Esteem is a term used to describe the fact of group approval of a certain kind of role. A well-behaved but not too docile child is esteemed. Prestige refers to the group-approval power of status: in fulfilling the patterns of a prestige status a person generally affects the behavior of others, usually subordinate to him in some degree, while in playing an esteemed role a person need not influence the reciprocal action of his fellows nor is subordination necessarily involved.

The subordination involved in prestige status need not be more than that of following the lead of those in prestige positions in certain particular activities. The leading fashion designers of Paris and New York have widespread prestige, but only in the realm of women's dress and not in, say, religion or politics. At the other extreme of prestige status may be the authoritarian father in a society which expects fathers to be sternly authoritarian. Within his family circle, his word is law on everything.

There are broadly two ways in which a person gets his status positions. Some are ascribed to him: these are assigned without much reference to his personal qualities. The status of male or female, of child or adult, of daughter or sister are ascribed statuses. Others he achieves by his own efforts. In our society, the status position of mayor, doctor, varsity fullback are achieved statuses. Among most peoples of India, the status of wife is ascribed rather than achieved because marriages are arranged by parents without much consultation of the prospective spouses. In American society there is a bit more achievement involved. Some status positions are partly ascribed and partly achieved, others are mostly ascribed or mostly achieved.

RANKED GROUPINGS: CASTE AND CLASS

More often among the nations we call civilized than among the tribes of primitive folk, there are social groupings according to caste and class. These are groups within a community which are graded so that one is considered to be higher in prestige and power than another. Each person has a class or caste status position which governs his behavior toward the other individuals. A person of the highest caste in an Indian village, because of his caste status, may not eat in the company of fellow villagers of lower caste rank, or associate with them freely, or take a wife of different caste status than his own.

There is no sharp distinction between a caste and a class. The term caste is used when a person's membership in the ranked group is ascribed and is so important that it affects every part of his life, his religion, his occupation, the life prospects of his children. A class is also a ranked group but one in which status may be achieved and whose members have social functions apart from their class status.

Caste groupings have been most highly developed in India where, as we have mentioned before, a villager is born into a caste, may marry only a woman of his caste, and often follows the occupation traditional for his caste. In the parts of India where the caste system is still important, a member of the highest caste, the Brahmins, may not even eat food that has been prepared by one of low caste. The Brahmins of a local community will often be the priests, or at least will be more educated in the sacred Sanskrit scriptures than their neighbors of other castes. A Brahmin boy who has undergone the rite of passage which initiates him into the status of a scholar will wear the sacred thread over his shoulder, the symbol of the higher castes. And a boy who has been born into a family of the blacksmith or musician caste—these occupations are among those lower in esteem—will generally be given little formal education and will probably follow the trade of his father.

Social classes are similar to castes in that one class is higher in the social scale than the others, as was true for the classes of nobles, commoners, and serfs in Europe of the Middle Ages. In modern societies, social classes are less definite and there is much more mobility by families and individuals between classes than there was. Wealth, family history, personal interests, and other factors enter into the determination of the class structure which can be found in present-day social organization.

In the United States, the class hierarchy is particularly fluid and most Americans think of themselves as belonging to a middle class. But class rankings do exist widely in America, although the gradations between classes may not be sharp and class distinctions may be fuzzy. In some sections of the American population, class status is relatively unimportant, in others it counts for a great deal throughout the life span of the individuals involved.

The social organization of the Deep South in the United States has sometimes been called a caste system. In some respect it certainly has been such. Intermarriage and interdining between the groups is forbidden; members of one group may not associate freely and openly with members of the other; mobility of individuals or families from one side of the community to the other is tabooed except where a few Negroes are able clandestinely to 'pass' into the other group; the status positions entailed in the respective groupings affect a large part of the individual's life. All this as in the classic caste system of India.

There are certain important differences. There was not the high religious sanction for caste in the South that there has been in India. Members of the lower caste in the South have increasingly rejected the assumptions necessary for caste differentiation. It is well to note that this occurred in India also, but in earlier centuries the rejection took the form of a new religion, as Buddhism. In India also, the caste system was not the rigid strait-jacket it sometimes is made out to be. There was mobility both for social groups and for individuals, although the opportunity to change one's caste status was much smaller than in a more open-class society such as that of the north or west of the United States. And the classic caste system of India has been undergoing change just as the traditional social system of the Deep South is changing.

Caste and class stratifications may exist together in the same community. In the South, there are quite clear class distinctions within the white group and within the Negro group. The criteria for, say, upper class status in the two groups are similar but there is little communication and informal association by members of the respective upper classes across the color—or if you like, the caste—line.

In Indian villages, the castes may be grouped into classes. There may be three castes which are called the lowest, 'untouchable' castes. The members of one of these castes may acquire some wealth, give up such degrading practices as beef eating, take on high caste customs and thus succeed in raising the position of their whole caste in that village to the next class of 'middle' castes. Each caste member retains his caste status, but the status of all members of their caste has been raised in the local hierarchy.

SOCIAL ORGANIZATION IN OUR SOCIETY

In western societies, there are many other types of social groupings, ranging from trade unions and medical associations to bridge clubs and parent-teacher associations. Each of these groupings is held together by a common interest, an interest arising from mutual participation in the same trades, the mutual enjoyment of a game, or mutual problems in relation to a set of children.

The primary social group, the family, remains basic in our social system. The local community, in the sense of a small set of people who know each other personally, is also essential in spite of the temporary weakening of this unit in large cities. The clan has probably disappeared from our social tradition for good, but its place has been taken partly by the social units which are extensions of the local group—the various state agencies within the nation—and partly by voluntary associations based on common interests.

The outline of social organization which has been sketched in this chapter, rudimentary though it is, nevertheless provides a basis for further questions of considerable theoretical and practical importance. For example, the subject of voluntary associations in our society has been relatively little studied. What kinds of voluntary associations are there in your community? What do they do for their members? Under what circumstances and for what people is one such association more important than another? How are voluntary associations related to age groupings, to class stratifications, to economic interests?

The study of these questions will necessarily lead to enquiry about other elements of social organization in the local and in the larger society because the various social units are interrelated and interdependent, because each person has various status positions. Therefore research on voluntary associations must take into account the factors of family and kinship, of age and social stratification, of community and state.

The political aspects of social organization are of special concern in our times. Great interest is devoted to setting up various kinds of new international organizations and in perfecting those we now have. Underlying all the detailed and technical discussions there are some broad problems which have been mentioned above. What makes a unified, co-operating political entity? Is a tribe only a collection of local bands? Is a state only a confederation of local communities? How can a union of sovereign states stay united? Much illuminating knowledge on such questions has been developed in the studies of social scientists. Much remains to be developed in future studies.

Religion

LESS THAN A HUNDRED YEARS AGO, scholars discussed with interest such questions as how men could have come to conceive of gods, whether there might be tribes so primitive as to have no religion, and how far the faiths and superstitions of savages could properly be related to the great universal religions.

No one who studies tribal religions today is interested in trying to answer such questions, nor even thinks that satisfying answers to them could be found. There is no evidence for any theory of an origin of religion in time or place; and most anthropologists have ceased to take their bearings in the study of religion from any religion practiced in their own society.

The publication of well-authenticated works of travel, and the growth of speculation about human nature at large, led in the eighteenth century to an increase in curiosity about tribal religions. In Boswell's *Life of Samuel Johnson* for example, we find Johnson—that firm churchman—rebuking a gentleman for wishing to spend three years living with the natives of New Zealand to find out what sort of a religion people denied a special revelation might have. 'And what account of their religion can you suppose to be learnt from savages?' asks Dr. Johnson. 'Only consider, sir, our own state. Our religion is in a book: we have an order of men whose duty it is to teach: we have one day in the week set apart for it, and this in general pretty well-observed; Yet ask the first ten gross men you meet, and hear what they can tell of their religion.'

Johnson thought that the fullness of religion lay in the presence of a theology and a church, a large measure of intellectual formulation and social formalization. For him, to learn about a religion was to find out

382

what people knew of its doctrines. 'Gross men' and savages could not know enough for their knowledge to form the basis of serious study.

This has not been the view of anthropologists. It is true that some of the main differences between the tribal religions of non-literate peoples, and those religions with literate traditions, are as Johnson stated; but a religion is something more than that part of it which appears in its sacred scriptures and in written commentaries upon them. These represent what people know and are prepared to say about their religion when they reflect upon it; we need also to understand how their religion figures in the ordinary conduct of their lives. To learn what a people say about their religion is not always the same thing as to know how they practice it.

Most tribes lack any formal theology, and in most of them there is no distinct religious organization, like a church, which can be studied in isolation from other forms of social organization. Faced with such difficulties, Professor Lowie suggested in his general work *Primitive Religion* (1925) that in the last resort religion could only be defined by reference to 'the subjective condition of believers and worshippers.' This view is strongly marked by the influence of William James's popular work, *The Varieties of Religious Experience*, published early in this century. James there dismissed some of the dogmatic features of religious thought and practice as 'phenomena of mere tribal or corporate psychology,' not to be confused, he said, with 'those manifestations of the purely interior life' in which he was then exclusively interested. In that study, he sought the grounds of religious phenomena in special conditions of the individual conscience, and understood religion as a matter of useful aspirations, rather than as an inevitable and formal duty.

This view has influenced many students of tribal religions. It is natural that it should have done so, for most tribes are without those very doctrinal and dogmatic elements of religion which James preferred to disregard, and an investigation of a tribal religion must therefore ultimately be based upon what individuals say and appear to think and feel. By regarding religion as grounded in features of a common human psychology, some students have thought themselves able to account for specific religious beliefs and practices by referring them to sentiments which they have recognized in themselves. They have thus tried to get over, in one way, a difficulty which is perhaps peculiar to the study of religion and magic in tribal societies, and which must be considered if we wish to understand the balance between fact and interpretation in most anthropological accounts of religion.

The difficulty may be thus explained. It is easy for a visitor to share the political sentiments or the economic interests of members of a tribal society, for he readily understands the nature of the reality upon which those sentiments and interests are based. If a tribesman says that his people have been attacked by an enemy, or that birds have spoilt the crops, our understanding of the situation is not fundamentally different from his own, for we do not doubt the reality of enemies or birds. The case is different if a man says that his people are being killed by a spirit, or that the birds which spoilt the crops were sent by witchcraft. Spirits, or witchcraft, are not directly known to us as are enemies or birds, and though we see the effects of course—the sick people, the spoilt grain— we do not attribute them to the same causes as does the tribesman. It is then that we come to ask ourselves what the spirits or witchcraft can be said to represent *for us,* as well as for the tribesmen who believe in them.

The most important differences in approach and interpretation arise between students of tribal religion at this point. St. Augustine (and perhaps also some missionaries today) answer this question in their own way by being able to regard foreign gods and spirits as daemons, powers other than the true God, but nevertheless conceivably real powers operating independently in the world, acting from without upon the human imagination and will and not merely created by those human faculties. This, at least, is not to deny to foreign gods some sort of real existence; and tribal peoples do indeed represent their gods to themselves as real powers existing apart from men, not as figments of human thought and feeling.

Most anthropologists, however, do not believe in daemons any more than they believe in the foreign gods, the spirits or the witchcraft they are trying to account for. Yet, they wish to bring the tribesman's thought and experience ultimately into one world with their own. If we cannot believe in the gods which other peoples accept as the basis of their religions, we seek for the basis in something other than those gods—in something we ourselves believe in. What is that something?

The answers which have been given to this question may be divided into three main groups, the theological, the psychological, and the philosophical or sociological.

St. Augustine's answer above was one example of a theological answer, but there are others, given from less well-defined theological standpoints and nearer to our present studies of religion. F. Max Müller, the scholar of comparative religious studies at the end of the last century, answered the question from the point of view of a liberal theology. 'However imperfect and however childish the conception of God may be,' he wrote, 'it always represents the highest ideal of perfection which the human soul for the time-being can reach and grasp . . .' So he fitted the pagan gods into his own theology, not by regarding them as daemons, but by regarding them merely as 'false or imperfect names for God'—for a God, that is, in which he himself believed.

Max Müller was praised by a missionary for having shown that heathen religions were not the work of the devil. In doing so, however, he also made them appear other than they seem to the tribal peoples themselves. Max Müller's conception of God was of an abstract ideal of primarily ethical perfection. There can now be no doubt that the gods of many tribal peoples are of a very different nature, and are thought of as active powers, willful, intelligent, capricious, jealous, and even, at times, greedy. Since for Max Müller God was an idea rather than an active power, he was surprised by a characteristic of primitive religion which he nevertheless intelligently noted—its preference for the concrete, its attachment to material symbols. He noted that there were

two distinct tendencies to be observed in the growth of ancient religion . . . on the one side, the struggle of the mind against the material character of language, a constant attempt to strip words of their coarse covering, and fit them, by main force, for the purposes of abstract thought. But . . . on the other side a constant relapse from the spiritual into the material, and, strange to say, a predilection for the material sense instead of the spiritual.

It is true that in primitive religions we find a preference for the local and specific understanding of divinity rather than for the general, abstract, and theoretical. Since Max Müller took his own abstract God to be the real basis of all religion, other conceptions of gods were interpreted as lowly conceptions of that God. He explained many gods as personifications of natural phenomena, such as the sky; what those who worshipped such gods thought to be personal agents, Max Müller explained as having originally been impersonal and general forces in which he also could believe.

The most famous examples of a psychological interpretation of tribal religions are those of what is sometimes called the 'English' school of anthropologists, and particularly those of the two great figures of nineteenth-century anthropology, Sir Edward Tylor and Sir James Frazer. To these we may add also the name of Malinowski, one of the first anthropologists to study a native people through their own language in the intimate way which is considered essential today.

Tylor put forward a theory of primitive religion which was widely accepted in his day, and which has had a great influence on the study of the subject until the present time. He claimed that what underlay tribal religions was a belief in spiritual beings, personal spirits which were thought to animate nature. This primitive faith Tylor called *animism*.

Tylor suggested that primitive man, reflecting upon his experiences in dreams and visions, and upon the differences between living men and corpses, concluded that man had a soul, which was a sort of spiritual counterpart of the body. The conception of a human soul then according to Tylor seemed to have 'served as a type or model on which primitive man framed not only his ideas of other souls of lower grade, but also his ideas of spiritual beings in general, from the tiniest elf that sports in the long grass up to the heavenly Creator and Ruler of the world, the Great Spirit.'

In so far as such theories pretend to be historically based, we know that they are not capable of proof. In so far as they pretend to describe the way in which all tribal peoples think today, they are misleading, thought not without a hint at truth. Let us consider the element of truth in them first.

It is well known that in many tribes material objects, such as bundles of sticks and roots or carved representations of beings, are treated with special reverence and are believed to have religious virtue. Such objects of religious and magical value are usually classed together as *fetishes*. (See Plate XI.) They are treated as sacred because they are objects in which deities are located or manifested. They *could* be regarded, however, as implying nothing more than the material of which they are composed, as when it is said in the hymn that

> "The heathen in his blindness
> Bows down to wood and stone. . ."

Tylor saw that this was a misunderstanding, and that no people worshipped material objects simply *as* the material objects which we see them to be. In this he took the view which every serious student has taken, and encouraged an interest in the distinction between material symbols and the divine beings they symbolized.

His theory had another virtue too. At a time when public opinion often represented savages as moved by almost subhuman instincts, unreasoning and perhaps incapable of reason, Tylor imputed reasoning to them as the very basis of their religion. It is true that there is an element of reason in tribal religions. They involve argument from effect to cause in some cases, such as the treatment of sickness, when a diviner may be called in to use his special insight to discover the spiritual reason for the complaint. The causes and treatment thus decided upon are not such as we should accept; but the conception of a cause which can be discovered by special investigation is certainly present. Tylor's error was not that he imputed the possibility of logical inference to primitive peoples, but that he assumed that they arrived at their religious beliefs by means of it. A little reflection upon the religion of his own society would have persuaded him that though reason and argument by analogy may support a faith, they do not found one. To show a religion to be reasonable, and to suggest that it is the result of reasoning from faulty premises, as Tylor and Frazer did, are not the same thing.

It is certainly wrong also to suggest that tribal gods and spirits are thought of as having personality analogous, in all important ways, to human personality, or that all spiritual beings are thought to resemble in kind the human soul. Some gods may be thought of in man's image, or may be deified men. Often, however, it would be truer to say that the force of tribal gods depends upon their being quite other than human in nature, and that it is this difference which is the basis of religious service offered to them. The Book of Job, with its emphasis upon God's transcendence of human knowledge and argument, indeed of the human scale altogether, is often nearer to the kind of understanding of the divine we find among primitive peoples than is the kind of crude anthropomorphism ascribed to them by some scholars of the last century.

Tylor's account of what *we* can regard as the basis of primitive religion thus grounds religion in processes of reasoning, found equally among savages and among ourselves. For the gods of the primitives, he substitutes something he can himself take for granted—logical processes, combined with primitive error and ignorance. The gods of the tribes need not then be supposed to correspond to any other-than-human reality, as Max Müller and St. Augustine both in their different ways thought possible; they may be seen to correspond to certain human mental processes.

This is one kind of psychological interpretation, based upon an intellectualist psychology. There are others more influential today; but before considering them we must take into account some attempts to modify Tylor's theory. Objections were raised to his notions of a primitive world filled with *personal* spiritual beings. These objections were based upon reports, from Melanesia, Polynesia, North America, and elsewhere, of native conceptions of an *impersonal* power active in the world. Tylor's theory of personal spiritual beings did not allow for this conception, which Tylor's successor Marrett was one of the first to investigate.

The Polynesian and Melanesian word for the conception is *mana;* that word has become almost as familiar a part of our vocabulary for the discussion of primitive religions as the North American Indian word, *totem,* and another Polynesian word, *taboo.* Each of these native terms sums up in a word a complex range of conceptions which many books have been written to explain.

The study of *mana* has produced so many general theories about religion and magic that it is interesting to see how it was described in the early accounts of those who studied it in its context of native life. The word became known primarily through R. H. Codrington's work *The Melanesians* (1891); but I quote an account of the meaning of *mana* in Polynesia from a slightly older source, *Old New Zealand* by a Paheka Maori. There the writer, a European who lived for long with the Maori, says of *mana* that:

Virtus, prestige, authority, good fortune, influence, sanctity, luck, are all words which, under certain conditions, give something near the meaning . . . *mana* sometimes means a more than natural virtue or power attaching to some person or thing, different from and independent of the ordinary natural conditions of either. . . I once had a tame pig which, before heavy rain, would always cut extraordinary capers and squeak and run like mad . . . all the Maori said that it was . . . a pig possessed of *mana:* it had more than natural powers and could foretell rain.

Many further examples of the situations in which *mana* is thought to operate are given:

The *mana* of a priest . . . is proved by the truth of his predictions . . . *mana* in another sense is the accompaniment of power but not the power itself . . . this is the chief's *mana* . . . the warrior's *mana* is just a little something more than mere good fortune . . ."

and so on.

It is clear that this is a conception for which no simple equivalent exists in our language. One way of giving an account of it is by giving lengthy descriptions of the contexts in which it is used. General theories of religion based upon the concept of *mana*, however, may omit much that is specific in the meanings of the term in its native context and try to give a general account of what it is. Goldenweiser, for example, explains *mana* as

a projection or objectivation of what, on the subjective side, is the religious thrill; *mana* is what causes the religious thrill. Now if the religious thrill is accepted as the basic emotional root of religion, then *mana*, a psychologically basic *mana* underlying its historic forms, becomes the fundamental idea of religion. *Mana* is but a term for an emotion, projected as 'something into the supernatural realm'. . .

This is a very clear example of the emotional kind of psychological interpretation of religious phenomena. The *mana* which the Polynesians and Melanesians conceive of as an objective reality is represented as being really certain special feelings or emotions which we are assumed to accept as being characteristically religious. Many anthropologists would doubt whether anything so undefinable as a 'thrill' should be regarded as forming the basis of religion; though we cannot ignore the work of Rudolf Otto, who in his book *The Idea of the Holy*, made out a case for the direct sensory and emotional apprehension of God by men. Otto, however, wrote as one who predicated the existence of a God. He was not content to allow religious 'feelings' to remain *mere* features of human psychology, but regarded them as a manner of apprehending divinity. The divine, and not the human mind, was for Otto the ground of religion and the final object of his study, and he wrote as a theologian, not a psychologist.

Other attempts to give an account of the grounds of religious phenomena emphasize the psychological *functions* of religious belief and practice. This approach is best seen in the writings of Malinowski, who built partly upon the theories of his English predecessors Tylor and Frazer, but much augmented their views through his own deep and first-hand understanding of some Melanesian peoples. Malinowski seemed to think that religion had its most important functions in the crises of life, and particularly in the situation of death, in which, he wrote:

the call to religion arises out of an individual crisis, the death which threatens man or woman. Never does an individual need the comfort of belief and ritual so much as in the sacrament of the viaticum, in the last comforts given to him at the final stage of his life's journey—acts which are well-nigh universal in all primitive religions. These acts are directed against the over-whelming fear, against the corroding doubt, from which the savage is no more free than the civilized man. These acts confirm his hope that there is a hereafter, that it is not worse than the present life; indeed better.

Anthropologists today would question such a broad generalization; it is by no means certain that anything corresponding to a sacrament for the dying is 'well-nigh universal,' and many primitive people neither seem acutely afraid of death, nor have any hope for or interest in a future life. It was Malinowski rather than tribal peoples who saw religion as a force for social and psychological integration, and it was in a human need for comfort and peace that he sought the grounds of primitive religions. So, after a death, the bereaved are, according to Malinowski

thrown into a dangerous mental chaos . . . torn between fear and piety, reverence and horror, love and disgust, they are in a state of mind which might lead to mental disintegration. Out of this, religion lifts the individual. . .

In such passages, Malinowski makes it clear that he regards the basis of religion, for the purposes of study, as the emotional needs of individuals, and the need for social integration. If the gods or ancestors of tribal peoples cannot have any real existence for us, we can recognize a universal validity in the human desire for individual peace of mind and social order; it is this which we are invited to substitute for the gods and the ancestors, as the grounds of primitive religion.

Malinowski stands between a psychological interpretation of religious phenomena, and the philosophical or sociological interpretation to which I now turn. While Malinowski sought the basis of religion in the emotional integration of the individual, and saw the integration of society as a function of the integration of its individual members, those who adopted a philosophical approach tended to reverse the argument. They sought the grounds of religion in the integration of the society, from which individual religious beliefs and practices were seen to derive.

Philosophical and sociological interpretations of religion are associated primarily with a group of French writers of the turn of the century. The best known of these are Emile Durkheim, H. Hubert, Marcel Mauss, and Lucien Lévy-Bruhl. They rejected the theories of the English anthropologists Tylor and Frazer because such theories assumed that all peoples had the same categories and processes of thought. Lévy-Bruhl attempted to show that this was not so. He maintained that there was a difference in kind between the experience of the world which characterized primitive peoples and that characteristic of the civilization of his own time. In his view, the thought of primitive peoples was what he called 'mystical'—

it proceeded less by logical inference and empirical verification than by imaginative and metaphorical associations of ideas and experience, in a way which we might regard as poetic. Their thought was not analytic, but synthetic, in intention.

Further, individuals accepted the very categories in which they thought, including the categories of religious thought and experience, from the societies in which they were reared. They did not choose their religious belief and practice; it was a product of social life, not of individual reasoning. Durkheim similarly maintained that just as a society must be regarded as something other than a mere collection of individuals living together, so its religion must be studied as something other than a feature of the psychology of individuals. A religion then imposed itself on individuals from without, from the society in which they were brought up and in which religious beliefs and practices were taken for granted.

What is the main difference between this philosophical approach and the psychological approach already mentioned? The psychological interpretation of religion requires the abstraction of such sentiments as those of fear, guilt, desire, awe, helplessness, or of certain reasoning processes, from the individual consciousness. It then relates these in a more or less systematic way to each other, and to religious beliefs and situations. Philosophical interpretation, on the other hand, requires the abstraction from our own thought of certain religious conceptions. Such conceptions are those of sacredness, divinity, cult, sacrifice, sin, truth, and many others. They are terms of our own thought, not words for sentiments or feelings, and whatever sentiments may be supposed to accompany them, the conceptions remain the same. So, for example, sacrifice may be studied in several societies irrespective of the feelings which may be supposed to precede and follow the act. Again, conceptions of sacredness—such as *mana*—may be studied in social and moral contexts, without assuming any special sensations or emotional experiences as their basis.

Much of the work done by those who have attempted philosophical interpretations of primitive religions has been in the study of congruences between particular forms of religion and the structures and values of the societies in which they are found. Durkheim's work on the religion and society of the Australian aborigines, *The Elementary Forms of the Religious Life,* is the most ambitious study on these lines. There he maintained that religion was characteristically a social and not an individual

matter, and that Australian aborigines' totemic animals were revered because they symbolized the unity of their social groups, their clans. In
regarding their totems as sacred, they were thus regarding the groupings
of their society as sacred, and in respecting their totemic animals and
objects, they were in fact expressing the relationship of individual members of society to the society itself, as a source of their moral traditions
and their very sustenance. The gods of the tribes might then represent,
for us, the order of tribal society itself. Other directions taken by philosophical enquiry have resulted in studies of the place of religious conceptions in wider contexts of primitive philosophy and symbolism. Two
very different examples are Professor Radcliffe-Brown's study of the
social significance of the beliefs and rites of the Andaman Islanders, and
a more recent book by Professor Henri Frankfort, *Kingship and the
Gods*, an interpretation of religion, philosophy, and art in ancient Egypt
and Mesopotamia.

In deriving religion ultimately from a God *we* believe in, or from psychological needs, or from society itself, we are substituting for tribesmen's beliefs in their gods something which we can take for granted—
whether our God, or psychology, or society—as sufficient grounds for
religion. Each general theory of religion is thus, in a way, a substitute
for any particular religion, an alternative way of giving an account of
those situations which different tribal religions give accounts of.

We may now see to what extent the kinds of theory discussed above
help us in understanding a specific situation. Livingstone, in his *Missionary Travels*, gives an account of a typical conversation between a
medical doctor and an African rain-doctor or rain-maker. Parts of the
conversation are as follows:

Medical Doctor: So you really believe you can command the clouds? I think
that can be done by God alone.

Rain-Doctor: We both believe the very same thing. It is God that make the
rain, but I pray to him by means of these medicines, and, the rain coming,
of course it is then mine. . . If we had no rain, the cattle would have
no pastures, the cows give no milk, our children become lean and die,
our wives run away to other tribes who do make rain . . . and the whole
tribe become dispersed and lost; our fire would go out.

Medical Doctor: . . . you cannot charm the clouds by medicines. You wait
till you see the clouds come, then use your medicines, and take the credit
which belongs to God only.

Rain-Doctor: I use my medicines, and you employ yours; we are both doctors,
and doctors are not deceivers. You give a patient medicine. Sometimes
God is pleased to heal him by means of your medicine; sometimes not—
he dies. When he is cured, you take the credit of what God does. I do

the same. Sometimes God grants us rain, sometimes not. When he does, we take the credit of the charm. When a patient dies you don't give up trust in your medicine, neither do I when rain fails. If you wish me to leave off my medicines, why continue your own?

Medical Doctor: I give medicine to living creatures within my reach, and can see the effect though no cure follows. . . God alone can command the clouds. Only try and wait patiently; God will give us rain without your medicines.

Rain-Doctor: Mahala-ma-kapa-a-a! Well, I always thought white men were wise until this morning. Whoever thought of making a trial of starvation? Is death pleasant then?

Almost all theories of primitive religion derive some support from this conversation, as we should expect if all had elements of truth in them. Theological interpretations receive support, since both Livingstone and the rain-maker are able to accept that they are referring to a single God, though thought of in different ways. A theory of Frazer, that the characteristic attitude of religion is that of supplication for benefits beyond human-beings' power and knowledge to achieve for themselves, is supported by the rain-maker's attitude. Interpreted psychologically, the conversation might permit us to say that in using his medicines and rituals the rain-maker is expressing a desire for rain and anxiety lest it should not come, and that the use of medicines and prayers releases the tension built up by desire and anxiety. Those who follow the interpretations of an intellectualist psychology may see in the argument a form of reasoning about the causes of rain, and an attempt at a rational justification of the use of medicines by one who is ignorant of 'natural' causation. The sacred medicines are also obviously used in situations which vitally affect the well-being of the whole society, and even the rain-maker has the theory that the tribe would disintegrate without them. Every interpretation—theological, psychological, or philosophical and sociological—may thus be placed upon the rain-maker's conversation: yet, none quite takes into account the whole of what he says.

The rain-maker's attitude is a blend of faith and skepticism, even cynicism, about his own medicines and about those of the medical doctor. It shows a grasp of the difference between what men can *know* and what they have been brought up to believe, and of the relations between experience and belief. It recognizes that experience sometimes contradicts belief, and it attempts to resolve that contradiction. The rain-maker is clearly not entirely 'mystical,' as Lévy-Bruhl would have us believe; nor, however, is he the logic-chopping savage of Tylor. It is left for modern students of primitive religion to show how beliefs are not simply the result of ignoring blandly the experience which contradicts them at times; nor are they arrived at by a kind of reasoning, though they may be defended by a kind of reasoning; nor are they just taken over, quite unthinkingly, from social tradition. They are supported by all three of these—by the will, by the reason, and by traditional teaching. We see also in the conversation other features of primitive religions: a respect for the seriousness of the concerns which religion, in its way, deals with, which excludes deliberate experiment to put faith to the test; and a concern for truth, though that truth may not be established by scientific methods of verification.

Two very recent works on the subject, *Nupe Religion* by Professor Nadel and studies of Nuer religion by Professor Evans-Pritchard, not yet published in book form, show how much nearer we have now come to understanding the complexities of tribal religions than did many of our predecessors. This is partly because those who study primitive religions today are required to have a good knowledge of the languages of the tribes they study, and can no longer mistake metaphorical or symbolic statements for literal assertions. Once the difficulty of full and subtle translation is overcome, a religion can be made to appear to us much as it does to those who practice it. We do not then have to substitute our picture, or 'explanation,' of it, for theirs. That stage—of giving our own explanation—comes later, when we have understood in their context what sacrifices, for example, or prayers, mean for the people themselves; then, by comparing their conceptions with our own and with those of other peoples, we can deepen our understanding of our own conceptions of sacrifice, or prayer, or whatever we choose to abstract for special comparative study.

Sacrifice is a good example. In many tribes blood-sacrifice is the central religious act; and sacrifice has been studied comparatively by two of the most able exponents of philosophical interpretation, Hubert and Mauss.

Hubert and Mauss, like Durkheim, thought that the two basic categories for our thought about religion were those of the sacred and the non-sacred or profane. All religions depend, in some way, upon the setting apart of certain objects, persons, and situations, as standing in a special relationship to the divine; these together compose the category of the sacred, as distinct from the profane objects, persons, or situations which are without any religious significance. I have mentioned earlier that these French sociologists equated this category of the sacred with the social world, but I do not further consider this wider implication of their theory here.

By examining several situations of sacrifice, Hubert and Mauss concluded that what sacrificial ceremonies had in common was the attempt to establish communication between the sacred and the non-sacred, through a victim which was consecrated and then destroyed for this purpose. The victim was killed and offered to the gods, who were thought to accept it perhaps as food, perhaps in other ways. By means of the gift of the victim, communication was established with the sacred, and those who offered sacrifice received in return spiritual, moral, and physical benefits which they could obtain in no other way. (See Plate XI.)

Such an analysis clearly fits the facts of blood-sacrifice as it is known among many peoples of the world. If, however, we compare the blood-sacrifice of the peoples of Africa with what is found in the very striking and well-described religion of the American Crow Indians, we see no immediate resemblance. In his chapter on Crow religion in his book on that people, Professor Lowie writes:

In a crisis an African Negro calls a diviner, who casts his sacred dice and by occult lore interprets the throw; such and such a one of his client's ancestors is angry, and so many head of cattle must be slaughtered to appease his wrath. The Crow had no system of divination, never worshipped their ancestors and made no bloody sacrifices. When hard put to it, the Indian tried to meet divinity face to face.

To do this, the Crow set out to mortify himself in various ways, in order to try to receive a vision or a revelation from a spirit guardian who would guide him and help him to prosper. One of the commonest forms of self-mortification was the cutting off of a finger-joint:

Most probably he would set out for a lonely mountain peak and fast, thirst and wail there. . . Rising at daybreak he sat down towards the east. As soon as the sun rose, he laid his left forefinger on a stick and chopped off a joint. This he put on a buffalo chip and held it towards the Sun, whom he addressed as follows 'Uncle (i.e. father's clansman) you see me, I am pitiable. Here is a part of my body, I give it to you, eat it. Give me something good. . .'

Later, when the man has suffered enough, the helping vision comes in his sleep and strengthens and guides him for his life.

Thus, although the Crow offer no animal victims, like many African peoples, yet they give over to the gods a part of themselves; this giving of the self in sacrifice is consistent with the analysis by Hubert and Mauss of the central feature of the sacrificial act. To observe a similarity be-

tween this act of the Crow Indians and some animal sacrifices is not to
minimize the great differences which exist between the religion of the
Crow Indians and those of many African tribes. It is merely to observe
that from one point of view we are dealing with one situation, not two,
when the Crow offers his finger-joint as a victim while the African offers
a sheep or ox. Further, recent investigations of animal sacrifice in Africa
have made it clear that underlying the offering of a victim to the gods is
the theme of offering a part of the self, for the victim is identified with
the person for whom the offering is made. The two cases may thus be
viewed in the light of single interpretation of the sacrificial act, though
the search for individual visions which is such a marked feature of Crow
religion is less prominent in much of Africa.

Even in this respect, however, there are some similarities which suggest further lines of investigation. Recent studies in Africa indicate that
since tribal societies began to disintegrate under foreign rule, there has
been a multiplication of individual 'spirits' and of individual religious
leaders, outside the traditional religious order, at least on such a scale.
Modern changes in Africa have resulted in a type of individual self-
sufficiency not previously possible, and it seems consistent with this trend
that private religious revelations and experiences should have increased.
A book by a Lutheran missionary, B. Sundkler, called *Bantu Prophets in
South Africa*, gives an account of the way in which even the original
Christian churches have now splintered into hundreds of semi-pagan
sects, each with its own leaders; and among the Nilotic peoples of the
Sudan, whose tribal integrity has begun to be undermined in comparatively recent times, many 'spirits,' thought to be also of recent origin,
have possessed individuals and through them become known in the society. These spirits are not spirit-guardians, as are those of the Crow
Indian; but they do represent a growth of a kind of individual and eccentric religious experience which the people themselves think to be on the
increase. Among the Crow Indians, whose cult of individual revelations
is now so marked as to seem to represent a distinct class of tribal religion, it is also suggested that at one time the emphasis was different.
Professor Lowie writes that:

. . . the hypertrophy of the individual vision represents an overlay that has
pushed other beliefs into the background, encroaching even on the widespread
American worship of the Sun. Visions themselves are doubtless very old, but
the one-sided stressing of individual visions as a source of power is a comparatively late development that largely remolded the rationale of Crow religion.

Only further research might establish whether there is a general correspondence between the dislocation of tribal life owing to an overwhelming conquest and an increased emphasis on individual self-sufficiency both in the religious and in the moral and economic situations of life. Such are some of the types of questions which a student of tribal religions today might ask himself.

I mentioned earlier that the anthropological study of tribal religions requires a different approach from that adopted by students of comparative religion who rely upon sacred writings for their knowledge. We study religious beliefs and practices in relation to particular social situations; and what people do in particular situations is not always consistent with what they are prepared, on reflection, to say they believe.

A little example of this occurs in an account by a missionary, John Roscoe, of the Kingdom of the Bakitara, or Banyoro, in Uganda. Roscoe wrote several valuable ethnographic accounts of peoples of Uganda, without attempting any elaborate theoretical interpretation of the facts, which he was content to report as he knew them. The honesty of his reporting makes it possible for us to note in his account an example of the discrepancy between theory and practice of religion which he seems himself to have overlooked.

Roscoe obtained native statements about the gods of the Banyoro, among which is an account of a god named *Ruhanga*. The Banyoro told Roscoe that *Ruhanga* was

> . . . the creator of things . . . people did not call upon him for assistance because he had done his work and there was no need to ask further favours of him. Other gods could assist in multiplying men, cattle, crops. . .

Such statements about a creator who, having finished his creation, takes little further interest in it, are common in other tribes. The Anuak of the Sudan, for example, say that when man was created, the creator gave instructions that he should at once be thrown away. These statements seem to depict a creator very different from, say, the Christian God; in writings on African religion, such gods who no longer have apparent functions in the world have been described as otiose.

But this statement about *Ruhanga* seems to represent only a part of the truth. A very few pages after Roscoe has reported the statement, he describes a rain-making ceremony, and there he writes

> A vessel of water was next brought from a spring near, and the rain-maker raised his hands and prayed thus to *Ruhanga*: '*Ruhanga*, bless us. Thou king of all the earth, hear us. The people are dying with hunger.'

Reports of such differences between professed notions and actual practice are obviously of importance for our understanding of tribal religions. When we see that sometimes, in practice, the creator of the Banyoro is asked for help and blessing, we see that their religion in practice is not always so very different from our own as the difference of doctrines might suggest. The behavior of people has often more in common than have their conceptions of gods.

Studies of tribal religions have so far had to treat the subject in very crude abstractions. It is as though we had not yet glimpsed what might be the elements which, in different combinations, would be seen to reappear wherever we recognized 'religion.' We write of 'ancestor worship,' 'sky-religion,' 'totemism,' and so on, though we well know that these words may be applied to religions which differ in very important ways, and that each is a crude compound term. This is true also of such terms as 'polytheism' and 'monotheism,' which are too general to take a proper account of what is actually found in any religion.

Again, the definitions we use tend to be ambiguous even in our own language. When we consider, for example, Tylor's minimal definition of religion as 'a belief in spiritual beings' we realize that we ourselves have no very clear idea of what such beings are; if we say that religion is the service of the gods, we are again faced with the difficulty of knowing what the gods are, for tribal peoples can often tell us nothing of their nature in themselves. They can only name them and indicate effects which they attribute to them. Durkheim seems to have recognized this difficulty when he wrote that

. . . a god . . . is a power of producing certain manifestations . . . which are related to a particular, determined subject. . . it does not matter whether this power be imagined as pure spirit, or whether it is attached to a material substratum; the essential thing is that it should be individualized. . .

A definition of this kind is useful in that it saves us from asking questions about the nature, in themselves, of tribal gods, questions to which tribesmen often have no answers. Such questions as 'is God good?' for example often cannot have the same meaning, in a tribal language, as it has in our own; for the gods are 'good' when they produce effects which human beings find good; in other situations, when suffering or sickness or death are attributed to them, they may just as easily be said to be bad. These are not comments on their nature, but upon the ways in which they are affecting human beings.

We talk also of religious 'belief'; and for us, the word has come to have the sense of an assertion about something which is admitted to be ultimately uncertain. But for tribal peoples, the *existence* of the gods is not a matter of uncertainty; they cannot be doubtful whether the gods exist, when they see everywhere effects which they attribute to them. Their faith is a matter of certainty about the operation of powers whose ways and nature are ultimately incomprehensible, not a matter of knowledgeable opinion about beings whose existence can ultimately be called into doubt. We often conceal this when we speak of religious 'belief'; in many cases it might be better to speak of religious knowledge. For, as I shall finally suggest, religion is a way of knowing about, and dealing with, certain situations of human life. Religious knowledge and practice are ways in which men apprehend some truths, and adjust themselves to their condition in the light of that apprehension.

A concern with knowledge of truth is an element we find among all tribal peoples, and one which is present in many religions. Let us consider a common feature of African religions, a sacrifice for a man who is sick. The man's relatives call in a diviner to attempt to diagnose the true ground of the illness, which the diviner's greater insight qualifies him to do. He may attribute the sickness to a particular spirit, or to a particular sin of the man or of his ancestors. To cure the illness, a beast must be offered in propitiation. Perhaps a priest is called to pray for the man's recovery and to offer the sacrifice. The prayer may be simply a statement of what *will* happen. Here is an example from the Dinka tribe:

And you, ox, it is not for nothing that we have tethered you in the mid-day sun, but because of sickness, to exchange your life for the life of the sick man. You, God, hear my words, and you, my totemic spirit, hear my words, and you, spirit of illness, I have separated you from the man. I have spoken thus: You leave the man alone. . . You, totemic spirit of my father, do not let me speak a lie. . .

The implication is that the words of the priest *must* be true and so they create the situation which they state. The true cause of illness has thus been diagnosed; the priest who speaks truth prays as though that which is desired is already accomplished, in the manner of a Hebrew prophet; and sacrifice is made in the light of this representation of the truth of the whole situation.

It was reported of the spiritual power *mana* that the *mana* of a priest was shown in the truth of his predictions; and from other parts of the world also it is clear that a divination and representation of truth, as a guide to action, is a part of the task of religion. Among the Crow Indians, who lack any of the African forms of divination, individuals search for visions of a truth which it is necessary and profitable for them to know. That truth often contains trivial and arbitrary elements, from our point of view—'capricious taboos of a dietary or ritualistic character' are what spirits often reveal to the Crow, according to Professor Lowie. It might be claimed, however, that it is in their very triviality and arbitrariness that they carry conviction, as being really revealed to a man and not merely thought out by him. Their peculiar and unlikely nature guarantees their divine origin. The relation of primitive religious practice to knowledge of truth is well conveyed by this charm spoken by a Maori diviner wishing to know the grounds of a sickness:

> A seeking a searching,
> To seek whither?
> To search the land, to seek the origin,
> To seek the base, to search the unknown,
> To seek out the *atua* [spirit]
> May it be effectual.

And we may think of other cases of the relation between religious practice and the definition of truth, such as oaths and oracles, in the first of which the divine is called in to guarantee the truth of men's words, and in the second of which men have truth revealed to them by operations over which, they suppose, they have no control.

Tribal religions then involve on the one hand a sense of human ignorance and weakness and on the other a means of guaranteeing the assumptions upon which are based a people's only means of dealing with the disabilities which follow from human ignorance and weakness. If there were no guarantee, for example, that a diviner was permitted an insight into the true grounds of an illness, there would be no means of dealing with that illness. As we know in our own civilization, it is not only in religion that a guarantee of such a measure of certitude may be sought, and what, for primitive peoples, is truth often seems to us to be a fallacy based upon ignorance. But it is a concern for truth, as they see it, which often prevents them from accepting assumptions upon which our own notions of truth are based, just as it is a concern for truth which prevents us from accepting what we see as their errors.

I do not suggest that tribal peoples see the world and their life in it as a puzzle, to which they anxiously seek an answer. But like ourselves, they sense that human life is lived within circumscribing conditions which they can discover but cannot alter; their religions are in part theories of what those conditions, moral and physical, really are, and means of adapting themselves as best they can to them. And if, from our point of view, their theories of the conditions are sometimes false and misleading, they share with us a concern for the truth of them.

DARYLL FORDE
in collaboration with
Mary Douglas

XVI

Primitive Economics

THE ECONOMIES of primitive peoples differ widely. The Australian aborigines, for example, or the Californian Indians live solely by hunting and foraging, without any knowledge of plant-cultivation or stock-raising. The Fula of the west Sudan or the Bedouin Arabs are herders and depend on cultivation only to a minor degree, or may themselves not grow any crops at all. There are hand-cultivators with no large livestock as in tse-tse infested districts in central Africa. There are stockraisers who grow cereals and supplement their larders by hunting, as do the Southern Bantu of Africa.

Agriculture appeared late in human history, and afforded a means of greatly increased production. But the food-gatherers do not necessarily all live at a lower level of subsistence than the cultivators. Some non-agricultural peoples developed elaborate techniques for exploiting the wild products of their environment. The fishing and hunting tribes of the northwest coast of North America not only made huge catches; they knew how to split trees into planks for their solidly built loghouses, how to construct ingenious dams and fishtraps, and even how to organize successful whaling expeditions. Technically they were more advanced than many cultivating peoples. Pastoral nomadism which is popularly believed to have preceded the development of agriculture actually appeared at a later stage in the Old World on the fringes of settled populations used to cultivation with the rearing of livestock.

The distinguishing features of a primitive economy are not to be found in any particular mode of securing a livelihood. The basic condition is
402

a low degree of technical knowledge. However favorable the climate, and rich the natural vegetation and animal life, peoples equipped with only simple techniques are limited in their exploitation of their country's resources.

The level of production of food supplies and the tools by which they are secured is everywhere vitally dependent on the amount of energy that can be harnessed for productive tasks, and it is important to realize the limited capacity for production of peoples lacking power-driven machines. An adult human being can directly exert energy equivalent to only about one tenth of a unit of horsepower and many primitive peoples have lacked any other prime source of power, apart from a limited use of fire. Without animal or water power for lifting and traction, their productive capacity is severely limited by their restriction to hand-tools such as the bow, the hoe, and the fishnet. These must remain mechanically simple and accordingly require little specialization in their manufacture and use. At the same time the level of output per man that they make possible is not great enough to release any significant proportion of the population from the common task of food-production, so that there is little scope for any considerable division of labor.

Advanced civilizations have tended to spread into the most favorable lands, so that there is also a tendency for the least well-equipped peoples to be found living in the most harsh and intractable regions.[1] To these they have adapted themselves as best they can—the Eskimos to snow and ice, the marsh-dwellers of the Euphrates to swamplands and flood, Bushmen and Bedouin Arabs to drought and desert. In many tropical lands, rapid exhaustion of the soil sets a basic limitation on cultivation by primitive methods.

Natural conditions restrict certain kinds of development and permit others, but they do not dictate in any precise way the lines on which an economy shall develop. Man by his skill and labor produces a kind of secondary environment, which is a function of techniques as well as of resources. This ecological framework, product of man's skill and his environment, varies widely from one people and region to the next, according to the different materials at hand and the individual bent of their interests and skills.

Preoccupation with the daily or seasonal food supply, the frequency

---

[1] On the other hand, some of the richest lands, the western forest and central plains of North America, were still occupied by primitives until the opening of the nineteenth century.

of hardship, and the risks of hunger are obvious characteristics of a primitive economy. So also are the limitations of transport, though this applies, of course, with less force to the livestock breeders such as the horse and camel nomads. Less obvious, but just as fundamental, are the difficulties of storage, which restrict the accumulation of food and other goods. Heat, damp, and the white ant effectively destroy any possessions which the Bemba of North Rhodesia or the Nambikwara of the South American Mato Grosso may succeed in amassing. In Polynesia the people of Tikopia did not know how to cure fish, and only one of their crops had good keeping properties. The Eskimo, admittedly, can freeze his meat, and keep it for indefinite periods, but the ice which makes food-storage possible for him causes other shortages, of vegetable foods, of wood for fuel and shelter. Pastoralists are better off in this respect, as herds provide a natural store of wealth, but cattle are vulnerable to disease, the onset of which may disrupt the whole economy.

Productive equipment is relatively simple and few durable goods of any kind are made. In short, the productive effort of a primitive economy is capable of anticipating its future needs only for a very brief span. Accumulation is difficult, long-term planning impossible.

Insecurity, then, is frequently the mark of a primitive economy. But on this score there is considerable variation from one primitive economy to another. Some food-gathering peoples, for example, the acorn-eating Yokuts of California, and the Kwakiutl fishers of British Columbia, were blessed with a natural abundance of basic resources.

Another common characteristic of a primitive economy, though also not a universal one, is a lack of diversity in the major resources. Some peoples are heavily dependent on a few products, which are processed so as to provide food, shelter, weapons, tools, and nearly all the main needs of the people. This tendency is particularly noticeable among hunters and herders. The Eskimo takes from the seals he kills meat to eat, fat for fuel and for lighting, fat for anointing himself, skins for covering, sinews for thongs, bones for harpoons and arrow heads. There is an economy of effort, but the risks are high. If, during a stormy winter, seals are absent from a usually sheltered bay, starvation and death for the whole community may result. The cattle-keeping Nuer of the southern Sudan turn the products of their cattle to meet most of their essential requirements: blood, milk, cheese, and meat for sustenance; horn and bone for weapons; dried dung for fuel; hides for covering and thongs and bags. But during the rinderpest epidemic at the end of the last century, when their cattle died wholesale, they were in desperate straits. Among such peoples enormous stress is placed on the value of their main resource, which tends to become the focus of their religious symbolism. For the Nuer, cattle play a central role in their religious life, being used for every ceremonial and sacrifice. Such a tendency to place exceptionally high value on a few vital resources may distort the development of an economy. Nuer country abounds in game and wild birds, yet they seldom exploit them, despising wild-game as food if they can get milk and beef. Conversely hunting peoples often disdain the meat of domesticated animals. One effect is that the full range of resources actually available with existing techniques are not exploited. Another is to inhibit internal and external exchanges. Thus the Nuer were averse to dealing with Arab traders, as these had no cattle and cattle were the only form of wealth which interested the Nuer.

We may sum up the basic characteristics of primitive economies as follows: preoccupation with the daily and seasonal food supply, limitation of transport, difficulties of storage, overdependence on one or two major resources. These restrictions derive mainly from a low level of technical knowledge, which severely limits productive capacity. Wherever these characteristics are found, certain consequences flow from them. The economic unit is small and, save for occasionally bartered specialities, does not transcend the population of a small village. Social relations are of the personal, face-to-face kind. Everyone has known everyone else from childhood, everyone is related to everyone else. The sick and unfortunate are able to depend on the kindliness of immediate neighbors. The sharing of tools and of supplies to meet individual shortages are matters of moral obligation between kinsfolk and neighbors. Impersonal commercial relations hardly exist. The group which lives and works together has strong feelings of solidarity, partly because they are isolated from other groups by poor communications.

The small size of the social group within which production is organized and exchange effected also reduces the opportunity for specialization. Such skills as are practiced are known to everyone of the appropriate age and sex [2] in the community. Certain kinds of work are traditionally assigned to men, others to women, but fulltime specialists are very rare. The work of the potter, boatbuilder, smith, or magician is a voluntary spare-time task.

[2] See Redfield's paragraphs on the sexual division of labor, p. 346.

In such a setting economic relations have not been separated out from other social relations. There is no question of one man working for another whom he knows only as an employer. Men work together because they are related to each other, or have other social obligations to one another. Important economic processes are thus embedded in wider social needs, and are inextricably mixed with politics, ceremonial, and general festivity. When the Blackfoot Indians of the Plains used to congregate in the summer for tribal buffalo drives, which were their main economic activity, a short period of intensive hunting was followed by feasts and dances, and the social life of the tribe reached its peak. The great annual ceremony of the Sun Dance brought not only the economic, but also the political and religious activities of the year to a grand climax.

In an economy for which these general conditions hold true, economic exchange is necessarily limited. Markets remain undeveloped because the advantages of internal exchange are slight. The household provides for its daily needs from its own production. Surpluses cannot speedily be sent to areas of scarcity because of the difficulties of transport. On the other hand, if the surplus is to be used at all, it must somehow be distributed at once, because of the technical difficulty of storage. As everyone produces much the same range of articles as everyone else, there will be little demand locally for any excess production. Often the only way an individual can dispose of a surplus is by holding a lavish feast or simply by giving it to kinsmen and neighbors who will feel bound to repay one day.

But primitive economics are not, as a rule, completely closed. Some external trade, however sporadic, is usually possible. Hunters may be in contact with cultivators and exchange meat for cereals, as did the Congo forest pygmies with their Negro neighbors in a silent trade in which the two parties to the exchange never came face to face. Shore-dwelling people may exchange fish for crops with inland cultivators. One community may produce a surplus of one speciality, a local delicacy, a raw material, or a prized ornament, and trade it with another speciality of another tribe. Among the Kalahari Bushmen there was a system of trade relations, both with their Bantu neighbors and between the different tribes. Centrally placed groups played the part of intermediaries, obtaining from their northern neighbors supplies which they bartered further south, and vice versa. In this trade eggshell beads and tobacco, because there was always a steady demand for them, had a fixed value according to which other goods could be 'priced.'

Internal exchange is also possible, as when four or five little communities meet regularly in a local market and cancel out small inequalities of output by exchanges. The difference between this kind of market and the markets of developed economies is that goods which are offered for exchange have not been produced primarily for sale, but are the fortuitous surplus of subsistence production. This is an essential difference between production in the primitive and in the developed economy. For these economies, instead of 'primitive,' the word 'subsistence' is often used, to emphasize the contrast with complex modern exchange economies. (See Plate XII.)

The production unit does not necessarily correspond to the unit of consumption; the size of the former is generally determined by technical considerations, while the size of the consumption unit may vary from a group of households to include the whole of the local community.

For production people co-operate in different groups at different seasons, according to the nature of the work. For some tasks the most efficient unit may be only one man: the Eskimo hunter waiting at his seal hole is better alone. The success of Bushman hunting often depends on fleetness of foot; in the wet season the sodden ground impedes the animals and even in the dry season the young buck can often be chased and run down, as the hot sand causes their hoofs to come off. For this kind of hunting, one man and a dog is the best team. At other times the whole male force of a large band may set barricades and pitfalls across a valley, and then drive a herd of wild animals into the great trap.

Other kinds of production can be broken up into a number of tasks performed by separate individuals. Only one man at a time can operate a Congolese handloom for weaving raffia. But the various processes for preparing raffia and the loom can be farmed out to different individuals to do in their own time: an old man may be the most suitable person for the intricate sorting of the strands, and a young man for the heavy work of actual weaving.

In agricultural work the pressure of the changing seasons may make it urgent for each farmer to get help in clearing the fields. In bush clearing a team is more efficient than a series of separate workers. According to local custom, a man may be able to call out a labor gang composed of his age-mates, his kinsmen, or all the able-bodied men of the district. The nature of the work tends to determine the size of the working unit, but because most tasks are not very complex, and because those few that do involve large-scale collaboration are of short duration, large working units are rare. (See Plate XIII.)

As to the reward of labor, there is little attempt to calculate the contribution of each unit, and to give it a corresponding share of the product. Among Bushmen, whether the game brought to the camp has been run down by an individual hunter, or killed in a communal battle, the rules for distributing the meat are still the same: all members of the camp are entitled to their share. A man who has killed a buck on his own, still has to hand it in to be divided by the camp leader according to fixed rules which set aside certain parts for the married men, others for the young men, others for women, according to their several status. The women of the band who collect the vegetables daily keep for their families the product of their own foraging, but meat represents an irregular supply of an important food, and the system of even distribution of game insures a share for all families of the community.

Where labor gangs are formed to clear land, each member in turn gets the benefit of the work of the whole group. In some cases a feast is offered as inducement to the workers, but the ultimate incentive is the maintenance of good will, which insures to each worker similar help in his need. In a primitive economy there are no wages (except for specialists' fees to healers, magicians, and smiths). A man does not normally earn his right to a particular share of output by contributing a particular piece of work. His claim to a share is based on his membership and on his status in the social group, household, camp, club, et cetera for which the work is being done. He works in order to fulfill his social obligations, to maintain his prestige and the status to which his sex, age, rank et cetera may entitle him.[8]

It is as difficult to distinguish a regular unit of consumption as a regular unit of production. Rights to enjoy certain things may be vested in individuals, in families, or in the community as a whole. Different kinds of sharing-situations may be set in the framework of different social groups, so that it is impossible to consider the society as divided into a fixed series of units of consumption such as the family. Food may be cooked by wives at their domestic hearths, but part of it is carried out to contribute to a general supply which the men share among themselves.

Among the Nuer, for example, the extended family is the cattle-holding unit, and each family's rights to cattle in payment of fines or at mar-

[8] See the analogy drawn by Professor Redfield with work and consumption within the family, Chapter 16.

riages are jealously guarded. But where the food-products' of cattle are concerned, men habitually eat in each other's homes to such an extent that the whole village seems to draw on a common stock. In agricultural communities, the land-rights of individuals are generally restricted by overriding rights vested in the village as a whole. A Bemba village, under its headman, owns its land by right of occupation; each male member has rights in the land he has cleared, by virtue of accepted residence. Each wife has her granary for storing the crop she has raised on the fields provided by her husband. But the whole village, with its fields, and granaries, is at the same time a kind of joint housekeeping concern, for the rules of hospitality and the habit of food-sharing distribute the product of the year's work over the whole village.

Such customs are common in most primitive economies, and tend to even out the inequalities of income that result from primitive techniques. Public opinion forces a household whose harvest has prospered more than those of the neighbors to share its advantages with them. Equality of distribution, then, according to status rather than reward allocated according to work, is another characteristic feature of a primitive economy. This does not mean that some economic privilege is not accorded to those who have high status.

The obligation to distribute income is supported by two factors. One, which brings home to all the importance of generosity, is the constant menace of want. Everyone is aware of his own insecurity and consequent dependence on his neighbors. The second, as we have already seen, is the technical difficulty of conserving goods for future consumption. Perishable goods constitute a major part of the wealth of these economies, and enjoyment cannot be postponed to an indefinite future. The man who distributes his surplus to his neighbors has the satisfaction of gaining prestige. And since the obligation to repay gift for gift is fully recognized, he is even laying up some security for himself for the future. By giving away his own surplus he is making a number of people beholden to him. This is an elementary form of credit. The recipients of his gifts will be expected to treat him likewise when occasion arises. They also accept his influence, and help to build up his standing in the community.

In a primitive economy political power is not related to economic control in the same way as in a highly developed economy. Since, as we have seen, the system of production is based on small independent units, it does not offer means for concentrating power through control of resources or productive equipment. A man can best satisfy the drive for power and prestige by attaching to himself a group of adherents: to them he affords protection and a lavish board; they give him status and authority. Competition, in a primitive economy, is not specifically economic, but social. On the other hand, economic advantages do often follow from high social status. Only a chief or a shaman among the Nambikwara can have more than one wife, and this is regarded as a reward for his responsibility. The chief of a district among the Bemba needs many wives, simply in order to organize the catering for councilors and visitors to the court. The payment of tribute to the chief, and the distribution by him of hospitality and largess are complementary aspects of his status. He needs the contributions of his subjects in order to fulfill his obligation to give lavishly to them. Thereby he also maintains his position. Although loyal villages send teams to cultivate his fields, and so ensure a grain supply commensurate with his responsibilities, the Bemba chief does not try to organize maximum production. He prefers to fill his granaries from windfall payments of tribute in kind. This illustrates a bias in the relation between economic and political organization in a primitive economy. It is not through control of production that political advantages and privileges in consumption can be acquired; rather it is that distribution can be controlled only by building up social status and gaining political authority.

The dominant institutions in a primitive economy, while predominantly political or religious, are nevertheless important channels for the redistribution of wealth. Where there is powerful chieftainship, what is brought in as tribute is quickly given out again as rewards and gifts: local inequalities of production over the chiefdom are thus evened out. It is usual for those who have met with disaster to ask for help from the chief, and he can call on his prosperous subjects to provide emergency supplies. In some societies one important channel of economic redistribution may be through associations of leading men, in the so-called 'secret societies.' As entrance to them is gained by payment of fees, which are shared by all members, the accumulated wealth transferred in fees receives wide redistribution.

Marriage, too, often has a prominent economic function as a distributing agency. Where descent is patrilineal, marriage transfers rights over a woman and her children from her father to her husband. As in many societies this transfer is secured by substantial gifts to the bride's kinsfolk, so through the constant succession of marriages redistribution of wealth takes place. A man may build up his herd of cattle until he has enough to acquire a new wife, for himself or for one of his sons. Negotiations are opened, and shortly his herd is reduced again to a few beasts.

Since all regular social obligations are channels of economic distribution in these ways, it is not exaggerating to say that social ties perform the function of rudimentary credit institutions in primitive economies. One tribe in South Africa has recognized this in their saying: 'A man is the bank of his father-in-law.'

Although labor is given for the sake of fulfilling social obligations, and although distribution similarly follows the same lines, this is not to say that there is not a keen sense of *quid pro quo* in particular transactions. A meanness is well-remembered and paid off at an early opportunity. A man who consistently fails to turn up at working parties is forfeiting his title to membership in the group in question, and losing any right to a share in its product. The idea of equivalence in giving and receiving is clearly recognized. There is no such thing as a free gift. Every act of generosity is expected to be repaid by an equivalent deed at some later date. Under this convention of strict reciprocity, what may seem at first sight to be reckless squandering can often be a prudent outlay of resources.

The crucial difference between gift and sale is that the first object of gift exchange is the building up of a social relationship, whereas in buying and selling, any continuous social relation between the parties is merely incidental. Even in a modern economy, a significant part of the distribution of wealth is by gift-exchange, although the main part is by trade. In a primitive economy there may be no trade, or it may account for very few of the transactions which take place, but there will certainly be a well-developed system of exchange through gifts, which distribute supplies at the same time as they cement social relations.

Most of the concepts devised for analysis in economic science, such as capital, investment, saving, interest, et cetera have been developed for the study of complex exchange economies. Entities and processes corresponding to these basic categories can be recognized in embryonic form in a primitive economy. But they are not necessarily significant for describing the economy of peoples who have few durable goods, no money, and few commercial exchanges. How, for example, should the distinction between liquid and fixed resources be applied to an economy where nearly all goods can be used in all kinds of transactions? Should cows be classified as producer or as consumption goods? Is any insight gained by describing a polygamist's wives in one context as capital investment for him, as his labor force in another, as the principal consumers in another? Conditions in these simple undifferentiated economies seem to make nonsense of fine distinctions elaborated for highly specialized modern economies. On the other hand, these fine distinctions apply to economic realities which have developed out of the less specialized economic relations of the primitive societies. In the latter one can, as it were, trace them back to their more generalized roots.

The simplest definition of capital, and one which is significant for any primitive economy, concentrates on the tools and equipment for production. A man, or a group, who gives up time and energy to make a special tool for a special task, be it a digging stick, or a fish weir, or canoe, expects to be able to use it for a considerable period. In a wider sense, not only tools, but any of the things which are produced in order to yield future services over a stretch of time such as houses, bridges, or granaries, are capital.

Primitive economies are, by definition, poor in capital equipment. The quantity, effectiveness, and variety of their tools and weapons, the durability of their houses, the serviceability of their roads and paths, are strictly limited by the low level of technical knowledge. Cultivators have their hoes and granaries, knives and baskets; hunters have their spear-throwers, harpoons, bows, hunting poisons, implements for curing hides and skins. Some fishing communities, and especially ocean-going peoples, maintain a greater amount of capital equipment for their exploitation of the sea. They have different kinds of canoes, elaborate fishtraps, nets, and lines, which all represent considerable outlay of labor in their manufacture, and which give valuable services over many years.

The fact that fishing communities invest in more capital equipment than cultivators, herders, or hunters, might be expected to put them in a class apart from other primitive economies, were it not for two things. First, all their equipment is directed to one kind of production only, the harvest of the sea. An economy which is heavily dependent on one main resource cannot develop the complexity and high degree of internal differentiation of the modern economy. For another, this main resource of a fishing economy is essentially perishable. Drying or smoking only preserves fish for a very limited period in all but the coolest climates. A community is incapable of developing a complex exchange economy so long as the greater part of its production is devoted to perishable goods. Only by mastering the technical difficulties of storage, and so being able to accumulate a variety of goods, can a community save. Saving is abstaining from consuming in the present, in order to consume in the future. If its wealth is in the form of perishable goods, a community cannot save. Thus low capacity to postpone consumption is the mark of a primitive economy.

In such an economy there can be little specialization of production and correspondingly little exchange. From this follows the absence or very limited development of money, which is essentially a medium of exchange. But primitive economies are not necessarily entirely without money. Some kind of currency, accepted for certain exchanges, was long in use in Melanesia, western North America, and parts of tropical Africa. (See Plate XII.)

Almost anything, from pigs, cowries, iron rods to strings of shells or tobacco, can be used as a standard for measuring relative values and as a medium of exchange. When some such object is used as money in a primitive economy, it is usually employed only for a restricted range of transactions. We find that by convention only certain kinds of goods or services can be bought and sold, or that only between certain categories of persons can there be a buying and selling relationship. Between other persons, or where other essential commodities are concerned, there are conventions of giving or sharing, not of buying and selling.

The existence of a monetary system, however rudimentary, gives the individual member of the economy an opportunity of saving. He accepts money in exchange for his products because it gives him a title to buy something else, at once, or in the future. So it enables him to postpone consumption to a time of his own choosing. It provides him with a link between the present and the future, extending the period during which his present wealth can be enjoyed. If an individual puts a store of money aside, he builds up a right to spend it in the future. Even if the borrower spends it all, the lender is still saving, so long, of course, as the borrower can be trusted to repay. When the debt is later repaid, the lender can enjoy the benefit of having refrained earlier from consuming his wealth. He will have saved for his own future, but as far as the economy as a whole is concerned there will have been no saving at all. The saving of one individual has been canceled by the spending of the other. Monetary savings of individuals do not imply that the total community will necessarily be saving anything. In a modern economy, savings correspond in this way to one type of spending, investment, or spending on durable goods. But where the economy is capable only of producing perishable goods, this cannot be so. Even if it has some kind of monetary system, the money saved by all the individuals is equivalent only to so much chalking up of claims against each other. Where the goods which can be acquired with the money are of a perishable kind, the people would, for all their individual saving of money, be no more secure against death or famine than if, without any monetary system, the rotting away of food were anticipated by great feasts. Money of itself does not give a closed economy any link between the present and the future. It does not enable the community to save, even though it makes individual saving possible. As saving simply means laying by wealth which is not immediately consumed, a community can only be said to save to the extent that durable goods are produced, houses, carved cups and bowls, well-tilled fields, canoes, fishing nets, spears, knives, et cetera. Such production in primitive economies is restricted in amount by the limited techniques available.

In a primitive economy the character of the distributive system can have adverse effects on the incentives to labor, and so on production. The incentive to work is derived not only from the simple need to provide subsistence, but largely from the drive for prestige, the satisfactions of working together, the pleasures of conviviality, and the common interest in the product of the work. The sum of these incentives may not necessarily secure maximum production. The obligation to share with neighbors any private windfall or surplus may have a deterrent effect on production. In the rural economy of Java, if a man wishes to become rich, it may be necessary for him to leave his home and settle in another village, as a stranger on whom the usual obligations of village membership do not fall. Otherwise every improvement in his own condition must be shared with all the village. A rank system may have a similar deterrent effect if a certain standard of living is considered suitable for a chief and another lower one right for a commoner. An ordinary man may be afraid of amassing riches for fear of seeming to aspire beyond his station, or be deterred by knowing that he will have to hand over a great part of his gains to the chief.

Many economies today lie at an intermediate stage between primitive and developed. There are still in Europe rural communities of farmers who mainly produce for their own needs, but send their surplus products to markets which link them with the world markets of modern capitalism. Through this link they are able to acquire tools, machinery, clothing, which they do not produce for themselves. Such dependent economies are found, for example, in rural Ireland, in Poland, and in the Balkans.

Other economies of an intermediate type are those which, though characterized by a simple technical knowledge, are only partly self-subsistent as a result of their access to the world market. They are able to produce some crop or offer their labor for sale in a modern market, and can satisfy many of their wants from that market. The fishing villages on the coast of Malaya are linked by Chinese middlemen with markets in Singapore or Indonesia. Cocoa farmers in the Gold Coast, or cotton growers in Uganda, are intimately affected by changes in world prices for their produce. These are economies that combine an important element of subsistence production with an important element of external exchange. They are not a new development. Coastal West Africa, for example, has had cash-crop economies of this type for over three hundred years.

The essential difference between the way affairs are run in a primitive economy and the working of a developed economy cannot be summed up by the absence or presence of the profit motive. Primitive peoples are as alive to the furthering of their own advantage as anyone in a capitalist economy. It is not true that they are devoid of economic sense. The most striking difference is the personal nature of all relations in a primitive economy, compared with the impersonal nature of most economic relations in modern society.

In the intermediate dependent economies, as in the truly primitive economies, all social relations are of the personal kind, but the people will also have some impersonal relationships with traders, moneylenders, and middlemen from the external economy. Such contacts give them access to valuables and capital goods produced by techniques that are far beyond their capacity. The technical difficulty of storing wealth may be overcome, partly by importing durable goods, partly by financial means. A banking system, or the mere circulation of money which has value in a nearby advanced economy, creates possibilities of postponing consumption, not only for the individual, but for the community as a whole. In these cases money put by can mean real saving, because at any time it can be used to import goods into the community.

Every contact which a primitive economy comes to have with a complex economy modifies its primitive characteristics. The feelings of village solidarity, the obligations of mutual aid and hospitality, will be present, but diluted. Family ties will still regulate production and distribution to a considerable extent, but the subsistence unit which shares a common board and common purse will be relatively smaller than in the primitive economy. It will be possible to distinguish within the total residential group regular units of consumption corresponding to family units. The social pressure forcing a man to share his gains with the whole community will still be there, but less pronounced, and the conflict between his economic ambitions and his responsibilities to the community will generate social friction. Inequalities of wealth will be tolerated. Some equivalence between the unit of labor and the amount of its reward will be increasingly aimed at. Wages will begin to be paid as one of the incentives to labor. These intermediate economies are not to be classed with modern capitalist economies, but they owe to their contact with them those features which distinguish them from the truly primitive.

ROBERT REDFIELD

XVII

How Human Society Operates

WHAT IS A SOCIETY?

A SOCIETY IS PEOPLE with common ends getting along with one another. A brawl in a barroom is not a society, nor is there yet a society when ten exhausted shipwrecked sailors clamber up on a lonely beach—at least there is none until they begin to work out their common problems of getting a living.and of living together. A society has, then, organization. It is people doing things with and to and for each other to the interests of each and all in ways that those people have come to accept.

In this sense a group of boys organized to play baseball or to exchange postage stamps is a society, but here we have in mind those societies in which people are organized not for some special purpose or interest, but for all the business and pleasure of living. The societies that are the subject of this chapter are composed of men and women and children living together, generation after generation, according to traditional ways of life. Such societies are whole societies, in that they exist for all human needs and interests. They are enduring societies in that children are born and raised to become adults with ways of life much like those of their parents and grandparents. A nation is such a society, and so is an Indian tribe. So, too, is a town or village, and even a single family in so far as its members have traditions that are transmitted to each succeeding generation and make that family, through time, distinguishable from other families. On the other hand groups of nations taken together are great societies; one speaks of Western society in contrast to Oriental society. In some sense all the people of the world taken together con-stitute a single society. But it is of the separate tribes and nations that we are chiefly thinking here. Because there have been and still are so many and so various primitive societies, one learns a good deal about society in general by referring, as will be done in this chapter, to one or another of these simple societies.

A society is easily seen as people doing work. It has other aspects, too. A society is also people sharing common convictions as to the good life. This is to say that it is not merely a system of production and of services—an anthill is that—but that a human society exists in the fact that its members feel that certain conduct is right and other conduct wrong, and act more or less accordingly. And a third aspect of human society is to be recognized in the sentiment its members have of belonging together as against other people who do not belong. A society is people feeling solidarity with one another.

A SOCIETY AS PEOPLE DOING WORK

In every society the work is divided. Everyone takes advantage from work done by others of a kind which he does not do and in exchange serves those others by doing useful things that are not done by them. The division of labor between men and women is universal, in that everywhere what women do is on the whole different from what men do; on the other hand what each sex does varies with the society: in Polynesia the men did the cooking; among the Hidatsa Indians the women did the farming. Equally obvious is the division of labor that goes with differences in age. Beyond these bases for the organization of work, there are those which depend on differences in temperament, or on training, or on the accidents of opportunity, or on the variations in demand.

In some small, isolated, primitive societies there is almost no division of labor except between the sexes and the age-groups, and except some individuals who act as magicians or as leaders of ceremonies. Every adult man does about what every other does, and so it is with women. With the development of tools and techniques, with increase in population, and with the advancement of communication and transportation, the division of labor has become far more complete and complex. In the Guatemalan village of San Pedro de la Laguna, fifty-nine different kinds of specialists are to be recognized in a population of less than two thousand. A classified telephone directory suggests but by no means completely lists the thousands and thousands of kinds of specialists that make up a modern city.

An obvious result of this increasing division of labor is the increasing ease in the number and kinds of commodities and services which people can enjoy. But another effect is to limit the view which any one individual has of the operations and goals of his society to a very small segment of the whole, with corresponding difficulties for industrial management, for democratic government, and for personal happiness. Another result is greatly to extend the number and distribution of people who divide labor with one another. Millions of people, from China to the Congo to Akron, come to depend upon one another for services and product s exchanged, and yet these people have no common purposes and understandings; they hardly know that one another exist. The organization of work tends to become worldwide while national and other local groups distrust, dislike, or fear one another. So men come to depend upon one another while yet without common sentiments and values.

A SOCIETY AS PEOPLE SHARING CONVICTIONS ABOUT THE GOOD LIFE

The organization of work takes place in ways other than the mere division of labor. Slavery is a way of organizing work. The market, to be discussed below, is another way. And a third, perhaps the basic form of the organization of work, arises from the fact that in a society people share common sentiments and beliefs as to what it is good to do. People work, not only because in most cases they are uncomfortable or even starve if they do not, but because work is a part of the meaning of life. To the primitive agricultural Indian, farming is a necessary part of decent and appropriate human existence, an essential way of maintaining relationship with the supernaturals, a test and duty of honorable manhood. In such a society one prays as one works, and work is, in part, religion. In aristocratic societies of recent times on the other hand, work was appropriate only to the underprivileged masses; while in modern Western society work is again a general positive value, and men work for wealth and power and to excel their neighbors.

The more general statement to make about society is that it consists of a plan of life. Society operates because its members have around them a universe which to them makes sense. Moreover, this plan is not merely a pattern without moral meaning: it is a plan for right conduct, an organization of conceptions as to the good, the true, and indeed the beautiful. The body of conventional meanings that are made known to us through acts and artifacts is by anthropologists called 'the culture' of a community. In the primitive societies the 'wholeness' of these meanings is more easily seen than in the case of large, complex, and rapidly changing societies. The customs and institutions fit together to make a single moral representation of the universe. The Papago Indians, for example, carry on warfare not as an opportunity for exploit separate from their other interests. The Apache scalp taken in a foray is the symbol of the supernatural power brought to the Papago camp by the warrior who killed, a source of spiritual strength, a form of divine power, solemnly to be welcomed into the camp, into the home of the killer. When the men are away on the expedition, the women and children, by abstaining from noisy or indecorous conduct, in effect share in the making of war, just as, in some primitive societies, men share in the importance and responsibilities of childbirth by 'lying in'—by restricting their behavior for the welfare of the newborn child. Labor is divided, but all members of the society act in terms of common conceptions and ideals. Commonly the myths of such a society are narrative representations of its moral values, as its ceremonies are dramatic expressions that correspond. So every culture is a provider of a course of action for the individual, a source of his motives, and validater of his convictions.

This is the way a simple and isolated society operates. But as societies have become larger and rapidly changing, with many different kinds of people in them, the customs and institutions no longer preserve this unity and harmony. There is then no single culture for all, even in one nation or town, but rather a great many incomplete cultures, so that what a man does at his office or in his factory is not always closely related to what he does when he plays or goes to church or visits the neighbors—if he does visit them. And what his children do and believe may be notably different from what he himself was brought up to do and believe. Then the sense of the meaning of life tends to be lost; men experience uncertainty, insecurity, and confusion. On the other hand as this happens men more and more come to think rationally and critically about the life around them and to act intentionally to change and to guide it. Science develops, along with rational administration and planning. The basis for the operation of society thus tends to shift, over the course of human history, from tradition to deliberate social invention and thoughtful choice.

A Society as People Feeling Solidarity with One Another

A society also operates by virtue of the confidence its members feel in one another and of the loyalty they have to their own group. It is said that the dangers of a great war between the present great powers of this earth would be quickly averted if Mars would attack this planet. Perhaps it would be sufficient for us earth-dwellers merely to know that there were Martians. We would feel a new sense of solidarity for all fellow earth-beings as contrasted with those inferior or iniquitous Martians. At any rate it appears that the members of every society, small or great, think very well of themselves as contrasted with the members of comparable societies. What is seen on a small scale in gangs, appears again in nations. Every tribe and nationality, in some parts of the world every valley or cluster of hamlets, refers to itself in favorable terms and to others unfavorably. Many primitive tribes reserve the term for 'people' or 'human beings' to themselves alone, while everywhere the terms used to refer to neighboring peoples are contemptuous, derogatory. It would seem, indeed, that the resentment and scorn shown toward other peoples are strongest with regard to neighboring people, as though, as Sigmund Freud remarked, one could least well bear to see what is so much like oneself and yet so different.

In cases where one society is divided into subgroups, each with its own loyalty, but yet a loyalty subordinated to that of the entire tribe or nation, this fact of appreciation of the lesser in-group and depreciation of the out-group contributes to the effective operation of the society. There is a special kind of strength in a tribe divided into clans, for each clan is a warm and supporting intimate group for every individual within it; its limited solidarity is intensified by the contrast and competition with other clans. A similar effect is brought about by the grouping of colleges within a university, and perhaps was realized among the nations of Europe in the nineteenth century, when all the nations were held together by a degree of common tradition and by common commercial and banking interests, so that national pride flourished while wars were limited to moderate destructiveness.

This sense of common membership, pleasant in itself and often referred to as *esprit de corps,* increases the effective operation of the society by making it possible for its members to withstand difficulty and defeat and to act together powerfully for the common good. Then we know it as morale. The sentiments are unifying when they attach to the same single society, or are qualified by limited attachments to balanced component units, as just indicated. The sentiments may, however, attach to groupings which cut across societal lines, and then may have a divisive effect. In-group sentiments may attach to religious groupings, or to racial groupings. When Christendom was a political and regional community as well as a religious community, the loyalties to the brotherhood of Christians as contrasted with infidels, however unchristian these loyalties were, may have served the solidarity of that part of the world that was Christian, as corresponding sentiments united the Islamic world, but the prejudice and conflict between Jew and Christian within a modern nation is disruptive of that nation. The disposition of a society or part-society to seek a basis for a revived solidarity in an intensification of hatred of some other group than itself is illustrated by the antisemitism, anti-Catholicism, or anti-foreignism of groups threatened or insecure in many a land in modern times. As a technique of waging war on an enemy, thus to be weakened by intensifying the ethnic and religious hostilities within it, the general principle was well understood by Hitler and Goebbels, as it is also employed for special advantage by occasional rousers of the masses everywhere. In peacetime also a nation may suffer when the in-group sentiment excludes some of a man's fellow citizens and neighbors, as appears in the racial prejudices of modern times, and especially in the prejudice and intolerance directed by white Americans or South Africans to Negroes. In these cases a large minority or even majority of fellow citizens are excluded in great measure from both the privileges of citizenship and from the sense of group solidarity corresponding to the nation. The result is a loss in man power, material and spiritual, for the dominating group is itself weakened by the unresolved inconsistency between its professed ideals and its evident practices. In these cases, then, the restriction of group-sentiments to only those racially qualified is to be recognized, in appraising the working of the society, as unfavorable to the effective operation of the nation.

WARFARE

Of many forms of organized violence, warfare is that one which has political consequences. The rivalry between closely related groups that is an aspect of the in-group sentiments just referred to, often leads, obviously enough, to organized violence. The brawls between gangs of boys in the city characteristically are regulated by custom and form; and this formal aspect of violence between closely related groups is marked in the primitive societies. Usually such violence, which is not war, follows upon the commission by some individual of an act which in a modern society would be called a crime. Among Australian aborigines the offender is required to stand and receive spears thrown at him. Among the Eskimo the quarrelers publicly sing insulting songs at one another. All these cases of limited and regulated fighting are ways to adjust differences between constituent groups of a larger unit; they are more closely related to law than to war. Distinguished also are the very common instances, in primitive society, of armed raids upon unfriendly groups to take heads, scalps, or other trophies, or to bring back human sacrifices. This resembles war, in that the groups engaged are persistingly hostile, and the military enterprises are organized and lethal. Yet in many of these cases there is a strong element of sport: such organized conflict is a dangerous game, in which glory may be won and lives lost. This element persisted in the warfare of western societies until very recently. Other cases of this general group involve a religious motive: the head or the scalp is taken to bring supernatural power to the taker's group, or the captive is brought home as an offering to the deities.

In none of these cases is warfare an instrument of tribal or national policy. True warfare is probably to be recognized in those military activities in which political power is extended to include culturally related peoples, and in those in which the rivalries of two culturally different groups are put to the test of armed conflict. In the operation of societies such warfare plays a double role. It both destroys and constructs societies. In ancient Mexico the Aztecs entered upon warfare with neighboring peoples; the object was in large part the obtaining of captives for sacrifice, but a result was the subordination of many neighboring peoples of similar culture to the Aztec military power. In ancient Peru warfare led to a much stronger political and administrative organization: a state over a thousand miles in extent was the result. Similar political consequences followed from warfare among the Maori of New Zealand and among several African tribes. With this political motive an economic motive enters in, not among the most primitive people, but where there is enough property and wealth to attract the military marauder. And mixed also, as causes, are the personal ambitions of military leaders. So fused into a well-established practice, warfare became an instrument of social development, an extension of political activity. In East Africa, especially, one can see how military conquest was culturally constructive. Hamitic cattle-breeders invaded this part of the primitive world and subjected to their domination the agricultural Bantus. There resulted a complex state, with a ruling class on top of the farmers below, and there resulted also an exchange and multiplication of inventions and ideas. The society that resulted after conquest was a society of classes, a society in which there was division of labor between ethnic groups, and a society in which the political institutions had developed far to provide for the regulation of these complexities. Under the impact of conquest and of cultures now included in a single polity, native custom is codified as law, and religious and scientific ideas are exchanged. One thinks of the history of Rome. How many new inventions, how many critical thinkers, arose in the mixing of peoples which followed upon warfare! At the same time, of course, the waging of war consumes immense quantities of goods and lives, destroys whole societies, and, with the accelerated destructiveness of weapons, threatens the very extinction of civilization.

THE ORGANIZATION OF PRODUCTION, DISTRIBUTION, AND CONSUMPTION

In the first part of this chapter the division of labor was emphasized as a universal method for organizing work. This aspect of the operation of society may now be examined more fully. The division of labor does bring it about that the whole society realizes the advantages of having some people do some things well through their freedom from necessity to do other things. But this is not all there is to the social organization of economic activity. In every society it is also necessary to determine, somehow, what resources shall be used in producing what products. How shall products and consumable commodities be distributed, and to whom? Who shall consume what commodities? The organized ways of accomplishing these ends may be called the economy of that society. The technology is the tools and techniques for producing and making useful things; the economy is the institutions and customs that get raw materials into products and that get both distributed and consumed.

It is easy for us, who read these words, to think of factories, markets, and money as principal social machinery for getting these things done. But looking at primitive and ancient societies shows that these three are recent and special devices for bringing about production and distribution. In most societies raw materials and manufactured goods get around to producers and consumers without markets and money. The ancient and the basic form of economy is one in which goods are made and goods are distributed not by buying and selling at all, but by virtue of the traditional rights and obligations that custom recognizes to exist between one individual and another in that society, or between one group in that society and another. This kind of economy is easily seen in most families. The product of the father's labor, whether it be meat from the hunt or a pay-check brought home from office or factory, is shared with his wife and children not because he sells something to them which they buy, but because it is recognized to be part of his role as father to share his produce with his wife and children. The allocation of the father's labor to daily work, of the mother's labor to cooking and sewing, and perhaps of the small son's labor to fetching firewood or going to the store for lemons and soap, is a matter which requires no competitive bidding to determine and in most cases no payment of money to compensate. It is fixed by the very relationships of the members of the family to one another. The word 'status' is conveniently used for all the rights and obligations which attach to an individual or a group, according to the customs of the society. The father's status, in our society, includes his right to choose the place to live, according to his need and ability to get work, and his duty to provide for his family, as well as to share in the practical and moral guidance of his children. The work he does and the sharing of what he earns are parts of his status, too. So we may speak of this kind of economy as a status economy.

The basic form of economy in human societies is a status economy. In primitive societies most of the production—whether by hunting or by farming or by raising cattle or by handicraft manufacture—is brought about not because somebody sees a chance to make a profit in some market, but because it is part of the traditional status of that man or woman to hunt or farm or make baskets. And what is made is shared with others according to status. In many South Pacific societies a man works, not to feed his own children, but to feed his sister's children; his own children will be fed by his wife's brother. In certain hunting tribes it is usual for the hunter to give certain parts of the slain animal to just certain relatives—perhaps eight or nine different parts go, respectively, to eight or nine different relatives. So goods are distributed and consumed. These are reciprocal exchanges according to status: what a woman's brother gives to his sister's son is balanced by what that same man, as sister's son, gets from his own mother's brother, in the long run, and on the average. It is also common for goods to be distributed in status economies by the gathering of these goods in one place and by their distribution to all from this center. In a certain Melanesian community every gardener brings some of his best yams and puts them into the chief's yam house. They are 'given' to the chief. As the large and beautiful yams pile up, the villagers take satisfaction in the richness and industry of their own community; the abundance of the chief's yams redounds to the credit and glory of all. At a certain festival, the chief distributes these yams, some to visitors, and some to the villagers themselves. So everyone participates, in both the pride and the eating. In many simple societies there is neither money nor market. The whole society is, in respect to this matter of the economy, like a family; the status relationships determine production and distribution. The medieval manor had an economy which was largely a matter of status.

In contrast with this is that economy which depends upon the market. For the beginnings of the market economy in primitive societies we must look outside of the local society to its relations with other societies. The beginnings of human social living must be thought of as taking the form of small groups scattered over a territory and pretty much isolated from one another. In the section above on warfare it might have been made clear that the relation between such groups is not ordinarily one of warfare. Organized aggressive violence against a neighboring society is not characteristic of the very simplest societies. Many such societies get along with one another in a more or less friendly way: both societies recognize customary visits, without hostile intention, from one to another. An occasional invader from the outside may be killed, but the formal visit is expected and is received without violence. Many such visits are the occasion of the exchange of goods.

More commonly, in primitive societies, people from one community pay a visit to another community, taking with them goods produced by the visitors and wanted by those visited. Then goods are exchanged, partly by barter, and partly by exchange of gifts. Something is given in the expectation that something will be given to the giver by the one to whom he gives. It is an equivalence of good will, rather than of precise market value, that determines the transaction. So in such a market personal relations, and the status of guest and host, affect the exchange. In larger communities, where people do not know each other personally, and more goods and more kinds of goods appear, the market may be more fully a matter of an effort to sell at the highest price and to buy at the lowest; then buyer and seller alike 'shop around,' and who the man is who buys or sells does not matter as compared with the opportunity to get the best price. Such a market can to some degree operate by the exchange of one sort of good for another, but money, as a universal measure of value, is an enormous help in facilitation of market exchanges. In some societies incomplete money appears: in some Melanesian communities certain strings of shell beads are used only in payment for pigs or wives. But in other places metal hoes or copper axes or coined metal or engraved certificates of promises to pay both serve as tokens of value that measure the value of one article against all others in the market, and also provide a way of temporarily holding buying power from one market or opportunity to buy to another.

In most societies of the world, and through most of human history, the production and distribution of goods has taken place chiefly as an aspect of the status relationships of the society: the market has been not the central mechanism for making society work, but a special or peripheral part of it. In modern times, and especially in the western world, the market became much more important. In our society the effort of the laborer is to a considerable extent bid for and offered to the highest bidder, and the use of land, paid for as rent, also enters into market competition. Now markets are very wide; for some goods, like wheat and rubber and tin, the market is worldwide; and, with rapid and universal communication, and with the machinery of banking and credit, what goes into production where and what goes where to what consumer are matters that the market 'decides,' rather than status and moral custom. So, in our society, the operations of the market have a principal and even determining influence on all sorts of affairs. Many a worker must live where the opportunity to get a job determines, and if suddenly the produce he makes ceases to be wanted, he may have no livelihood at all, and perhaps cannot keep his family together; in parts of the world men starve because the market no longer needs their labor. Where a family goes to live, perhaps its own solidarity, perhaps even whether its members live at all, follow from what happens in an immense impersonal market, and the actions of a nation, from its form of government to its remaining at peace or its going to war, may be shaped by what happens in markets.

The operation of the economy may also be regarded from the point of view of the organization and regulation of productive effort. Even in the simplest societies there is more to this than the mere separate work of single individuals. The household economy is in many cases under the leadership or direction of someone: the husband of several wives, as among the Hidatsa Indians, an older woman in a large matrilineal family of the Iroquois. When the Chukchee of Siberia go to hunt seal or walrus, the builder of the boat is master: he gives the orders and he receives the largest share of the meat. In modern societies with highly developed markets, the enterpriser may be one or a group that brings together a very great amount of money and credit, labor and raw materials, in order that automobiles or steel plate may be made. Furthermore, with the development of the state as formal government, its own efforts enter largely into production and distribution. The state may itself be the principal producer, as in Russia, or it may supplement private production, or it may impose regulations upon the conduct of private enterprise, either to limit the operations of a free market, as in granting a monopoly to a single telegraph company, or in helping a freer market to operate, as in legislation against trusts.

PROPERTY

Among the common understandings which constitute the ultimate basis of society are those which attach to things that may be used, enjoyed, or disposed of. Where the understandings limit or otherwise define such rights and obligations of one individual or one group as to others, we speak of 'property.' Property operates to keep use and enjoyment and disposal in expected channels; it contributes to the working of society in wide and far-reaching ways: to confer and to limit power and the basis for getting more power; to serve as a criterion for status; to provide motives for effort. Wanting to own things, men may work, steal, or go to war. Owning things, men may enter social groups otherwise barred to them, exercise influence over political decisions, or assume correspondingly great responsibility for serving the common good.

Property is thought of most immediately in connection with such tangible goods as tools, automobiles, houses, and land. It exists also, with respect to such intangibles as magical spells, power-inducing songs addressed to supernaturals, hunting and fishing rights, patents and copyrights. In some societies personal names are owned in that they may be disposed of by sale or gift; in our society, a trade name may be registered and so owned. On the whole, the conceptions of ownership have become more complex with the developing complexity of society. Land, in particular, has become subject to private and exclusive ownership, with rights of sale and disposition by will; in most primitive societies such precise and exclusive rights to land are not recognized; nevertheless, individual or familial rights over hunting and fishing territories may be sanctioned in custom in some very simple societies.

In primitive societies, and to an extent in modern society that is not always recognized, property does not consist of a single all-embracing bundle of rights held by one man as against all the world. On the other hand, thoroughly communal ownership of important goods, in the sense that every individual has the same right in most goods as has every other, is not to be found. What is usual, rather, is that every species of ownership turns out to be the exercise of certain rights as to the thing owned subject to other rights in that thing held by others, at least in possibility. The Melanesian canoe-maker does not completely 'own' his canoe: he is expected to share it with certain others, and to share the catch it helps to bring about. The owner of land on Main Street may own it subject to zoning regulations, and to the right of the state to take it from him for certain public uses. Beyond this, furthermore, are the claims on property which are made outside of the law, but through expectations resting on custom. The primitive fisherman may share his catch with the whole settlement, as a matter of course. The rich American is expected to do something useful and generous with his riches; and everywhere the claims of the nearest of kin constitute a real limitation on ownership of many kinds of goods. And still further it is to be recognized that property rights are deeply associated with attachments that are sentimental and outside of the rights of control and disposal. It is not so much that the aborigine, long established on the desert or in the forest, owns the desert or the forest; he is attached to it, is a part of it, almost 'is owned' by it. And the reader of these pages may feel similarly about his home, if he happens to live in a home and not simply in a house, or about an heirloom of tender memories, or about a familiar old garment.

STATUS, PRESTIGE, AND RANK

Society operates through the division of labor and the social organization of production and consumption. Society operates through understandings as to proper conduct which have become traditional. Society operates through the guidance provided by conventional rights and obligations connected with the individuals and the groups making up the society. These, as already indicated, constitute the 'status' of the individual or the group. What is expected of any particular person, or group of them, or of the occupier of any particular role or office, is known in advance, and this foreknowledge enables the people of the society to do what is expected and what is consistent, more or less, with the ideals that the people have in common. In this way, too, society operates.

Society may thus be seen as a system of status relationships. Many of these take the form of relationships of kinship, and are described in Chapter XII. Also mentioned already is the status of the members of the in-group as contrasted with that of the out-group. And easily added are the differences in status of a man as contrasted with a woman, or a priest, policeman, or potentate as contrasted with a man who is none of these things. Conduct is expected of the one, and is due to him, different from that expected of or due to the other. In every society there are status-groups connected with differences in age. Any school reveals them, where they are connected with the grades through which the child passes. In many primitive societies this sort of classification in terms of status is made without schools; boys and men pass through a series of ranked groups, each perhaps with its name, its rights and duties, its growing prestige. In many cases certain of these age-groups enjoy a special clubhouse, or have special secrets or ceremonies. Such a ladder of attainment defines what is expected of everyone according to successive categories, from birth to death.

The attitudes that make up the status of any one individual, or group, in a society include, it will be noticed, authorization of various degrees of approach and intimacy. If someone has the status of 'best friend' I may go close to him and claim his sympathies as he may claim mine. They also include attitudes of superiority and inferiority. A cat—or a commoner—may look at a king, but he must look up when he looks at him. The 'place' in which an American Negro is thought by most white men to be 'all right' is a place that is down, not up, with reference to the white man. These differences of ranked status, of 'vertical' social position, are apparent as one individual is compared with another. In any gang or small school group the individuals with superior prestige are well known as such, and it may be possible even to rank all the members in an order of 'up-or-down.' There is no society in which the relative vertical status of the individual does not depend in some degree on himself—on his own conduct and personal chances. On the other hand in many societies the vertical position of any one individual is that of a great many others who are associated with each other more than they are associated with contrasting groups that are 'above' or 'below' their own. Such social classes make of the society a sort of column of layers: the vertical status of every individual is in large part determined by his birth. He takes the degree of prestige associated with his class, and as he works, plays, and probably marries within it, the classes remain distinguishable. On the other hand, the exceptional son of a nineteenth-century English workingman might 'become a gentleman,' and in societies nearer the frontier movement between classes is much less 'sticky' and the classes may be hard to see at all. Where the classes are very rigid, so that there is no possibility of escape to a superior class, they are, after the East Indian example, described in an earlier chapter, known as castes. All these organizations of society into persisting layered groups are ways of defining the rights and obligations of people with regard to one another, and so contribute to its operation. In most cases, there are special kinds of occupations appropriate to each of the classes in a society so organized; thus classes constitute an aspect of the division of labor. In India the correspondence between inherited social position and the kind of work or useful function performed is very close. In America it has been the immigrant or latest arrival who has done the most unpleasant work. And also social classes are ways of maintaining an unequal distribution of wealth and power that is to the advantage of the dominant classes. The upper layers get more than their share of prestige, social influence, and wealth. At the same time, in societies where class or caste is well established, the glories of the privileged provide a certain second-hand satisfaction to the less privileged. In many societies that include conspicuously different racial groups, relative vertical social positions correspond with the racial groupings, and as the skin color or other racial mark is permanent, the racial classes become caste-like, with the taboos against contact and the ceremonial separation of the racial groups which are characteristic of castes.

CUSTOM AND LAW

The simplest answer that can be made to the question, how does society operate, is that it operates because on the whole people do what is expected of them. But why do people do what is expected of them? To this question there are many true answers. It is easier to do what one has done before than to do something else; a habit that everyone in a society has we call a custom. Further, the things that one has done, and that one's father's father has done, as well as some things that have been thought over and struggled for, have come to be so rooted in sentiments and in explanations and justifications that they have the force of what we speak of as conscience: they are felt to be right, ultimately and necessarily right. And still further, one does what is expected of one because it is often extremely inconvenient, even dangerous, if one does not. That is why I do not start out tomorrow to drive on the left-hand side of an American road. There is an efficiency, an ease, about doing what is expected of one. In a more special form, the expediency of doing

what other people expect appears in the exchanges of services and benefits which help us all to get along. I do a thing helpful to another
knowing that he is then more apt to do something helpful to me. If I
pay my bills, lend my lawnmower, keep out of those of my neighbor's
affairs which correspond to those of mine that I want him to keep out of,
and yet listen to enough of his troubles so that I may tell him mine, we
all get along pretty well. It is, however, to be emphasized that it is the
nature of human society to regard these considerations of expediency,
important as they are, as less worthy than those which are rooted in
conscience and the sense of duty. Society is not, basically, so much a
body of traffic rules and favors exchanged as it is a system of moral
convictions.

At a more obvious level society operates because conduct is sanctioned. A sanction is a consequence, pleasant or unpleasant, that follows
the doing of something and is known to follow it. Some such consequences are internal—the pangs of conscience—but others fall upon the
transgressor from without. Of those that so fall, many are imposed by
almost anybody in a diffuse and generalized way, as is illustrated by the
looks I receive from the people who know me if I do something of
which they disapprove. Perhaps what I do is not otherwise punishable.
If a specific consequence follows through the exercise of some centralized authority, we begin to think of the transgression and its consequence as an affair of the law. Legal sanctions have a quality of precise-
ness about them: the misconduct is defined in advance in clear terms,
and the consequence is also precisely known. Commonly the procedure
for matching the transgression to its appropriate consequence—complaint
or arrest, charge, hearing, trial, judgment—is specific and formal. Also,
for the matter to be one of law and not just custom, the consequence
that is the sanction is carried out not entirely if at all by the particular
person that suffered from the transgression, but by someone or some body
that stands for the society as a whole and acts for it. Law is the whole
society settling a local dispute or punishing or redressing a wrong in the
interests of the whole society and according to its common conscience.
When in a Plains Indian tribe a society of warriors finds a wrongfully
wounded man and sees to it that the wrongdoer heals the wound and
pays horses as a fine, law has begun. One may recognize law-making
and law-administering in groups smaller than the whole society: there is
something like law in some families; and there is certainly law in many
gangs. But there is a tendency for that group which is the principal

in-group, the tribe or the nation, to insist on its chief or exclusive power and right to make and enforce law. So law appears more clearly in the centralized and monopolizing force of the state.

POLITICAL INSTITUTIONS

In the simplest societies there is nothing that is 'political' if we use that word for institutions to express or enforce the common will or the ruler's will formally and publicly. In the Andaman Islands the natives lived in small bands without chief, council, law, or administrative regulation. If a man lost his temper and smashed things, the rest of the people just let him alone till he got over it. No one exercised any general authority to rule or to decide or to negotiate on behalf of the community. In such a society there is no state, no political government. Political institutions do clearly appear, however, in many tribal societies; there is a chief who has power to decide issues or to lead in the making of decisions; there may be a council; there may be groups to police the people.

The dependence of modern complex societies upon political institutions for their operation is obvious. The making, enforcing, and interpreting of law is the manifold business of thousands of individuals and hundreds of bodies: from legislatures, courts, and executives to the citizens who vote or obey orders, bring law suits or defend them, pay taxes, and discuss public issues with their neighbors or write a letter to some newspaper. These political institutions keep people's behavior more or less within the rules. They also are a means to the reconsideration of the rules and for the changing of the rules. They operate in that frontier of rule-making and rule-observing where conflicts occur, or at least differences of opinion, and the enforcement and interpretation of the rules helps to keep at least some of the people conscious of them, and so pushing to change them. Formal political institutions not only keep societies going in the good old ways; they also provoke a challenge of those ways.

What is, then, not so obvious is that political and administrative acts have an effect upon moral custom. It is commonly said that the laws express the customs and grow out of them. This is true, but it is also true that the passage of a law or the making of an administrative decision has an impact upon the sentiments and convictions of the society. To punish a criminal is to make a solemn gesture renewing the collective moral judgment with regard to the conduct for which the criminal is punished. Sometimes the law stands for a sort of theoretical or ideal norm which the society does not really mean to have realized, at least without exception, as when a Southern jury of white men find confessed lynchers of a Negro not guilty. Then the decision expresses a moral judgment that is inconsistent with the letter of the law. At the same time such a decision sharpens the conflict between the general principles and the exception, and helps either to remove the exception, or to weaken the principle. The decision and act whereby American citizens of Japanese descent were locked up during the war had one effect in strengthening the prejudices of those who were prejudiced against Orientals, for by conspicuous and effective public action a discriminatory act was performed. On the other hand, it aroused or strengthened sentiments of condemnation of the act. It is true that the customs make the law. It is also true that legal and administrative acts help to change the moral judgments of the society.

RELIGION

Some of the sanctions that keep men doing what is expected of them are neither the exterior sanctions of the law or of public opinion, nor the wholly interior sanctions of conscience. The sentiments that arise within a man that prevent him from doing that of which he would be ashamed, or that condemn him for doing it, in certain situations seem to come from outside him, yet not to come from this earthly world. Then it is a religious sanction that affects him. The convictions about the good are associated with unseen powers; these powers *are* the good, or represent it. A man's relationships to them have a unique quality; they are supremely critical for his ultimate welfare; and before the powers or their symbols he feels awe. The consequence of his action that is the sanction in this case may be a punishment, a suffering here on earth or a suffering in some other life. It may be a hand withered, or a soul damned. The suffering—or the reward, should his conduct be right, not wrong—may be simply the sense that the unseen powers are satisfied or dissatisfied, the feeling that one is or is not in harmony with ultimate goodness, final and unearthly authority.

Religion has been briefly defined as the adoration of goodness. It is goodness that is its essence; religion is not concerned with the trivial, nor with the morally neutral. It is about what most matters. But though an aspect of the moral life, it is not the same as morals. There are peoples—and many of these are primitive, uncivilized—whose religions are the worship or propitiation of supernatural beings who do not enforce the rules of good conduct among men. In such religions it is the worship and the propitiation, the ritual and the relationship between man and god, that matter; earthly morality is supported by conscience and the interplay of reciprocal obligations among people. In other religions, of which Christianity, Islam, and some primitive ones are examples, what a man should do to or for another *is* a matter of divine concern. On the whole, the ethical aspects of religion have grown stronger in the course of human history.

Religion is, moreover, activity; it is something going on in mind and in overt act; it is belief and rite. The power that is beyond men and that holds the welfare of men, mundane and spiritual, is thought about, conceived in certain forms and powers, and approached in prayer and offering and sacrifice. Commonly the power is conceived with qualities that are personal; the god may be angered, appeased, gratified. But in some religions, as in forms of Buddhism, the rites and beliefs have to do with conduct and with spiritual qualities. A religion is yet a religion even though it does not center about a god or gods.

Religion thus contributes to the operation of society through the power and authority and sacred meaning which it provides to the support of man's conduct and to his understanding of his place in the universe. In the totemic societies of aboriginal Australia groups of men carry on rituals at water-holes in their arid land to bring about the multiplication of the wild animals which the natives hunt for food. These rituals act out events and evoke sacred beings that were there before man was, and that were man's ancestors and benefactors. So the life of today is, through religion, conceived as an outcome of powers mysteriously greater than men's powers; they are greater, and yet men today share in that power through the goodness of these beings and the effectiveness of the rites. Similarly, the heavenly hierarchy of Christian faith is a version, in religious thought, of the hierarchies of earthly power of medieval times. These divine beings provide help to the worshipper; and the rite of the Mass, solemnly commemorative of the great act of sacrifice of God become man, is effective in bringing to the worshipper a benefit and strength which only religion can give.

THE EXPRESSIVE LIFE: PLAY, ART, CEREMONY, MYTH

In many of the preceding pages of this chapter the operation of society has been described as a matter of work and discipline. It has been suggested how people become and continue as a society by virtue of the fact that they labor together for common ends, and how they are kept

at it by the convenience of co-operation and by the rewards and penal-
ties which are provided by law, the general opinion, or the conscience
of the individual. In this account the sober, the practical, and the con-
straining have perhaps been too strongly emphasized. Perhaps the impression has been given that society gets along wholly or chiefly because
people do what they are compelled to do, or that work is the sole or the
basic form of activity.

As a matter of fact, a very great part of human social behavior is
quite the opposite of work. In work one does what a particular end demands in just the way it demands it and when the end requires it. To
hoe corn effectively is usually work because one must move the hoe just
so, one must do the hoeing just when the weather and the weeds make
it necessary, and one may not stop when one would care to. But a very
great deal of human activity is simply expressive. It is activity which
responds to the impulse of the individual to be active; it is activity which
takes a form that shows what the individual is thinking and feeling; it
is a fruit of the human impulse to create. Some expressive activity takes
place when it occurs to the individual to express himself; much takes
place at times fixed by the expectations and rhythms of society, but even
then without having to meet the demands of practically useful effort.

Laughing, joking, improvising with language, storytelling, praying,
arranging flowers, painting pictures, enjoying or playing a ball game or
Beethoven, and dancing are all forms of expressive activity. The expressive forms of behavior in large part give each society its own special
character as they give special flavor to each personality. Different societies may have the same tools and the same work habits, but if their art
and storytelling are different, the societies are then different. 'What do
you dance?' is the first enquiry a man of a certain Bantu tribe puts to
a stranger. What a man dances in that part of Africa is the key to a
man's whole life, the way to ask about a foreign society.

The relations between expressive activity and work appear in considering magic. If a man has something immediate and practical to accomplish he may do a little work to get the thing done. If the pipe leaks, I
may unscrew the faucet and put in a new washer. If the pigs are eating
the Melanesian's yams, he may fence the yam patch to keep out the pigs.
What is done is done in just the way that the end requires. The putting
in the new washer and the building of the fence are technically 'correct'—
that is, in both cases what is done is responsive to the demands of the
situation outside of the state of mind of the worker. I may not express

my anxieties or my annoyance too vividly and originally in putting in the washer or building the fence; if I attempt to express my sentiments I may not do a good job with the washer or the fence. These are practical actions appropriate to the mechanical solutions of the problems.

But in some cases there is room for expressing the way one feels besides doing the appropriate practical acts, and in other cases no appropriate practical acts are known and one expresses the way one feels, believing that what is done is effective, instead of doing something really effective in getting the result desired. The Melanesian who wants his yams to grow may fence them and cultivate them; he may also recite little spells expressive of his desire for a good crop. Tom Sawyer knew how to get rid of warts by putting water from a decaying stump on them while reciting a charm imploring the warts to go away. We call these actions 'magical.' Magic is that activity directed toward accomplishing some special limited end and done in a form which is determined not by the real effectiveness of the act to bring about the result but by the desires and fears and general thinking and feeling of the man who performs them. Magic is practical action in that it is done for a certain limited end, like work; but it is expressive action, and work is not. Magic is characteristically colorful, even dramatic. Magical rites are little pictures of what one wants. One sticks pins into a figure of one's enemy. One sacrifices not just any hen; it must be a black hen. If a problem bothers a deliberating assembly it may appoint a committee; the result may be practically effective, or it may in part just express the concern and desire to do something about the problem; it is then not so different from many acts recognized as magical.

While magic is unusual among expressive forms of action in that it is directed to some limited practical end, like work, other forms of expressive activity are less closely directed to such an end. Play is a familiar case of those expressive acts which are carried on for their own sake. If what is done carries with it no satisfaction from the mere doing of it, it is not play. Play is doing what is fun, and what is done does not have to bring about some immediate useful result. The contributions of play to the operation of society are apart from the immediate goal, which in many cases is put there only as a stimulus to the carrying on of the activity. In 'playing house' and in playing 'cops and robbers' the housekeeping and the criminal-catching are of course only pretenses to provide form and zest to what is done, although the playing may help to develop in children qualities or capacities needed in their later life. In competitive games the apparent end—the winning of the game—is not a real accomplishment, as work is; it is there, again, in order to give zest to what is done; it is there to make the doing important, not the result. If all one cares about is winning, the play is no longer play.

Art is like play in that it has its justification in itself, not in getting something done by its means. In art the limitations set around what is done are not rules for contestants and make-believe goals, as in play; the limitations that give art its character are the expectations and satisfactions of a technique mastered, a creation made or appreciated. There are standards, as in play; but in art they are the standards of craftsmanship and the conceptions of the beautiful that prevail in that society and as they are modified by the creative artist.

Until modern times artist and artisan were thought of as the same. Art, in general, makes something. If a wall is built, a shoe made, or a room set in order, in this generous sense of the word, there is a work of art. Most works of personal making give the maker some scope to express himself. The expression may be of no particular idea, and there may be no conscious aesthetic judgment, but there is often expression in the sense that the imagination shapes and varies and so creates. In so far as a work made, whether a useful product or not, is ordered to beauty, it is a work of art in a more limited sense. Where the work is ordered first for beauty, as in sculpture, painting, or poetry, we nowadays speak of it as belonging to the 'fine arts.' So far as a made thing is beautiful it is self-sufficient; it is a delight in itself. As there is no tribe or nation that has no way of making, as in every case there is some shaping, drawing, or speaking in forms that are for themselves enjoyed beyond the usefulness of the thing done, so it must be that art makes apparent some impulse or quality present in all societies of mankind. The relation of artist to society includes, therefore, the expression he gives to the more ultimate values and standards of that society. With the priest, and the thinker, the artist makes known the collective character of a people, and so unites and directs it by stating its nature and its ideals.

All these forms of expressive action help in the operation of society by providing opportunities for carrying out the expectations which are the basis of society and by depicting to its members the related conceptions and ideals. Games involve the ideas and ideals as to sportsmanship which the society entertains; playing them disciplines player and audience toward these ideals and tests each player by them. In many primitive societies some games are representations of religious ideas. A game played by the ancient Maya represented the movement of the divine sun through the heavens; yet the game was sport too. 'Pure art' is a relatively new and unusual conception; in most times and places art is or has been a form for the expression of the religious conceptions, or for the earthly ideas and ideals. The totem poles carved by Indians of the Northwest Coast proclaimed the social position and divine connections of the family connected with the pole.

In ceremony and in mythology the expressive side of life appears in forms plainly related to the persistence of society. A ceremony is a meaningful formal act that signalizes an occasion of special importance. It is a little drama to underline the significance of a person or a moment that is out of the ordinary and that the society wishes to recognize. Some ceremonies are in ancient forms of deep religious meaning, like the Mass; others are unconnected with the church but yet are public and solemn, like the pledge of allegiance before the national flag; still others are domestic matters and not solemn at all, like the merry little ceremonies of a birthday party. All of them are representations of beliefs that the people hold; they are ways in which people together show that they care about something. Although not every society has well-developed myths and also well-developed ceremonies, myths are the stories that correspond to the ceremonies. Myths are ways in which the institutions and expectations of the society are emphasized and made dramatic and persuasive in narrative form. Myths show that what a people has to enjoy or endure is right and true—true to the sentiments the people hold. It does not so much matter whether or not little George Washington really cut down the cherry tree and told his father about it; what matters is that the story expresses some ideas the tellers had about telling the truth when it goes against you. The religious myths are true to the moral and sacred ideas that inspire them; they need not be true as legal evidence must be true. Myths and ceremonies, like much of art and some of play, are collective and traditional forms in which the people of a society remind themselves of what matters to them and why it matters. They are gestures made by a people to itself. Work and sanctions alone do not suffice to keep a society in operation. It is also needful that the tendencies of people to leap, move, shape, and tell fall into representations that satisfy and intensify the conceptions which, held in common, make that people a society.

This chapter suggests some of the answers to the question expressed in its title: How does a human society operate? In its first pages the answer given was that a society is kept in operation by arrangements whereby a number of people can do the work that needs to be done to keep them going and whereby they can feel that they belong together and share a kind of life which they believe to be good. There is a world of necessity into which people are born; to survive they must live together; to live together they must have tacit agreements as to who does what, and is what. They must, in short, regulate their common life. The regulation is a matter of conventional understandings partly as to what each one should do, and partly as to what is, generally and for everybody, the good life. The plan of the good life finds expression, it was then added, in religion, myth, and art. We can think of the operation of society as machinery for social control and also as a sort of charter or drama of a scheme of all things.

But there is another way to think of the operation of society that is, probably, implicit in what has been written here. We may also think of society as operating so as to realize impulses and meet needs of human beings. Instead of asking, as we have, What operations keep this society going? we can ask, What is there about society that keeps human beings going? Any human being must have protection and food, and we can see society as providing for these necessities. Human beings have also sexual demands or needs, and every society provides some arrangement for meeting these. Moreover, beyond this, human beings have characteristics that are not shared with the animals but are peculiarly human. The foregoing discussion of the 'Expressive Life' rests on the assumption that there is an 'impulse of the individual to be active,' that it is the nature of human nature to use the imagination and to shape things that please themselves. While it is perhaps not possible very definitely to describe the human impulses and needs beyond those that are shared with animals, it is hardly possible to deny that there are some; and society may thus be seen as a way of providing for the development and expression in everyone of human nature. In this sense, society operates by doing for us what our natures, given society, demand.

LIST OF SUGGESTED READINGS

Benedict, Ruth
Patterns of Culture. Houghton Mifflin Co., Boston, 1934.
Bennett, Wendell C., and Junius B. Bird
Andean Culture History. Handbook Series No. 15, American Museum of Natural History, New York, 1949.
Boas, Franz
The Mind of Primitive Man. Revised edition. The Macmillan Company, New York, 1938.
Buettner-Janusch, John
Origins of Man. John Wiley and Sons, New York, 1966.

Campbell, Bernard G.
Human Evolution. Aldine Publishing Co., Chicago, 1967.
Childe, V. Gordon
Man Makes Himself. Library of Science and Culture No. 5, Watts and Co., London, 1936 (also: New American Library, New York, 1951).
Clark, J. G. D.
Prehistoric Europe. Philosophical Library, New York, 1952.
Clark, W. E. LeGros
History of the Primates. An Introduction to the Study of Fossil Man. Second edition. British Museum (Natural History), London, 1950.
The Fossil Evidence for Human Evolution. An Introduction to the Study of Paleoanthropology. The Scientist's Library. Biology and Medicine. University of Chicago Press, Chicago, 1955.

Dobzhansky, Theodosius
Genetics and the Origin of Species. Third edition, revised. Columbia Biological Series, No. XI, Columbia University Press, New York, 1951.

441

Forde, C. Daryll
Habitat, Economy and Society. A Geographical Introduction to Ethnology. Methuen and Co., Ltd., London, 1934.

Gelb, I. J.
A Study of Writing. University of Chicago Press, Chicago, 1952.

Griffin, James B., editor
Archeology of Eastern United States. University of Chicago Press, Chicago, 1952.

Herskovits, Melville J.
Economic Anthropology. A Study in Comparative Economics. Alfred A. Knopf, New York, 1952.

Hill, Archibald A., editor
Linguistics Today. Basic Books, New York, 1969.

Honigmann, John J.
Culture and Personality. Harper and Brothers, New York, 1954.

Howell, F. Clark
Early Man. Life Nature Library, Time Incorporated, New York, 1965.

Howells, William W.
The Heathens. Primitive Man and His Religions. Doubleday and Co., Inc., Garden City, 1948.

Jennings, Jesse D., and Norbeck, Edward, editors
Prehistoric Man in the New World. University of Chicago Press, Chicago, 1964.

Langacker, Ronald W.
Language and Its Structure. Harcourt, Brace and World, New York, 1968.

Murdock, George Peter
Our Primitive Contemporaries. The Macmillan Company, New York, 1935.
Social Structure. The Macmillan Company, New York, 1949.

Oakley, Kenneth P.
Frameworks for Dating Fossil Man. Aldine Publishing Co., Chicago, 1964.

Redfield, Robert
The Folk Culture of Yucatán. University of Chicago Publications in Anthropology, Social Anthropology Series. University of Chicago Press, Chicago, 1941.

Sayce, R. U.
Primitive Arts and Crafts. An Introduction to the Study of Material Culture. The University Press, Cambridge, 1933.

Underhill, Ruth Murray
Red Man's America. A History of Indians in the United States. University of Chicago Press, Chicago, 1953.

Vaillant, George C.

The Aztecs of Mexico. Origin, Rise and Fall of the Aztec Nation. Penguin Books, Harmondsworth, 1950 (also: American Museum of Natural History Science Series, Vol. 2, Doubleday, Doran and Co., Inc., Garden City, 1941).

White, Leslie A.

The Science of Culture. Grove Press, Inc., New York, 1949.

Willey, Gordon R.

Introduction to American Archaeology. Vol. 1, *Meso America and North America.* Prentice-Hall, Englewood Cliffs, New Jersey, 1966.